Hitchcock at the Source

THE SUNY SERIES

HORIZONS OF CINEMA

MURRAY POMERANCE | EDITOR

Hitchcock at the Source

The Auteur as Adaptor

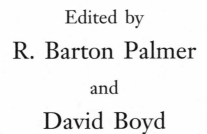

Edited by

R. Barton Palmer

and

David Boyd

"John Michael Hayes discusses with Alfred Hitchcock on location in Monaco his script for *To Catch a Thief* (1955)," publicity photo courtesy of the Academy of Motion Pictures Arts and Sciences Library.

Published by State University of New York Press, Albany

© 2011 State University of New York

For information, contact State University of New York Press, Albany, NY
www.sunypress.edu

Production by Eileen Meehan
Marketing by Fran Keneston

Library of Congress Cataloging-in-Publication Data

Hitchcock at the source : the auteur as adapter / edited by R. Barton
   Palmer and David Boyd.
      p. cm. — (SUNY series, horizons of cinema)
   Includes bibliographical references and index.
   ISBN 978-1-4384-3748-4 (pbk. : alk. paper)
   ISBN 978-1-4384-3749-1 (hardcover : alk. paper)
   1. Hitchcock, Alfred, 1899–1980—Criticism and interpretation.   2. Film
adaptations—History and criticism.   I. Palmer, R. Barton, 1946–   II. Boyd,
David, 1944–

   PN1998.3.H58H558 2011
   791.43'60019—dc22   2011003059

10 9 8 7 6 5 4 3 2 1

Contents

Illustrations

Introduction

Recontextualizing Hitchcock's Authorship

DAVID BOYD AND R. BARTON PALMER

"AFTER YEARS OF BEING STUCK IN the backwaters of the academy," asserts Thomas Leitch in a recent survey of the field, "adaptation studies is on the move." In part, this movement is a retreat from, at least in principle, the approach that has dominated the field since the beginning of serious academic study of the cinema, what Leitch terms "fidelity discourse," or critical analysis devoted to measuring, and evaluating, the relative faithfulness of an adaptation to its literary source. Instead, scholars have begun to focus more on "Bakhtinian intertextuality," acknowledging that adaptations, like all other texts, are "afloat upon a sea of countless earlier texts" from which they "cannot help borrowing" (63). So transformed, adaptation studies would offer a way in which both literary and film scholars might radically transcend a traditional focus on unitary, self-sufficient individual texts and the supposed one-to-one relationship between sources and secondary versions. The study of adaptations would direct itself instead toward accounts of the unlimited, multiform permeability of intertextual relations, perhaps even finding ways, Leitch muses, to dispose of any substantial consideration of an adaptation to its official, acknowledged, and (in some fashion) perpetuated "sources."

But perhaps this celebrated reorientation of the field is just wishful thinking, at least in part, because adaptation studies remains "haunted" in Leitch's view by "the assumption that the primary context within which adaptations are to be studied is literature." That context constitutes a "dead hand" impeding fruitful progress toward understanding adaptations in themselves rather than as secondary, less valuable versions of honored originals (64). Most scholars working in adaptation studies today would agree, as do we. Although they otherwise take up a variety of critical approaches, the contributors to this book do uniformly reject any literary paradigm that might be summoned up to organize this series of essays and case studies. With its focus clearly on cinematic rather than literary authorship, *Hitchcock at the Source* aims to help loosen the grip of the "dead hand" of literature and of literary study on the field. This is entirely appropriate for the subject at hand. For Alfred Hitchcock's cinema is by no means a "literary" cinema. The mostly popular, rather than highbrow, novels, plays, and short fiction that provided the source material to be reworked in his films bear limited cultural cachet. These cinematic versions are valued for the most part because of their connection to Hitchcock's authorship. With a notable exception or two (*Rebecca* immediately comes to mind), Hitchcock's films do not circulate now as adaptations, nor were they marketed as adaptations during their initial releases. Quite the contrary. In order to promote Hitchcock's authorship, the connection of these films with their written sources has been quite deliberately occulted.

This is somewhat exceptional in that Hitchcock did sometimes work with canonical literary texts. We must remember that few commercial screen adaptations of honored fiction and drama are not marketed as such. In the course of a long career in Britain and then in Hollywood, Hitchcock produced adaptations of works by such acknowledged modern masters as Joseph Conrad, W. Somerset Maugham, and Sean O'Casey, and by writers considered important in their own time such as Daphne du Maurier and Patrick Hamilton. But Hitchcock was unlike directors with stronger, deeper literary interests, such as his Hollywood contemporary John Huston. Huston built a long and productive career by screening the fiction of an amazing number of celebrated authors, including Dashiell Hammett, James Joyce, Flannery O'Connor, Stephen Crane, Malcolm Lowry, Herman Melville, Carson McCullers, Tennessee Williams, and Rudyard Kipling. Unlike Huston, however, Hitchcock never conceived of himself as a literary adaptor, nor did he want his public to perceive him as one, even though undeniably the majority of his films are literary adaptations. This fact, we submit, has not been sufficiently recognized by Hitchcockians. But is it important that they do?

By adopting a cinematic rather than a literary perspective, *Hitchcock at the Source* proves able to address a central definitional problem that many scholars barely acknowledge. While the term *adaptation* seems fairly straightforward, it turns out in practice to be more complex. To be sure, any text that borrows centrally and substantially from another text (including, most often, taking over its "identity" in some fashion) is what is generally understood as an adaptation. As Julie Sanders remarks, "adaptation . . . constitutes a more sustained engagement with a single text or source than the more glancing act of allusion or quotation, even citation, allows" (4). So much is clear. The correlative of this definition is also beyond argument. Not all intertextual connections or relations are "sustained," and therefore not all intertextual connections are equal. We would surely not want to use the term adaptation to describe allusions and minor borrowings.

It is certainly true, as Leitch reminds us, following a central development in modern theory, that all texts, cinematic and literary, including (and perhaps especially) adaptations, can be usefully understood as constituted by a multiplicity of other texts. But, as a way of offering a given text an identity, adaptation is a relational term, privileging one particular intertextual relation. Adaptations in this sense are always reworkings of preexisting texts, whose cultural mode of being they continue in some other form. In this regard, it becomes crucial to discriminate between two different meanings of adaptation. On the one hand, adaptation is a matter of textual ontology, a result of, in Sanders' terms, a derivative text's "sustained engagement with a single text or source." On the other, adaptation is a feature of textual rhetoric, a matter connected not only to formal transformations but also to "branding" or reception. Adaptations are not always circulated and consumed as adaptations. Identifying a film as an adaptation is in effect a protocol of reading that directs viewers' attention toward the film's connection to its source, inviting them to engage in what Sanders appropriately terms "the ongoing process of juxtaposed readings that are crucial to the cultural operations of adaptation, and the ongoing experiences of pleasure for the reader or spectator in tracing the intertextual relationships." Adaptations not positioned to be appreciated as such thus deny consumers "the connected interplay of expectation and surprise." They do not invite readers to share in the same kind of "ongoing experiences." The several generations of filmgoers and critics who have taken pleasure from viewing Hitchcock's films have for the most part not been invited to indulge this "inherent sense of play" since such an invitation is a matter of rhetoric rather than ontology. As Sanders suggests, this play "is produced by the activation of our informed sense of similarity and difference between the texts being invoked" (25). But neither Hitchcock himself nor the majority of those writing about his films have done much to activate (and elaborate upon) that "informed sense of similarity and difference."

A connecting thread in the chapters of this volume is an exploration of the various reasons that Hitchcock's films have not been understood as the adaptations they in fact are. And the central theme of the book is the recovery and anatomizing of those hitherto occulted relationships. *Hitchcock at the Source* is very much *dans le vent* of contemporary adaptation studies in privileging a cinematic paradigm, reversing the customary directionality of inquiry, which begins with the page and ends with the screen. But in Hitchcock studies this book also breaks new ground by restoring to critical focus the shaping power of the director's literary sources, which constitute an important element of his cinematic authorship. We hope that the exciting work collected here will contribute substantially to the ongoing reevaluation of Hitchcock as an auteur begun by scholars such as Tom Ryall, who justly complained in 1986: "Auteur criticism has wrenched films and their directors from the historical circumstances of production and has defined the expression of the author's consciousness as responsible for the shape, form and meaning of a text" (1).

Ryall demonstrates how Hitchcock's authorship can be usefully measured by invoking the film cultures within which he worked, which provide "the critic with an overarching sense of a context for cinema, an indication of the options available in principle to a film maker at a particular point in time" (2). He is much in agreement with Charles Barr, who has recognized, speaking of Hitchcock's early work in the British cinema, that these "options" include ideas, values, and themes current in literary culture, as well as the particular texts in which these are embodied:

> A film criticism centred on directors . . . has not been concerned to follow up Hitchcock's statements . . . of indebtedness to English literary figures. Still less has it been concerned to explore the influence of his predominantly English source materials or of his English scriptwriters, to whom Hitchcock was far less inclined to give credit. His readiness to claim full authorship of the films, at the expense of his collaborators, can be seen as an unattractive egoism or as an astute marketing ploy, or as a mixture of both, but there is no reason for critics to continue to go along with it unquestioningly. (8)

Much the same, of course, may be said of Hitchcock's work for the Hollywood cinema, which is better known but equally misunderstood in terms of its literary context. Here also is a well-known body of films that can usefully be claimed for an "ongoing process of juxtaposed readings," problematizing the received fiction of Hitchcock's "full authorship" but also enriching our understanding of these works in their cultural context and of artistry exercised by their director in transferring the written word to the screen.

Somewhat paradoxically, then, this volume, while privileging in a traditional fashion the role of Hitchcock as an honored auteur, also directs critical attention away from the films in themselves as products of his undoubted genius. Simply by reading Hitchcock's films as adaptations, the chapters in this volume reject the customary neoromantic construction of Hitchcock as a self-sufficient genius, bringing into critical focus the director's engagement with literary sources, including his collaborative work with screenwriters. *Hitchcock at the Source*, to be sure, promotes a different model for adaptation studies, one that privileges the cinematic over the literary. But our aim here is also literaricizing, in the sense that this volume explores the deep roots of Hitchcockian cinema within Victorian and modern literary culture. Or, to put this another way, this book explores the often complex interconnections between the terms *Hitchcockian* and *adaptation*, problematizing but enriching the sense in which we understand his films to be authored.

"Hitchcockian . . . Characteristic of or Resembling Sir Alfred Hitchcock, British Director of Suspense Films (1899–1980), or His Work"

The authority of the *Oxford English Dictionary* notwithstanding, up until the mid-1930s the work which members of the British filmgoing public would probably have thought most characteristic of Alfred Hitchcock was not suspense films but rather literary adaptations: more specifically, as Thomas Leitch points out in the opening essay of this volume, theatrical adaptations, screen versions of recent hits by such West End luminaries as John Galsworthy, Noël Coward, and Ivor Novello. But with the release of the "thriller sextet" that established his international reputation, starting with *The Man Who Knew Too Much* in 1934, Hitchcock was transformed forever into the "Master of Suspense." Interestingly enough, this career redirection was managed through a deep engagement with a then-popular literary and cinematic series: the spy thriller.

Two of the British thrillers, in fact, bring to the screen notable literary sources: W. Somerset Maugham's *Ashenden* (1928) and Joseph Conrad's *Secret Agent* (1907). But these literary connections are carefully downplayed as the films in question, through a retitling that emphasizes genre, were not marketed as adaptations. Both released in 1936, *Ashenden* emerged as *Secret Agent* and *The Secret Agent* as *Sabotage*—a confusing bit of nomenclature musical chairs that was perhaps deliberate. In any event, Hitchcock continued throughout the remainder of his career to be a Master of Adaptation—and to do his best to deny any dependence of literary sources. Of the fifty-four feature-length films that he directed, forty-one were based on previously published or produced works (see appendix). His involvement with adaptation, furthermore, both preceded and extended beyond his feature films. As Leitch points out, the twenty films on which Hitchcock worked in various capacities prior to his directorial debut were all, without exception, adaptations. And the great majority of the seventeen episodes of his television shows *Alfred Hitchcock Presents* and *The Alfred Hitchcock Hour* that he himself directed between 1955 and 1962 were also derived from previously existing works (including no fewer than four from stories by Raoul Dahl).

Why, then, have Hitchcock's adaptations generally received so little attention *as* adaptations? After all, as we have suggested, the adaptation of literary works to the screen has been the subject of increasing, and increasingly sophisticated, critical and scholarly attention in recent years. But with a few notable exceptions, such as Charles Barr's *English Hitchcock*, already noted, relatively little notice has been taken of Hitchcock's sources. Possibly part of the reason lies in the diverse nature of those sources, ranging as they do across the sociocultural spectrum from the highest of highbrow (*The Secret Agent*, an established classic of modernist fiction), through middlebrow bestsellers such as *Rebecca*, to the lowest of lowbrow (a short story published in *Dime Detective* magazine). Many, perhaps most, of Hitchcock's important and successful films were adapted from the lower end of that spectrum, but the attention of film scholars has generally tended to focus on the upper end. *Rear Window*, for instance, based on that story from *Dime Detective* magazine, is only one of more than two dozen films (from France, Italy, Germany, Spain, Argentina, Brazil, and Japan, as well as Hollywood), adapted from the works of Cornell Woolrich. But there is as yet no volume of essays on "Cornell Woolrich on Film" sitting on library shelves alongside those addressing the screen versions of fiction by Jane Austen and Charles Dickens.

The sources, furthermore, are often obscure; certainly the nature and extent of Hitchcock's indebtedness is not always adequately indicated in the screen credits of the films. *Secret Agent* is ostensibly based on a Somerset Maugham novel, but *Ashenden* is actually a collection of short stories, several of which were, it seems, turned into an apparently unproduced stage play of the same name (now unfortunately lost). This initial remaking likely influenced Charles Bennett's screenplay decisively, but in ways that are now beyond recovery. The credits for *Spellbound*, to take another example, inform us that Ben Hecht's script was "suggested by Francis Beeding's novel *The House of Dr. Edwardes*." That vaguely suggestive "suggested" is perhaps fair enough, given the radical nature of the transformation involved (although no more radical, surely, than those involved in some other Hitchcock films, such as *The Birds*, which takes little more than its narrative premise from the Daphne du Maurier story on which the film's screen credits unproblematically announce it is based). In other cases, though, the credits for a film leave its ultimate origins not merely obscure, but wholly unacknowledged, as Matthew Bernstein demonstrates in tracing the relationship of Hecht's screenplay for *Notorious* to a long-forgotten story that appeared in *The Saturday Evening Post*.

In still other cases, the influence of particular texts extends far beyond the films for which they serve as acknowledged sources. For instance, Hitchcock directed only one film openly based on a novel by John Buchan, *The 39 Steps* (1934), but he frequently acknowledged Buchan's wider impact on his work. And quite rightly: Mark Glancy convincingly demonstrates the extent to which *The Man Who Knew Too Much*, released the year before *The 39 Steps*, was influenced by Buchan's novel *The Three Hostages*, and many critics have pointed out that *North by Northwest*, putatively based on an original script by Ernest Lehman, is virtually an updated and Americanized version of *The 39 Steps* itself. Similarly, Marie Belloc-Lowndes's influence on Hitchcock extends beyond his 1926 version of her novel *The Lodger* to inform, in a general way, many of the director's exercises in female Gothic in the 1940s, and in a very specific way *Shadow of a Doubt*, which picks up not merely the general narrative premise of a family home invaded by a serial killer but such telling details as a landlady remarking on the money left strewn on the killer's bedside table. Any adequate attempt to deal with Hitchcock's relationship to his sources has to confront those sources in all of their diversity: highbrow, middlebrow, and lowbrow; acknowledged and unacknowledged; direct and indirect. That "sea of countless earlier texts," to invoke Leitch's canny formula, upon which the director draws for his films includes those to which he returns again and again.

But that diversity is not the only reason for the relatively scant attention that this subject has previously received. If from the mid-1930s on it became increasingly difficult to think of Hitchcock as anything other than a "director of suspense films," with the rise of the auteur theory in the 1950s, it became increasingly difficult to think of him as anything other than a director of "Hitchcockian" films. His films came to be seen as constituting, in effect, a genre in themselves. And understandably, of course, since no filmmaker has ever produced a body of work more coherent (narratively, thematically, and stylistically) than Hitchcock's. But the idea of directorial authorship so firmly imposed itself on the study of Hitchcock's films that it tended to suppress alternative or complementary approaches. Any film demands to be understood in more than a single context. *Psycho*, for instance, may most immediately present itself for understanding in terms of its parallels with other Hitchcock films stretching back to *The Lodger*. But it also holds a pivotal place in the history of the horror film, and it therefore needs to be considered within its generic context; it marked a shift in the history of American film production, from the studio system to the package system, so it can be useful to look at it within an industrial context; and, not least, it is based on a novel by Robert Bloch, and it can therefore be illuminating to examine it, as Brian McFarlane does here, as an adaptation.

Moreover, the study of Hitchcock's films in relation to their sources can help to illuminate more than the individual films. As noted earlier, studies of adaptation have often tended to privilege literature over film simply by virtue of taking the literary sources as their starting point and their organizing principle. This volume reverses the common pattern, and rather than examining the centrifugal process by which a given author is adapted into a variety of films by different filmmakers (Austen on Film, Dickens on Film), it considers the centripetal process by which a diversity of literary sources are transformed into a coherent body of work by a single filmmaker. In other words, it raises the question of how works by authors as utterly different as, say, Joseph Conrad, Daphne du Maurier, and Cornell Woolrich all manage to end up transformed into films as unmistakably Hitchcockian as *Sabotage*, *Rebecca*, and *Rear Window*.

According to Hitchcock himself, there was nothing in the least mysterious about this alchemy: the sources, he explained to interviewers whenever given the opportunity, were of no real importance at all. "What I do is to read a story only once," he told François Truffaut, "and if I like the basic idea, I just forget all about the book and start to create cinema." But as the essays in this volume demonstrate again and again, it was not the books that Hitchcock tended to forget, but rather his indebtedness to them. That is not to say that his films are ever simply recyclings of their sources, any more than Shakespeare's history plays are merely retellings of Holinshed's *Chronicles*. The radical process involved in Hitchcockian remaking often moves beyond adaptation proper to what Julie Sanders usefully terms "appropriation," which "frequently effects a more decisive journey away from the informing source into a wholly new cultural product and domain." (26). Nevertheless, what survives from page or stage to screen is, however radically transformed, generally something more than just "the basic idea." The conditions under which Hitchcock went about "creating cinema," furthermore, as he himself frequently complained to interviewers, often played as crucial a role in the process as his own artistic vision.

The process of adaptation, as Robert Stam concisely describes it, is always "mediated by a series of filters: studio style, ideological fashion, political constraints, auteurist predilections, charismatic stars, economic advantage or disadvantage, and technology" (68). Hitchcock's films were no exception. It was the interference of studios and censorship boards, for instance, that transformed the murderers in *The Lodger* and *Rebecca* into falsely accused men and that denied Hitchcock the darker conclusions for *Suspicion* and *The Birds* that he claimed he would have preferred. The importance of these various filters varied, naturally, from film to film, as did the nature and extent of the changes involved (changes of tone, style, and point-of-view, as well as of character and event). Accordingly, the authors in this volume differ in the approaches that they take and the matters on which they focus. Collectively, however, they offer a view of the relationship of Hitchcock's films to their sources which reflects both the diversity of the sources and the complex coherence of the films.

Works Cited

Barr, Charles. *English Hitchcock*. Moffat: Cameron & Hollis, 1999.

Leitch, Thomas. "Adaptation Studies at a Crossroads." *Adaptation* 1 (2008): 63–77.

Ryall, Tom. *Alfred Hitchcock and the British Cinema*. Urbana and Chicago: University of Illinois Press, 1986.

Sanders, Julie. *Adaptation and Appropriation*. London and New York: Routledge, 2006.

Stam, Robert. "Beyond Fidelity: The Dialogics of Adaptation." In James Naremore, ed., *Film Adaptation*. New Brunswick, NJ: Rutgers University Press, 2000.

1

THOMAS LEITCH

Hitchcock from Stage to Page

*T*HE *PLEASURE GARDEN* (1925), THE FIRST feature Alfred Hitchcock directed at Gainsborough Pictures, was based on a novel. So was his third film, *The Lodger* (1926), and his ninth, *The Manxman* (1929). In the context of Hitchcock's early work, however, these three films are anomalies. Although *The Mountain Eagle* (1926), *The Ring* (1927), and *Champagne* (1928) were produced from original screenplays, all the other silent films Hitchcock directed at Gainsborough or British International Pictures—*Downhill* (1927), *Easy Virtue* (1927), *The Farmer's Wife* (1928), *Blackmail* (1929)—were based on theatrical plays rather than novels. Once Hitchcock began making films with synchronized soundtracks at British International, only *Murder!* (1930), its German-language version *Mary* (1930), and *Rich and Strange* (1931) were based on novels. All the others—the synch-sound version of *Blackmail* (1929), along with *Juno and the Paycock* (1930), *The Skin Game* (1931), *Number Seventeen* (1932), and *Waltzes from Vienna* (1933), produced by Tom Arnold for Gaumont-British Pictures—were adaptations of plays. All told, eight of the first sixteen films Hitchcock directed (counting the two versions of *Blackmail* and the two versions of *Murder!* as one film each) were based on theatrical sources.

There is nothing unusual about these proportions. Hitchcock grew up only a few miles from the greatest theatrical district in the world, and he was an avid playgoer from his youth. When he came to direct films, he undoubtedly found that plays offered source material more readily

11

adaptable to the cinema than novels, since they were already conceived as an evening's entertainment whose characters and plots were dramatized by conventionally coded external action. It might seem odd that theatrical adaptations would play so large a role in Hitchcock's silent filmography, where spoken language was replaced with more sparing intertitles. But they had played an equally prominent role in the earlier films on which Hitchcock had worked as a designer of intertitles, art director, scenarist, assistant director, or codirector. Two of these earlier films were based on short stories, seven on plays, seven on novels, and two on theatrical adaptations of novels. Contemporaneous films such as Ernst Lubitsch's *Lady Windermere's Fan* (1925) and F. W. Murnau's *Last Laugh* (1927) showed, after all, that silent films could dispense with the sparkling dialogue of their theatrical originals, in Lubitsch's case, or with any dialogue at all, in Murnau's. Small wonder, then, that Hitchcock's early work "draws from novel and theatre in equal measure" (Barr 14).

The wonder is what happened afterward, beginning with the 1934 version of *The Man Who Knew Too Much*, which was based on an original screenplay by Charles Bennett and D. B. Wyndham Lewis, who took as their inspiration the Bulldog Drummond stories of H. C. McNeile. The film's highly episodic structure marked a break with the more tightly woven theatrical models of *Easy Virtue*, *The Farmer's Wife*, *Juno and the Paycock*, and *The Skin Game*. And this break became decisive with *The 39 Steps* (1935), based on an already picaresque espionage novel that became in the hands of Hitchcock and his scenarists Charles Bennett, Alma Reville, and Ian Hay even more episodic. Every one of the remaining films Hitchcock directed in England—*Secret Agent* (1936), *Sabotage* (1937), *Young and Innocent* (1937), *The Lady Vanishes* (1938), *Jamaica Inn* (1939)—was based on a novel rather than a play. The only partial exceptions are *Sabotage*, which drew its inspiration from both Joseph Conrad's 1907 novel and his 1923 play of the same title, and *Secret Agent*, whose credits identify it as "From the play by Campbell Dixon, based on the novel *Ashenden* [1928] by W. Somerset Maugham." Hitchcock elaborated the relationship in an interview *Film Weekly* published on 30 May 1936: "*Secret Agent* consisted of two of the Ashenden stories, 'The Traitor' and 'The Hairless Mexican,' and also a play written by Campbell Dixon. We switched the two stories round, made Caypor the innocent victim, turned the Greek into an American, introduced a train smash for dramatic purposes, and obtained the love interest from the play" (qtd. in Barr 236). Even though Dixon's play may never have been published or produced, *Secret Agent*, together with *The Lodger*, *Sabotage*, and *The Manxman*, which was based on *Pete*, Hall Caine's 1908 theatrical adaptation of his 1894 novel, is notable as one of four Hitchcock films based on novels, or in

Maugham's case cycles of stories, that were dramatized for the stage before they were adapted to the cinema.

Once Hitchcock had begun to rely mainly on novels rather than plays as source material for his films, he never looked back. Only three of the films Hitchcock directed after *Secret Agent*—*Rope* (1948), *I Confess* (1952), and *Dial M for Murder* (1953)—are based on plays. Of the remaining films, *Foreign Correspondent* (1940) is based loosely on a memoir; *The Wrong Man* (1957) on a magazine article; *Rear Window* (1954) and *The Birds* (1963) on short stories; *Saboteur* (1942), *Aventure Malgache* (1944), *Notorious* (1946), *North by Northwest* (1959), and *Torn Curtain* (1966) on original screenplays; *Mr. and Mrs. Smith* (1941), *Shadow of a Doubt* (1943), *Lifeboat* (1944), and *Bon Voyage* (1944) on stories written directly for the screen; and *The Man Who Knew Too Much* (1956), though once again crediting a story by Bennett and Wyndham Lewis, on an original screenplay drawing primarily on Hitchcock's 1934 film. All the others—fifteen of the thirty-two films Hitchcock directed after coming to America in 1939—were based on novels, five times as many as were based on plays.

This move from theatrical to novelistic adaptations is even more pronounced if it is defined as a move from adapting works from the stage to adapting works on the page (novels, short stories, stories written directly for film studios without going through an earlier theatrical incarnation). Not only does Hitchcock shift from depending primarily on theatrical sources to depending primarily on prose fiction, but that shift corresponds precisely with his identification in the later 1930s with the thriller as his chosen medium. Of the four thrillers Hitchcock directed before the 1934 *Man Who Knew Too Much*, two (*The Lodger* and *Murder!*) were based on novels and two (*Blackmail* and *Number Seventeen*) on plays. But most of Hitchcock's early theatrical adaptations are forgotten except by Hitchcock scholars. In committing himself to adapting novels and stories rather than plays, Hitchcock seems to have found the creative voice he maintained had eluded him in the adaptations of *Juno and the Paycock* and *Waltzes from Vienna*. Although all the three later films he based on theatrical sources—*Rope*, *I Confess*, and *Dial M for Murder*—are highly characteristic, none of them is among his most highly regarded. In a fundamental sense, the Hitchcock acknowledged around the world as the Master of Suspense is also a master of novelistic adaptation.

Hitchcock's increasing dependence on novels as source material for his films is not surprising, especially after his move to America. Although the United States offered a theatrical culture nearly as rich in its way as England's, that culture was based in New York, three thousand miles from the Hitchcocks' home in California. By his own account, the director rarely attended the theater once he had settled in America. His contact with Broadway was mostly limited to the paternal eye he cast over his daughter Patricia's theatrical training and his affinity for writers familiar with the theater, from playwright Samuel Taylor, who worked on the screenplays for *Vertigo* (1958) and *Topaz* (1969), to critic John Russell Taylor, who became Hitchcock's authorized biographer. At the same time, Hollywood showed an increasing interest after 1940 in adapting novels that had not yet been adapted to the theater. Hitchcock's shift from stage to page in search of material for his films could doubtless be paralleled among many other American-based filmmakers once the demand for theatrical material and theatrically trained writers ushered in by the arrival of synchronized sound had crested. What remains surprising is Hitchcock's continued fondness for source material for whose customary strengths he had so little use, material that offered enduring challenges for filmmakers in general and Hitchcock in particular.

An obvious advantage novels are commonly observed to have over plays, for example, is their more generous scope. *Antony and Cleopatra* and *The Skin of Our Teeth* apart, most novels feature larger casts of characters developing over longer periods of time in a broader range of locations than most plays, offering filmmakers a wider range of photogenic backgrounds. But although Hitchcock films from *The Manxman* to *To Catch a Thief* (1955) attest to the director's interest in eye-catching location shots and films from *Foreign Correspondent* to *North by Northwest* to his ability to handle large casts, most of his films focus on small groups of characters in circumscribed locations. The contrast between *North by Northwest* and *Torn Curtain*, on the one hand, and the series of James Bond adaptations starring Sean Connery that they bookend, on the other, is instructive. Compared to the Bond films, these two spy films, neither of them based on a novel, take place in a much more restricted set of locations and shun pictorial effects. When Hitchcock adapts the plays *Rope's End* (1929) and *Dial "M" for Murder* (1952), he does not open them out in the fashion prescribed by adaptation textbooks, but rather emphasizes their sense of claustrophobic enclosure by confining the action to a single set, imposing in the case of *Rope* the additional discipline of shooting only in long takes that generally imply a single, unbroken, eighty-minute shot. If Hitchcock's increasing reliance on novelistic sources reflects a special affinity his films have with novels, then it is not the obvious sort of affinity that depends on the pictorialism of John Ford or the epic scale of Cecil B. DeMille. Indeed, the fact that Hitchcock developed two other one-set films from nontheatrical sources, *Lifeboat* from an original screen story and *Rear Window* from Cornell Woolrich's 1942 short story "It Had to Be Murder," suggests that he was less attracted to prose fiction by the freedom it provided than by the challenges it offered.

Many of these challenges have been catalogued in general studies of adaptation. Novels are longer than movies, so adapting novels to the screen requires extensive pruning of subsidiary characters, subplots, and long speeches. Novels are normally more discursive than plays, so adapting them to the movies involves imposing tighter structural constraints than the form of the novel demands. Novels abound in generalizations, accounts of habitual actions, and descriptive passages that must be either lost or translated into the very different expositional strategies of cinema. Novels are designed to be absorbed discontinuously, at each reader's own speed; they are free to weave dense webs of signification through which readers can move at their leisure, free to ponder or ignore specific implications. Novels and movies mark tone and style in ways that are often parallel but never quite congruent. Novels can draw on an extensive variety of verb tenses; movies are restricted to the present tense. The verbal signifiers in novels communicate to their readers by means of concepts that require abstract thinking to assimilate, the visual signifiers in movies by percepts that require no such abstract thought. Hence even the visual and auditory images in novels that might seem to make them most cinematic operate differently in novels than in movies, in which every picture and sound is a potential locus of meaning. Novels tell, and movies show.

Some of these differences are truisms of adaptation theory; some are canards that have been repeatedly debunked (e.g., by Cardwell, Leitch, and Hutcheon); some contradict each other. Instead of using Hitchcock's adaptations to test these general principles in general terms, I wish to consider a narrower range of challenges the adaptation of novels, and short stories as well, posed to Hitchcock in particular. Hitchcock unfailingly presented himself as unintimidated by his literary sources, partly no doubt because they were so often subliterary. François Truffaut, interviewing Hitchcock, observed that "[y]our own works include a great many adaptations, but mostly they are popular or light entertainment novels, which are so freely refashioned in your own manner that they ultimately become a Hitchcock creation." When he suggested that "many of your admirers would like to see you undertake the screen version of such a major classic as Dostoyevsky's *Crime and Punishment*," Hitchcock tartly responded, "I'll have no part of that!" and explained that he had no desire to join "Hollywood directors [who] distort literary masterpieces," and added that he paid little attention to his alleged sources anyway: "What I do is to read a story only once, and if I like the basic idea, I just forget all about the book and start to create cinema" (70–71).

Most Hitchcock scholars, echoing authors such as Robert Bloch, have greeted the last of these claims with skepticism, and with good reason. *Murder!* borrows much of its dialogue nearly verbatim from Clemence Dane and Helen Simpson's novel *Enter Sir John* (1928). Thanks in large part to David O. Selznick's intervention, *Rebecca* (1940) is equally faithful to Daphne du Maurier's novel. Even *Spellbound* (1945), whose source novel, Francis Beeding's *House of Dr. Edwardes* (1928), Hitchcock dismissed as "melodramatic and quite weird" (Truffaut 163), takes from Beeding two central ideas: the criminal who disposes of the director of a mental asylum (by abduction in Beeding, by murder in Hitchcock) and takes over the position himself, and the hero rescued by the love of a female therapist. It is clearly true, however, that once he saw himself as having graduated from close stage adaptations like those of *Juno and the Paycock* and *The Skin Game*, Hitchcock treated his sources with increasing freedom. He lightened the tone of John Buchan's novel *The Thirty-Nine Steps* (1915) when he filmed *The 39 Steps*, Conrad's *The Secret Agent* when he filmed *Sabotage*, and Victor Canning's *Rainbird Pattern* (1972) when he filmed *Family Plot*. He changed both the proportions and the ending of David Dodge's *To Catch a Thief* (1952) when he filmed it in 1955, extending both the opening and the closing scenes into major sequences and having his hero turn the real thief over to the authorities instead of covering up for her. He introduced new murderers into Josephine Tey's *Shilling for Candles* (1936) when he adapted it as *Young and Innocent*— Tey's murderer does not even appear in the film—and Selwyn Jepson's *Outrun the Constable* (1948) when he filmed it as *Stage Fright* (1950). He added romantic subplots to each of the adaptations he made between 1935 and 1939: *The 39 Steps*, *Secret Agent*, *Sabotage*, *Young and Innocent*, *The Lady Vanishes*, *Jamaica Inn*. His adaptation of Daphne du Maurier's 1952 story "The Birds," perhaps the only Hitchcock adaptation fairly described by the procedure he indicated to Truffaut, borrows only the story's central idea—a series of apparently unmotivated but apocalyptic attacks by masses of birds against humans—while changing its characters, setting, scope, duration, and tone.

Readers skeptical of Hitchcock's claims to have forgotten all about the book so that he can start to create cinema will rightly be suspicious of many of the claims of my previous paragraph as well, for its repeatedly active singular verbs ("Hitchcock treated . . . he lightened . . . he changed . . . he introduced . . . he added") ascribes a decisive agency to Hitchcock that is more properly shared among many of his collaborators. *The Lady Vanishes*, the film whose mixture of humor and suspense brought Hitchcock to Selznick's attention, is perhaps the most influential of all his English films on both the course of his own career and his distinctive contribution to the thriller. Yet Frank Launder claimed that he had written the screenplay together with Sidney Gilliat substantially as it was eventually filmed "not [for] Hitchcock at all but Roy William Neill" (Brown 89) before Hitchcock expressed an interest in the adaptation after the original production was abandoned. It seems likely that early and late in his career, the screenwriters Hitchcock acknowledged as his closest collaborators did much of the work of shaping adaptations for which he was increasingly ready to take credit.

Charles Barr has done a great deal not only to illuminate the contributions specific screenwriters made to the films Hitchcock directed in England but to provide a useful way of framing the distinctive nature of the problem of authorship in Hitchcock. He quotes a representative assessment of the problem by David Sterritt: "Although [Hitchcock] never wrote his own screenplays . . . he exercised great care in shaping the screenplays that others wrote for him. He was able to do this because of the extraordinary degree of personal power he gained in the film industry . . . As much as any major filmmaker ever has, he channeled the talent of his collaborators and the temper of his times into coherent narrative/aesthetic patterns dictated by his own deepest instincts" (2).

Acknowledging the force of this assessment, Barr adds an important disclaimer: "It deals with the phenomenon that Hitchcock became. I deal here with the English period, with the gradual and uneven process of his becoming (or anyway starting to become) the Hitchcock we all think we know" (11).

In a fundamental sense, of course, Hitchcock is always becoming Hitchcock. The 1934 *Man Who Knew Too Much* marked an important new direction in his career that the earlier Hitchcock would have found well-nigh unrecognizable. So did *Rebecca, Notorious, Rear Window*, and *Psycho* (1960). Indeed Hitchcock has continued to develop posthumously at the hands of critics who have discovered so many different tendencies in his body of work that a thousand Hitchcocks have bloomed. At the same time, it seems clear that even before *The Pleasure Garden*, Hitchcock was unusually intent on enlarging and consolidating his professional power as he moved from designing intertitles to decorating sets, writing screenplays, and codirecting films in what his commentators eventually came to describe, in Sterritt's terms, as an attempt to impose patterns dictated by his own deepest instincts on his films. So the relationship between Hitchcock the established phenomenon and the Hitchcock under construction is dialectical and evolving. An important point of potential agreement between Sterritt and Barr, though neither of them considers it directly, is that after a certain point in his career, Hitchcock the phenomenon can be stipulated by producers, screenwriters, performers, and other collaborators who can anticipate what the director is likely to want because they know his work, know his reputation, know what it means for a film to be what Truffaut called "a Hitchcock creation." Although Hitchcock directed only a small number of episodes of *Alfred Hitchcock Presents* (1955–62) and *The Alfred Hitchcock Hour* (1962–65), the entire run of both programs feels thoroughly Hitchcockian, or perhaps more precisely Hitchcockized, because a tone was established, properties were chosen, teleplays were written, and performers were cast and directed as expressions of a persona he no longer needed to assert directly himself.

In sum, then, a phrase such as *Hitchcock chose* or *Hitchcock changed* a given property for adaptation can carry three different meanings. It can indicate, as Sterritt does, that Hitchcock himself was responsible for the choices and changes. It can imply, as Barr does, that writers such as Launder and Gilliat or producers such as John Maxwell and Michael Balcon made the decisions that history has reassigned to a Hitchcock who was still in the process of becoming Hitchcock—and became Hitchcock more completely by benefiting from and internalizing those decisions. Or it can identify decisions that were made by others on behalf of a Hitchcock that had already become a recognizable persona, albeit one that might be still further developed by these decisions.

It is a commonplace of Hitchcock criticism, more often assumed than asserted, that Hitchcock's identification with the suspense genre marked a crucial development in the process of becoming Hitchcock. To this Barr adds the argument that Hitchcock's association with both a specifically English literary and theatrical culture and a series of screenwriters headed by Eliot Stannard and Charles Bennett helped make him Hitchcock. Without wishing to diminish the force of either of these arguments, the rest of this chapter will explore a third proposition: that Hitchcock's metamorphosis into the Hitchcock we all recognize, the Hitchcock that could be stipulated by his collaborators and marketed by his studios, depends on his turn away from plays and theatrical models to novels and novelistic models for his films.

This turn is peculiar, as I suggested, because Hitchcock's films based on novels continue in important ways to feel histrionic, theatrical, or stagy in eschewing the novel's clear invitation to pictorialism, variety of tone or incident, and temporal or geographical sweep. But it is even more peculiar because Hitchcock, along with the collaborators who worked on his many adaptations of novels, evidently continued to regard novels as posing specific narrative problems plays did not pose. Hitchcock, who never shrank from challenges as long as they were imposed by himself or his subordinate collaborators and not by a producer with veto power, seems to have found in the novels he adapted a series of particular challenges and an invitation to a general discipline that went far to define his distinctive contribution to the cinema: an unprecedented and deeply influential emphasis on focalizing a divided consciousness.

In 1963 Hitchcock told a *Cinema* interviewer that *"Rear Window* is purely subjective treatment—what Jimmy Stewart sees all the time" and then agrees with the interviewer's suggestion: "Could we say that a strong point in your style would be this subjective treatment?" by adding, "Subjective treatment. As against the objective. You see, the objective is the stage. Is the theater. We are audience looking at people on the stage. We aren't with them, we aren't getting any viewpoint you see" (Hitchcock 291). Discovering and exploring the possibilities of a divided subjectivity in each of the properties he adapted began the process of Hitchcockizing the source. Despite his movement away from theatrical models, however, Hitchcock rarely imitates prose fiction's ready access to his characters' subjectivity. In this regard none of his films, not even *Rear Window*, is "purely subjective." Instead, he makes each of them, even his heroes and heroines, just opaque enough to make the search for cues to their emotions and development interesting.

Barr notes that Eliot Stannard's screenwriting primer places special "emphasis on the potential of cross-cutting" as a means to "tight organic construction" (25). Stannard's emphasis on cutting between related actions in two separate locations as a way of generating suspense reflects a staple device in D. W. Griffith's imperiled-heroine films, from *The Lonely Villa* (1909) to *Orphans of the Storm* (1921), a device Griffith brings to an apotheosis in the intermingling of four widely separated historical periods in *Intolerance* (1916). However great Stannard's influence on Hitchcock may have been, however, he did not persuade him to make crosscutting an important part of his own cinematic grammar. Even Hitchcock's earliest suspense films are notable for their departure from the Griffith model of suspense. It is true that Hitchcock can use crosscutting effectively to ratchet up suspense. Everyone remembers the episode in which Sam Loomis cross-examines Norman Bates in *Psycho* while Lila Crane is searching the Bates house for Mrs. Bates and the bravura sequence in which Bruno Anthony strains to retrieve Guy Haines's cigarette lighter as Guy is struggling to win his tennis match so that he can rush off to prevent Bruno from planting the lighter at the crime scene in *Strangers on a Train* (1951). But these sequences are exceptions to Hitchcock's customary rule of crosscutting within a particular location: the event-reaction sequence as Sir John Menier watches Handel Fane's last trapeze act in *Murder!* the Albert Hall sequence in the 1934 *Man Who Knew Too Much*, the agonizing cuts from the series of clocks outside the bus Stevie is riding to the interior of the bus to the timer on the bomb he is carrying just before the explosion in *Sabotage*, the episode in *Foreign Correspondent* in which Huntley Haverstock, hiding in the windmill, is almost revealed to the spies when his raincoat is caught in the machinery, the finales atop the Statue of Liberty in *Saboteur* and Mount Rushmore in *North by Northwest*. And at least one Hitchcock film, *Number Seventeen*, concludes with a sequence whose crosscutting between the imperiled heroine and the rescuer riding a series of startlingly unexpected vehicles to her side is so extended that it seems to parody the Griffith model. But once he shifts from plays to novels as his primary source material, Hitchcock prefers to restrict himself to a single primary point of view, creating suspense by dramatizing the contradictions with the consciousness that point of view implies, instead of intensifying suspense along Griffith's lines by cutting between different centers of interest. By the time he comes to make *Vertigo* and the films that follow, "Hitchcock has let go of the need to link his hero's character development to a conventional suspense plot. The suspense no longer pretends to centre on how a man deals with an external event; it now focuses directly on his struggle with an internal one" (Cohen 24).

Because his most successful films are rooted in the consciousness of a single leading figure, adapting novels that unfold from a series of different points of view, even if these viewpoints are not presented in the first person, poses specific problems for Hitchcock that it would not pose for many another filmmaker. A number of the novels Hitchcock adapted— Joseph Conrad's *The Secret Agent* (1907), Robert Hichens's *The Paradine Case* (1933), Helen Simpson's *Under Capricorn* (1938), Jack Trevor Story's *The Trouble with Harry* (1950), Robert Bloch's *Psycho* (1959), Leon Uris's *Topaz* (1967), Victor Canning's *Rainbird Pattern*—move freely among multiple points of view. Hitchcock deals with such novels in several different ways. He is most comfortable with *The Trouble with Harry*, which creates a gently comic tone that requires no considerable psychological penetration by taking its characters very much on their own terms. In *Psycho*, he retains the same centers of narrative interest as Bloch's novel—Marion Crane (Mary in Bloch), Norman Bates, Lila Crane, Sam Loomis—but deepens the sense of intimacy with Marion and remains more distant from all the others, especially from Norman, within whose consciousness Bloch often, albeit deceptively, remains. Hitchcock's adaptation of Conrad shows his ability to shift viewpoints from one character to another, though his selection of characters so favored in *Sabotage*— Verloc, Stevie, Mrs. Verloc, Ted—is both different and narrower than Conrad's. He pares away asides in *Enter Sir John* like the moment when Martella Baring's barrister, watching Handell Fane, reflects: "He'd give his ears to be standing there instead of her. Poor devil!" (Dane and

Simpson 56) and in *To Catch a Thief* in which Claude warns Danielle that Jack Burns, the pseudonym under which John Robie has hired her as an escort, "will massage your legs under the table" (Dodge 46).

Hitchcock similarly narrows the number of what Henry James would call the "centers of consciousness" in adapting *Under Capricorn* (1949), focusing more narrowly on Charles Adare's point of view than Helen Simpson's novel does, and in adapting *The Rainbird Pattern*, marginalizing Grandison and Bush in order to concentrate on George Lumley and Arthur Adamson in *Family Plot* (1976). And he clearly relished the challenges of remaking the Albert Hall sequence in the 1956 *Man Who Knew Too Much*, this time from the rapidly alternating point of view of his hero and heroine and of cutting freely between Adamson's kidnappings and Lumley's search for the missing heir who turns out to be Adamson in *Family Plot*, whose working title was *One Plus One Equals One*. But his general habit of framing each story from a single point of view makes the scenes in which Sir Simon Flaquer and his daughter, Judy, comment on Antony Keane's marital woes seem like gratuitous expository interruptions in *The Paradine Case* (1947), and his shifting between Michael Nordstrom and André Devereaux's viewpoints, with occasional forays into Tamara Kusenov's, Philippe Dubois', and Juanita de Cordoba's, prevent *Topaz* from establishing the strong narrative center characteristic of Hitchcock's best films.

Hitchcock's preference for exploring a single divided consciousness often attracted him to first-person novels and stories. But although John Buchan's novel *The Thirty-Nine Steps*, Daphne du Maurier's *Rebecca* (1938), Selwyn Jepson's *Outrun the Constable* (1948), and Winston Graham's *Marnie* (1961), as well as Cornell Woolrich's "It Had to Be Murder," are all presented by first-person narrators, none of the films based on them—*The 39 Steps, Rebecca, Stage Fright, Marnie* (1964), and *Rear Window*—retains this narrator. Filmmakers have sometimes employed first-person narrators either discontinuously (as in *Sunset Blvd.* [1950]) or continuously (as in *Personal Velocity* [2002]) or restricted the cinematic field of vision to a particular character's point of view (*Lady in the Lake* [1946]; *The Blair Witch Project* [1999]). And the presence of a first-person narrator whose retrospective commentary frames the apparently contingent action ironically by casting it as foreordained from the beginning is a staple of film noir. Apart from retaining some of the famous opening paragraph of *Rebecca* as an introductory voiceover at Selznick's instance, however, Hitchcock makes no attempt to turn his films into first-person equivalents of the first-person narratives he adapts. In changing the first-person novels he sometimes adapts to what is usually called the "objective, third-person narrative" of cinema, Hitchcock

does no more than follow industry standards that generally discourage
first-person filmmaking.

Nonetheless, except for *Marnie*, which alternates between the viewpoints of Mark Rutland and the compulsive thief he has knowingly hired
as a bookkeeper, Hitchcock's adaptations of first-person novels are anything but objective. They continually imply a close, though not uncriti-
cal, identification with a single character's point of view. The obvious
exception to this rule provides its most striking illustration: Hitchcock's
adaptation of *Outrun the Constable* as *Stage Fright* (1950). The one thing
everyone remembers about *Stage Fright* is "a flashback that was a lie"
(Truffaut 189): the sequence in which Jonathan Cooper tells Eve Gill that
the police are chasing him because when his lover, Charlotte Inwood,
after killing her husband, came to him and begged him for help, he went
to her flat, planted new evidence designed to suggest that an intruder had
killed Inwood, and was spotted leaving the flat. Only at the climax does
the film reveal that the long flashback illustrating Jonathan's story, the
one extended episode at which Eve is not present, was a lie designed to
conceal the fact that Jonathan killed Inwood himself. Hitchcock expressed
a low opinion of both the film and the sequence, which he said was
something "I never should have done" (189). Yet he never mentions how
closely the sequence follows Jepson's novel, with one crucial difference.

Outrun the Constable, originally serialized in *Collier's* between 9
August and 13 September 1947 under the title *Man Running*, is the
first of Jepson's novels to feature amateur sleuth Eve Gill. It opens,
appropriately enough, with her reflections on her father's misfortune in
having no sons and a wooden leg that forced him to press his daughter into service when he wanted to climb a ladder through a window
in order to steal a painting from a relative. "But for this I would not
have met Jonathan [Penrose], nor taken upon myself the thankless task
of saving him," says Eve before the story abruptly shifts to Jonathan's
point of view: "Jonathan's daydream about Charlotte Inwood that same
unlucky evening was improbable enough for any miracle to embellish it,
for he was making it up as he went along" (Jepson 12). This ambiguous introduction of Jonathan's viewpoint is complemented by an equally
ambiguous shift to Charlotte's point of view after he leaves her: "One
can imagine how Charlotte Inwood came out of the ladies' room at the
Paradise and went back slowly to her table. She would have renewed
her make-up and taken another aspirin or so; Jonathan had been gone
about four minutes" (38).

The use of "daydream" and "making it up as he went along" in the
first passage and the subjunctive constructions "one can imagine how"
and "would have renewed" in the second seem to set up both passages as

lying flashbacks. Yet both present the absolute truth, for Jonathan really is innocent, and Charlotte really did confess the murder to him in order to secure his help, even though the end of the second episode reveals that the actual murderer was her lover, Freddy Williams, who killed her husband in her presence. In retaining Jonathan's flashback narrative even though he plans to undercut its authority in the end, Hitchcock provides a textbook illustration of the dangers that await him both when he departs from the single point of view both novel and film establish as normative and when he experiments with overtly first-person filmmaking. Hence his bewildered question to Truffaut: "Strangely enough, in movies, people never object if a man is shown telling a lie. . . . So why is it that we can't tell a lie through a flashback?" (189)—a question made even more pointed by the lack of protest that had greeted *Crossfire* (1947), whose flashback by the murderer had merely lied by omission. Hitchcock is at once most characteristic and most successful when he follows Henry James's formula in framing a story such as *The Lady Vanishes* or *Rear Window* or *Vertigo* "not as my own impersonal account of the affair at hand, but as my account of somebody's impression of it" (1322).

The novels and stories most readily turned into Hitchcock creations were those that found a middle way between first-person narration, which threatened to undermine each story with what James aptly terms "the terrible fluidity of self-revelation" (1316), and multiple points of view, which threatened to dissipate both the audience's rooting interest and the film's anatomy of consciousness. Not every such novel could be successfully Hitchcockized. Daphne du Maurier's *Jamaica Inn* (1936), for example, is a third-person novel that remains consistently close to the consciousness of its heroine, Mary Yellan. But despite occasional suggestions of moral or psychological complexity—for example, her sense that Francis Davey, the vicar of Altarnun who will turn out to be her uncle's partner in murder and robbery, has "something about him that made her untrue to herself" (177)—Mary is not an especially interesting character, simply a spirited young woman placed in an extraordinary situation. In this respect she resembles Richard Hannay, the hero of *The 39 Steps*, who "makes no declarations and has none to make" (Rothman 119). Unencumbered by any loyalty to period detail, Hitchcock can make Hannay's adventures more interesting than Mary's. But both films are essentially adventure films of a sort Hitchcock would leave behind after *Saboteur*. Although his early films focus on extraordinary situations, Hitchcock's adaptations of novels increasingly become anatomies of exactly the sort of consciousness neither Mary nor Hannay possesses.

This development in Hitchcock's career is all the more remarkable in view of the fact that Hitchcock's focus is never as psychological as that of, say, Ingmar Bergman's in films from *Wild Strawberries* (1957) through *Cries and Whispers* (1972) because his characters are never as complex as Bergman's. The heroine of *Rebecca* is more complex than Mary Yellan, and Roger Thornhill in *North by Northwest* is more complex than Richard Hannay. But even in *Vertigo*, Hitchcock's most profound exploration of subjectivity, the process by which the hero's consciousness is revealed is more interesting than the nature of that consciousness, which emerges from an ordinary enough subjectivity's confrontation with extraordinary circumstances rather than the revelation of an extraordinarily fine or subtle or sensitive subjectivity. However gripping the relations among his characters may be, Hitchcock's mature films are always more interested in the relation between the unfolding story of the film and its audience.

The device novels most often use to render a commonplace consciousness such as Emma Bovary's interesting, free indirect discourse [a technical literary term, a translation of "*style indirect libre*"] is often assumed to be the exclusive property of prose fiction. But several Hitchcock adaptations show how resourceful the director was in finding cinematic equivalents for this apparently literary device. Many of the novels that provide the basis for Hitchcock's most distinctive films—*The Lodger, Sabotage, Suspicion* (1941), *To Catch a Thief, Vertigo, Psycho*—present their stories in a third-person narrative couched largely in free, indirect discourse that inflects the narration with the judgments and internal language of a particular character. *D'entre les morts*, which Pierre Boileau and Thomas Narcejac published in 1954 under the name Boileau-Narcejac, freely intersperses Roger Flavières' surveillance of Madeleine Gévigne with Flavières' reflections, as when Madeleine visits the grave of her great-grandmother:

> She went on along the path which presently took her right into the heart of the cemetery. She stooped to pick up a red tulip, fallen from a vase, and still with the same leisurely gait went up to one of the graves and stopped. Hidden behind a mausoleum, Flavières was able to watch her at his ease. Madeleine's face showed neither exultation nor sorrow. On the contrary, the expression on it was one of peace and happiness. What thoughts were running through her mind? Her arms hung limply at her sides; her fingers still held the tulip. Once again she looked like a portrait, her whole being turned inwards, lost in some interior contemplation. (Boileau and Narcejac 26)

In presenting Scottie Ferguson's surveillance of Madeleine Elster, Hitchcock, eschewing as usual voiceover commentary, cannot indicate his hero's thoughts nearly so precisely. But he does pick up both certain details of presentation and interpretation (Madeleine's unreadable face looks like a portrait) and Flavières' bewilderment. In fact, Boileau and Narcejac simplify the job of their adapter by making their hero's uncertainty about how to interpret Madeleine's behavior the keynote of the sequence:

> Crossing the Seine, she stopped on the bridge and leant with her elbows on the parapet, stroking her cheek with the tulip. Had she given someone a rendezvous? . . . Or was she simply resting? . . . Perhaps she was only nursing her own ennui, as she watched the swirling wake of a steamer or the fascinating undulations of the reflections in the water . . . She leant over the parapet, looking at herself far below in the water, with the whole sky above her and the long curve of the bridge cutting across her shoulders. (Boileau and Narcejac 28)

The way in which Hitchcock films this sequence, alternating long shots of Madeleine's trancelike actions with medium close-ups of Scottie's facial reactions, faithfully reproduces both the heroine's unreadability and the hero's puzzlement. But it adds a new complication not present in the novel. Boileau and Narcejac keep their heroine at a distance, presenting her as the hero sees her, but provide direct access to the hero's mind. But Hitchcock, although he may seem to be following the same procedure, is actually doing something quite different by keeping not only his heroine but also his hero at a distance. It may be obvious that Scottie is bewildered by Madeleine's behavior, but bewilderment is not all he feels; without knowing it, he is falling in love with her, as he reveals when he passionately murmurs her name after rescuing her from an apparent suicide attempt. Peter Lev has aptly observed that although Scottie, unlike Flavières, has "no privileged interior monologues," Hitchcock's view of him is filtered through "colors, movement, setting, pacing, speech rhythm, music—indeed, the entire palette of cinematic creativity—[which] turn this superficially objective view into a richly subjective experience" (179). At the same time, as Richard Allen puts it, "we can only understand the nature of the character's emotional state through the reaction shot that objectively renders the character's emotional response to what it is that he or she sees" (185). Viewers generally assume they can read the thoughts and emotions of characters shown in close-up reaction shots. As Hitchcock observed to Truffaut, however, these reaction shots are often objective in the sense established by Lev Kuleshov: they are essentially blank slates onto which viewers project their own desires (215–16). The challenge of reading Scottie's growing obsession with Madeleine through representational codes which, like Madeleine's actions, seem more transparent than they are makes the film's presentation both intensely subjective and critically detached.

This combination of intimacy and detachment is hardly unique to Hitchcock. Many of the novels he adapted include passages of psychological description that depend on free indirect discourse to create a combination of intimacy and distance. Here is Mrs. Bunting, the landlady in Marie Belloc Lowndes's *The Lodger*, distraught by her suspicions that her mysterious lodger is a murderer:

> She pressed her hot forehead against the cool bit of looking glass let into the hat-and-umbrella stand. "I don't know what to do!" she moaned to herself, and then, "I can't bear it! I can't bear it!"
>
> But though she felt that her secret suspense and trouble were becoming intolerable, the one way in which she could have ended her misery never occurred to Mrs. Bunting.
>
> In the long history of crime, it has very, very seldom happened that a woman has betrayed one who has taken refuge with her. The timorous and cautious woman has not infrequently hunted a human being fleeing from his pursuer to her door, but she has not revealed the fact that he was ever there. In fact, it may almost be said that such betrayal has never taken place unless the betrayer has been actuated by love of gain, or by a longing for revenge. So far, perhaps because she is subject rather than citizen, her duty as a component part of civilized society weighs but lightly on woman's shoulders.
>
> And then—and then, in a sort of way, Mrs. Bunting had become attached to Mr. Sleuth. A wan smile would sometimes light up his sad face when he saw her come in with one of his meals, and when this happened Mrs. Bunting felt pleased—pleased and vaguely touched. In between those—those dreadful events outside, which filled her with such suspicion, such anguish and such suspense, she never felt any fear, only pity, for Mr. Sleuth. (Belloc Lowndes 129)

Here Belloc Lowndes begins with a readily adaptable bit of exterior action in the opening paragraph, shifts in the first half of the one-sentence second paragraph to free indirect discourse, and then shifts again in the second half of that paragraph to an idea specifically excluded from Mrs. Bunting's consciousness before continuing in the third paragraph with a long excursus from an Olympian point of view far removed from Mrs. Bunting's and returning in the fourth paragraph to a free indirect discourse clearly flavored with Mrs. Bunting's own viewpoint and rhetoric.

Hitchcock told Truffaut that when he came to adapt *The Lodger*, which he knew through Horace Vachell's 1916 stage adaptation *Who Is He*, "I treated it very simply, purely from [the landlady's] point of view" (43). Once again, this is not really so, though for different reasons than in *Vertigo*. Unlike Belloc Lowndes's novel, Hitchcock's film includes many scenes from which Mrs. Bunting is absent, especially the scene in which the lodger "make[s] himself agreeable" to Daisy—Mrs. Bunting's step-daughter in Belloc Lowndes, her daughter in Hitchcock—and the final sequences, in which the lodger first sits with Daisy and tells her the story of the sister's murder he has been determined to avenge, then is joined with her in a happily-ever-after epilogue. There are many moments that strongly imply Mrs. Bunting's point of view, notably the shot of the lodger pacing overhead on a glass ceiling and the sequence in which Mrs. Bunting sits up in bed and listens to what a series of crosscuts reveal to be the sound of the lodger descending the staircase in the dead of night.

More to the point, Hitchcock never needs to adapt the quoted passage from Belloc Lowndes because although his landlady also suspects that her lodger may be a murderer, she harbors no particular desire to protect him from the police. Indeed, the moment she becomes certain that he is a murderer, she is single-mindedly frantic in her desire to protect her daughter from him. True, Hitchcock's lodger is not the murderer that Belloc Lowndes's lodger is. But this change is almost beside the point of the film's handling of subjectivity. A much more important change in this connection is that Hitchcock's landlady is greatly simplified psychologically. She is not torn between suspicion and loyalty to her lodger; she merely suspects something menacing of which she remains uncertain. Hitchcock's landlady never shows any inclination to protect a man she thinks is a killer. The most important difference between the novel and its film adaptation is not a difference in strategies of focalization but a difference in the subjectivity being focalized.

This difference is thrown into sharper relief by Hitchcock's adaptation of a third episode, a more complex and savagely ironic passage in Joseph Conrad's novel *The Secret Agent*. This passage, which Hitchcock adapts far more directly than the passage in Belloc Lowndes, shows Winnie Verloc avenging the death of her brother, Stevie, sent to his death by the husband who had given the unwitting young man a bomb that exploded before he could leave the package in which it was hidden at the Greenwich Observatory:

> "Come here," [Mr. Verloc] said in a peculiar tone, which might have been the tone of brutality, but was intimately known to Mrs. Verloc as the tone of wooing.

She started forward at once, as if she were still a loyal woman bound to that man by an unbroken contract. Her right hand skimmed slightly the end of the table, and when she had passed on towards the sofa the carving knife had vanished without the slightest sound from the side of the dish. Mr. Verloc heard the creaky plank in the floor, and was content. He waited. Mrs. Verloc was coming. As if the homeless soul of Stevie had flown for shelter straight to the breast of his sister, guardian, and protector, the resemblance of her face with that of her brother grew at every step, even to the droop of the lower lip, even to the slight divergence of the eyes. But Mr. Verloc did not see that. He was lying on his back and staring upwards. He saw partly on the ceiling and partly on the wall the moving shadow of an arm with a clenched hand holding a carving knife. It flickered up and down. Its movements were leisurely. They were leisurely enough for Mr. Verloc to recognize the limb and the weapon.

They were leisurely enough for him to take in the full meaning of the portent, and to taste the flavour of death rising in his gorge. His wife had gone raving mad—murdering mad. They were leisurely enough for the first paralyzing effect of this discovery to pass away before a resolute determination to come out victorious from the ghastly struggle with that armed lunatic. They were leisurely enough for Mr. Verloc to elaborate a plan of defence involving a dash behind the table, and the felling of the woman to the ground with a heavy wooden chair. But they were not leisurely enough to allow Mr. Verloc to move either hand or foot. The knife was already planted in his breast. It met no resistance on its way. Hazard has such accuracies. (262–63)

What makes this such a virtuoso passage is the abrupt transition from Winnie's point of view ("a loyal woman bound to that man") to Verloc's ("raving mad—murdering mad") even as Conrad maintains a vertiginous distance from them both by emphasizing details neither of them sees (the sudden physical resemblance of Winnie to her brother) or apparently notices (Winnie's taking the carving knife). Even once the narration settles definitely within Verloc's point of view, Conrad presents it in sharply ironic terms by couching his most private thoughts in a rhetoric clearly remote from his "plan of defence involving a dash behind the table" before it withdraws definitively from him in death ("hazard has such accuracies"). At the same time, the narration's pronounced lack of intimacy with both Mr. and Mrs. Verloc, who are called "that man" or "Mr. Verloc" and "his wife" or "that armed lunatic" rather than by their first names, emphasizes their alienation from each other and ultimately from themselves ultimately expressed by the death blow, into which Winnie Verloc "put all the inheritance of her immemorial and obscure descent, the simple ferocity of the age of caverns, and the unbalanced nervous fury of the age of bar-rooms" (263).

Hitchcock begins filming this climactic episode by cutting between a midshot of Mrs. Verloc (whom the movie gives no first name) beginning to carve the roast for her husband's dinner and a midshot of Verloc absently sitting across from her, congratulating her on having "pulled yourself together a bit." He returns to a slightly longer shot of Mrs. Verloc staring at the knife as Verloc begins to eat and complain about the overcooked greens, then tilts down to a close-up of the knife as she takes it up. The following three low-angle midshots of Mrs. Verloc carving, then thrusting the knife away from her, and finally taking it up again alternate with (1) a close-up of Stevie's vacant chair, (2) a close-up of Mrs. Verloc's hands holding the knife and fork, and (3) a full shot of the caged bird the film has consistently identified with Stevie. A track-in to a tight close-up of Mrs. Verloc, followed by another close-up of her hands on the knife and fork as she holds a potato in unnatural stillness above the plate and a third close-up of Verloc as his brows rise and his eyes widen in alarm, indicate that first the wife, then the husband, realizes what she is about to do. Verloc rises from his chair, the camera tilting up with him, and slowly comes around the table, moving so close to the camera that, as Hitchcock told Truffaut, "the spectator in the theater gets the feeling that he must recoil to make room for him" (111). Although his wife has laid the knife back down in distaste, another tilt down following both their eyelines shows her seizing it again before he can take hold of it. The camera tilts back up to a shot of their faces in profile as they regard each other wordlessly. As the camera tightens on this shot, Mrs. Verloc cries out, and her husband gasps. A waist-level close-up cutting off both their faces shows the knife plunged into his stomach before Hitchcock cuts to a final shot of their facing profiles, Verloc grimacing in death, his wife in revulsion from both him and herself.

Hitchcock told Truffaut that the reason he did not "have the heroine convey her inner feelings to the audience by her facial expressions" in this scene was that "in real life, people's faces don't reveal what they think or feel. As a film director I must try to convey this woman's frame of mind to the audience by purely cinematic means" (110–11)—a remark as relevant to his adaptation of *D'entre les morts* as to his adaptation of *The Secret Agent*. But in fact there was a still more compelling reason for the "purely cinematic means" Hitchcock chose than simple realism: they communicated so precisely the same state of somnambulistic action as

Conrad's decidedly noncinematic passage. In Conrad, Winnie's murder of her husband, so detached that it seems virtually without conscious agency, is part of a larger pattern of calamitously unauthored actions by secret agents from Verloc to the Assistant Commissioner; in Hitchcock it is a more limited rhetorical strategy to build sympathy for a heroine the film will rescue from the legal consequences of her action. Both sequences, however, depend on a combination of exceptional intimacy and exceptional detachment that would become the hallmark of Hitchcock's psychological thrillers, as opposed to Griffith's chase/adventures, and the director's most influential legacy to commercial cinema.

This amalgam of emotional intimacy and ironic detachment extends beyond Hitchcock's treatment of characters to his handling of adaptational frames. *Murder!*, like *Enter Sir John*, concerns murder among a company of actors who give their best performances off the stage. Accordingly, Charles Barr contends that instead of observing that "Hitchcock sets *Murder!* in a theatrical setting in part to dramatize the fact that, in the world of a film as in reality, acting is not confined to the stage" (Rothman 99), William Rothman might better have written, "Hitchcock may have been attracted to the novel *Enter Sir John* . . . by a story that plays on the shifting possibilities between theatre and life" (Barr 9). Barr is surely correct in reassigning credit for the story's theatrical setting from Hitchcock to Dane and Simpson, and the reassessment that follows from this reassignment is decisive.

Yet Barr makes too little of an important point. Although both the novel and the film deal centrally with actors, acting, and theatricality, they frame these figures in very different ways. Dane and Simpson frequently satirize or comment ironically on the many theatrical figures in *Enter Sir John*, from the tableau in which Magda Druce's body is discovered to Handell Fane's attempt to play innocent to actor/impresario Sir John Saumarez's comparison of the ruse by which he means to expose Fane to "the Mousetrap" in act 3 of *Hamlet* (Dane and Simpson 11–12, 233). Indeed, every one of their twenty-three chapters is headed by a Shakespearean epigraph. But although the novel is constantly aware of the characters' theatricality, it always presents its own narrative strategies as clear-eyed and superior, never complicit in the world of the stage whose machinations it exposes.

The film, by contrast, constantly emphasizes the parallels between the characters' theatricality and its own. Hitchcock and his coscenarist Walter Mycroft rework the dialogue scene in which Sir John first becomes convinced of Martella's innocence as a histrionic monologue in which Sir John, while shaving, goes through the same logical steps alone, accompanied by the prelude to act 1 of *Tristan und Isolde* as it is broadcast over the radio. The novel ends with a press agent's query about Sir John's announcement of his engagement: "For publicity?" "Naturally!" Sir John replies against a background of excited theatrical personalities who all play roles offstage as well as on (315). The implication is that although the characters constantly essay duplicitous roles, the novel has the power to see beneath their artifice. But the last shot of the film, in which the camera pulls back to show Sir John's romantic final scene with Diana Baring to be part of the new show in which he has cast her, suggests that no one, certainly not the film or its viewers, can ever be certain when a particular character is giving a performance and where a given performance ends. Although it borrows its central metaphor from the novel, the film gives that metaphor a more subversive and self-conscious turn that looks forward most obviously to *Stage Fright*, which makes Eve Gill a student at the Royal Academy of Dramatic Arts, adds a scene in which Jonathan interrupts her in the middle of a performance by clumsily trying to fit his entrance into the scene, and repeatedly revels in the opportunities to quibble in ways Jepson's novel never does on the gossamer line separating Charlotte's performances onstage and off.

There was nothing unusual about Hitchcock's growing preference, as a crucial stage in the process of his becoming Hitchcock, for novels over plays as sources for his films. But the surprisingly single-minded use to which he turned those novels—generally rejecting their opportunities for a broader canvas and more pictorial effects and concentrating instead on the models they offered for focalizing the adventures of a single divided consciousness which could be developed in ways more interesting than the consciousness itself—marks his deep affinity, for all his emphasis on the "purely cinematic means" into which he sought to translate the literary devices he borrowed, with the novel. It seems a pity that he never overcame his superstitious reverence of literary classics long enough to film *Crime and Punishment*. With its obsessive focus on a hero torn between the desire to act out violent fantasies, his moral revulsion from the consequences of his actions, and his terror of getting caught, it could have been Hitchcockized far more successfully than *Juno and the Paycock*, *The Paradine Case*, or *Topaz*.

Works Cited

Allen, Richard. *Hitchcock's Romantic Irony*. New York: Columbia University Press, 2007.

Barr, Charles. *English Hitchcock*. Moffat: Cameron & Hollis, 1999.

Belloc Lowndes, Marie. *The Lodger*. 1913: rpt. Doylestown, PA: Wildside, n.d. [2003].

Boileau, Pierre, and Thomas Narcejac. *Vertigo*. Trans. Geoffrey Sainsbury. 1956; rpt. London: Bloomsbury, 1997.

Brown, Geoff. *Launder and Gilliat*. London: British Film Institute, 1977.

Cardwell, Sarah. "'About Time': Theorizing Adaptation, Temporality, and Tense." *Literature/Film Quarterly* 31 (2003): 82–92.

Cohen, Paula Marantz. "James, Hitchcock and the Fate of Character." In *Alfred Hitchcock: Centenary Essays*. Ed. Richard Allen and S. Ishii-Gonzáles. London: British Film Institute, 1999, 15–27.

Conrad, Joseph. *The Secret Agent: A Simple Tale. The Concord Edition of the Works of Joseph Conrad*. Garden City: Doubleday, Page, 1921.

Dane, Clemence, and Helen Simpson. *Enter Sir John*. New York: Grosset and Dunlap, 1928.

Dodge, David. *To Catch a Thief*. 1952; rpt. London: J. M. Dent, 1988.

du Maurier, Daphne. *Jamaica Inn*. 1936. Rpt. New York: Sun Dial Press, 1937.

Hitchcock, Alfred. "On Style." 1963. Rpt. in *Hitchcock on Hitchcock: Selected Writings and Interviews*. Ed. Sidney Gottlieb. Berkeley: University of California Press, 1995.

Hutcheon, Linda. *A Theory of Adaptation*. London: Routledge, 2006.

James, Henry. *Literary Criticism: French Writers, Other European Writers, the Prefaces to the New York Edition*. New York: Library of America, 1984.

Jepson, Selwyn. *Outrun the Constable*. Garden City: Doubleday, 1948.

Leitch, Thomas. "Twelve Fallacies in Contemporary Adaptation Theory." *Criticism* 45 (Spring 2003): 149–71.

Lev, Peter. "*Vertigo*, Novel and Film." In *The Literature/Film Reader: Issues of Adaptation*. Ed. James M. Welsh and Peter Lev. Lanham, MD: Scarecrow, 2007, 175–86.

Rothman, William. *Hitchcock—The Murderous Gaze*. Cambridge: Harvard University Press, 1982.

Sterritt, David. *The Films of Alfred Hitchcock*. Cambridge: Cambridge University Press, 1993.

Truffaut, François. *Hitchcock*. Revised ed. New York: Simon & Schuster, 1984.

2
_____

SIDNEY GOTTLIEB

Hitchcock and the Three *Pleasure Gardens*

ITCHCOCK'S HABIT OF REFERRING TO *The Lodger* (1926) as the first "Hitchcock film" has perhaps unduly distracted us from serious consideration of the first completed work that he directed on his own, *The Pleasure Garden* (1925), made at the Emelka Studios in Munich, Germany, with some sequences shot on location in Italy. It is mentioned in at least some detail by some critics but has not attracted extensive attention—less even than Hitchcock's other silent films, as a group the least noticed and watched of his films.[1] And while it was based on a very popular novel, that text is even harder to come by than the film.

All this makes my task in the present chapter particularly difficult: writing about a film that few have seen in the context of a novel that almost no one nowadays has read or will be able to consult. I will address this difficulty by including more expository information than I might — otherwise in order to help prepare for what I hope will be for some the thrill of discovery in confronting a "new" work by Hitchcock. And to get a full view of what should be recognized as not just chronologically but also substantively, in terms of its themes and techniques, the first "Hitchcock film," I will focus extensively on three *Pleasure Gardens*: the novel and the two strikingly different versions of Hitchcock's film that exist. The copy held by the National Film, Television, and Video Archive of the British Film Institute (hereafter called the NFTVA version) is the one most often referred to in critical discussions. But what is described as a restoration distributed by the Rohauer Archive in 1981 (hereafter called the Rohauer version) contains several important sequences not in the NFTVA version, including a radically different ending. Also, the artfully designed credit sequence and intertitles of the NFTVA version are reshot and reworded in the Rohauer version. It is often necessary to qualify specific critical comments by keying them to one or the other version, and at present there is no way of knowing for sure how these two different versions came to be, what role Hitchcock himself played, if any, in shaping each, and whether they derive from some longer "original" version, now lost.

The Novel

Examining the novel can give us a great deal of insight into the roads taken and not taken in the film by Hitchcock and screenplay writer Eliot Stannard.[2] *The Pleasure Garden* was published in 1923 under the name Oliver Sandys, the male pseudonym used by Marguerite Florence Hélène Jervis (1894–1964). The primary focus is on Gaynor Brand, a young woman of indomitable optimism, determination, and compassion, renting rooms from a kindly, down-to-earth couple, Mr. and Mrs. Sidey, while barely making ends meet as a chorus girl. Gaynor's lack of means does not prevent her from taking in a procession of stray animals and then a similarly needy young woman, Jerrie Cheyne, who is Gaynor's foil throughout the novel. At first glance, Jerrie is the country innocent, newly arrived in the dangerous city, but we soon realize that she is not only pretty and talented but flirtatious, ambitious, completely self-involved, insensitive, and shrewdly manipulative—altogether far from helpless. Both she and Gaynor are hired by Gus Hamilton, the proprietor of a theater that Gaynor repeatedly characterizes as a metaphorical "pleasure garden" (22, 55, etc.), where women are the flowers to be displayed, used for male enjoyment, and inevitably discarded.

Jerrie is uniquely well prepared to play in the garden without harm: her physical beauty and vivacity give her power and capital; she is without any morals to restrain or shame her; and she has no heart to break. She is engaged to a man stationed in India and also dangling a married man back home who is infatuated with her, but once in town she immediately focuses on turning Hamilton's desire to set her up as a kept woman to her advantage, all the while pursuing someone who will give her what she truly wants: attention, status, and luxury, without emotional responsibilities. Prince Shamshud Singh is the answer to her dream of being a queen (53), and she is not deterred by conventional concerns, voiced especially by Gaynor, that he is a nonwhite foreigner who will take her to a distant culture to be one wife among others. She in fact prefers an arrangement where she will have the jewels and others will have the babies. Near the end of the novel, she literally rides off happily into the sunset in India in a gilt coach. She is never harshly condemned by Sandys, but we rarely lose sight that every step on the way to what for Jerrie is a fairy-tale ending is a misstep: no further authorial commentary is needed as we watch her cause the suicide of her married lover, fail to help Gaynor when she needs her most, and in all ways lead a life of glittering but ultimately barren independence and selfishness.

The contrast of Gaynor and Jerrie is at the heart of this character-driven novel, but Gaynor gets most of the attention. She is notable for her down-to-earth "goodness," evident in her charmingly open and familiar manner with everyone, including Mrs. Sidey, whom she calls "Ma," and God, whom she talks to regularly, addressed as "Big Pal." Gaynor is unambitious, other-directed, and principled, never susceptible to the temptations of the "pleasure garden" because she dreams of a real garden, a humble country retreat where she could live simply, raising chickens for the eggs. If Gaynor is "touched by the divine" (136), it is not because she is other-worldly, but rather because she lives a life of sympathy and charity, caring sincerely for others and constantly imagining herself into the lives of people who are under duress. Despite her own trying circumstances, she is inveterately cheery and steadfast, as captured in her "creed," a poem she wrote and recites at several key points in the novel: it begins "Life is a test; give of your best; / Fight with your back to the wall. / Never say die, Laugh and don't cry; Get up again if you fall" (12). Gaynor's poetic spirit is that of Kipling, who is mentioned and quoted numerous times in the story: practical, wary of romanticism and sentimentality, but attuned to hearty emotions and reachable ideals of honor, love, inner and outer strength, and trust. Nothing mars her goodness and beauty: even her disdain for nonwhites like the Indian Singh, Jews like Hamilton, and the natives in the Far East setting of the last part of the story is presented as a sign of her admirable good judgment. Race, but not racism, is an issue in the novel. As we shall see, neither surfaces substantively in the film.

But there is more to Gaynor than charitable impulses and haloed beauty. Part of the reason she is so wary of romance is that she is a believer in its overwhelming power. Rather than dispersing herself in a series of trivial affairs with temporary benefits, a fortune teller's prophecy, serendipitous glance at a photo in an album, and chance meeting at a social occasion lead her to the mysteriously vibrant and compelling red-haired man who is to be the one great love of her life. She never regrets this experience, although it leads her to reject the proposal of the one truly admirable man in the story and tie herself to a painful marriage with a rousing but unworthy bounder. One of the key differences between the film and the novel revolves around the character of Oscar Levett (Levet in the film) and the nature of Gaynor's attraction to him (she is named Patsy in the film). In the novel Levett is an imposing physical presence, and he stimulates something "primitive" (105) in Gaynor. Gaynor moves closer to him, in part out of loneliness after Jerrie suddenly leaves her to live in a more stylish apartment in keeping with her growing success on stage and with her suitors. But it is also clear that she gives herself to an irresistible passion. Her first kiss, we are told, blots out the whole world (110), and she enters a world made familiar by operas, melodramas, and both great and cheap romances: "She had no choice. Love had descended upon her and she was filled with the fiery sweetness" (111).

Gaynor makes an error in judgment in marrying a man with so many soon-to-be-revealed "warps and twists" of character (112), but the resulting pain proves to be inconsequential. What is truly important is Gaynor's "spiritual" experience of "first love" (113), which helps enlarge her "instinct to outpour herself; to expend, to keep nothing back" (113). Marriage to Levett allows Gaynor many opportunities for sacrifice, sympathy, charity, and fidelity. She never regrets her marriage or repudiates Levett, even when she travels to care for him in his Far East post and discovers him with his native wife, Leulhi, and young child, Baba. She nearly faints at this sight and barely escapes Levett's continuing abuse as he attempts to take her back as his wife, but she is the least damaged by this operatic turn of events: Leulhi, abandoned and distraught, drowns after a fall into a well that is perhaps as much willful as accidental; Levett, haunted by visions of Leulhi, falls ever further into a drunken fever and subsequently drowns himself; and Baba, constitutionally unable to survive the transition to English climate and culture, withers and dies when Gaynor takes him "home."

Gaynor is by no means promiscuous, but her passion finds another suitable object: she nurses Hugo, Jerrie's abandoned fiancé, back to health even as she tries to protect herself from Levett's feverish advances. Hugo is the second man that she kisses, this time out of sympathy and "innocent intent" (246), and while it rouses Levett's jealousy as he stumbles into the scene, it is a foreshadowing of the new focus of Gaynor's life. After she returns to England, and Levett dies, she is free to accept the true love and devotion of Hugo and live the rest of her life with him in peaceful and pleasant domestic retreat on an estate he has inherited. The book ends with Gaynor acknowledging the force of first love—Kipling's poem "Virginity" is quoted for the second time in the novel with the force of scripture—but then giving her heart to her new love, "the greatest gift of all" (283). Perhaps much of the popular appeal of Sandys's tale derives from her attempt, sealed by this happy ending, to reassure her readers that it is possible for women like Gaynor to truly have it all by marrying first a Heathcliff and then a Mr. Knightley.

The Film(s)

Yacowar's fine analysis of Hitchcock's film is not supported by any mention of Sandys's novel but lends itself very well to a comparative analysis by commenting on the four key settings of the action, each charged with moral significance and presenting key problems to be overcome (20). Although there are cross-references and oscillations, the film, like the novel, basically moves from one to the next: from the pleasure garden to the home to the honeymoon and then to the East.

Much of the action in the early part of the novel takes place in a theatrical setting, which Gaynor repeatedly describes, using an extended metaphor, as a place lorded over by men where women are "grown to be looked at" (108), plucked, and discarded. Constantly witnessing this spectacle makes her well aware that "[w]e're supposed—we girls—to understand all the rules of their game and never to cry 'How's that?' if they haven't played fair" (22). Hitchcock eliminates the discourse but keeps the imagery. While this allows him to use pictorial means to very effectively tell a tale of a broken blossom, it radically diminishes key elements of Gaynor's character in the novel, especially her insight into and ongoing commentary on the "rules of the game" and corresponding determination to protect herself. In the novel, we see what Gaynor, experienced and observant, sees. In the film, we see what Patsy, not entirely aware of the kind of garden she inhabits, very often does not see.

The Pleasure Garden becomes a literal place in the film where a musical revue titled "Passion Flowers" is being presented, and Hitchcock, far more than Sandys, is interested in visualizing and analyzing the complex dynamics of the theater. The film begins with a sequence that highlights women as spectacles on display and anatomizes how the spectators look at them. Costumed women descend a spiral staircase onto a stage. The camera shows them dancing but also shows the audience watching. One older man is a particularly energetic viewer and uses binoculars and eyeglasses to bring one of the dancers, Patsy, close and into sharp focus, shown by point-of-view shots that enmesh the viewer of the film with the viewer in the film. Patsy is no passive subject of the gaze: after a moment of being looked at, she stares back boldly. But the iris shot showing this action presents an emblematic minidrama of woman's hope and woman's fate: Patsy's resistant gaze and assured laugh are part of a cameo of containment. As it turns out, there is little she can do throughout the film to keep herself from being perceived, pursued, and overtaken.

Hitchcock is fascinated by more than spectacles on stage and the audiences that watch them. He is particularly interested in behind-the-scenes views showing how stage shows are constructed. The opening sequences take place during a rehearsal, and the camera is positioned primarily backstage, revealing the making of the world of make-believe and mystery (elements at the core of two of his most important works many years later, *Rear Window* and *Vertigo*). Related to his interest in star-gazing and the dynamics of spectatorship, he also focuses on the process and spectacle of star-making. In the second scene near the beginning of the film set in the theater, we see Patsy transform herself very quickly from an off-stage victimized waif to a side-stage opportunist to an onstage star attraction. This is paralleled by a different kind of choreography as Patsy, instead of separating from others and gravitating to front and center stage like Jill, recedes into the background and group shots, happy and best-suited to be part of the chorus. Using very economical cinematic touches, Hitchcock characterizes the theater as a place of danger (Jill is robbed outside the theater door, and each time she enters and exits, she runs a gauntlet between stage-door johnnies on either side), transgression (when the manager Hamilton puffs away at a cigar in front of a sign stating "No Smoking Allowed," this tells us something about his character but perhaps also identifies the theater as a place where all kinds of violations are the norm), and ambitious mutual seduction. Jill's greatest success comes when she moves from the stage of the Pleasure Garden to become a star in a different setting: the luxurious apartments of Hamilton and then Prince Ivan (the film's foreign and exotic but still European replacement for Shamshud Singh in the novel), both of whom became attracted to her in the theater. Ironically but fittingly, Jill is at her most theatrical—as a well-dressed spectacle and vamp, complete with a cigarette at the end of a long holder used as a fashion accessory and a weapon—when she is at "home," fitted out as a theater in all but name. As we know from other films as well, for Hitchcock theatricality is associated with victimization but also certain kinds of empowerment.

In the novel, Gaynor repeatedly retreats to the Sidey's as an idyllic haven in a heartless world. Hitchcock's view of the home is much more complicated. Especially in the Rohauer version, the film shares with the novel the sense that domesticity is a reliable source of comfort and security for Patsy and provides the model of life as it should be lived. The Sideys are in effect her parents, and Patsy shares her emotional ups and downs with them, accepts their generously offered help when she needs money to visit her husband, and—at least in the Rohauer version—returns to them at the end when she resolves her marital affairs. But domesticity in *The Pleasure Garden*—as in all of Hitchcock's films—is far from untroubled, to say the least. In this respect Hitchcock perhaps follows the model of the German *kammerspielfilme*, as Garncarz suggests (68), which focus on individuals under extreme duress in the context of beleaguered households and unstable intimacies, and also illustrates his debt to Griffith, the presiding cinematic influence on this film in a variety of ways.[3] As in Griffith's melodramatic fables, home in Hitchcock's *The Pleasure Garden* is a place of warmth and refuge but also of eccentricity and strain: unlike the novel, the Sideys are occasionally somewhat ridiculous in the film, with the husband hobbling along and fussing with his radio (in the Rohauer version) and the wife at several points appearing fierce, even menacing as she lords over the household. And there is much loneliness and anxiety as well as comfort in the home: a shot of Patsy sitting alone washing her stockings in her room is a lightly comical return to mundane reality after scenes of the glittering world of the theater, with footlights replaced by a box of Lux soap, but also a stunning evocation of Patsy's fundamental isolation.

The home appears to be less a fortress than a place of vulnerability. Hitchcock's first film sets up a template that he returns to repeatedly in some of his most powerful works: as in *The Lodger, Blackmail,* and *Shadow of a Doubt,* for example, *The Pleasure Garden* is structured around a disturbing force entering into the home, threatening a young woman. The first disturbance is Jill, who despite Mrs. Sidey's stern disapproval is welcomed by Patsy into the home and into her bed. Some of the disturbance is erotic, suggested playfully but palpably as Patsy and Jill talk and disrobe in a scene that is part pajama party and part striptease. Hitchcock's treatment of this woman-to-woman relationship is much more condensed and peripheral than Sandys's. Gaynor's emotional although not necessarily sexualized connection with Jerrie is one of the key themes in the novel, and when Jerrie suddenly moves to an apartment of her own, Gaynor is deeply upset and cries; in the film, Patsy simply looks out rather blankly after reading Jill's farewell letter, and the shot fades out. But we are perhaps meant to intuit that Patsy is affected: immediately afterwards, she complains of loneliness, and this—part an existential condition and part a result of her failed intimacy and friendship with Jill—draws her to the second disturbing force who enters the home: Levet.

Hitchcock loads the scenes of their "courtship" with warning signs. Levet is a physically unattractive character, with nervous gestures and a cynical smile, and surrounded by smoke and shadows like the mysterious lodger in Hitchcock's film of that title made not long after this one. His proposal to Patsy is intercut with carefully structured parallel scenes of Prince Ivan attempting to romance Jill, and the contrast is instructive: Jill is in the kind of brightly lit environment that she desires and is fully in control of the man who makes this possible, laughing gaily even as she burns him with a cigarette when he attempts to kiss her. Patsy's romance takes place in a grim, claustrophobic environment, and she is progressively enveloped by a man taking advantage of her to make a marriage that is convenient to him. When he kisses her (in the Rohauer version) Hitchcock cuts quickly several times to reverse angles to show how ominous and unsettling this experience is for Patsy. The wedding day, which follows immediately, is similarly foreboding, heralded by the large question mark that appears in the background of the intertitle (in the NFTVA version) that introduces the festivities: in the extended Rohauer version of the sequence, Levet takes Patsy away from her home into a relentless rain storm, leaving behind her dog, Cuddles, who provides the most prescient commentary on the events by howling and scratching at the door, the earliest example of the Hitchcockian "dog who knew too much" who will appear again in *Secret Agent* and *Rear Window*.[4]

The setting of the honeymoon that immediately follows is much different in the film than in the novel and initially seems more promising. In the novel, after the wedding, Levett takes Gaynor to Brockenhurst, and although the country atmosphere actually suits her very well, Levett's intention was not to please his new wife but to get on with their physical intimacy as quickly and cheaply as possible. In the film, the honeymoon is in the much more luxurious and romantic setting of Lake Como, but the overall tone of this part of the film (substantially longer in the NFTVA version) is more ironic than celebratory. Long shots show the scenery but dwarf the two main characters and emphasize their lack of intimacy even when they are shown together. And Hitchcock uses parallel action and intercutting to underscore their unbridgeable differences as well as distance: shots of Patsy examining the honeymoon suite, perhaps with at least some sense of hopeful anticipation, are intercut with Levet standing outside against a wall, nervously smoking one cigarette after another and talking to himself. The next day, Patsy stands reverently in front of a religious statue—the intertitle says "Unspoken gratitude"—but this is intercut with Levet lying impatiently on the grass under a tree, chewing on grass and spitting. And in the final vignette of the honeymoon, Patsy plays with a baby, surrounded by other little children, but this is intercut with shots of Levet walking alone through the city. When he finally joins up with her, it is only to call her away from the children, criticize her for being "sloppy and sentimental with these filthy brats," and then throw the flower she had given to him into the water, noting that it had "wilted." Literally and metaphorically, the honeymoon is over, and they are soon waving goodbye as Levet sails away to the East. Sandys punctuates this farewell with a rather blunt "presage of disaster" (145): as Gaynor waves her hand and shields her eyes in the bright sunlight, her wedding ring falls into the water. Hitchcock's cinematic "touch" here is perhaps more subtly imaginative and effective: Gaynor's waving arm gives way to that of the native woman who will be her replacement in the next section of the story.

The Far East setting in the novel is clearly identified as a place of the Other who should remain so. Kipling is Gaynor's guide on these matters, and when she quotes him, moral complexities disappear: "He says: 'For East is East and West is West, and never the twain shall meet.' And he's right" (153). She is consistent in her thoughts about keeping East and West apart and disapproves not only of Shamshud Singh's pursuit of Jerrie but also of the convention of English men taking a native "wife" while in India, an issue that becomes very concrete and personal when she surprises her husband "lolling in a chair" (221) with Leulhi. Sandys also pictures the Far East as a place of physical discomfort and danger: of tropical heat and incipient fever, like the one that afflicts Hugo. But there is no elaborate portrayal of this as a place harboring some mysterious heart of darkness, and although several disturbing events occur there, the setting is not blamed. The East is ultimately no more—and no less—a dangerous pleasure garden than the West.

In contrast with Sandys's dedramatization in this part of the novel—the most shocking events, the deaths of Leulhi and Levett, are only briefly reported, not shown—the film noticeably increases in drama and intensity in the closing sequences. It may be a bit of boldness on Hitchcock's part to disregard the general objections specified by the British censors at this time against "scenes in which British officers and officials in India and elsewhere [are] shown in invidious circumstances" and scenes of "white men in state of degradation amidst native surroundings" (Low 64). But he does not seem particularly interested in using the East for any commentary on British colonial activities or as a setting particularly likely to release implacable and inscrutable forces: for Hitchcock, any setting is suitable for this, and while his recurrent association of exoticism with disorientation and a variety of threats throughout his films (e.g., *Downhill*, *Rich and Strange*, *The Man Who Knew Too Much* [1956], and *Vertigo*) deserves close attention, in *The Pleasure Garden* it is largely atmospheric and subsidiary rather than thematic and analytical. At the end, his main concern is driving the film toward a dramatic conclusion that shows the disintegration of an increasingly unstable character, Levet, his murder of

Leulhi when she no longer suits his purposes, and his final descent into mad hallucinations and an assault on Patsy that, in true melodramatic fashion, is miraculously thwarted only at the very last moment.

The ending of the film diverges radically from the novel and, like the opening, seems particularly loaded with inventive cinematic techniques and special effects. While Sandys is more interested than Hitchcock in Levett as an elemental romantic force, Hitchcock is more interested in him as a shady character and ultimately a murderous manipulator and study in guilt, obsession, and decompensation. When Patsy discovers Levet and Leulhi together, she is, of course, shocked but recovers quickly, laughs (in the novel, it is Levett who laughs), and comments disdainfully on the awkward scene, calling Leulhi "that child" and Levet a "beast." She threatens to leave him and in fact walks out to care for Hugh in a cabin nearby.

Levet has already been shown as drunk and enervated, but from this point on he rapidly deteriorates even further, conveyed by some startling shifts in point of view that disorient the viewer and give us brief glimpses of the unstable world as Levet sees it. Most memorably, Hitchcock cuts to an underwater image of whirling bodies as Levet drowns Leulhi and later shows hallucinatory images of her return to haunt and torment him. But we should also note that Hitchcock embeds these attention-getting shots in a broader structure of alternating scenes that sets up a complex counterpoint. There are several layers of connection, contrast, and commentary at work here. Shots of Patsy comforting Hugh alternate with Levet's abuse of Leulhi in his room and frame the scene where he drowns her in the ocean. Hitchcock thus reinforces the obvious distinction between those who care and those who kill but also subtly reminds us that there are different levels of victimization: Patsy's survival at the end of her ordeal with Levet seems like more of a real achievement when we remind ourselves of Leulhi's fate. And after the murder, shots of the growing intimacy of Patsy and Hugh highlight his return to health and underscore the irreversible downward turn of Levet, shown alone in his room. While he uses parallel editing here mostly for contrast, Hitchcock also establishes an interesting link between Levet and Hugh as men tormented by love. He cuts from shots of Levet haunted by guilty visions of Leulhi to shots of Hugh as delusional as well, imagining that Patsy leaning over him is Jill. Kissing her seems to break his fever and end Jill's spell on him, allowing him to recognize Patsy and transfer his love to her. Later Hitchcock characters will not be so fortunate in their experiences of love's vertigo and the magical but also punishing exchange of one woman for another.

The kiss is witnessed by Levet, and Hitchcock uses this moment as a kind of fuse that sets off a concluding sequence that is far more threatening and exciting than what Sandys envisions. Patsy lights a candle in Levet's room, and while this dispels the darkness, it also contributes to a kind of magic lantern effect. Leulhi's ghost appears, as a superimposed image, advancing on Levet, pointing to a sword on the wall, which gives him the idea that, as an intertitle says, "She won't let me rest until I've killed you too." Patsy retreats, as in a Griffith film, into an inner room, and Levet pursues her, lunging at her with the sword through a lattice, and then finally pushes through the door and stands over her with the sword, poised to strike. The image blurs quickly, and Hitchcock cuts to a shot of a man's hand with a gun that he has just fired. Then in a long-shot tableau, we see the man's hand with the gun, Patsy cowering in the background, and Levet immobile, frozen between life and death. In a Hitchcock touch that will be reprised in *The Man Who Knew Too Much*, the gunshot is both a death wound and a curiosity.[5] Levet smiles and speaks, looks down at the blood on his shirt quizzically, remains standing for longer than one would expect, and then topples to the floor.

We now come to the ending of the film—or, as I have indicated earlier, the endings. In the NFTVA version, Hugh is carried onto Levet's porch, and he and Patsy embrace, acknowledging that each has saved the other's life: Patsy by curing his fever, Hugh by warning Carruthers, the most reliable man at the outpost, of Levet's threat to her. Each has survived a disastrous relationship, and they are at last safely in each other's arms, but the future is uncertain. Honest and realistic as always, Patsy looks down and says: "We've both suffered . . . what have either of us got to live for?" Hugh's response is hopeful, but far from enthusiastic: "We have one of the greatest things of Life . . . Youth." Patsy nods, and the muted affirmation that their life together will continue is followed immediately by the closing title that proclaims, "The End." It's an equivocal conclusion, and quite Hitchcockian, at least in tone, especially as it looks ahead to the far more elaborately envisioned mixed messages at the close of such films as *The Lodger* (where the couple formed in traumatic circumstances overcome is still juxtaposed with the neon sign blinking out the words "To-Night Golden Curls" that were an invitation to murder at the beginning), *Blackmail* (where the dour expression and stiff movements of the newly consolidated couple convey the unlikelihood of keeping the past behind them), and *The 39 Steps* (which resists the pull to end like a joyous comedy by concluding with a complex emblem: the clasped hands of the reunited lovers, with a handcuff dangling from one).

In the Rohauer version, though, the tone is much different. The intertitles quoted above are replaced by ones that are far more buoyant: Patsy voices her hope that "you'll get over her [Jill], as I must try to get over this," and Hugh responds, "You're the only woman for me, Patsy—I was blind not to see it before!" The fade out is then not to the end title but to a scene of their joyous return to London, where they are enthusiastically welcomed back by the Sideys: Mrs. Sidey embraces Patsy; Mr. Sidey is distracted by the radio but maintains his place as the genial and somewhat ridiculous man of the house; and Cuddles affirms his position as the guardian of good sense as he excitedly greets Hugh and, in the final shot of the film, bites the wires of Mr. Sidey's radio and wags his tongue vigorously, confirming as perhaps nothing else could that everything is back to normal and that the world is indeed a good place. There is Hitchcockian wit and humor in this sequence, not out of line with the ending of some of his other films, where there are turns to unexpected lightness (e.g., the remake of *The Man Who Knew Too Much*); and this ending is consistent with that of the novel, where much is made of Gaynor's return to London and subsequent marriage to Hugo, which promises nothing but happiness spent in their country home. Still, I am not sure whether this should be accepted as the preferred and legitimate ending of Hitchcock's *Pleasure Garden*. Much textual, historical, and archival work remains to be done to determine, if we can, the "authority" of the NFTVA and Rohauer versions of the film. Until then—and perhaps even after then—our interpretations of the film must take into account that there are two endings for the film, each of which is arguably, although somewhat differently, Hitchcockian.

I would like to conclude not with a textual and interpretive crux but with a final reiteration of what a comparative study of the film and the source novel reveals about Hitchcock's reconceptualization of the main female character and her experience of love. To put it most simply, in the novel, Gaynor is quite assertive, verbal, and resourceful, and while she goes through a prolonged love trial, there is nothing damaging about what she endures, and through it all she remains the steadfast moral center of an occasionally swirling world. While Patsy certainly retains some of these characteristics, she is not particularly expressive (the fact that this is a silent film contributes to this but does not account for the change), is beleaguered in love without having Gaynor's experience of the kind of passion that makes life worth living despite its inevitable pain, ends up in a situation where she needs to be rescued from imminent danger, and at least in the NFTVA version of the film, is left somewhat suspended, not rewarded.

It is worth noting that this particular kind of transformation of a source text occurs repeatedly in Hitchcock's early films (for example, in *Easy Virtue*, *The Manxman*, and, perhaps most interestingly, *Blackmail*), where the main woman character in the film version typically loses some of the resourcefulness, independence, and vitality that she had in the novel or play, her confusion and victimization become more prolonged and painful, and her triumph more equivocal. I take this not as a sign of misogyny but rather as an indication that Hitchcock approached the situation of women in the world with sensitivity and high seriousness; was more alert to the precariousness and danger rather than the steadiness, comfort, and joys of their relations with men, other women, and family members; and was altogether more interested in following the path out of rather than, as in Sandys, back to Eden. If one of his guiding principles even this early in his career was, as he said in various interviews, "Torture the women! . . . The trouble today is that we don't torture women enough"[6]—a highly quotable phrase that unfortunately lends itself to misunderstanding Hitchcock as more a perpetrator than an analyst of torture and other kinds of suffering—he evidently felt that his source texts often did not accomplish this satisfactorily and set out to remedy this in his films, beginning with *The Pleasure Garden*.

Notes

1. Maurice Yacowar, *Hitchcock's British Films*, 19–29; Charles Barr, *English Hitchcock*, 18, 27–31, 215–16; Ken Mogg, "*The Pleasure Garden*," 16–27; Joseph Garncarz, "German Hitchcock," in *Framing Hitchcock: Selected Essays from The Hitchcock Annual*, 59–81; and Marc Raymond Strauss, 11–25. For Hitchcock's comments on his experiences making *The Pleasure Garden*, see "My Screen Memories" and "Life among the Stars" (1937), in *Hitchcock on Hitchcock: Selected Writings and Interviews*, 7–13, 27–33.

2. While I will use the conventional shorthand of referring primarily to Hitchcock as the adapter, I acknowledge the likelihood, as Charles Barr argues, that Stannard in particular and Hitchcock's screenwriters in general contributed far more than we usually recognize to plotting and structuring his films and even shaping the "Hitchcock touch." See *English Hitchcock*, esp. 6–26, and "Writing Screen Plays: Stannard and Hitchcock," 227–41.

3. For further comments on this subject, see my essay "Hitchcock on Griffith," which introduces Hitchcock's own essay on Griffith, "A Columbus of the Screen."

4. Barr comments on "Hitchcock & Dogs" in *English Hitchcock*, 186–89. In pursuing the role of dogs in Hitchcock's films, and especially *The Pleasure Garden*, I think it would be valuable to follow up on Peter Brooks's brief observations about the recurrent appearance of dogs in melodramas as "clear indicators of the significant message to those who can read their non-verbal signs." See *The Melodramatic Imagination*, 45–46.

5. This may well be a DeMille touch: there is an extended sequence in *Old Wives for New* (1918) where a man is shot and remains standing, apparently unaffected, for a surprisingly long time until he collapses. Bill Krohn makes a strong argument for the influence of DeMille on Hitchcock in *Alfred Hitchcock*, although he does not include this particular example.

6. Quoted from several sources by Donald Spoto, *The Dark Side of Genius*, 483; see note on 606–07.

Works Cited

Barr, Charles. *English Hitchcock*. Moffat: Cameron & Hollis, 1999, 227–241.

———. "Writing Screen Plays: Stannard and Hitchcock." In *Young and Innocent? The Cinema in Britain 1896–1930*. Devon: University of Exeter Press, 2002.

Brooks, Peter. *The Melodramatic Imagination: Balzac, Henry James, Melodrama, and the Mode of Excess*.(1976; New Haven: Yale University Press, 1995, 45–46.

Garncarz, Joseph. "German Hitchcock." In *Framing Hitchcock: Selected Essays from The Hitchcock Annual*, ed. Sidney Gottlieb and Christopher Brookhouse. Detroit: Wayne State University Press, 2002, 59–81.

Gottlieb, Sidney. "Hitchcock on Griffith." *Hitchcock Annual* 14 (2005–06): 32–45.

Higson, Andrew, ed. *Young and Innocent? The Cinema in Britain 1896–1930*. Devon: University of Exeter Press, 2002, 227–241.

Hitchcock, Alfred. *Hitchcock on Hitchcock: Selected Writings and Interviews*. Ed. Sidney Gottlieb. Berkeley and Los Angeles: University of California Press, 1995.

———. "A Columbus of the Screen." *Hitchcock Annual* 14 (2005–6): 46–49.

Krohn, Bill. *Alfred Hitchcock*. Paris: Cahiers du Cinéma, 2008.

Low, Rachel. *The History of the British Film 1918–1929*. London: Allen & Unwin, 1971.

Mogg, Ken. "*The Pleasure Garden*." *The MacGuffin* 29 (2004): 16–27.

Sandys, Oliver. *The Pleasure Garden*. London: Hurst & Blackett, n.d.

Strauss, Marc Raymond. *Alfred Hitchcock's Silent Films*. Jefferson, NC: McFarland & Company, 2004.

Sandys, Oliver. *The Pleasure Garden*. London: Hurst & Blackett, n.d.

Spoto, Donald. *The Dark Side of Genius: The Life of Alfred Hitchcock*. New York: Ballantine Books, 1983.

Yacowar, Maurice. *Hitchcock's British Films*. Hamden, CT: Archon Books, 1977.

3

Mary Hammond

Hitchcock and *The Manxman*

A Victorian Bestseller on the Silent Screen

B Y THE END OF 1927 ALFRED HITCHCOCK had been poached from
Gainsborough by British International Pictures and at twen-
ty-eight years old was the highest paid director in the United
Kingdom. However financially rewarding it may have been, though, the
move was not immediately creatively successful; several of his films from
this period were temporarily shelved before release as in need of further
work, and his development was uneven at best. Donald Spoto puts this
down to the fact that a less nurturing atmosphere for young talent pre-
vailed at BIP than at Gainsborough, arguing that as a result Hitchcock's
films between 1927 and 1932 "do not reveal the passion and intensity
associated with his later British films and most of his American films"
(100), that they have no "overarching vision" (107–08), and that they are
probably only retrospectively successful because Hitchcockian touches
are evident in parts of the structure or content.

He might well be correct about the different atmosphere prevailing
in the two studios, and one might argue fruitfully enough over the various
merits and demerits of the films produced in each period in terms of their
place in the young director's developing autonomy over his oeuvre. But in
searching for some essentialist notion of Hitchcockian value—appearing
early on only in the odd splash of brilliance, coming to fruition during

the more independent Hollywood years—Spoto perhaps embraces too readily an auteur theory that privileges genius over context. The fact is that signature "Hitchcockian" motifs were developed over a period of time during the director's formative years (some of the most important of which span the years at BIP), and they drew on his experiences of growing up in the early twentieth century and of reading, watching, and listening to the work of others.

Some recent critics have posited a more holistic view, considering Hitchcock's British silents in light of their wider literary, theatrical, filmic, and illustrative influences. Sidney Gottlieb goes some way toward unpacking the politics of Hitchcock's cinematic influences, arguing with reference to a film that will be central to this chapter—*The Manxman* (1929)—that it "subtly announces its political subthemes by stylistic allusions to Eisenstein" (161). Charles Barr's ground-breaking *English Hitchcock* adds a further contextual dimension, suggesting that early Hitchcock is essentially English (rather than British) and that its influences, its production values, and its modes of address owe a great deal not only to the Soviet and German filmmakers with whom he worked as a young assistant but also to the prevailing cinematic climate in the city of London where he was born, lived, and largely worked until his departure for Hollywood in 1939. He adds to this a crucial acknowledgment of the debt Hitchcock owed to the novelists of his parents' generation whose narratives would furnish much of his material (6). More recently still, Christine Gledhill has interpreted *The Manxman*'s stylistic effects in terms of what she calls "the poetics of British cinema"—by which she means its "rootedness . . . in [British] pictorial-theatrical practices and the powerful and distinctive cinematic language they can generate" (119).

These critics are assuredly right to consider Hitchcock's early work as inseparable from the cultural moment in which it was formed. But the underlying debate over whether the strongest influences came from theater, from literature, or from art, from Europe, America, or England (or Britain), is perhaps a touch overdetermined. The early British film industry might have been nationalist and even parochial in many respects—based largely in the south of England, concerned with its own national image (as witness the 1927 Cinematographic Act, which insisted on a quota of "British" films to counteract the prevailing American import trend), but it was also at least partially transnational and necessarily engaged with several different media. For one thing, it followed in the footsteps of a well-established and highly successful nineteenth-century global trade in narrative and illustrative techniques. Successful writers and the agents who had begun to represent them had been negotiating adaptation, translation, and distribution deals with much of Europe and the United States at least since the 1880s—the more vigorously after international copyright agreements were finally ratified in 1891. Magazine illustrations were often syndicated and circulated over much of the world. Novelists were long accustomed to adapting their work for the international stage, and—as I will demonstrate—the sharpest among them recognized early on the cinema's adaptive potential.

In its turn, cinema (like the cheap reprint book trade before it) plundered a long international history of story-telling, recasting many old narratives in new ways. By the mid-1920s the U.S. and U.K. book trades had cottoned on to cinema too and begun producing what we would call "film tie-ins": cheap novelizations of popular films that illustrated a given story with stills from the movie and were widely circulated across Europe and the Atlantic. It follows from this that early twentieth-century readers and viewers—Hitchcock among them—had access to texts originating from far outside their own geographical locations and well beyond their own historical moment, and they were readily able to assimilate these into a broad personal canon of favorites. The works Hitchcock admits to being influenced by and/or at some point adapted for the screen (including those from his parents' generation)—works by Edgar Allan Poe, John Buchan, J. B. Priestley, G. K. Chesterton, the brothers Grimm, E. T. A. Hoffman, Mrs. Belloc Lowndes, Hall Caine, Gustave Flaubert—were an eclectic mix of literary and popular, British and non-British, old and new. Moreover, their influences were not purely narrative: the publishing industry in this period was intensely visually aware, and as a former graphic illustrator Hitchcock is likely to have been particularly responsive to this fact. Most of these works would have been available to him not only in hardback in public libraries but also in cheap paper covers (often with pictures, almost always with cover illustrations) in shops and at railway bookstalls. They were advertised with illustrated posters. They were often accessible via the London stage and/or in London cinemas. Hitchcock also admits to an early penchant for both U.S. and U.K. trade papers, which means time spent in the magazines section of his local bookstore just off Leicester Square and further exposure to international illustrated fiction (Spoto 38–39). In light of this well-established pattern of cooperative circulation and the multiple reception possibilities provided by the different available media, the notion of "influences" takes on a somewhat more complex dimension. Perhaps we need to look further than the "text" of a particular source novel or the "works" of a particular writer or the "techniques" of a particular filmmaker and consider the wider pattern of experiential possibilities to which a young Hitchcock looking for ideas for an adaptation would have been exposed.

One potentially fruitful way in which we might tackle the subject of influences in the absence of complete documented proof is to unpack the paratext as well as the text of a particular adaptation, to examine its pre-Hitchcock public appearances (particularly their illustrative modes) alongside his treatment of it, and wherever possible to note stylistic similarities. What I want to do in this chapter is to examine *The Manxman* (novel 1894–95) in exactly this way in the hope that I can shed some light on the illustrative and narrative tropes from which Hitchcock may have been learning at this point in his career. There are several reasons for my choice of text here. *The Manxman* was Hitchcock's last silent movie and, while later dismissed by the director himself as "banal" (Truffaut 61), it has since deservedly engendered the kind of critical interest quoted above.[1] In addition, as a book historian working on Victorian bestsellers, I have recently come across some hitherto unexamined information on *The Manxman*'s publication, adaptation, and illustrative contexts that seems to me to be of significant value to film scholarship. *The Manxman* is, however, only an example. It is useful as a case study, but the principles applied here would, I believe, readily transfer to other adaptation histories.

"It belonged to a tradition," the director told François Truffaut of *The Manxman*. "It was not a Hitchcock movie" (61). In separating out the traditional (and insignificant) from the personally innovative (and noteworthy), Hitchcock was here running true to form, but he was wrong. *The Manxman* did indeed come from a strong narrative and pictorial tradition, but the unmistakably Hitchcockian motifs in the film draw so heavily on that tradition that it is hard to see how they could have existed without it. *The Manxman* is high Victorian melodrama: it was not Hitchcock's choice perhaps, in a studio system in which budding young directors (even highly paid ones) pretty much did as they were told, but some of its strongest elements are remarkably close to his longest lasting preoccupations. It is worth setting out the work's pre-Hitchcock history here, as a way of demonstrating the ways in which certain tropes—material and commercial as well as aesthetic—fed into its final appearance onscreen under Hitchcock's direction.

Published in serial form in *The Queen* between January and July of 1894 and appearing in book form later that same year, *The Manxman* was the seventh major best-selling novel from the pen of one of the most famous authors of the Victorian age, Sir Thomas Henry Hall Caine (1853–1931). Published simultaneously in the United States, it went into many editions and was translated into twelve languages, easily outselling contemporary rivals such as George du Maurier's *Trilby*, George and Weedon Grossmith's *Diary of a Nobody*, Anthony Hope's *The Prisoner of*

Zenda, and Kipling's *The Jungle Book* (Allen 434, 234). Unusually for a Caine novel, it was also a critical success, even outranking Hardy's *Tess of the D'Urbervilles* in some quarters (Allen 234). It was also quickly adapted for the stage. This was a less unusual development; keenly aware and ever-watchful of his copyrights, Caine's usual practice was to hold an informal rights performance of each new novel as he finished it and later send the play on tour to Drury Lane, New York, and the provinces. His plays made him further fortunes, partly because his books lent themselves easily to the melodramatic mode then in vogue; typically the novels were biblical parables set in some visually spectacular location, and they usually revolved around betrayal, guilt, and final redemption through repentance. *The Manxman* is no exception. The story—set in the Isle of Man—focuses on his favorite theme of two men (boyhood friends in this instance: Pete the fisherman and Philip the lawyer) in love with the same woman (Kate the innocent Manx maiden). Kate promises herself to Pete in a moment of youthful impetuosity, but in spite of the well-respected Philip's intervention on his friend's behalf, Pete is rejected by her ambitious innkeeper father as too poor, and he sets sail for South Africa to make his fortune leaving Kate in the care of his trusted best friend. The inevitable happens: Kate and Philip fall in love, and when word is received that Pete has been killed in a mining accident, they are free to consummate their relationship—though outside wedlock as Philip's family (even more ambitious than Kate's) object to their lawyer son's planned union with an innkeeper's daughter. Kate becomes pregnant just as Pete arrives home to tell them how he has cheated death. Trapped by her promise, Kate marries him, and her child is born without Pete knowing he is not the father. Kate cannot live with her guilt and attempts to drown herself in the harbor. Rescued in the nick of time, she is brought before the island's highest judge, the "deemster"—who happens to be Philip, now at the pinnacle of his career. He cannot bring himself to sentence her, knowing he is the cause of her shame and despair, and he renounces his office. The novel in both serial and book form ends with the pair leaving together through a jeering crowd of townsfolk—socially outcast but spiritually cleansed now that they are free of their burden of guilt.

Caine's plays tended to change the denouements, replacing the novels' characteristically down-beat endings with happy ones in line with long prevalent ideas about what was acceptable and expected on stage. *The Manxman* followed this pattern, the surviving original play script (later titled *Pete*) providing two possible upbeat endings. In the first, Philip refuses to give up his position as deemster at the plot's denouement and instead offers to pay Kate's father to have her back and take care of the child. Pete is shocked and delivers a speech in which he declares how wrong it is that only the woman should be punished for a couple's wrong-doing; Kate hears him, realizes she loves him, and they are reconciled. In the second version (which also contains lighting cues, perhaps indicating that it was in the end the version chosen for performance), Philip returns Kate to her father, and Kate banishes both him and Pete from her life, choosing single-minded devotion to her child over life with either man.[2] These endings are typical of Caine changes (he provided no less than four possible endings for another of his plays, based on the 1904 novel *The Prodigal Son*). *The Manxman* differs in only one interesting respect: in the end, two very different versions actually circulated close together (a point missed by Barr in his survey of the film's antecedents). The first, dramatized by Caine's long-time collaborator Wilson Barrett and given the same title as the novel, was a skewed recasting of the moral characters of the two men so that the novel's fallen man uncomplicatedly became the play's hero, no redemption required. After a short provincial tour, it opened in London to dire reviews, among them a severe panning by George Bernard Shaw, and was taken off after only thirteen performances (Allen 235–36). The second, dramatized in part by Caine himself and titled *Pete* to distinguish it from Barrett's version, reinstated the balance between the novel's characters and was far more successful, touring on and off until 1916 in both Britain and the United States and helping to keep the novel in print long afterward.

The differences between novel and play are significant—as we shall see—when it comes to Hitchcock's adaptation for the screen; for the moment though, my point is merely to emphasize that despite its first appearance before Hitchcock was born, *The Manxman* was still around and still a culturally viable commodity when he was of an age to have encountered it, being by the age of fifteen an avid theater-goer and consumer of popular fiction (Barr 13). We have no way of knowing whether he read or saw it at this time; it is not in his list of favorites. But it was in the ether, proof that the Victorian melodrama died a long and lingering death. Nor did *The Manxman*'s last stage appearance mean that it was on its last legs in 1916; in fact, the primary reason for its final disappearance from the theater was the release of George Loane Tucker's successful film version in 1916.

Caine had quickly figured out that the new medium of cinema could make him more money and—equally important for him—keep his name before the public. He leased the film rights to his novels for vast sums—far greater than theatrical agreements provided: just by way of a few examples, in 1919 he leased the rights to *The Christian* (novel 1897) to Samuel Goldwyn for £40,000[3] and in the same year Famous Players-Lasky paid $30,000 for *The Woman Thou Gavest Me* (novel 1913).[4] In

1923, Goldwyn also purchased the rights to *The Eternal City* (novel 1901) for £25,000.[5] The contracts with Loane Tucker or BIP for *The Manxman* do not appear to have survived, but it seems reasonable to assume that since the canny and still popular Caine was still alive, both versions would have commanded high figures. The odd scrap of information that does emerge from the archives demonstrates that Tucker's version was still bringing in money as late as 1919, when Caine received £343.4.0, from its producers the London Film Co., his share of the film's Scandinavian profits.[6] Hitchcock was entrusted, then, with a property that might have been old-fashioned, but was still eminently bankable, its author still alive and rights-watching, its audience still interested. "The novel had quite a reputation and belonged to a tradition," Hitchcock told Truffaut. "We had to respect that reputation and that tradition" (61). The manner in which Hitchcock chose to exercise his respect is worthy of further study. It had long-lasting consequences in terms of the development of his individual style.

The tradition to which *The Manxman* belonged was in some senses essentially Victorian but in others contains aspects that feed easily into the *avant garde* of the early twentieth century. Caine's novels were overwhelmingly melodramatic, being scenically atmospheric, containing overblown emotions, adhering to a form of Christian socialism that privileges spiritual over worldly rewards but deals unflinchingly with very human concerns. His writing style was high Victorian, his frames of reference largely biblical. The illustrations that accompanied the serialized installments of his novels were, however, like many such periodical illustrations, of an order that both reinforces an essentially Victorian moral universe and in some ways foreshadows the *noir* techniques of early European filmmakers. *The Manxman* illustrations by Fred Pegram that appeared in the *Queen* serialization (figures 3.1–3.8 below) are typical of their kind.

The private moral dilemmas of the characters are emphasized with the use of dark shadows and small pools of bright light (only figure 3.2 representing sunlight—appropriately enough since it depicts a prelapsarian moment of innocence between Kate and Pete). Significant plot moments are framed with doors and windows (e.g., figure 3.3), in which the postwedding departure of Kate and Pete is figured as the leaving behind of everything bright in her childhood home and the hurtling toward an unforeseeable future). Kate is frequently pictured in or near a sort of shadow cage (figures 3.2 and 3.4), emblem of the moral trap into which she has fallen. The massive fireplace in many of the interiors (figures 3.4, 3.5, 3.7, and 3.8) yawns like the mouth of hell, the characters teetering on its brink and lit by its brimstone glare. There are an astonishing number of cradle scenes, which tend to feature the cradle itself (heavy symbol of Kate's shame) rather than the child (whose

Figure 3.1. "Backwards, slowly, tremblingly." The *Queen*, 20 January 1894, p. 88.
All *Queen* images reproduced by kind permission of the Manx Heritage Museum,
Isle of Man.

Figure 3.2. "Bend down so the ould man won't hear.'" The *Queen*, 20 January 1894, p. 89.

Figure 3.3. "And they drove away." The *Queen*, 7 April 1894, p. 515.

Figure 3.4. "You will be all he thinks I am, but never have been. Farewell, my sweet Katherine." The *Queen*, 28 April 1894, p. 640.

Figure 3.5. "Sitting on a stool with the little one on his knees, he sobbed while the child cried." The *Queen*, 5 May 1894, p. 681.

Figure 3.6. "As the clock was striking nine, Pete was squaring himself at the table, pen in hand." The *Queen*, 12 May 1894, p. 737.

60

Figure 3.7. "Suddenly, while he knelt there, he was smitten as by an electric shock." The *Queen*, 16 June 1894, p. 964.

Figure 3.8. "'Don't you know me, Pete?' she said in a helpless way." The *Queen*, 28 June 1894, p. 1005.

appearance presumably might soften the reader's heart). This illustrative tradition—moody, atmospheric, utilizing a powerful moral chiaroscuro—had a long reign.

Loane Tucker's 1916 version of the novel was given Caine's full backing, even to the printing of his congratulatory endorsement on the publicity pack.[7] No known copy of the film survives, but while the extant publicity stills show a series of wide-angle shots of a sunny island with characters in traditional costume as though this were a simple period drama, if Tucker's earlier white slave-trade film *Traffic in Souls* (1913) is anything to go by, it seems likely that his version of *The Manx-man* [sic] utilized some trademark rapid editing for effect and some atmospheric lighting. In terms of treatment and moral tone, too, it seems likely that the illicit sex theme was paramount. One shot certainly stands out from the extant stills: significantly, it is a cradle scene in which Kate stares into space, an oblivious Pete dozes, and only the baby looks at the camera (figure 3.9). On the side of the cradle the shadow of a pot about to boil underscores both the scene's explosive tension and Kate's emotional turmoil.

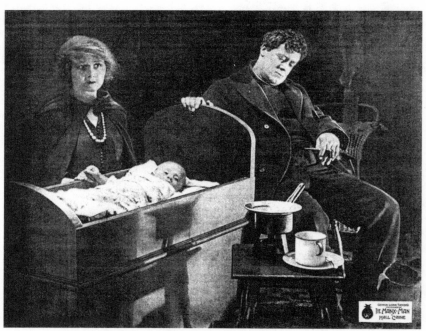

Figure 3.9. Still from George Loane Tucker's *The Manx-man* (1916), produced by the London Film Company. Reproduced courtesy of the Billy Rose Theatre Division, New York Public Library for the Performing Arts, Astor, Lenox and Tilden Foundations.

We do not know for sure whether Hitchcock ever saw Tucker's film, either of the play versions, or (surely unlikely) the original *Queen* illustrations. But Victorian and Edwardian theatrical and illustrative traditions were clearly strongly imprinted in his visual memory; despite the fact that cradles make only incidental appearances in the novel, his *Manxman* too contains a cradle scene. In it, Kate is sitting contemplating her guilt beside a huge gaping fire reminiscent of the fires in the Pegram illustrations. The slowly rocking cradle casts a pulsing shadow, back and forth, echoing Kate's vacillating thoughts and reinforcing the larger motif of a flashing lighthouse used by Hitchcock to punctuate the night scenes (a device used to equal effect in an earlier film, *The Lodger*). Hitchcock's use of frames is also in some ways reminiscent of this earlier tradition as important plot moments and the dilemmas they signal are starkly picked out with windows and doorways. Philip's loyal attempt to convince Kate's father to accept Pete as a suitor (when he's in love with her himself) is filmed through a window from Pete's point of view as from outside a cage. In Figure 3.10 a rock frames Philip at his appointed rendezvous with Kate, dwarfing him and adding immense dramatic weight to the moment in which he must tell her that Pete is still alive and on his way home to reclaim her.

Figure 3.10. *The Manxman*, Alfred Hitchcock (UK, 1929). Source: British Film Institute.

At this point in his career Hitchcock had already made *The Ring* (1927), *The Farmer's Wife* (1928), and *Champagne* (1928) for BIP, and only on the first of these had he been given anything like authorial control, having come up with the scenario and written the script. He is unlikely to have had a great deal of control over *The Manxman* either; if John Maxwell (head of BIP) exercized a firm hand in his studio, Hall Caine exercized an equally firm one outside it, though in this case the interference was unofficial. In almost all his theatrical and film contracts, Caine insisted on the insertion of a clause giving him final say over the script and often some say in the choice of cast too. He was every bit as obsessive as Hitchcock when it came to control over his creations. Unusually, however, and against the advice of his agent and manager, on this occasion he had sold rather than leased the rights to *The Manxman*, perhaps sensing that this was likely to be its last outing and opting for the higher amount outright sale commanded (Allen 416). This meant he had no official control over any part of the shoot. But Hitchcock's original plan to make the film on the Isle of Man was thwarted almost as soon as the two men met; in spite of the contract Caine interfered to such an extent that after a couple of weeks Hitchcock decamped to Cornwall with his entire cast and crew and finished the filming there. Caine hated the film, objecting most of all to the choice of Anny Ondra to play Kate. Though he attended the premiere at the Hippodrome he walked out halfway through, absenting himself despite the film's apparent success and repeated calls for the "Author" (Allen 416).

In some ways, Caine's disgust is hard to fathom: Hitchcock's *Manxman* is truer to the book than any of Caine's own dramatizations for the theater had been. The scenes in which the fishermen go on strike for fairer wages are handled as sympathetically as Caine might have wished. Philip's struggle with his conscience throughout means that the dynamic between the two best friends revolves—in a very Cainelike way—around individual responsibility, rather than intrinsic notions of right and wrong as represented by the polarization of the characters in the plays. Hitchcock and his scenario writer Eliot Stannard put back the original denouement, having Philip resign his high office and leave the courtroom for a future with Kate and their child through a disapproving crowd of neighbors. But on another level, despite the adherence to a strong Victorian pictorial tradition, *The Manxman* demonstrates that it is part of the new century: post-Great War, acutely conscious of the Depression and of more ambiguous moral values. The settings dwarf the actors. The framing is capable of trapping or excluding anybody. The pulsing lighthouse is both reminiscent of nineteenth-century tropes and at the same time disturbingly innovative, since it occurs relentlessly, almost without reference to the action, presaging nothing and yet everything. In Hitchcock's world, shadows fall on the just and the unjust alike. Similarly, the ending might reflect the novel's action, but his direction of it is quite different. In the novel—in true high Victorian/Hall Caine fashion—Philip turns his face away from the jeering crowd and towards Heaven:

> The door opened and Philip and Kate came out. There was no other exit, and they must have taken it . . . Under the weight of so many eyes, her head was held down, but those who were near enough to see her face knew that her shame was swallowed up in happiness and her fear in love. Philip was like a man transfigured . . . It was the common remark that never before had he looked so strong, so buoyant, so noble. This was the hour of his triumph . . . this, when his sin was confessed, when conscience had no power to appal him . . . Once for a moment she halted and stumbled as if under the hot breath that was beating upon her head. But he put his arm about her, and in a moment she was strong. The sun dipped down from the great tower on to his upturned face, and his eyes were glistening through their tears (439).

This is pure Caine, but it is not Hitchcock. In his movie, Philip and Kate seem crushed rather than buoyed up by the publication of their shame; their faces express grim determination rather than spiritual release—or even love. In fact, the direction is often so unsympathetic toward local characters and traditions (Kate's father, Caesar, for example—the novel's endearing local—comes across in the film as a grasping patriarch) that we feel the onlookers are hypocrites, and Philip and Kate are to be pitied, rather than that they have transcended earthly temptation and achieved a spiritual reward. Hitchcock also adds one final scene—a long take of Pete at the helm of his fishing boat, heading out to sea as though, having lost a wife and child on whom he doted, solitude and the elements are all that are left to him, the corruption and disappointment of the land and all its inhabitants now more than he can bear. It is a curious ending with no precedent in any other version that we can now detect, but it reinforces the film's overall sense that stringent Victorian morality has a hidden personal cost, and it makes this film less about spiritual triumph than about the devastating betrayal of a friendship. This is all the more significant when we recall that the love triangle—two friends in love with the same woman, heartbreak for all—was the theme of Hitchcock's only previous solo venture, *The Ring*, and that Carl Brisson starred in both.

Deeply embedded though it was in the "tradition" that Hitchcock felt he had to respect, his film of *The Manxman* is nonetheless a useful example of the ways in which the new medium of film straddled two centuries and a wide—even global—range of influences. It is also a reminder of how much a visual style that is too often described as unprecedented owed to its creator's formative years.

Notes

1. It is worth mentioning here that in addition to the critical attention paid to the film by Gledhill and Gottlieb, Charles Barr calls the movie "a consummate illustration of the rich expressive potential of the medium to which he was saying farewell" (67).

2. Drafts of *The Manxman* play by Hall Caine and Louis N. Parker. Papers of Sir Thomas Henry Hall Caine (1853–1931) (MS 09542) held on deposit in the National Library and Archive, Manx Museum, Isle of Man.

3. Hall Caine Letters and Contracts, Berg Collection, New York Public Library, Ref: Box 22, 68B4095, Folder 1, No. 49. Letter from H. A. Hubman to John W. Rumsey, n.d.

4. Ibid., Folder 7, No. 740. Contract between Famous Players-Lasky and H. C. for film rights to *The Woman Thou Gavest Me*, 2 January 1919.

5. Ibid., Folder 3, No. 147. Contract between Samuel Goldywn and H. C. for film rights to *The Eternal City*, handled by the American Play Company, 6 June 1923.

6. Letter from the London Film Company to Hall Caine, 18 July 1919. Hall Caine Archive, the Manx Heritage Museum, Isle of Man. Letters to Hall Caine (1853–1931) (Letters to Hall Caine 1900–1919, Box 64, Ref: 9542) held on deposit in the National Library and Archive, Manx Museum, Isle of Man.

7. Prepublicity brochure for George Loane Tucker film, clippings file of *The Manx-man*, Billy Rose Theatre Division, New York Public Library. Ref: "Cinema, 1917."

Works Cited

Allen, Vivien. *Hall Caine: Portrait of a Victorian Romancer*. Sheffield: Sheffield Academic, 1997.

Barr, Charles. *English Hitchcock*. Moffat: Cameron & Hollis, 1999.

Caine, Hall. *The Manxman*, 9th ed. London: Heinemann, 1898.

Gledhill, Christine. *Reframing British Cinema 1918–1928: Between Restraint and Passion*. London: BFI, 2003.

Spoto, Donald. *The Life of Alfred Hitchcock: The Dark Side of Genius*. London: Collins, 1983.

Truffaut, François. *Hitchcock*. New York: Simon & Schuster, 1984.

4

CHARLES BARR

Blackmail

Charles Bennett and the Decisive Turn

THE AUTHOR OF *BLACKMAIL*, CHARLES BENNETT, is, I will argue, the most important of all Hitchcock's writers—not in literary stature, but in his influence on Hitchcock's work. In the critical literature, Robin Wood is of comparable importance, and his writings are relevant to the case of Bennett in a double-edged way. The imperious dismissal, in his original book of 1965, of the British films as utterly minor compared with most of the Hollywood ones helped to divert critical attention from them for a long time; his auteurist indifference to the input of Hitchcock's collaborators was equally influential. In 1989, in *Hitchcock's Films Revisited*, Wood apologized for his earlier "indefensible attitude to the British period" and offered a close, positive, and insightful reading of three films: *Blackmail* (1929), *The 39 Steps* (1935), and *Young and Innocent* (1937). On the question of collaborators, however, there was no change. Those three titles have a writer in common, as well a director, but that writer, Charles Bennett, is never mentioned.

Bennett wrote the play on which *Blackmail* is based, and he was the main screenwriter for the other two. He is unique among all Hitchcock's writers, across his directing career of fifty years and more than fifty films, for the way he combines these two functions, supplier of original material and adaptor of the work of others. The only other writer who even begins to qualify is Helen Simpson, co-author of the novel on which *Murder!* (1930) was based and author of the novel *Under Capricorn* (filmed in 1949); she is credited alongside two others for contributing dialogue to *Sabotage* (1936), but did no other screenplay work for Hitchcock or indeed for anyone else.[1] The main writer on *Sabotage* was again Charles Bennett, just as he was for *Secret Agent* (also 1936) and *The Man Who Knew Too Much* (1934)—the first in that remarkable run of five successive collaborations that ended with *Young and Innocent*.[2]

Bennett thus helped, on two separate occasions, five years apart, to set Hitchcock on a new path: first with *Blackmail*, which became his first sound film, and then with the decisive switch into the thriller genre with which he would become so identified. Of course a number of Hollywood screenwriters would also be important to Hitchcock, but by then he had essentially been "formed." In some ways his first collaborator, Eliot Stannard, must have been the most formative influence of all, working on each of his first nine (silent) films, usually with solo screenplay credit as adaptor, but he provided no original novel or play.[3] Likewise, authors of key texts that, like *Blackmail*, had a long-term impact on Hitchcock— Marie Belloc Lowndes for *The Lodger*, John Buchan for *The 39 Steps*, Daphne du Maurier for *Rebecca*—did no work on Hitchcock screenplays. Only Bennett, to repeat, did both, and it was clearly his appreciation of *Blackmail* that caused Hitchcock to welcome the prospect of working with him when the chance arose at Gaumont-British five years later, and then to prolong the association. As I have traced elsewhere, the period between the two link-ups with Bennett was characterized by a strategy of close adaptation of plays and novels—rather different from the more radical strategy adopted previously on most of the Stannard films, and then on the Bennett ones, a strategy that Hitchcock would thereafter adopt as official policy and advocate with great eloquence. When doing his own adaptations in the interim, along with his wife, Alma Reville, he had used a more tentative and respectful approach (Stannard 98).

Hitchcock himself is the sole writer credited for adapting *Blackmail*, though the sound version also credits the playwright Benn Levy for dialogue. Some sources give Bennett a share in the script, but he always denied this in interviews (Server 18). Michael Powell's uncredited input is discussed later in this chapter.[4] This is, of course, the transitional film that Hitchcock shot in two versions, silent and—the word appended in brackets to the title by the British Board of Film Censors—"synchronised." From the time of its release, the sound version, the one that got all the publicity, was justly celebrated for the ingenuity with which it not only negotiated the technological clumsiness of the new synchronized medium but also exploited the soundtrack positively through aural expressionism and counterpoint.[5] Later, when the forgotten silent version became more accessible, there was fresh cause to admire the ingenuity with which Hitchcock had stitched together the two parallel versions from a varied range of material, in an often inspired work of *bricolage*. All this formal attention has tended to distract from the subject matter of the film, which influential critics of the time saw, in any case, as somewhat trivial. Paul Rotha admired the film's technical inventiveness but considered it essentially shallow and ephemeral: it would be "completely forgotten in a few months by those who saw it" (405–06). And it was on the basis of *Blackmail* and of *Murder!* that John Grierson was moved to make his notorious rhetorical appeal to Hitchcock—seen as "the world's best director of unimportant pictures"—to create a film about an industrial city, "with the personals in their proper place and the life of a community instead of a benighted lady at stake."[6]

"A benighted lady": in *Blackmail*, this is Alice White (Anny Ondra), victim of an attempted rape, who in panicky self-defense stabs her attacker with a fortuitously placed bread knife and kills him. The remainder of the narrative keeps us in suspense as to what will follow. Will she confess to the killing? When others realize her guilt—the tentative blackmailer and then her policeman boyfriend—will they reveal it? What will happen if they do? And is "guilt" the right word?

The very fact that Grierson and company could so easily dismiss all this as unimportant is an index of how far ahead of its time *Blackmail* was. The derogatory reference to "the personals" is characteristic of his polemical pro-documentary aesthetic, then so influential in British film culture; to an obsessive extent, his writings use *personal* as a dirty word, long before the counter-argument that "the personal is political" had become easily available. Grierson could also, then, make with impunity his at least semi-serious plea that separate cinemas be established for men and for women so that the "personal" themes and modes preferred by women should not be allowed to get in the way of the serious concerns of the male audience (in Hardy 33). In 1988, in *The Women Who Knew Too Much*, Tania Modleski anatomized the trivializing tone adopted in subsequent decades by a succession of other male critics writing on *Blackmail*, who hinted that a woman who went alone with an artist to his studio was in effect "asking for it." The subtitle of her book is *Hitchcock and Feminist Theory*, and it was soon followed by the new edition of Robin Wood's book containing extensive new material centered likewise on the sexual politics of Hitchcock's films. Criticism had at last properly, and persuasively, caught up with *Blackmail*. For both Wood and Modleski, this is the film that launches "their" Hitchcock, his tenth film but the earliest that they discuss; Modleski starts with it, and Wood goes back to it, as the first film in the revised edition of *Hitchcock's Films* (the earliest film discussed in any detail in the 1965 text is the 1952 Hollywood film *Strangers on a Train*).

But Bennett is mentioned by neither of them. They really do both write as if Hitchcock had made the whole thing up himself, and they do not feel the need to justify this; such an approach has not, of course, been unusual in author-centered criticism, before or since. The boldest and most explicit defense of this strategy that I have found comes in Wood's early monograph on Arthur Penn. The emphasis on the two adverbs here is my own:

> I am perfectly aware of quoting lines from *The Miracle Worker* as if Penn, not William Gibson, had written them . . . Ideally, one would wish *constantly* to be introducing little qualifications and acknowledgments into one's text when quoting lines of dialogue. This is, however, a study of Arthur Penn, not of [Gibson and others] . . . When the genuineness and intensity of a director's response are as evident as they are in *The Miracle Worker*, the film becomes his. These are Arthur Penn's films; the lines in a very real sense belong to him even if he didn't write them. One cannot *always* be acknowledging collaborators, but this doesn't imply unawareness or denigration of their contributions. (40)

Well, yes, up to a point. But there is a big gap between "constantly" or "always" acknowledging the writer (or other collaborator) and never doing so, which is Wood's frequent practice, notably with Hitchcock. I quote this at some length both because it makes such a valid point in principle about directorial imprint and also because it seems so relevant to the project of this volume, that of giving due weight to Hitchcock's literary and dramatic sources and considering the complex process by which he did, generally, take them over successfully, make them "belong to him," without, however, ceasing to be dependent on them. To adopt Wood's vocabulary further, Hitchcock did often *denigrate* his writers' contributions, or more often ignore them, when he could get away with it, but he cannot have been *unaware* of them, least of all Bennett's.

Far from being a hit, as many writers on Hitchcock claim, *Blackmail* had a mixed reception and a short run when it was staged in the West End of London. Its subject matter seems to have made both reviewers and audience uneasy; one paper reported "If Mr. Charles Bennett has a rather tawdry story to tell, it certainly deserved a kindlier reception, as presumably a 'prentice effort, than it obtained from gallery first-nighters at the Globe . . . We shall probably hear of Mr. Bennett again."[7] The disturbing thematic elements that lead one to call the film of *Blackmail* "ahead of its time" are unequivocally there in the play text.

According to Michael Powell, it was during the location shooting for his previous film *The Manxman*—his last all-silent one—that Hitchcock gave him the text of *Blackmail* to think about as a film possibility (191).[8] Hitchcock may or may not have already seen the play staged in London, and he may or may not have been looking, at this point sometime in 1928, for a subject with potential as a sound film; but its immediate appeal to him is understandable, not least because of the strong continuity between its central female role and that of *The Manxman*. Robin Wood refers to *Blackmail's* "privileged status as the first of Hitchcock's guilty woman films." His extreme alienation from the repressive climate of the Britain of the period, into which he himself was born and against which he rebelled, leads him into writing as though only he and Hitchcock had the measure of it, but of course there were others. Already in *The Manxman*, set in a more remote environment and somewhat earlier, Hall Caine (novel) and Eliot Stannard (adaptor) had anatomized a similar climate and had between them created a poignant role for Anny Ondra as a "guilty woman," stifled by a repressive family and caught disastrously between men in different ways unworthy of her. Bennett's play offered the same structure, highly sympathetic to the woman's situation, in a contemporary London environment. It is not surprising that Hitchcock, with Powell's encouragement, seized on it.

He was worried, though, about the play's third act. In it, all the action that resolves the story occurs off-screen, reported in messages and phone calls. Powell, by his own account, reassured him: "To hell with the third act. We'll make it a chase" (192). Hence the long sequence of the pursuit of the blackmailer, culminating in his fall to his death from the dome of the British Museum, a passage echoing very deliberately the film's long opening section of another aggressive police operation. Most of the drama in between takes place in the two settings of the play. Act 1, in the artist's studio, ends with his death and Alice's catatonic exit, after a scene of attempted seduction, which turns into attempted rape. Acts 2 and 3 are set in her home, where she lives with her shopkeeper parents and a brother whom the film will omit. The film devotes large chunks of its running time to these two settings, and much of the ground it covers is close to the play in action and tone. It is in these interior settings that the sound version of the film is least mobile, with the still-crude recording technology making for some lengthy takes and carefully enunciated dialogue.

It would be much too simple, however, to regard the play material as "theatrical," redeemed by the "cinematic" of the framing action sequences and by the occasional interpolation of spectacular sound devices ("knife . . . knife"). Leaving aside the question of whether long static takes are necessarily uncinematic in the first place, there are many elements in the play text that already seem to be ready for, and even to invite, more mobile cinematic adaptation; these help to explain why Bennett would become such a congenial and effective screenwriting collaborator.

Here is part of the exchange between Alice and her family early in act 2, following her return home. In the film she returns just before breakfast, and her long absence has been undetected; in the play, she does not return until 4 p.m., and her family members launch into a long process of prurient interrogation.

> MRS. JARVIS: Oh! So you've come home, have you? Well . . . where have you been?
>
> [Alice is looking at her mother. She is obviously at the end of her tether. Her movements are quick and nervous, and there is a hunted look in her eyes. She looks at her father and then at her brother. Finding no sympathy with either of them, her eyes come back to the questioner. She speaks quietly.]
>
> ALICE: Walking
>
> MRS. JARVIS: Walking?
>
> ALICE: Just . . . walking
>
> MRS. JARVIS: And last night?
>
> ALICE: [after a momentary pause] Walking.
>
> MRS. JARVIS: What?
>
> [Alice can't bear it any longer and lowers her eyes. Mrs. Jarvis stares at her for a moment . . . then follows up her attack]
>
> What do you mean . . . walking?

This very precisely charted exchange of looks may well have been reasonably effective on stage, depending on the spectator's position in the auditorium, but can be much more so in cinema, whether taken in a shot-reverse-shot series or in a wider shot which leaves it to the audience to follow the movement of glances within the frame. While this scene obviously has no direct equivalent in the film, there are many others involving the exchange of meaningful glances, sometimes in shot-reverse-shot (Alice and the artist in the café, the first time we see him), more often within the frame. Then there is the five-fold repetition of the single word, "walking"—a good example of the less-is-more principle, giving great scope to the actors, the subtext of the family's skepticism being brought out more eloquently than by having it explicitly articulated. Moreover, the repetition of the word, within such a slow-paced exchange, invites us to imagine, to see, the walk itself, which we, unlike the family—who are all certain that she has been involved in the unforgivable: sexual activity—know that she will have taken and at agonizing length. Hitchcock and Powell must assuredly, likewise, have seen the walk as they read (and maybe also saw) the play, and they indeed take Bennett's cue in constructing, for the film, the trancelike walk, linked with dissolves, that Alice takes through London, bridging the gap between her late-night departure from the artist's studio and her early-morning return home.

Soon after this comes an exchange that surely confirms, if it is still necessary, that Hitchcock's angle on the repressive culture and sexual politics of the time was already present in the stage play. Here, it is not just her parents but her own brother too who bully her. Italics and ellipses are in the original:

ALBERT: D'yer mean . . . you're goin' to 'ave a kid?

ALICE: Worse than that.

ALBERT: Worse . . . ?

MRS. JARVIS: It couldn't be.

Powell—again by his own account—sold Hitchcock on the idea of the chase, to replace, or at least to break up, the third act. Like the walk, this is obliquely or potentially present in the play text. Tracy, the blackmailer, has in act 2 established a hold on Alice and her policeman boyfriend (named Harold in the play, though he is Frank in the film); in act 3, after becoming a suspect sought by the police, he returns to Alice's home to be sheltered by her and gives a vivid account of being chased by them: "Then I saw a couple of them coming down Imperial Road . . . looking over the fences and flashing lights into the doorways. I knew what that meant, so I hopped it up this way again. There was one of them on the bridge and he spotted me as I came by against the wall. Any other time he wouldn't have noticed me . . . but I suppose I'd got the hunted look all right. Anyway he blew his whistle and chased me down Lots Road."

Again, this monologue, which goes on for a lot longer, invites us to visualize and offers a cue to the filmmakers who take it up in displaced form at a later point, making the police pursuit of Tracy into the action climax of the film. Nor is it just a chase; the psychology is more complex. On stage, hearing Tracy's narrative, Alice is already tormented by knowing that he is being pursued for a killing for which she, not he, was responsible—and by knowing that he knows this. One obvious way of staging the scene would be to have Alice downstage left or right, staring out into nowhere, while Tracy speaks. At the film's climax, this effect is again displaced into cinematic terms through editing: immobile close shots of Alice sitting at home, staring ahead of her, are cut into the sequence of the pursuit of Tracy, which ends in his death. There are nine such shots in all, and they are so weighty, and have such an intense interior quality to them, as to create the sense that the pursuit is, at some level, still a visualization, pictures from her feverish imagination. And indeed they are that, at the same time as being pictures of what is happening "out there."

This merging of, or hesitation between, subjective and objective is one of the great defining aspects of Hitchcock's cinema, supremely illustrated in the dreamlike narratives of such later color films as *Rear Window* and *Vertigo*; it is anticipated already in silent films, notably *The Manxman*, but nowhere more powerfully than in *Blackmail*. The stage play has provided a potent springboard for this, both in these scenes of narrative superimposition—the words that cue visualization—and in its many nightmarish dramatic moments when time seems to freeze. Bennett's stage directions for the exit of Alice from the studio, after the death of the artist, are almost like a script for the sequence that Hitchcock makes of it.

All this helps to explain why Bennett teams so effectively with Hitchcock at Gaumont-British, five years later. As before at the time of *Blackmail*, he is there just at the right time to enable Hitchcock to build upon a new element that he has lit upon and responded to from elsewhere, in source material that otherwise would not easily lead anywhere. After *The Manxman*, he had no wish to make period films in fringe locations; nor is there now a future in continuing to adapt the tongue-in-cheek melodramas of Jefferson Farjeon after *Number Seventeen* (filmed in 1932). But this Farjeon text was a liberating one in important ways, notably in supplying Hitchcock's most oneiric narrative to date, his first real action thriller, his first true "MacGuffin," and his first "overnight" romance, adding up to a narrative skeleton on which Bennett would show himself well equipped to put flesh in a succession of five scripts.[9] The insight into power and gender relationships, so evident in *Blackmail*, are evident again in all of them, as is the skill of which Bennett was proudest, that of being a "constructionist" (McGilligan 26).[10] Repeatedly, in the course of narratives constructed with a satisfying flow and dramatic logic, he maneuvers sympathetic women into painful entrapments, in scenes to which Hitchcock's direction can fully respond: Jill in the Albert Hall in *The Man Who Knew Too Much*; Margaret in her loveless marriage to the crofter in *The 39 Steps*; Mrs. Verloc facing her husband over the dinner table in *Sabotage*; Erica defying family and the law in *Young and Innocent*.

Bennett felt bitter that the collaboration with Hitchcock did not go on longer than it did, telling McGilligan, "You'll find that no writer ever gets any credit from Hitch. I think that since I had written seven of his top movies, for a while he resented me, and then he became my friend again." Despite the friendship, and the fact that they both worked continuously in Hollywood for several more decades, there were no more collaborations after *Foreign Correspondent* in 1940.

Here, despite my evident partisanship for Bennett, I sympathize with Hitchcock. It is not just that Bennett had broken the partnership first, by moving to Hollywood ahead of him, still in the middle of the planning of *Young and Innocent*; one can understand Hitchcock wanting to move on, to avoid the danger of going stale, to expose himself to new American writers. Those encounters with other writers and other material belong elsewhere in this volume and take us far beyond *Blackmail*, which remains one of the key films in Hitchcock's career. On it, Bennett deserves the last word. He may overstate the case, but he is surely entitled to, after so many decades of neglect: "I didn't actually work on the screenplay, but I'm not kidding myself about that—the film was my play" (qtd. in McGilligan 24).

Notes

1. I am not counting Frederick Knott, who is credited in 1954 for adapting his own play *Dial M for Murder* but did no other writing for Hitchcock, or Robert Bloch, author of the novel *Psycho*, who wrote some teleplays for the series *Alfred Hitchcock Presents*.

2. After writing *Young and Innocent*, Bennett took up a contract in Hollywood, two years ahead of Hitchcock; they had a final collaboration on Hitchcock's second Hollywood film, *Foreign Correspondent* (1940).

3. I have argued for Stannard's importance in *English Hitchcock* and then more thoroughly in "Writing Screenplays: Stannard and Hitchcock," in *Young and*

Innocent? The Cinema in Britain 1896–1930, ed. Andrew Higson., The latter draws upon a series of articles by Stannard in the British trade paper *Kinematograph Weekly*, written years before Hitchcock started to direct, which in some respects combine to construct an anticipatory "template" for his filmmaking.

4. See for instance the Bennett interview in Lee Server, *Screenwriter: Words Become Pictures*.

5. A key document here is the article "As Is," in the intellectual film magazine *Close Up*, October 1929, by its editor Kenneth Macpherson: reprinted in *Close Up 1927–1933: Cinema and Modernism*, ed. James Donald et al.

6. John Grierson, in *The Clarion*, October 1930, reprinted in Hardy, 108, 110.

7. The review is from the *Illustrated London News*, 10 March 1928.

8. Powell has no screen credit for the work he describes having done on the script, nor was his involvement ever mentioned by Hitchcock; and he was writing more that half a century after the events he claims to recall in such detail. But this is typical of his book's style, and there is no reason not to accept the broad truth of his account. If he exaggerates his input, one might say it serves Hitchcock right for his tactic of always being so silent about the contribution of others, when he thought he could get away with it, as he so often could.

9. This somewhat unorthodox line on *Number Seventeen* is developed further in *English Hitchcock*, 122–27.

10. See McGilligan, *Backstory*, 26, among many other instances.

Works Cited

Barr, Charles. "*Blackmail*: Silent and Sound." *Sight and Sound*. Spring 1983.
———. *English Hitchcock*. Moffat: Cameron & Hollis, 1999.
Hardy, Forsyth, ed. *Grierson on the Movies*. London: Faber & Faber, 1981.
Higson, Andrew. *Young and Innocent?: The Cinema in Britain 1896-1930*. Exeter: University of Exeter Press, 2002.
Macpherson, Kenneth. "AS IS." In James Donald et al., eds., *Close Up 1927–1933: Modernism*. Princeton, N.J.: Princeton University Press, 1998, 90.
McGilligan, Patrick. *Backstory: Interviews with Screenwriters of Hollywood's Golden Age*. Los Angeles: University of California Press, 1986.
Modleski, Tania. *The Women Who Knew Too Much: Hitchcock and Feminist Theory*. New York: Methuen, 1988.
Powell, Michael. *A Life in Movies*. London: Heinemann, 1986.
Rotha, Paul. *The Film Till Now*. 1930. 3rd ed. London: Vision, 1960.
Server, Lee. *Screenwriter: Words Become Pictures*. Pittstown, New Jersey: Main Street, 1987.
Wood, Robin. *Hitchcock's Films*. London: Tantivy, 1965.
———. *Hitchcock's Films Revisited*. New York: Columbia University Press, 1989.
———. *Arthur Penn*. London: Movie Paperbacks, 1969.

5

MARK GLANCY

The Man Who Knew
Too Much (1934)

Alfred Hitchcock, John Buchan,
and the Thrill of the Chase

URING THE FIRST HALF OF THE twentieth century, John Buchan
was a prominent figure in British life. He was Director of
Intelligence during the First World War and later served as
the Lord High Commissioner of the Church of Scotland, a member of
Parliament, and the Governor General of Canada. Remarkably, during
this life of service and prominent posts, Buchan was also a prolific and
popular author. His books included respected biographies of historical
and literary figures, as well as many contributions to a literary genre
that drew little respect, the thriller. Buchan slipped from prominence
in later decades, but his best-known thriller, *The Thirty-Nine Steps* (first
published in 1915), has never gone out of print, and it is now considered
a cornerstone of the thriller genre. To a significant degree, its extended
life can be attributed to the film and stage productions based upon it,
and none has proven as popular, enduring, and influential as the earliest
adaptation, Alfred Hitchcock's *The 39 Steps* (1935).[1]

Hitchcock was always ready to cite Buchan as an important influence on his work, and he once observed that he most admired the "multiple chases" in Buchan's stories and also the "understatement of highly dramatic ideas" (Truffaut 122). Arguably, though, the clearest and most evocative indication of Buchan's influence on Hitchcock can be found in the opening dedication of *The Thirty-Nine Steps*. There, Buchan refers to his story as a "shocker" and defines this as one "where the incidents defy the probabilities and march just inside the borders of the possible." It is an apt description of the fast-paced story that follows, with its thrilling chases, narrow escapes, wild coincidences, assumed identities, and an international conspiracy that threatens to undermine an entire nation, if not the whole world order. It is also, of course, an apt description of a distinctive strand of Hitchcock's films: those centered on international intrigue and espionage that began with *The Man Who Knew Too Much* (1934) and ran throughout his career, up to and including *Topaz* (1969).

This chapter examines Buchan's influence on *The Man Who Knew Too Much*, the first film Hitchcock made under a new contract at Gaumont-British Studios and the film that immediately preceded *The 39 Steps* (1935). It must be noted that the credits for *The Man Who Knew Too Much* make no mention of Buchan, and in fact they indicate that the story was based on an original scenario and a script written by no fewer than five screenwriters.[2] This is undeniably correct, yet Buchan's signature is apparent throughout the film. In terms of plot devices, story elements, and characterization, the film owes a significant debt to the four thrillers centered on the character Richard Hannay that Buchan had published by this time: *The Thirty-Nine Steps* (1915), *Greenmantle* (1916), *Mr. Standfast* (1918), and *The Three Hostages* (1924). One concern, therefore, is to consider what Hitchcock drew from Buchan's stories for this film. Another concern is to consider why Hitchcock turned to Buchan in 1934. This was a decisive moment in his career. Previously, he was not so strongly associated with the thriller genre. The sixteen films he directed between 1926 and 1933 had included various shades of melodrama, comedy, and even a musical, but only a few films that are now recognizable as Hitchcock thrillers. *The Man Who Knew Too Much* changed that. Its success with critics and audiences led Hitchcock to make five further thrillers, consecutively, over the next four years, and it was these films that secured his reputation as the "master of suspense." *The Man Who Knew Too Much* was also the first of Hitchcock's films to demonstrate a concern for the world of current events and political issues. This was not an easy leap for a British filmmaker to make in the 1930s, when the British Board of Film Censors (BBFC) maintained that films should be entertainment only and avoid any kind of controversy.

However, Hitchcock's spy thrillers proved able to circumnavigate the censors' rules, defying them by stealth if not challenging them directly, and Buchan's influence was crucial in this regard. Thus an account of how and why Hitchcock turned to Buchan is also an account of how Hitchcock became political and in turn how he politicized the thriller.

The Man Who Knew Too Much was initially conceived while Hitchcock was still under a contract at British International Pictures (BIP) that lasted from 1927 until 1932. At this stage, it was planned as a Bulldog Drummond story. Drummond was a fictional detective at the center of a series of novels written by H. C. McNeile (under the pen name of Sapper). The first, simply titled *Bulldog Drummond*, was published in 1921, and eight years later Samuel Goldwyn produced a film version in Hollywood. With the debonair Ronald Colman in the leading role, the film was a huge international success. McNeile, meanwhile, produced a steady stream of books chronicling the detective's further adventures. There was a marked disparity between the tough-talking, violent, and xenophobic Drummond of McNeile's books and the more gentlemanly figure portrayed by Colman in the film, but by 1932 Bulldog Drummond was nevertheless a well-known figure in popular culture. Hence, John Maxwell, the chief production executive at BIP, bought the rights to produce original films centered on the character. Hitchcock was assigned to develop the first of these original stories, and for this project he was paired with the writer Charles Bennett. Although Hitchcock's *Blackmail* (1929) was based on a play by Bennett, they had not collaborated before this. Maxwell brought the two together for the first time—and they would go on to collaborate on six highly regarded films—but this first, preliminary effort met with a dead end. Their scenario, entitled "Bulldog Drummond's Baby," was shelved by BIP (McGilligan, *Backstory* 24–26).

There are differing versions of what happened to "Bulldog Drummond's Baby." Years later, Hitchcock blamed the second-in-command at BIP, Walter Mycroft, and accused him of "intriguing against me" (Truffaut 107). Mycroft's recently published memoirs tell a different story. According Mycroft, John Maxwell ran the studio like "an absolute and complete dictator," and by 1932 he had little admiration left for Hitchcock. Maxwell did not object to the storyline—in which Drummond's own child is kidnapped by his nemesis, the master criminal Carl Peterson—but to a single, early scene within it. Set in a nightclub, the scene would show a ball of yarn gradually unwinding as it becomes hooked on a single dancer's jacket, and wraps around the legs of the dancers. This scene was eventually realized in *The Man Who Knew Too Much*, and it serves as an apt metaphor for the tangled web of conspiracy that ensnares the characters at the outset of the story. Maxwell, however, thought it was too whimsical for fans of Bulldog Drummond, and Mycroft recalled that he did a "slow burn" about this single scene, taking it as a definitive sign that Hitchcock's "wayward genius" had strayed too far (131–33). It has never been revealed whether he jumped or was pushed, but Hitchcock left BIP shortly thereafter.

Hitchcock's career had lost its momentum. He had not had a popular success since *Blackmail*, and although he had made his reputation primarily as a critics' favorite, his most recent films had disappointed even the critical fraternity. Cast adrift, his next assignment was as a freelance director, filming the costume musical *Waltzes from Vienna* (1933). The result was another film that scarcely registered with either the critics or the public, but its failure at least had the effect of forcing Hitchcock to make a "very sobering self examination" of his career to date. Henceforth, he would choose his projects with greater care, rather than moving from one assignment to the next at the behest of producers, and he would ensure that he had an "inner feeling of comfort" about each film before he embarked on it (Truffaut and Scott 107–09). These are of course convictions that any filmmaker should have, but there are two important points about the vows he made in the wake of *Waltzes from Vienna*. First, when Hitchcock signed a new contract at the end of 1933, it was to work with the producer Michael Balcon at Gaumont-British Pictures. Balcon had given him his first opportunities in the film industry, and now, as the chief production executive at this ambitious studio, he was willing to grant an unusual degree of creative control to Hitchcock. Second, when given this creative control, Hitchcock immediately chose to return to the thriller genre and the story that Maxwell had rejected at BIP.

Balcon was certainly a more supportive producer than Maxwell. At Hitchcock's request, he bought the rights to "Bulldog Drummond's Baby" and also hired Charles Bennett to develop the scenario further. In February 1934, the story was submitted to the BBFC. It was now called "The Hidden Hand," but it was still centered on McNeile's characters: the main character is the detective Bulldog Drummond; he investigates with his friend Algy; and the villain is Carl Peterson. Despite these names, the story described in the BBFC's brief report is recognizable as *The Man Who Knew Too Much*. It begins in Switzerland, where Drummond is vacationing with his wife and young daughter. In a hotel nightclub, they witness the killing of a friend, the Frenchman Louis Bernard, and Bernard's dying words lead them to discover a cryptic secret code hidden in a shaving brush. Before they can determine its meaning, their daughter is kidnapped, and they are warned not to reveal the code to the police. Back in London, Drummond realizes that the code alludes to the assassination of a foreign diplomat at the Royal Albert Hall, and with the help of Algy, he manages both to prevent the assassination and to save his daughter.[3] This story line, together with the nightclub scene (recalled by Walter Mycroft) and the title of "The Hidden Hand" (surely a reference to the close-up shot of the assassin's pistol emerging from behind the curtains at the Royal Albert Hall) indicate that key aspects of *The Man Who Knew Too Much* were already in place when it was conceived as "Bulldog Drummond's Baby."

Gaumont-British submitted the story to the BBFC again in May 1934, this time under the title of *The Man Who Knew Too Much*. All references to McNeile's characters had been dropped. The Drummonds were renamed Bob and Jill Lawrence, and Bulldog Drummond's sidekick, Algy, was now known as Clive.[4] The change may have been made simply for legal reasons: McNeile's characters were under copyright, and Mycroft recalled that Maxwell was eager to retain them for films made at BIP. Nevertheless, taking the Drummond name out of the story fundamentally altered it. The need to shape the main character to fit the mold of McNeile's blunt detective was now null and void. Whimsy and humor need not be banished from the film, and one of the most influential aspects of *The Man Who Knew Too Much*, and Hitchcock's subsequent 1930s thrillers, is their innovative mixture of tones: dark, menacing characters and events are combined with light, ironic comedy.

While the story undoubtedly benefited from its disassociation with Drummond, the change may also have been made because the filmmakers realized that, even while writing "Bulldog Drummond's Baby," they had been drawing more from Buchan than from McNeile, and specifically from Buchan's most recent Hannay story, *The Three Hostages*. This was the first of the Hannay stories to be written after the First World War, and the opening finds Hannay living quietly with his wife, Mary, and their young son, Peter John. A more reflective, intelligent and less violent character than Drummond, Hannay is enjoying his peacetime idyll, and he initially refuses a request to take on a new case. After wartime service (chronicled in *The Thirty-Nine Steps*, *Greenmantle*, and *Mr. Standfast*), he has retired to a quiet farm in the Cotswolds and feels himself to be "anchored at last in the pleasantest kind of harbour." Yet there is conspiracy that is baffling the government—three children of prominent parents have been kidnapped, apparently as a prelude to some form of international tyranny—and one of the children is a boy who is Peter John's age. Hannay's sympathy for the boy's heartbroken father compels him to help, and he soon arrives at the heart of the conspiracy. There he finds Dominic Medina. Ostensibly a charismatic and charming young politician who is destined for great things, Medina is beneath the surface a corrupt egotist of vaguely foreign origins, who uses hypnosis to bring people under his control. Hannay overcomes Medina's powers and, with the assistance of his friend Sandy Arbuthnot (who features in the other novels as well) and his wife, Mary, (introduced as a leading figure in the British security services in *Mr. Standfast*), the kidnapped children are saved, the conspiracy is thrown off track, and Medina is killed.

The Man Who Knew Too Much borrows and reworks key elements of *The Three Hostages*, as well as elements that recur in Buchan's other stories. One of Buchan's favorite story devices, for example, was the cryptic clue that, once decoded, solves the mystery. In *The Three Hostages*, the only clues come from a seemingly nonsensical verse of poetry. Hannay describes the verse as "doggerel" at first, but one by one, each of its lines slowly leads him a step further to unraveling the mystery. The more striking parallel for *The Man Who Knew Too Much* can be found in *Greenmantle*. In this story, Hannay sets out to uncover a German conspiracy in the Middle East, but his briefing by a British intelligence officer is minimal. He is told that his predecessor, an English spy working undercover in Turkey, stumbled back to his camp with bullet wounds and died before he could reveal what he had discovered. Only a piece of paper in the dead spy's pocket—reading "Kasredin," "cancer," and "v.I"—offers any indication of his findings, and decoding these clues eventually leads him to fulfill his mission (Barr 148). In *The Man Who Knew Too Much*, it is Louis Bernard who is killed by a sniper's bullet, and his dying words are whispered to Bob. He instructs him to examine his shaving brush and retrieve a message left hidden inside of it. The clues that Bob finds there ("Wapping G Barbor make contact A Hall March 21st") represent the knowledge referred to in the film's title: Bob Lawrence now knows too much. The spies kidnap his daughter, Betty, to ensure that Bob will not reveal the clues to Scotland Yard, so Bob must decipher them himself in order to find and save his daughter. Hence his first destination is Wapping, where he and Clive find that G. Barbor is a dentist hiding the spies (in a scene that prefigures the sadistic dentistry in John Schlesinger's *Marathon Man* [1976]). These cryptic clues represent what Hitchcock termed "the MacGuffin": the details of the story that set the characters' quest in motion, that matter most within the world of the story, and that matter least to the audience, who are more absorbed by the chase, the suspense, and the action. This was a definitive feature of Hitchcock's thrillers and, when he discussed "the MacGuffin" in interviews, he reminded critics and audiences that there was more at stake in his films than secret messages, wine bottles filled with "vintage sand," or hidden rolls of films.[5]

Other key aspects of *The Man Who Knew Too Much* also have their origins in *The Three Hostages*. Some of the novel's most memorable and disturbing scenes involve hypnosis. At one point, Hannay feigns being under Medina's spell and therefore has to obey his orders to crawl around the floor on all fours like a dog. Hitchcock later said that he thought scenes like this would be very difficult to put across on the screen ("visually speaking, there would be no difference between someone who is really hypnotized and someone who's pretending") and indicated that this was a significant obstacle to adapting the novel (Truffaut and Scott 472–73). Apparently, though, he could not resist trying his hand at representing a hypnotic state cinematically. Bob and Clive stumble from the dentist's office into a meeting house, the "Tabernacle of the Rising Sun," where hypnosis is used in bizarre religious services. The spies hold sway here, too, and in the midst of a service, Clive is called forth to be hypnotized. Both his woozy acquiescence and the hypnotist's menacing power are effectively conveyed via Hitchcock's camera work and special effects.

Mary Hannay is perhaps the most surprising character in *The Three Hostages*. Richard Hannay is initially unaware that his wife is involved with the hunt for the kidnapped children. While he is pursuing Medina, he imagines that Mary is at home and worrying about him. It comes as a shock to him, then, when he finds the spies' north London base, concealed behind a dance hall, and he sees that Mary has already infiltrated this hideaway and is among the dancers. The film's Jill Lawrence is certainly as formidable as the novel's Mary Hannay. Jill is first seen in Switzerland, competing against Ramon (Frank Vosper) in a clay-pigeon-shooting competition. She is distracted and loses the competition, blaming Betty and declaring, "Never have children!" with mock anger. But in the film's finale she proves her skill by shooting her daughter's pursuer with perfect marksmanship. Thus it is Jill rather than Bob who ultimately saves Betty and kills the menacing Ramon. This outcome is entirely in keeping with Mary Hannay's abilities in *The Three Hostages*, but it was rare in a 1930s film thriller to find a woman as level-headed, capable and effective as Jill Lawrence.

The most significant parallel between *The Three Hostages* and *The Man Who Knew Too Much* is the storyline itself: a kidnapping that has international political ramifications. In both stories, the central characters are initially complacent and disengaged with the wider world. Hannay, as in the earlier novels, is exhausted at the outset of *The Three Hostages* and resists pleas for his help but then rediscovers his energy and purpose amid the thrill of the chase. The Lawrences go along a similar, if more jaded, narrative trajectory. Where Hannay acts entirely from altruism (to save the children of other parents) and patriotism (to save his country), the Lawrences are involved only because their own daughter has been kidnapped. The political implications of the plot scarcely register with them. This is demonstrated in the film's climactic scene, which has no parallel in *The Three Hostages*. At the Royal Albert Hall, Jill watches as Ramon, her daughter's kidnapper, prepares to assassinate a foreign diplomat attending a concert. As a full orchestra plays the "Storm Cloud Cantata," and this highly dramatic piece (written specially for the film) builds to a climax, she sees the assassin's gun emerge from behind the curtains and take aim at the diplomat. It is only at this point that the full weight of the dilemma descends upon her. If she intervenes, her daughter will probably be killed in retribution; if she does not, the diplomat will be killed and an international crisis will follow. The dilemma overwhelms her, and when she finally screams, it seems an involuntary, hysterical response rather than a decisive end to a moral quandary. It is only later, when she sees Ramon stalking her daughter across the rooftop of the spies' hideaway, that she proves decisive and shoots him. Then in the film's final frames, when the traumatized family is reunited, we see that their complacency has been shattered. While Jill once joked about not having children, and Bob feigned indifference while his wife flirted with Louis Bernard, the three are clinging together in the film's final shot.

Hitchcock had long been interested in exploring the complacency of his characters, but in previous films the characters' complacency involved only their personal or romantic lives. *The Man Who Knew Too Much* represents the first time that a Hitchcock film mounts a critique of political complacency. The Lawrences refuse to reveal Louis Bernard's message to a Foreign Office official. The official is adamant: the clues refer to an impending assassination attempt on a foreign statesman who is visiting London. "Why should we care if some if some foreign statesman we've never heard of were assassinated?" Bob Lawrence asks, with his wife's agreement. The man from the Foreign Office replies: "Tell me: in June 1914 had you ever heard of a place called Sarajevo? Of course you hadn't. I doubt if you'd ever heard of the Archduke Ferdinand. But in a month's time, because a man you've never heard of killed another man you've never heard of in a place you've never heard of, this country was at war."

The statement may seem mild now, but in 1934 this was the closest a British filmmaker could come to alluding to the threat of another European war and to implying that current unrest could spread to Britain. The BBFC maintained that film was a medium of light entertainment, and any overt treatment of political issues, whether related to domestic or foreign matters, was rejected. However, the censors apparently found it difficult to grapple with implication and allusion, and in this regard *The Man Who Knew Too Much* skillfully evaded their restrictions. The film may not have constituted an explicit warning against the growing danger of fascism. Nevertheless, it offered a timely suggestion that political complacency ultimately hits home.

Neither *The Three Hostages* nor *The Man Who Knew Too Much* suggests that the threat to Britain comes entirely from abroad. In the novel, Dominic Medina's political philosophy and his long-term plans for subversion are never explicitly stated. Buchan apparently found a vague threat to be more effectively sinister than a specific one. Yet it is made clear that Medina is a respected and trusted MP and one headed for higher office, until Hannay stops him. In the film, the domestic dimensions of the threat seem vague on the surface, but they have some interesting connections with actual events. In the scene set at the Tabernacle of the Rising Sun, for example, the quasi-religious service quickly descends into a violent free-for-all in which chairs are thrown. This would appear to be inspired by the violence that regularly occurred at meetings of the British Union of Fascists, who were gaining strength in the East End at the time the film was written. Indeed, while the script was being prepared, the *Times* reported on one typical fracas with the headline, "Free Fight with Chairs: Uproar at Fascist Meeting" (*Times*, 25 November 1933, 14).

This may be a coincidence, but the film's denouement was an obvious recreation of the Siege of Sidney Street in 1911, a notorious episode of East End history, in which foreign anarchists engaged in a prolonged gun battle with the police. The film stages this in the manner of a Hollywood gangster film, but such violence was still rare in 1930s British films. The BBFC insisted that Britain must be portrayed as a law-abiding, peaceful and orderly country. The censors, in fact, seized upon this scene and insisted that it was "quite prohibitive": British Bobbies should not be shown using guns. In negotiations with the studio, it was agreed that the dialogue would stipulate that the police do not normally have guns and that they had to find a local gunsmith to supply them. The censors were not happy with this compromise and gave the film an "A" (for "adult") rating, but Gaumont-British apparently backed the filmmakers and refused to accede further to the BBFC's demands.[6]

Gaumont-British was a cosmopolitan, politically aware studio. Its owners, the Ostrer Brothers, were Jewish; so too were both the executive producer (Balcon) and the associate producer (Ivor Montagu). Balcon and Montagu were also founding members of the British Relief Committee for the Victims of German Fascism, and over the course of the 1930s the studio became the home of many filmmakers fleeing the German film industry (McGilligan, *Alfred Hitchcock* 158). Furthermore, Montagu was a committed and outspoken Communist, and his efforts to import Russian films for British screenings had given him extensive experience of the practices of the BBFC. Thus it is not surprising that Gaumont-British stood behind the film, and Montagu's skillful hand might be detected in numerous other ways. The casting of Peter Lorre as the leader of the spies, for example, was highly suggestive: Lorre was a Hungarian, but he was best known at this point for his role as a child killer in the German film *M* (1931) (Robertson 94). So, too, was the casting of Frank Vosper as the assassin Ramon. Vosper was a British-born actor, but his most recent film had been Gaumont's *Jew Süss* (1934), a portrait of anti-Semitism in eighteenth-century Würtemberg, in which Vosper played the cruel Duke Karl Alexander. In *The Man Who Knew Too Much* his nationality is never stated, but the association with this previous film, as well as his accent and bearing, point to Germany. In fact, one of the film's earliest scenes offers a clear alignment of nationalities: the Lawrences (played by English actors Leslie Banks and Edna Best) represent Britain, and they are friendly with Louis Bernard (played by the French actor Pierre Fresnay) and compete against the menacing Ramon (representing Germany). On the neutral ground of Switzerland, they meet for a shooting competition. When Jill Lawrence loses the competition, she tells Ramon, "We must have another battle one day," and he replies, "I shall live for that moment."

If Hitchcock's political awakening and the new timely relevance of his films are largely attributable to the collaborators he found at Gaumont-British, his penchant for Buchan's fiction was pivotal in mobilising the thriller for political purposes in the 1930s. *The Man Who Knew Too Much* may not be a direct adaptation of *The Three Hostages*, but it is a "shocker" inspired by Buchan. The story's picaresque structure, the characters' progression from complacency to commitment, the notion that respectability can be a mask for subversion, the easy slippage from ordinary life to terrifying danger, and of course the vast foreign conspiracy were all elements of his best-selling stories. As Montagu undoubtedly realized, the "shocker" was associated with the First World War, and revelations of German conspiracies and aggression in that conflict. Setting a "shocker" in the present day of the 1930s was itself heavy with implications. This is not to say that the film's only value resides in its specific historical context. *The Man Who Knew Too Much* reinvigorated Hitchcock's career and set him on a path that led not only to *The 39 Steps* in the following year but also to some of the most notable entries in his oeuvre, released over the next three decades. Ironically, he was never able to fulfill his ambition to make a more direct adaptation of *The Three Hostages*, but to a significant extent, he was inspired by this book, and Buchan's other thrillers, throughout his career.

Notes

1. Hitchcock's *The 39 Steps* was followed by two further British adaptations: director Ralph Thomas's version in 1959 and Don Sharp's 1978 version. In 2007, a stage adaptation of the story opened in London's West End, and this transferred to Broadway in 2008.

2. The credits attribute the story to Charles Bennett and D. B. Wyndham Lewis, the scenario to Edwin Greenwood and A.R. Rawlinson, and additional dialogue to Emlyn Williams.

3. "The Hidden Hand," 27 February 1934; *The Man Who Knew Too Much*, BBFC Scenario Reports, Special Collection, British Film Institute, London, UK. Hereafter BBFC/BFI.

4. *The Man Who Knew Too Much*, 10 May 1934; BBFC/BFI.

5. I am thinking here of three classic MacGuffins: the secret message memorized by Mr. Memory in *The 39 Steps*, the uranium found in wine bottles in *Notorious* (1946), and the film hidden in a statue in *North by Northwest* (1959).

6. Negotiations between the BBFC and Gaumont-British are recounted (briefly) in the BBFC's scenario reports: *The Man Who Knew Too Much*, 10 May 1934; BBFC/BFI. Hitchcock discussed the dispute in an interview with Leslie Perkoff, originally published as "The Censor and Sydney [sic] Street" in *World Film News* in 1938. This is reprinted in Sidney Gottlieb's *Hitchcock on Hitchcock*.

Works Cited

Barr, Charles. *English Hitchcock*. Moffat: Cameron and Hollis, 1999.

Gottlieb, Sidney, ed. *Hitchcock on Hitchcock*. London: Faber, 1995.

McGilligan, Patrick. *Alfred Hitchcock: A Life in Darkness and in Light*. New York: Regan/HarperCollins, 2003.

McGilligan, Patrick, ed. *Backstory 1: Interviews with Screenwriters of Hollywood's Golden Age*. Berkeley, C.A.: University of California Press, 1986.

———. *Alfred Hitchcock: A Life in Darkness and in Light*. New York: Regan/HarperCollins, 2003.

Mycroft, Walter C. *The Time of My Life: Memoirs of a British Film Producer*. Ed. Vincent Porter. Maryland: Scarecrow, 2006.

Robertson, James. *The British Board of Film Censors: Film Censorship in Britain, 1896–1960*. London: Croom Helm, 1985.

Truffaut, François and Helen G. Scott. *Hitchcock*. Revised edition. London: HarperCollins, 1978.

6

R. Barton Palmer

Secret Agent

Coming in from the Cold, Maugham Style

The Emergence of the Hitchcockian Thriller

THE 39 STEPS (1935), SO JUDGE Eric Rohmer and Claude Chabrol, is Alfred Hitchcock's "most famous English film." There is certainly no contesting their view that it is this production "that made his name known all over the world and got him his first offers from Hollywood." Based on John Buchan's popular adventure novel (*The Thirty-Nine Steps*), published in 1915, *The 39 Steps* is, as they point out, an "ambitious commercial film." But, according to Rohmer and Chabrol, *The 39 Steps* also allowed the director to square his "personal circle." Hitchcock, in short, proved able in this case to make a film that was not only profitably entertaining but also artistically satisfying (43).

And, so the argument runs, this narrative became a template that Hitchcock used again and again with considerable success. *Saboteur* (1942), *North by Northwest* (1959), and *Torn Curtain* (1966) are virtual remakes, while such otherwise thematically diverse films as *Strangers on a Train* (1951), *Frenzy* (1972), and *Shadow of a Doubt* (1943) creatively recycle what is perhaps this early thriller's most distinctive feature: a protagonist who unwillingly, but perhaps deservedly, finds him(or her)self occupying a dangerous middle ground between the villain and the official police and is thereby forced to act decisively in order to be exculpated and save his (or her) life. It is thus hardly surprising that most Hitchcock scholars agree that *The 39 Steps* is thoroughly Hitchcockian, in the sense of establishing a narrative formula that would be often repeated in his other suspense thrillers, while, as Rohmer and Chabrol observe, also engaging the morally substantial theme of the wrong man, which was to become quickly the director's most easily recognizable signature.

This understanding of the evolution of the Hitchcockian thriller seems accurate enough, at least from the distant vantage point of his completed oeuvre, but it is clearly not the whole story. Intriguingly, the two thrillers that follow *The 39 Steps*, while imitating this ur-text closely at times, also depart from it significantly and substantially. These two productions form something of a diptych, being both rather closely based on source texts that are determinedly highbrow and literary, in pointed contrast to Buchan's entertaining page-turner. Somewhat confusingly, *Secret Agent* adapts W. Somerset Maugham's *Ashenden* (not a novel, but a collection of short stories), while *Sabotage* offers a screen version of Joseph Conrad's *The Secret Agent: A Simple Tale*. A correlative of this fundamental shift in source material is that both films develop fictional worlds that, as Charles Barr points out, are "short on humour and adventure." It is certainly telling that they feature nothing like the consistently suspenseful and fast-paced action that had made *The 39 Steps* such a smash hit with audiences (Barr 162). So in retrospect it seems somewhat understandable that both *Secret Agent* and *Sabotage* performed poorly at the box office, as they failed to mine effectively the rich vein of popular taste that Hitchcock had discovered with the release of *The 39 Steps*.

A Double Failure?

The director blamed this double failure on his own miscalculation of audience reactions. In his famous interview with François Truffaut, he confessed to not anticipating the difficulty viewers would find in identifying with the protagonist of *Secret Agent*, who is not only reluctant and generally unresourceful, but also blundering. Richard Hannay (Robert Donat) in *The 39 Steps* rarely miscalculates, but, when he does, he always finds himself saved from disaster by barely credible good fortune. Sent to eliminate a German agent determined to deliver war-changing intelligence to the enemy Turks, *Secret Agent's* Richard Ashenden (John Gielgud), in contrast, manages to have the wrong man killed before, more or less accidentally, presiding over the death of the real villain, whose impersonation of a frivolous American student had hitherto completely fooled him. In this film, melodramatic coincidence (the good luck that guarantees a happy ending) rectifies the failure of the protagonists rather than, as in *The 39 Steps*, rewarding their heroic efforts. Ashenden's competence is more called into question than ratified by the film's finale, which emphasizes his powerlessness as an individual in the face of a larger and inscrutable destiny.

Similarly, Hitchcock did not foresee the distaste that viewers of *Sabotage* would feel at the blowing to bits of an innocent child, for whom much sympathy is developed, or their unease at the guiltless speed with which the wife of the ostensible villain becomes romantically involved with the investigating detective (Truffaut 73–80). These miscalculations beg a much larger question. Why did these two films go so far wrong (at least commercially speaking) when *The 39 Steps* had clearly marked out the generic path worth following? Did Hitchcock nod, as Homer was famed to do? Perhaps, but then some kind of transitory incompetence seems only barely credible as an explanation, given the director's well-established reputation for thorough preparation. Furthermore, that the same kind of "error" was perpetrated across two closely related projects suggests that this experiment with a different form of affect was intentional. Hitchcock seems to have been attempting something quite different. Audiences simply did not approve.

Blaming the films' source material seems an attractive explanation. And it is true enough, as Barr observes, that the story elements mentioned above are "integral . . . to the literary texts" upon which the films are based and become "integral to the respective films as well" (162). The implication is that Hitchcock and screenwriter Charles Bennett were perhaps reluctant to depart too radically from such respected authors as Maugham and Conrad. But an immediate problem arises with this explanation in that, somewhat paradoxically, the titling of the films marks them as belonging more deeply to the thriller genre than to their ostensible sources, whose relationship to the films is substantially obscured. It does not appear, in fact, that either project was constrained by the protocol of faithfulness, as we would expect viewing these films from the perspective of the completed oeuvre. As the critical commonplace has it, Hitchcock's well-established approach to adaptation was to consider source material eminently disposable.

But let us presume that, as Barr suggests, these projects are marred by an insoluble compositional difficulty: the reliance on source material that was resistant, despite the best efforts of those involved, to being remolded in the image of the recently established Hitchcockian thriller. Such an explanation—of *Secret Agent* at least—seems wrong. In fact, a reading of the filmscript against the fictional source quickly establishes that the opposite is true. The evidence discussed in this chapter establishes that the Maugham material was remolded to enhance, not lessen, its particular qualities, all of which stand in opposition to the Buchan model. My point is that Hitchcock and Bennett set out to produce a film that, arguably, is even more Maughamian than its source, even as, paradoxically enough, it became thoroughly Hitchcockian.

In a sense, this is hardly surprising. It bears keeping in mind that Hitchcock was in no way coerced to make a film from Maugham's fiction (as passed down to him in the form of an apparently unproduced stage version by Campbell Dixon based mainly on two of the stories). With considerable freedom granted by producer Michael Balcon to choose an appropriate project, he could well have followed *The 39 Steps* with another film version of Buchan. He was especially partial to the novel *Greenmantle* (1916) and did at times think of bringing it to the screen. As the second of the five novels to feature Richard Hannay as a main character, *Greenmantle* would have had much to recommend it as a sequel. The book had been extraordinarily popular upon initial publication and was still in print two decades later. Another alternative would have been for Hitchcock to seek out something generically quite similar in the works of such popular writers as the immensely prolific William Le Queux, Eric Ambler, and "Sapper" (H. C. McNeile), all three of whom very much wrote in the Buchan vein.

Moreover, there seems no good reason to call into question the considerable abilities of Charles Bennett to confect a scenario that would please the director. Barr's expert and thoroughgoing examination of this important collaboration between screenwriter and director has convincingly established not only their quite simpatico working relationship but also Bennett's considerable skill. With faithfulness to the source text not an issue for those involved in the production, the necessary changes, however substantial they would have had to be at points, could have been carried out. And, of course, we should remember that Hitchcock confessed himself to miscalculating viewer reaction, suggesting that the problem with the two films lay with his formal and thematic design and the kind of emotional response thereby evoked, rather than with unworkable source material.

So the key question seems to be: why did Hitchcock decide on a literary source so different from *The Thirty-Nine Steps*? The modernist Maugham, it is useful to remember, figures much more centrally in the later history of the spy thriller than does Buchan, whose literary roots are late Victorian (the Hannay novels offer an interesting amalgam of H. Rider Haggard and Arthur Conan Doyle). Indeed, Maugham is usually credited as effecting with the Ashenden stories a thoroughgoing transformation of the genre. John Le Carré, among more recent practitioners of spy fiction, cites Maugham as a major influence and pays him the sincere compliment of close imitation. Le Carré's *Spy Who Came in from the Cold* (1963) is thoroughly Maughamian, dominated, like *Secret Agent*, by a reluctant and flawed protagonist, whose morally questionable mission "succeeds" only *malgré lui*.

Like both Maugham and Le Carré, Hitchcock was interested in probing the ironies and discontents of the human condition, as both *Blackmail* (1929) and *Murder!* (1930), among other early films, make clear. It is hardly surprising, then, that Hitchcock found Maugham an attractive model, albeit one that in some ways deconstructed the formula developed in *The 39 Steps*. *Secret Agent*, in fact, seems to point toward an emerging alternative pattern for the Hitchcockian thriller, one that was further explored in *Sabotage* (Conrad also takes a decidedly unromantic approach to the depiction of the spy or *agent provocateur*). That pattern was then subsequently abandoned, but it might not have been had viewers not clearly demonstrated their indifference. Late in his career, however, when Le Carré's spy fiction was beginning to attain a world-wide popularity, Hitchcock determined to adapt Leon Uris's *Topaz* (1967, film version 1969), a novel that treats the complexities of Cold War politics and shows the heavy influence of both Le Carré's *Spy Who Came in from the Cold* and also *The Looking-Glass War* (1965). Like *Secret Agent*, *Topaz* is another neglected and underappreciated film, often unfairly dismissed as unHitchcockian because it does not fit the Buchan pattern. It too is the story of feckless agents, devastating betrayals, appalling violence, and morally questionable national politics.

But *Secret Agent*'s often disturbing dramatization of the darker, more morally problematic aspects of experience finds other echoes in the director's oeuvre. As Raymond Durgnat suggests, Hitchcock seems eager in this early project to explore the possibilities of heroism being "shorn of its levity," which would then become "a little more sensibly unwilling. In terms of theme, the story would conclude irresolutely, with "an incomplete expiation of its guilts" (Durgnat 131). This Doestoevskyan concern with guilt and responsibility, and the impossibility of expiation, is to be found as well in those later films that are generally recognized as among his masterpieces: *Strangers on a Train* (1951), *The Wrong Man* (1956), *Vertigo* (1958), *Marnie* (1964), *Psycho* (1960), and *Frenzy* chief among them. From this perspective, *Secret Agent* seems very much a harbinger of the darker side of Hitchcock's genius that was (perhaps better, could be) on more prominent display during the last decades of his career.

Debunking Derring-Do

Filled with narrative leads that erupt but then go nowhere, and characterized by puzzling anticlimaxes, the *Ashenden* stories lack the one-directional suspenseful, adventurous action of which Buchan was a rich source. Maugham presents espionage as a disagreeable, murkily dangerous, and thoroughly mundane enterprise that, paradoxically enough, deeply engages the reader because of the insights it yields into the mysteries of human sensibility and motivation. Unlike the romantic and patriotic fantasy at the center of *The 39 Steps*, the tale of irresolution, failure, and moral disgust in *Secret Agent* did not make for an easy liking. In fact, Maugham refuses to provide the customary pleasures of spy fiction, especially debunking its claim to promote heroes. Maugham's protagonists, instead, are more often pawns; they seldom learn their true role (even when it seems of some importance) in the intrigues in which they take part. Ashenden, in fact, is best conceived as Richard Hannay's antiheroic and ironic double—a weak and often unsubstantial figure with whom film viewers could not identify as easily as they had with Hannay.

Moreover, as if to announce its break with *The 39 Steps*, *Secret Agent* self-reflexively embodies the turn away from engaging, humorous adventure. The film's most striking feature is its thoroughgoing change of tone about half-way through from devil-may-care games-playing on the part of the three self-indulgent, blasé, and comic protagonists to deadly serious, and morally questionable, murderous plotting. *The 39 Steps* features no such transition; it artfully maintains its light-heartedness throughout by draining the affect from necessary scenes of violence (the stabbing of Annabella Smith [Lucie Mannheim], the shooting death of Mr. Memory [Wylie Watson]) and by refusing to meditate on questions of guilt and responsibility. *Secret Agent*, in contrast, gradually heightens its presentation of the moral horror of violence in a fashion that audiences could hardly have missed: through the innovative deployment of unpleasant, disturbing sound effects. Discordant organ notes presage the discovery of a murdered agent; the miserable howling of a dog anticipates the anguish all involved will feel at the mistaken killing of a supposed enemy spy; and the annoying rattle of coins jiggled in a dish, through sound association, recalls the misleading "clue" that condemned the innocent man to death.

What is most significant, however, is that this change of tone finds its reflex in the "arcs" that the screenwriters designed for both Ashenden and Elsa Carrington (Madeleine Carroll), his erstwhile companion. In what seems an attempt to link the two films, Carroll was asked to reprise the role of Pamela, the hero's at first reluctant companion and then lover that she played to such perfection in *The 39 Steps*. Ashenden has no wife furnished him as "cover" in the Maugham stories, and it appears that a love interest had been added in the stage adaptation. Hitchcock and Bennett, however, were likely the ones who decided to develop Elsa in ways that closely parallel, but then starkly diverge from, her model in the earlier film. Interestingly enough, Elsa becomes the figure who most closely embodies the novelist's major themes as the film explores them. In fact, Bennett and Hitchcock arguably make Elsa the moral (and then narrative) center of the film, effectively displacing Ashenden. The film emphasizes the profound disillusionment with violence she comes to feel, effectively debunking any linkage of heroism and adventure. Despite growing moral qualms, Ashenden finds himself unable to resist his patriotic urges and complete the mission; but the moral impulse in Elsa proves much stronger than national loyalty. Elsa, in fact, decisively intervenes to save the real German agent, Marvin (Robert Young), when Ashenden and his partner, the general (Peter Lorre), are about to execute him, thereby frustrating, if only temporarily, what the agents have been informed is the necessary safeguarding of a British attempt to achieve final victory against the Turks in particular and the Central Powers more generally. We are asked to believe that if Marvin lives and delivers the British plan of attack to the Turks, the war may be lost. But for Elsa the threat of national failure proves less compelling than her profound distaste at having to murder, essentially in cold blood, a man whom she (and the viewer as well) has come to know intimately.

The Barely Possible and the Mundane

Consider the only superficially similar plot development in *The 39 Steps*, where Carroll's Pamela also plays a key role. This film finds its narrative structure in a complex double pursuit that energizes, even as it unifies, a quite disparate collection of episodes, providing the plot with a strong sense of forward motion. Only by finding and correctly identifying the real villains will Hannay be vindicated for the supposed murder of the spy Annabella Smith—and his country's military secrets kept safe. Pursued by the police, Hannay pursues the spies, who, in an interesting reversal, come to pursue him once they realize the threat he poses to their mission. *The 39 Steps* appropriately concludes with a spectacular sequence in which the two lines of pursuit intersect. With significant help from Pamela, Hannay locates the master spy and his accomplice just as they are about to make the vital transfer of information—and just as the police catch up to him. The improbable hero then ingeniously forces his enemies to reveal their plans to one and all, including the amazed authorities, thereby effecting the capture of the true villains and establishing his own innocence.

Thanks to the rewriting that Buchan's novel received at the hands of scenarist Charles Bennett and the director himself, however, the film version features another vital source of dramatic tension that is of equal if not greater importance than its much-remarked double pursuit: the character of Pamela. Interestingly enough, this addition is in keeping with the novelist's avowed aesthetic, even as it fulfills the intention of the filmmakers to provide viewers with a customary form of cinematic pleasure: a romance from which sparks (erotic and otherwise) continually fly. Hannay first meets Pamela while on a train to the remote Scottish village where the dying spy Annabella Smith had said a vital contact must be made. He asks Pamela to help him escape the police searching the train by pretending to be his lover. Quite sensibly she refuses to believe the preposterous tale Hannay briefly relates. She prefers the more conventional and probable explanation for Annabella's murder accepted by the police. And Pamela persists in that mistaken belief even when, meeting up with Hannay once again, she finds herself handcuffed to him by men who say they are from the police, but who, it seems increasingly likely, are members of the same gang Hannay says is pursuing him. Now joined by a physical tie that cannot easily be broken, the seemingly ill-sorted pair effect an escape into the Scottish wilderness despite her persistent reluctance.

Taking refuge later in a country inn, Hannay and his erstwhile companion find a way to remove the handcuffs, after which Hannay, exhausted by his ordeal, falls asleep. Seeing her chance, Pamela then attempts to escape. As she is about to alert the innkeeper about her companion's true identity, however, she comes upon the same faux policemen, who are looking for them. From their conversation, she learns that Hannay's story is no self-serving fantasy but the truth, which she now has no trouble believing because she has had the chance to take Hannay's true measure. Pamela returns immediately to "their" room, now eager to help the eager young man as their romantic connection, previously restrained by her distrust, begins to deepen. Pamela's "conversion" marks a crucial turning point in the narrative as it is only through the joint efforts of the couple that the villains are eventually defeated.

We can see another meaning in Pamela's eventual acceptance of Hannay's oft-repeated insistence that everyday reality is not what it seems. For what she learns is that there is another, more exotic and exciting meaning to events that otherwise must be seen as thoroughly without redeeming purpose and ordinary (if we can call a "sex murder" ordinary, that is, as it is perhaps for readers of *The News of the World*).

The essential appeal of Buchan's novel, captured neatly in this aspect of Bennett's script, connects, to quote the novelist's own words, from his confection of a "romance where the incidents defy the probabilities" but "march just inside the borders of the possible" (qtd. in Barr 148). Because the relevant events are dramatized, the viewer knows that Hannay has truly been launched on a mission to save his country and himself after innocently attending a musical hall show and foolishly allowing a fellow member of the audience, Annabella, up to his room. Skeptical at first, Hannay is convinced when he sees that she is being followed by two men.

Pamela's conversion mirrors Hannay's even as it reenacts that of the viewer. In the sequence at the inn, the film artfully dramatizes how the improbable may indeed be proven barely possible, thus emphasizing a central, ontological aspect of the romance aesthetic that Buchan—and Charles Bennett—invokes throughout so cunningly and to such great effect. The slightly magical aura of romance is expressed by the pervasive, decisive, and ostentatious role of coincidence, which figures as the secular equivalent of destiny. The apparent sordidness of a grisly killing (Hannay as murderer), along with its heavy baggage of immorality and pathology, is dismissed by Pamela's discovery. In its place, she now is able to believe in a Manichaean struggle between the forces of evil and goodness. The criminal is unmasked as the hero, as she, formerly his prisoner, almost without thinking assumes the role of the heroine.

Like the man now able to inhabit fully his desired role as her partner and lover, Pamela allows herself to be caught up in a narrative that is motored by the idealizing and intoxicating power of adventure. During his interview with François Truffaut, Hitchcock said this of the thriller form: "[I]n an adventure drama your central figure must have a purpose. That's vital for the progression of the film, and it's also a key factor in audience participation. The public must be rooting for the character" (Truffaut 73). One way of looking at Pamela's conversion is to see it as an intratextual enactment of this crucial psychological dynamic. For, in finally accepting Hannay's purpose, Pamela accommodates herself completely to the supportive role that the viewer has been offered to occupy from the outset. Viewers accept the logic of the "barely possible" in order to enter a fictional world in which everything means much more (and much more gloriously) than initially seems possible. So does Pamela.

Ashenden, in contrast, rejects absolutely the possibility of any transcendent, redeeming meaning to human experience. From this point of view, that there is something like "adventure" is just a cruel mystification, for it can only conceal the brutal force and disagreeable reality of the mundane. Instead, it is the real world that such fiction intends to represent, unmasking the idea of "adventure" to reveal an unexciting, even morally disgusting reality. This aesthetic, which discards the accustomed pleasures of a well-established genre, proves somewhat problematic, as Maugham himself recognized. In the novelist's own description, *Ashenden* is "a batch of stories dealing with the adventures of an agent in the Intelligence Department during the First World War," an agent very much like Maugham himself, who served the British government in the same capacity (*Ashenden* 7). But the novelist disavows, perhaps disingenuously, not only any autobiographical but also any journalistic strain in this fictionalizing. These stories are by no means *reportage*, he asserts. The reason is simple. "Fact," Maugham proclaims, "is a poor story-teller": "It starts a story at haphazard long before the beginning, rambles on inconsequently, and tails off, leaving loose ends hanging about, without a conclusion. Because the work of an agent, moreover, is 'on the whole monotonous,' perhaps even 'uncommonly useless,' the author has to work even harder 'to make it coherent, dramatic, and probable'" (7).

This shaping process poses further difficulties, which, in the self-reflexive fashion characteristic of Maugham, merit discussion in the first story of the collection, "Miss King." Conferring with his spymaster "R," who is attempting to turn the well-known writer into one of his operatives, Ashenden is informed of a recent incident that, he is told, might well be "material that would be very useful to you in your work" (10). R tells him the somewhat sordid tale of a certain French minister, who, escaping the capital to recover from a cold, finds himself at a Nice hotel for the weekend. Encountering a beautiful blonde in a nearby restaurant, he proceeds with her to his room, where he is drugged and then robbed of his briefcase, which contains important documents. Expecting Ashenden to agree that the story is "dramatic," R is disconcerted that the writer, who does not dispute that judgment, underlines instead the utter conventionality of such a sequence of events: "We've been putting that incident on the stage for sixty years, we've written it in a thousand novels" (*Ashenden* 10). And what this means, as Ashenden tells R, is that "we really *can't* write that story much longer," even though it proves to be true (11).

The implication is that the writer must overcome both the anxiety of influence and the resultant loss of reader interest in overexploited material. Such overuse problematizes the willing suspension of disbelief. But a rejection of literary convention in favor of unshaped experience will not do either because "fact is a poor story-teller." Thus a hitherto unexploited form of the real constitutes the only feasible subject matter, whose unengaging inertness, however, needs to be transformed. So the writer must deal in the dramatically undramatic, in actions that are probable but, surprising and new in their rejection of established convention, are not easily recognized as probable. In his world-weariness, thoroughgoing rejection of idealisms, and yet perpetual openness to the unanticipated strangeness of those he meets, Ashenden effectively embodies this aesthetic. As the teller of his own tales, he remains committed to exposing the dark underside of the spy's dangerously mundane *moyen de vivre*, eagerly telling the "truth" that deconstructs the convention of the very genre he writes within, even as he continually writes himself out of the hero's role.

In *Secret Agent*, John Gielgud's low-key impersonation nicely captures Ashenden's ennui, as well as his writerly detachment. During the course of pursuing the mission assigned by R, he becomes confirmed in his moral disgust at what patriotism requires, voicing something like the disillusionment of a Wilfrid Owen or Siegfried Sassoon. As opposed to a middle-aged novelist called upon to do his small bit for our side, the script turns him into a serving officer from the Western front, who has killed many men from the distance of "a half-mile." It is quite credible that Ashenden experiences profound anguish at having to witness, if not actually assist in, the cold-blooded killing of Caypor (Percy Marmont), the result of no fair fight or battle of wits between equals. The unsuspecting victim is simply shoved off a mountain ledge by the general as Ashenden watches the ghastly scene unfold through a telescope, involuntarily telling Caypor to "Look Out!" as the fatal moment approaches. No notion of patriotic adventure relieves this sequence of its horror, which Hitchcock and Bennett strongly emphasize. The death of Caypor in *Ashenden*, by way of contrast, is only imagined not represented, as Ashenden convinces the man to cross the Swiss border into France, where, unbeknownst to the traitor, Allied agents are waiting to murder him.

The film rejects the notion of patriotic adventure much more forcefully and thoroughly with its focus on Elsa. She begins her assignment as Ashenden's "wife" fully believing in the possibilities of exactly the kind of thrilling adventure that Buchan's fiction promises. When she meets her husband for the first time in their Swiss hotel room, she eagerly confesses, in response to his question about her motives for taking on such a potentially dangerous assignment, that she is doing so for the "excitement, big risks, danger, even a bit of . . . ," finishing her sentence by turning her hand into a pistol, pulling the trigger, and broadly smiling. When Caypor, misidentified as the agent, is to be murdered by Ashenden and the general, she is greatly disappointed at being left behind "when you go out hunting and have all the fun."

But, like Pamela, she too experiences a sudden conversion. The difference is that it breaks her attachment to the mission rather than cementing it. As events unfold on the mountaintop, she sits with Caypor's wife, and the two listen with horror as the man's dog lets out an earsplitting howl, giving disturbing aural form to the anguished disgust Pamela's face suggests she is feeling. As her crisis of conscience deepens the next evening, she confesses her change of heart to Ashenden, who shares his similar feelings. The pair determine to abandon the mission and their commitment to espionage. If, joining forces, Pamela and Hannay resolve to foil the attempt of enemy agents to compromise British air defenses, Elsa and Ashenden, their relationship cemented by a shared disgust, find themselves unable to perpetrate another cold blooded murder. Or so they think at this point.

But Bennett's plot, which owes nothing to Maugham, rejects such an easy and premature resolution, giving Elsa instead a chance to demonstrate forcefully her resolution to avoid further involvement in bloodshed, while Ashenden finds himself reluctantly resuming his official role, though ultimately to no effect. Their mission apparently stalled, the general suddenly discovers that the young American Marvin, whom they had gotten to know quite well, is the German agent they are after, and Ashenden, full of moral uncertainty, sets off with the general in pursuit. Meanwhile, Elsa, who is thoroughly disillusioned by Ashenden's violation of their "resignation" from the mission, intends to leave Switzerland, as it happens, with Marvin, who she does not yet know is the German spy. Looking for Marvin, Ashenden and the general meet Elsa by chance at the train station. Sensing her erstwhile partners intend Marvin's death, Elsa accompanies the three on the train heading for Turkish territory.

In the showdown between Marvin and the British agents, she seizes a gun and prevents Marvin's murder, but the train, bombed by British planes summoned by R, crashes, fatally injuring the German spy, who, before he dies, manages to kill the general. The mission is completed, but its success owes nothing to Ashenden's reluctance, while even Elsa's opposition proves ineffectual. If the question of the guilt Ashenden and Elsa must bear for Caypor's killing is left unresolved, they are spared the necessity of taking another life, even as the film provides the happy ending demanded by the genre by staging the victory of "our side."

Maugham must have chuckled at the self-consciously paradoxical politics of the cinematic denouement, so similar to that of several stories collected in *Ashenden*. Documentary footage of General Allenby's successful Jerusalem campaign, flagged by a huge "Victory in the East," is followed by the light-hearted postcard resignation of Ashenden and Elsa, who vow "Never again," echoing the famous pledge of the British Peace Pledge Union (founded in 1934 and rapidly gaining adherents when *Secret Agent* was released). Hitchcock's characters seem in perfect agreement with those who pledged: "I renounce war and will never support or sanction another." To echo Le Carré's striking metaphor for the rejection of a politics that sanctions reprehensible, if undoubtedly expedient, murder, Ashenden and Elsa come in from the cold. The film's jarringly juxtaposed final sequences, with their contradictory moral tones, fittingly conclude its deconstruction yet perpetuation of the spy fiction genre, much the same aesthetic balancing act managed by Maugham himself with *Ashenden*.

Works Cited

Barr, Charles. *English Hitchcock*. Moffat: Cameron & Hollis, 1999.

Durgnat, Raymond. *The Strange Case of Alfred Hitchcock: Or the Plain Man's Hitchcock*. Cambridge, MA: MIT Press, 1974.

Rohmer, Eric, and Claude Chabrol, *Hitchcock: The First Forty-Four Films*. Stanley Hochman trans. New York: Ungar, 1979.

Maugham, W. Somerset. *Collected Short Stories Volume 3*. 1951. London: Penguin Books, 1977.

Truffaut, François. *Hitchcock*. New York: Simon & Schuster, 1967.

7

NOEL KING AND TOBY MILLER

The Lady Vanishes, but She Won't Go Away

You are a spy!

—Margaret Lockwood

Oh, I always think that's such a grim word.

—May Whitty, *The Lady Vanishes*

❧

ALFRED HITCHCOCK'S *LADY VANISHES* (1938) traces the adventures of cross-European train travelers who variously befriend, lose, imprison, conceal, seek, ignore, rescue, and chase a little-old-lady English governess who is also His Majesty's spy. A comedy-romance-thriller, it stands alongside *The 39 Steps* (1935) as the high watermark of Hitchcock's postsilent cinema English filmmaking and displays his quaint mix of affection and contempt for imperial hypocrisy and insouciance.

In a *Sight and Sound* piece written to coincide with a screening of *The Lady Vanishes* at the British Film Institute's Southbank London complex in January 2008 as "part of a Margaret Lockwood series" (Fuller 40),

Graham Fuller alerts readers to the fact that the event "coincides with the centenaries of Michael Redgrave and Sidney Gilliat, who wrote the screenplay with his partner Frank Launder" (37). In the seven decades since it appeared, this little film has provided innumerable intertexts and tropes. When Fuller mentions that "2008 is also the anniversary of the film itself, and of Neville Chamberlain's disastrous 'peace for our time' speech, which he made on returning from Munich on 30th September 1938, three months before *The Lady Vanishes*'s Christmas day premiere," he joins the many commentators who have inscribed the film into various original and subsequent contexts of explanation, appropriation, and rewriting.

Set in and between the fictional nation of Bandrika and the (quasi-)factual nation of Britain, *The Lady Vanishes* has traveled a long way since its maiden voyage, leaving a mark on everything from twenty-first century congressional politics to contemporary transportation. For the *New Yorker*, "The Lady Vanishes" refers to the impenetrability of Hillary Rodham Clinton's character (Kolbert). For the *Journal of Bioethical Inquiry*, it encapsulates the absence of women from debates about somatic-cell nuclear transfer and embryonic stem-cell technologies (Dickenson), while the *Journal of Organizational Change Management* tropes the movie to account for obstacles to women becoming leaders (Höpfl and Matilal), and *Film Quarterly* understands that it connects to a deep-seated fear of women (Fischer). Remade in 1979 (Anthony Page), *The Lady Vanishes* provided an obvious inspiration to *Flightplan* (Robert Schwentke). And when Virgin Trains was promoting its new rail franchises across Britain in 2005, it did so through a campaign called "The Return of the Train," deploying what it called "the golden era of British cinema" as a marketing tool whereby stars of yesterday were digitally manipulated to marvel at the company's 125 mile per hour tilting Pendolino train rocketing across country. *The Lady Vanishes* figured prominently.

This complex intrication of the factual and the fictional forms the backdrop to our argument: that *The Lady Vanishes* is a conservative text because of its faith in the "talented amateur" and "Little Englander," but is equally a liberatory one in the contradictions of gender, class, sexuality, and national difference that it discloses; and that this is not a case of spy fiction allegorizing or adequating to the real, but of contributing to it—hence the subsequent tropes. To explain how this worked, we engage the film by considering the nature of espionage fiction; the function of the railway as a signifier of modernity; and the play of gender, class, and sexuality in the text and its source—Ethel Lina White's 1936 novel, *The Wheel Spins*, where the vanished lady is prized because she is "against the Red element" (White 105).

Espionage

In *The Lady Vanishes,* Redgrave, the male lead, says "British diplomacy—'Never climb a fence if you can sit on it.' It's an old Foreign Office adage." Redgrave represents the muddling, talented amateur in the film, the charming, raffish, almost rakish, cheeky, naughty-but-nice scholar (Gilbert the ethnomusicologist) who moves whimsically between recreating and recording bizarre folk rituals and romancing, ironizing, doubting, aiding, comforting, and leading his love interest. He is an appealing hero. Of course, male amateurism of this kind has certain economic and social preconditions. A clubbish atmosphere, as per Redgrave and his account of statecraft, is clear in the nicknames that early members of the British secret service used to refer to one another: "Woolly, Buster, Biffy, Bubbles, Blinker, Barmy, [and] Tin-Eye" head one list. Apart from attesting to the claim that the public schools produce children rather than developing them, this roll call signifies joie de vivre, not taking things too seriously, and never losing a sense of self that can transcend its environment—the stereotype of the phlegmatic all-rounder (Porter 169, 171–72).

Despite—or perhaps as a consequence of—this background, Gilbert and his ilk move easily between comedy and crisis, amity and action, emotion and intellection. They embody a structural homology with international politics in the light touch they apply to everyday life, which can rapidly transmogrify into fierce aggression as required. That flexibility both hides and enables the play of diplomacy and its shadowy alter arts. Similarly, wherever we turn in the comparatively anarchic world of states, we find deceit and treachery, with espionage the alpha and omega of means-ends rationality. Unlike the domestic lives of governments, where lawmakers struggle for the means of control over their citizens and vice versa, the field of international relations is constitutively chaotic. Exploitative espionage runs alongside affable entertaining.

Espionage involves surreptitiously conveying information about a country, company, or union to its enemy or rival. Much of this information is "official," in that it is deemed to be of national-security significance to a state or economic value to a firm. Von Clausewitz saw war as "a real political instrument, a continuation of political commerce, a carrying out of the same by other means" (119). He regarded "the knowledge which we have of the enemy and his country," however compromised it may be through the "multiplier of lies and untruths," as the key to war (162–63). This blend of fabrication and fact, along with the glamor and romance of undercover work, has characterized espionage for a very long time, making for a complex interplay of life and art. Nicholas Hiley argues that the period up to the 1930s saw most British intelligence officers "[take] the greater part of their ideas of secret service directly from fictional sources" (57).

Espionage fiction's nexus of "spectacular violence and social vacuousness" has led to accusations that it models antisocial conduct, heroicizes the capitalist state, or delights in base consumerism (Westlake 37; Kerr 2; Morrison 21). But it also has champions. Reactionaries argue that the espionage genre models the struggle between bad and good and displays democratic values. This seems difficult to sustain given the shadowy parallel universe occupied by spies, which is messily complicit with despised others and frequently involves indulgent evacuations to exotic locales (Hiley 68). For centrists, the success of espionage fiction demonstrates that its consumers approve of their governments acting covertly in the interest of state security. Other critics find a romance of citizenship in it, a drama where readers and viewers test and enjoy the limit cases that are regularly presented by the comparative anarchy of international relations. Loyalty, patriotism, and even the mundanity of public employment are suddenly reforged as plays with death and doom. The genre is equally associated with the question of subjectivity under technologization and bureaucratization, an existential dilemma derived from the material relations that form everyday life (DerDerian 53–54, 57–58).

Espionage fiction took off in the decade following the Dreyfus affair in France, when a Jewish officer was falsely accused of espionage in a racially charged case. Wesley K. Wark traces connections in Britain among cheap popular fiction, journalistic and governmental campaigns of xenophobia, shifts in class formation and the division of labor, and the emergence of moral panics about foreigners and spying: "The enemy could be the Jew, the foreigner, the not-quite gentleman, the corrupted, the bomb-throwers, women. Why the day needed to be saved was very much a product of national insecurities that began to mount at the turn of the century. At their heart were fears about the pace of technological and societal change caused by the impact of the industrial revolution. In the wake of its manifold upheavals, traditional measures of the international balance of power were threatened and the domestic structures of government upset" (275).

Ernest Mandel describes the period between the two world wars as an epistemological watershed when perceptions of the power of organized crime shifted to engage new forces that were directed against sovereign states rather than property or individual people. These were crimes by one state against another, with the body of governments personified in shadowy, undercover figures. The element of mystery in espionage derives from identifying the enemy and her or his alliances, supporters, methods, and reasons. There is always a "triple search for identity: who has done it; under what assumed identity is the villain hiding; what is the murderer—or spy, or mad billionaire, or conspirator—like as a 'person'[?]" (Mandel 62, 65).

Espionage plots usually follow a brilliant plan that has been devised and executed by the enemy but is foiled in the lonely hour of the last instance by the brilliant counterstroke of a lone operative within the enemy's own sphere of action. The agent is successful because of superior beauty, physique, technology, and flexibility. Mandel ties these developments into the split subjectivity and increased alienation produced by consumer capitalism. Superheroes must be raised to a higher level with the general development of bourgeois society: mounting mechanization, greater diversification of commodity production, hyperconsumerism, further alienation of the individual—and new, unforeseen dimensions of that alienation (61).

Mandel argues that this search for identity is a necessary process for fiction produced in bourgeois societies, where individuals are divided among a variety of selves. The worker, the buyer, and the capitalist are utilitarian figures who calculate the maximum benefits to themselves of all their actions. As property owners, they uphold and even materialize laws of ownership of both objects and people. As citizens, they are concerned with the general good rather than their own. And as sexual subjects, they are driven by needs that take them beyond reason, the family, and property. The spy story enacts the dilemmas posed by this contradictory, split subjectivity (Mandel 65). It also brings up all the mystique of law and order, the where and why of sovereignty, in a physical, material way, via the daily actions of spies. They act as delegates of the people, the monarchy, or the army in foreign camps. The arbitrariness of this delegation, and its reliance on instant decision and action, is paradoxically cynical. Loading up one person with such power and responsibility, and hence signing away the right to democracy, makes the myth of bourgeois society—popular endorsement of overt governmental processes under the publicly ratified rule of law—unsustainable. Binary divisions between good and evil, police and felon, spy and counterspy, West and East, become unstable and a grudging respect and recognition of mutuality and doubling appears (Mandel 122). A weird mix of hyperbourgeois individualist, technocrat, and empty signifier, the spy can never relax, never truly know who he/she is, other than a sign of the malleable shape of state labor. No wonder she can vanish, her very existence becoming the subject of debate.

Gender, Class, and Sexuality

Margaret Lockwood plays Iris Matilda Henderson in the Hitchcock film, the young woman who meets and subsequently loses the vanishing lady, Miss Froy (May Whitty). Her feminist counterpublic sphere galpals, Googie Withers as Blanche and Sally Stewart as Julie, resist any notion of passive, decorous women through their overbearing occupancy of each hotel room they enter while voyaging across "the Continent." As a group, they are indomitable, using their wit and sex to dominate seemingly any context.

Effortlessly flirty, moneyed, sophisticated, and self-confident, Iris stands in her underwear on a table addressing the hapless help. She is to be married back in London later that week. The girls ask why her bridegroom can't change his name. After all, we are told, she's played baccarat at Biarritz and eaten both "caviar at Cannes and sausage rolls at the docks . . . What is there left for me, but—marriage?" Blanche retorts, "Little thing called love." The girls claim to have complete and diurnal social mobility. Able to shift easily between a cosmopolitan international elite and organic intellectuals of the working class, they pick up and discard cultural signage as easily as pie.

White's novel spends some time exploring what constitutes "ladyness" among the group, a concept and social type that involves particular codes of behavior and dress and at all cost avoiding exhibitions of "bad form" and "abandon" (86). Some of Iris's fellow passengers explain why they wear evening dress for dinner on the Continent: "If we didn't dress we should feel that we were letting England down" (26). Nevertheless, Iris's friends are derided as "a party of near-nudists, who drank all day and night" (112). They are the frothy superstructure of empire's bite.

This rather risqué side to Lockwood's screen characters became encrusted in her portrayal of the dubious Hesther in *The Man in Grey* (Leslie Arliss, 1943), the scandalous Lady Barbara Skelton of *The Wicked Lady* (Leslie Arliss, 1945), who spirits away her best friend's husband and embarks on a remorseless campaign of robbery and gambling, and *Bedelia*'s serial-killer bride (Lance Comfort, 1946). Her career developed along the tracks of the new-moneyed snob at the opening to *The Lady Vanishes*, rather than the wide-eyed naïf who emerges into a world of international intrigue. Even there, her extraordinary self-confidence relies on a casual imperialism, as when the novel finds her convinced of the rightness of her cause thanks to an image in her mind's eye and a sound in her mind's ear of "the Union Jack fluttering overhead" to "the strains of the National Anthem." Even if she "can't speak a word of this miserable language" (presumably Bandrikan) all will be well because "I expect foreigners to speak English" (87, 72, 59). At an early point in her adventure, exasperated by her inability to master European languages sufficiently to make her situation known, Iris thinks "of Basel on the milky-jade Rhine, with its excellent hotels where English was spoken and where she could be ill intelligibly and with dignity" (40).

But there are limits to the girls' gleeful, giddy independence, set not only by their gender but also by the class of birth versus mobility. Iris's fiancé is referred to as a "Blue-blooded cheque-book chaser." She plaintively confides, "Father's simply aching to have a coat of arms on the jam label." For despite the hauteur with which she and her gay friends address the international proletariat (Iris witheringly moans, "Don't tell me Cooks are running cheap tours here") their self-confidence plainly derives from "commerce" rather than formal station: the girls are spending new money. The quid pro quo is that they are expected to bring respectability to their house via a peerage. The nouveaux riches crave lineage to beef up merit.

Alongside these fascinating elements that crop up at the intersection of female autonomy and drudgery lie other gender commentaries. Gay issues form a recurrent theme in Hitchcock's work, drawing both on the heady sex of the English public school and his own more violently expressed Catholic background (Wollen). A queer reading might see Redgrave's private life of bisexuality referenced when he says, "We've got to search this train. There's something definitely queer in here." And this was the first of several films where Basil Radford and Naunton Wayne played homosocial cricket obsessives, perhaps most notably in *Night Train to Munich* (Carol Reed, 1940). Wayne says, "It seems a bit queer," in reaction to a question as to whether there is something to Redgrave's story about abduction, just minutes after he and Radford are seen in bed together. The contemporary viewer may well read this rather differently from her 1938 counterpart, or not.

Train Travel

These destabilizing moments and characters emerge in environments of flux—a hotel and a train—where everybody and everything is on the move, unmoored from norms and ready for crisis as much as pleasure, notably an adulterous couple (Cecil Parker and Linden Travers). It seems as though each middle-class subject stands ready to fabricate a story, for petty reasons (cricket scores or philandering) that point to gendered British suburban hypocrisies and falsehoods. They are home-counties counterparts to "European" duplicity, which is at least driven by the desire for geopolitical advantage. Disappointed by her boyfriend barrister's inconstancy, Travers's character sees through class distinctions to gender likeness: "[A] professional man did not differ so greatly from a tradesman in essentials . . . they looked much the same before shaving and without their collars" (130).

In White's novel, train travel is analogized both to horse riding and air travel; but the most consistent descriptions are of an experience that is "screaming through darkness" (30), "monstrous metallic," "scorching," "rushing," "jerking," "shooting," "explosive," "ripping," "rattling," "sweeping," and "insensate, maddened" (150). And the train is at the center of the film's dynamism. Hitchcock was fascinated by the railway experience, its bizarre amalgam of imprisonment and mobility. Train travel is a key player in many of his most famous texts, from *The 39 Steps* to *North by Northwest* (1959) (Wollen 82). Fuller discusses cinema's wider fascination with trains at the time of the original release of *The Lady Vanishes*, mentioning *The Shanghai Express* (Von Sternberg, 1932), *Rome Express* (Walter Forde, 1932), *Orient Express* (Paul Martin, 1933), *Night Mail* (Herbert Smith, 1934), and *Night Train to Munich*. And train-spotting film critics are well aware that every kind of cinema from this point on, be it French genre or avant-garde (Costa-Gavras' *The Sleeping Car Murders* [1965] and Robbe-Grillet's *Trans-Europe-Express* [1966]) through to US independent filmmaking (Jim Jarmusch's *Dead Man* (1995) and Wes Anderson's *The Darjeeling Limited* [2007]) testifies to the enduring imbrication of train travel and film. Wim Wenders has commented perceptively on the connections:

> Trains, in a way, are related to filmmaking insofar as it's completely mechanical—a mechanical thing of wheels and speed and movement, and you have this wonderful view, like the movie screen. Trains are even more related to movies than cars are. When you sit in a train it's so much like the situation of sitting in a movie—sitting with other people. Trains are complete dream machines. They're very relaxing and they're very comfortable, and you really lose yourself—all the same qualities good movies have. And of course there's the constant movement and sort of little rattle, like the noise from the projection booth. (Wenders 74)

Between 1850 and 1920, a vast array of culturally significant machines appeared, such as planes, railways, typewriters, lights, radios, and phones. These devices were the very image of a mechanical dream or nightmare, depending on where you stood. The counting house became the modern office in the 1870s, when new technologies, education systems, and labor hierarchies emerged, helping the United States overtake Britain as the center of world productivity in a general shift from

personalized, customized, low-volume production to anonymous, stan-
dardized, high-volume manufacture (Broadberry and Ghosal, Grantham
13). The expansion of rail lines was a critical site for the emergence
of new relations of space and power that joined industry, science, and
the body in a complex of power and knowledge as never before. The
human railway body came to be subjected to a medical gaze, with workers and passengers pathologized. Speed, jolts, and noises were found to
produce pain, anxiety, and poor verbal communication. Railway "spine"
and "brain" were invented. By the turn of the century, these complexes
had been comprehensively theorized, with bodies succumbing to stresses
supposedly produced by mechanical reconfigurations of time and space.
As science became applied, transportation businesses referred to middle-
class travelers as packages, and the Left complained that workers were
now commodities (Schivelbusch 113–14, 118, 136, 121, 145).

In the film, Iris is pathologized by all and sundry on the train as
an amiable but disturbed young woman. Her seemingly definitive diag-
nosis comes from a scheming brain surgeon, Egon Hartz (Paul Lukas).
His duplicity embodies the railway's ambiguity, facilitating the speed of
modernity and the discipline of the psy-function, all at one and the
same time. The train is a paradoxical object, a source of both prison
and freedom, incarceration and flight. In the novel, Iris has a "sense of
nightmare." Her travails are augmented by "maniac shrieks of the engine
and the frantic shaking of the train" and the confusion surrounding Miss
Froy's whereabouts—and her very identity—in the flux of motion. For
all the world trapped in a mechanical vortex, Iris deems herself to be "in
the grip of an insensate maddened force, which, itself, was a victim to
a relentless system" (150–51). At the same time, the railway had turned
"the everyday business of transport" into "a temporary rapture" (43).

For Fuller, *The Lady Vanishes* displays and is predicated on "speed—
of narrative, wit, motion and emotion." He suggests that the element
of the film most likely to resonate with viewers today "is Hitchcock's
manipulation of Iris's consciousness and, through the use of the train as a
vehicle for dreaming, the idea that she, not Miss Froy (the literal disap-
pearee) is the lady who vanishes" (Fuller 38) Although Fuller describes
White's novel as "tepid," as merely following "Graham Greene's *Stamboul
Train* and Agatha Christie's *Murder on the Orient Express* into bookstores"
(38), the book is of interest in its own right and in fact contains the
essence of what Fuller finds still contemporary in Hitchcock's film.

For example, in White's novel, Iris suffers sunstroke and loses consciousness at the end of chapter 5 ("The Night Express"). Come the end
of the book, we learn that as a child she had "dreams of power" that
enabled her to overcome an "inferiority complex." The eventual discovery of Miss Froy is made possible only because Iris has regressed to one

of these childhood states, having "passed from unconsciousness into one of her childhood dreams of power . . . Instantly she staggered to her feet—half-awake and half in a dream—and walked directly into the next compartment." There, "still under the influence of her dream of power and secure in the knowledge of immunity which raised her above the fear of consequences," Iris tears plaster bandages from the face of "the invalid" and shows her to be Miss Froy (185). These actions, undertaken in a childhood-regressive hypnogogic state, complete the novel's exploration of a "dream theme" introduced when the vicar had asked, "What is a dream? Is it stifled apprehension?" (28).

White's novel shows almost as much interest in referencing cinema, its products, stars, and glamor (11, 25, 33, 52, 56, 92, 108, 109) as in discussing train travel. When characters speculate on the true identities of individuals, analogies with cinema are always available as an assistance to thought:

> "I wonder who they really are," remarked Miss Flood-Porter. "The man's face is familiar to me. I know I've seen him somewhere."
>
> "On the pictures, perhaps," suggested her sister.
>
> "Oh, do you go?" broke in Mrs. Barnes eagerly, hoping to claim another taste in common, for she concealed a guilty passion for the cinema. (19)

At one point on her train journey, "Iris . . . had the impression that the whole scene was flickering like an early motion-picture" (52). Later in the novel she explains the urgency of their quest by reference to movies: "We must find her . . . It sounds exactly like some sloppy picture, but her people are expecting her home. They're old and rather pathetic. And the fool of a dog meets every train" (92). The dog is named "Sock" (from "Socrates"), and at one point he is said to resemble "a Walt Disney creation" (108) as he performs the family task of "herald and toastmaster . . . barking excitedly to tell her [Miss Froy's mother] that the master was coming home" (108). This scene is reprised at the novel's end when "somewhere in the distance a dog barked. Again and again in frantic excitement . . . It was the herald who had run on ahead to tell her that the young mistress had come home" (191).

Metafiction and Storytelling: "You Know the Sort of Thing"

In the novel, the disappearance of Miss Froy occasions various acts of logical-inductive analysis, with "the Professor" an exemplar of logico-scientific naysaying. (At one point Iris compares her relation to the

Professor as that of Watson to Holmes). Metanarrative moments abound as characters seek either an explanation for the lady's disappearance that would corroborate Iris's story or disprove it. References are made to "magazine stories" (147) as possible narrative models for the situation in which Iris finds herself, but it is Iris's romantic interest, Hare, a Cambridge academic (the ethnomusicologist Gilbert of the film) who offers the most sustained metafictional moment when, at Iris's suggestion he concocts a "yarn" (144) to support her contentions. His usual specialty, he tells us, is "golf stories" (144), but he summons forth an "original story called 'The Disappearance of Miss Froy'" (142). This metanarrative exchange between Iris and Hare assists the formation of the novel's romantic couple and also permits some metafictional punning, evident when she asks him "[I]s the whole train in on the plot?" (143). Hare promises that his story will deliver certain generic elements that "my readers will adore" (145). Miss Froy will "be put in an ambulance and taken to some lonely house, overlooking deep deserted water—a creek, or arm of the river, or something. You know the sort of thing—black oily water lapping a derelict quay. Then she'll be weighted, and all that, and neatly dumped among the mud and ooze. But I'm not altogether ruthless. I'll let them keep her drugged to the bitter end. So the old dear'll know nothing about it" (145).

It is tempting to see this as a reference to the form of storytelling on offer in Collins' Crime Club to which White's novel was a contribution in its 1936 original publication, and later when it was chosen as one of ten books to appear in a Penguin publication event intended "to celebrate the twenty-fifth anniversary of Collins' Crime Club." Among the ten republished titles were works by Nicholas Blake, Agatha Christie, Ngaio Marsh, and Rex Stout. Collins had launched its series "twenty-five years ago on the wave of new-found public enthusiasm for the various delights of the detective story. Its two principal objects were: to provide a steady flow of detective novels to satisfy the voracious and critical demands of the most devoted readers . . . and to maintain a standard which would represent for the reader a hall-mark of quality" (inside back cover).

The coda to this metafictional aspect of White's novel comes at the conclusion. Miss Froy, safely rediscovered and shown to be veridical, tells Iris, "I'm just making up my story to tell them at home. Mater will be thrilled" (189). Miss Froy assures Iris that she would not tell her mother the truth ("I'm going to keep mum about that") for fear both of shocking her too greatly in her dotage, and of being confined to regional-national quarters when she has plans for further European travel. Instead, Miss Froy will offer up a story "about you—and your romance" (189). (Readers have by this point learned that the heterosexual romantic couple has formed. Iris and Hare will be together "on his next trip" (189)). And when we read that, "somewhere in the distance a dog barked. Again and again, in frantic excitement . . . It was the herald who had run on ahead to tell her that the young mistress had come home" (191), we realize that the Walt Disney dog is now barking to announce the arrival back in Little England of the once vanished lady, who will tell her aged parents a story of romantic love to substitute for the story we have just read.

Conclusion

We began by mentioning the seventieth anniversary of Hitchcock's film of White's novel, and citing some of the many intertexts and tropes that have become attached to this beloved, iconic film. We should add that White's novel has also enjoyed an ongoing life: "The plot . . . was later utilized on such varied television programs as *The Adventures of Superman*, *The Big Valley*, and *The Rockford Files*" (Eder), and more recently, "a stage adaptation of *The Lady Vanishes* toured Britain from March to July 2001," and "a recent abridged reading of the same story on BBC radio 4 has introduced [White] to a new audience" (Pollinger).

As for the achievement of Hitchcock's work—filmed "on a 90 foot set on a small stage at Islington studios" (Fuller 38) after he inherited the project from a failed attempt one year earlier by Roy William Neill to film the story (as *Lost Lady*) in Central Europe for Gaumont Studios— we can say that the sign is truly disarticulated from its referent in *The Lady Vanishes*. Was there a lady? Could Iris ever become one? Which lady vanished? The sense of mobility and destabilization, of opportunity and constraint, are ever-present—the conditions of existence for both Iris and Gilbert are the frippery of empire, which relies on the secret services of Miss Froy. They are all bundled together on a cross-class, cross-continental train, unsure of anything but their unshakeable chauvinism. And the title of the film is itself disarticulated from its referent, for redisposal as a trope to describe everything from stem-cell struggles to Clintonista speculations. Just as train tracks laid out new forms of dominion, they also delivered difference and newness, where vanishing points could be resumed as new metaphorical baggage.

Works Cited

Broadberry, Stephen, and Sayantan Ghosal. "From the Counting House to the Modern Office: Explaining Anglo-American Productivity Differences in Services, 1870–1990." *Journal of Economic History* 62, no. 4. (2002): 967–98.
DerDerian, James. *Antidiplomacy: Spies, Terror, Speed, and War*. Cambridge, MA: Blackwell, 1992.

Dickenson, Donna L. "*The Lady Vanishes*: What's Missing from the Stem Cell Debate." *Journal of Bioethical Inquiry* 3, nos. 1–2 (2006): 43–54.

Eder, Bruce. "All Movie Guide: Ethel Lina White." *The New York Times*: http://movies.nytimes.com/person/311782/Ethel-Lina-White/biography (accessed January 8 2008).

Fischer, Lucy. "The Lady Vanishes: Women, Magic and the Movies." *Film Quarterly* 33, no. 1 (1979): 30–40.

Fuller, Graham. "Mystery Train." *Sight and Sound* n.s. 18, no. 1 (2008): 36–40.

Grantham, Bill. "*Some Big Bourgeois Brothel*": *Contexts for France's Culture Wars with Hollywood*. Luton: University of Luton Press, 2000.

Höpfl, Heather, and Sumohon Matilal. "'The Lady Vanishes': Some Thoughts on Women and Leadership." *Journal of Organizational Change Management* 20, no. 2 (2007): 198–208.

Hiley, Nicholas. "Decoding German Spies: British Spy Fiction 1908–18." *Spy Fiction, Spy Films, and Real Intelligence*. Ed. Wesley K. Wark. London: Cass, 1991, 55–79.

Kerr, Paul. "Watching the Detectives." *Primetime* 1, no. 1 (1981): 2–6.

Kolbert, Elizabeth. "The Lady Vanishes." *New Yorker* 11 June 2007.

Mandel, Ernest. *Delightful Murder: A Social History of the Crime Story*. London: Pluto, 1984.

Morrison, Grant. "Un Monde de Miraculeuses Métamorphoses." Trans. David Fakrikian and Bruno Billion. *Chapeau Melon et Bottes de Cuir*. Ed. Alain Carrazé and Jean-Luc Putheaud. Paris: Huitième Art, 1990, 21–22.

Porter, Bernard. *Plots and Paranoia: A History of Political Espionage in Britain 1790–1988*. London: Unwin Hyman, 1989.

Pollinger Limited. "Ethel Lina White." http://www.pollingerltd.com/estates/ethel_lina_white.htm (accessed January 8 2008).

Schivelbusch, Wolfgang. *Railway Journey: The Industrialization of Time and Space in the 19th Century*. Trans. Anselm Hollo. Berkeley: University of California Press, 1977.

von Clausewitz, Carl. *On War*. Trans. J. J. Graham. Ed. Anatol Rapoport. Harmondsworth: Penguin, 1983.

Wark, Wesley K. "The Intelligence Revolution and the Future." *Queen's Quarterly* 100, no. 2 (1993): 273–87.

Wenders, Wim. "Wim Wenders' Guilty Pleasures." *Film Comment* 28, no. 1 (1992): 74–77.

Westlake, Mike. "The Classic TV Detective Genre." *Framework* no. 13 (1980): 37–38.

White, Ethel Lina. *The Wheel Spins*. Harmondsworth: Penguin, 1955.

Wollen, Peter. "*Rope*: Three Hypotheses." *Alfred Hitchcock: Centenary Essays*. Ed. Richard Allen and S. Ishii-Gonzalès. London: British Film Institute, 1999, 74–85.

8

DAVID BOYD

The Trouble with *Rebecca*

ALFRED HITCHCOCK COULD SCARCELY have hoped for a more propitious beginning to his Hollywood career. Not only was his first American film a great success both commercially and critically, but it collected the Academy Award for best film of 1940 and garnered for Hitchcock himself the first of his five Oscar nominations. Yet *Rebecca* remained over the years possibly the director's least favored child. He not only spoke of it dismissively in interviews, but he virtually disowned it, insisting to François Truffaut, for instance, that "it's not really a Hitchcock picture" (127). And for Hitchcock that was the trouble with *Rebecca*: its paternity was in doubt. Although the idea of directorial authorship, later to be formulated by Truffaut as a *politique des auteurs* and so successfully propagated as an "auteur theory," was not to be popularized until the 1950s, Hitchcock had been actively promoting himself as an *auteur avant la lettre* virtually from the beginning of his career. But with *Rebecca* there were just too many other authors vying for attention.

The screenwriters posed no real threat to Hitchcock's authority. He was accustomed to working closely with writers on the preparation of his scripts, and of the four listed in the film's screen credits—Robert E. Sherwood and Joan Harrison for the screenplay, and Philip MacDonald and Michael Hogan for adaptation—all but Sherwood had been chosen by Hitchcock himself. And Harrison, MacDonald, and Hogan worked so harmoniously alongside the director and his most constant collaborator, his wife, Alma, that they effectively comprised, as Patrick McGilligan puts it, "five Hitchcocks collaborating on the script" (236). But there were other collaborators, and two of them impertinently claimed pride of place in the film's opening credit: "The Selznick Studio presents its production of Daphne du Maurier's celebrated novel." There it was for all to see: not really a Hitchcock picture, but a Selznick production of a Du Maurier novel. And that seems to have been pretty much the way the filmgoing public in 1940 understood the situation: a survey of viewers during the film's opening weekend revealed that around 70 percent said that they had attended in part because it was a Selznick production (this was in the immediate wake of the unprecedented ballyhoo surrounding the premiere of *Gone with the Wind* just three months earlier), 60 percent because they had read or at least heard about the book, and less than 10 percent because it was directed by Hitchcock.[1]

Neither Daphne du Maurier nor David O. Selznick had reason to be much more sanguine than Hitchcock about the collaborative challenges posed by the project. Du Maurier had been so distressed by Hitchcock's adaptation of her *Jamaica Inn* the previous year that she wept "bitter tears" when she saw it (qtd. in Leff 345). And Selznick's "rich and strange collaboration" with his new star director, as Leonard Leff aptly describes it in the subtitle of his invaluable *Hitchcock and Selznick*, was a relentless battle of wills from the beginning. Hitchcock had never before worked with so obsessively interventionist a producer, accustomed to overseeing every aspect of the production process, and the two clashed at every stage. They clashed over casting: Selznick initially wanted Nora Pilbeam, the star of *Young and Innocent*, for the female lead, but Hitchcock considered her just *too* young and innocent and succeeded in persuading Selznick to name an American actress "in order to stress her isolation at Manderley" (Leff 51). They clashed over Hitchcock's persistent failure to shoot enough "coverage," threatening to deny Selznick the opportunity to recut scenes as he saw fit. They clashed over Hitchcock's editing style, which Selznick thought too "cutty."

But most of all, they clashed over the issue of adaptation. By the time they came to *Rebecca*, both men were old hands at turning books into movies (only four of Hitchcock's preceding two dozen films had been originals, and many of Selznick's most successful films of the thirties had been adaptations, either of canonical classics such as *David Copperfield* and *Anna Karenina* or of current bestsellers such as *Gone with the Wind*). But they had arrived at positions that were diametrically opposed, as Hitchcock later explained to Richard Schickel:

There are two schools of thought there. One producer I worked for insisted that a novel be followed meticulously, especially if it was a best-seller, because then the public, having read the scene, would want to see it come to life on the screen. And I felt, myself, that when you consider the vast world audience, a best-seller—I don't care how big it is—doesn't reach anything like the same number of people or meet the same conditions as a film. For example, if you take your, say, Japanese market, it's very possible that the novel hasn't reached a Japanese audience. So my instincts are to go with the visual and not follow the words of the novel. Follow the story line if you like, but retell it in cinematic form. (283)

The producer in question was Selznick, of course, and Hitchcock states his position perfectly accurately. He could scarcely have suffered under any misapprehensions on the matter: when "the five Hitchcocks" submitted their first treatment of *Rebecca* in June 1939, Selznick responded with a memo in which he professed himself "shocked and disappointed beyond words" before proceeding to expend several hundred words spelling out his view that if "a book has caught the fancy of the public" (as Du Maurier's spectacularly successful bestseller undeniably had) "the only sure and safe way of aiming at a successful transcription of the original into the motion-picture form is to try as far as possible to retain the original" (Selznick 307).

The only exceptions to his rule that Selznick would countenance were "omissions necessitated by length, censorship, or other practical considerations." A number of episodes from Du Maurier's novel were eventually omitted from the film, some of them presumably on the grounds of length (uncomfortable visits the second Mrs. de Winter has to endure from the bishop's wife and other neighbors at Manderley, for instance, and an even more excruciatingly uncomfortable visit to Max's senile grandmother, culminating with the old lady peevishly asking, "Why did Maxim not bring Rebecca?"), and censorship was to play a crucial part in shaping the film. But Hitchcock's treatment had gone far beyond the sort of alterations Selznick might find permissible. And while many of his proposed changes were indeed designed in the interests of retelling the story line "in cinematic form," others seemed unmistakably designed to transform a Du Maurier novel into something that would be immediately recognizable as a Hitchcock picture by anyone familiar with the thriller sextet that had established his international reputation during the 1930s: in particular, the introduction of a comic element almost wholly absent from the novel and the recasting of the second

Mrs. de Winter more in the mold of the livelier heroines of *The 39 Steps*, *Young and Innocent*, and *The Lady Vanishes*. Selznick was having none of it. "We bought *Rebecca*," he bluntly told Hitchcock, "and we intend to make *Rebecca*."

And make *Rebecca* they did—up to a point. Much of the film's dialogue comes verbatim from the novel, and many of its most memorable visual touches, including some of those that might seem most unmistakably "Hitchcockian," such as Mrs. Van Hopper "mashing her cigarette in a jar of cleansing cream," are in fact also taken directly from the book (Du Maurier 38). Some moments from the novel are almost uncannily realized on screen, such as Mrs. Danvers' first appearance: "Someone advanced from the sea of faces, someone tall and gaunt, dressed in deep black, whose prominent cheek-bones and great, hollow eyes gave her a skull's face, parchment-white, set on a skeleton's frame" (72). Other moments survive into the film, but displaced and transformed. Its memorable final image of the monogram on Rebecca's pillow disappearing in flames, for instance, is clearly derived from an episode early in the novel in which the heroine tears out Rebecca's dedication from a book of poetry she had given to Max and burns it: "The letter R was the last to go, it twisted in the flame, it curled outwards for a moment, becoming larger than ever. Then it crumpled too: the flame destroyed it" (62).

Despite Du Maurier's fond desire that her novel might be faithfully realized on screen, however, and Selznick's determination that it would be, both were ultimately going to have to accept changes far more radical than anything proposed by Hitchcock. For yet another author entered the scene: the Motion Picture Association Production Code Administration, in the person of its head, Joseph I. Breen. After the submission of the screenplay to the Administration, Breen wrote to Selznick:

> We have read the temporary script . . . and I regret to inform you that the material, in our judgement, is definitely and specifically in violation of the Production Code . . . The specific objection to this material is three-fold: (a) As now written, it is the story of a murderer, who is permitted to go off 'scot free'; (b) The quite inescapable inferences of sex perversion; and (c) The repeated references in the dialogue to the alleged illicit relationship between Favell and the first Mrs. de Winter, and the frequent references to the illegitimate child-to-be. (qtd. in Berenstein 17)

Breen apparently managed to come to terms with two of these three concerns. The references to Rebecca's affair with Jack Favell and her (phantom, as it turns out) pregnancy remain perfectly explicit in the film as released, and the "inescapable inferences of sex perversion" remain inescapably clear to all but the most innocent of viewers. The implications of a lesbian relationship between Rebecca and Mrs. Danvers are, in fact, considerably clearer in the film than in the novel, which goes no further than to have Maxim hint discreetly to his second wife that his first "was not even normal" (283). The actual dialogue of the film is no more explicit, but Hitchcock was a dab hand at inserting illicit innuendos into his staging. The implications of the scene in which Mrs. Danvers displays Rebecca's lingerie to the heroine were not lost on Breen, a man with a sharp eye and a dirty mind, who specifically complained to Selznick in a later letter about Mrs. Danvers' "handling of the various garments, particularly the night gown" (qtd. in Berenstain 18). Nevertheless, he let it pass.

The possibility of a murderer getting off "scot-free," however, was something to which Breen was not prepared to turn a blind eye. And the novel is unequivocal that Maxim is, indeed, a murderer. "There never was an accident," he confesses to the heroine. "Rebecca was not drowned at all. I killed her. I shot Rebecca in the cottage in the cove" (278). Ever-helpful, however, Breen had a solution to the problem: Rebecca's death would be accidental, the result of a fall during her final confrontation with Maxim. Selznick found the suggestion absurd ("The whole story of *Rebecca* is the story of a man who has murdered his wife," he indignantly complained, "and it now becomes the story of a man who has buried a wife who was killed accidentally!"), and seriously considered challenging Breen's decision and leading his fellow producers in a mutiny against "so insane and inane and outmoded a Code as that under which the industry is now struggling" (qtd. in Behlmer 326). In the end, though, he had little choice but to accept Breen's proposal and make the best of it. Robert E. Sherwood made the crucial suggestion that the scene of Maxim's confession be shifted from a sitting room to the seaside cottage where Rebecca's death occurred. Hitchcock "used a subjective camera to etch in film the geography of the first wife's death," as Leonard Leff describes it, "counterpointing the agitato of de Winter's narrative and the legato of the camera's languorous movement," and the result was a scene that works wonderfully well on screen (53–54), but not one that has any basis whatsoever in the novel. In fact, the moral imperative of the Production Code that murder must not go unpunished actually resulted, ironically, in a film that manages to evade the far harsher moral calculus of its source. For although Du Maurier's novel is, indeed, "the story of a murderer," he is decidedly not "permitted to go off 'scot-free.'" The book is, in fact, a cautionary tale of crime and punishment. The book of poems that Rebecca had given Maxim, Francis Thompson's *Hound of Heaven* ("I fled

Him, down the nights and down the days;/ I fled Him down the arches of the years"), points to an element of divine retribution in the eventual fate of Maxim the murderer and the second Mrs. de Winter, his willing accessory after the fact, who are left, after the destruction of Manderley by fire, living in self-imposed exile in a hotel on an "indifferent island" somewhere in Europe. "Granted that our little hotel is dull, and the food indifferent, and that day after day dawns very much the same, yet we would not have it otherwise," the heroine insists, but it is difficult to believe her. Maxim talks "quickly and eagerly about nothing at all, snatching at any subject as a panacea for pain," and she admits that "his premonition of disaster was correct from the beginning" (9). Even in Cornwall, the postman always rings twice.

The nemesis in Du Maurier's original draft took a considerably more overt and more familiar form, an automobile accident (that reliable Hollywood standby) as the couple return to Manderley from London after discovering the truth about Rebecca's supposed pregnancy: "Perhaps Rebecca will have the last word yet. The road narrowing before the avenue. A car with blazing headlights passed. Henry [as Maxim was] swerved to avoid it, and it came at us, rearing out of the ground, its huge arms outstretched to embrace us, crashing and splintering above our head." The accident leaves Maxim, like his prototype, Rochester in *Jane Eyre*, maimed physically as well as psychologically ("You see then that he is crippled, he walks slowly and awkwardly with the aid of sticks") and possibly impotent. But unlike Rochester and Jane, there is no final suggestion of a redemptive healing for Maxim and his bride. Instead, they are left sharing the consequences of their crime, "shorn of our little earthly glory," as the heroine says, "he a cripple and his home lost to him, and I, well, I suppose I am like all childless women, craving for echoes I shall never hear, and lacking a certain quality of tenderness" (13) Nothing could be further in tone and implication, surely, from the embrace that ends the film.

The film makes two other changes to the novel's narrative that are almost as fundamental as the exoneration of Maxim, one at the beginning of the film, and the other at its end. Novel and film alike begin, of course, with the heroine announcing, "Last night I dreamt I went to Manderley again." The time present of the film from which the heroine's offscreen voice emanates remains unseen, and despite the wistful tone of the voiceover, we are free to assume, if we wish, that our Cinderella and her prince are off somewhere living happily ever after. In the novel, however, we quickly learn that it is from her exile on that "indifferent island" that she dreams of Manderley. Du Maurier's description of that exile figures in her original draft as an epilogue, but it became instead the opening chapter of the novel, and that, as Avril Horner and Sue Zlosnik point out, crucially influences the tone of all that follows: "This opening 'frame narration,' which is typical of Gothic writing, alerts the reader to the fact that there is to be no simple or happy ending to the plot about to unfold" (84).

When the ending to the novel arrives, it is, indeed, neither simple nor happy. Driving back from London, Maxim and the heroine see in the distance what they first mistakenly take for the dawning of a new day (literally and metaphorically) but that turns out to be Manderley aflame. Since Maxim has received word earlier that Mrs. Danvers has abruptly and mysteriously "cleared out . . . gone, disappeared," readers are free to assume that she was responsible for the fire, but there is no certainty (and there are those persistent suggestions of divine retribution). In the film, of course, there is no doubt at all: we see the wild-eyed Danvers, clearly mad, walking ominously, candle in hand, through the darkened rooms and, more ominously still, standing over the sleeping heroine, who has remained at Manderley. Moments later the awakened heroine tells Maxim that Danvers had told her that "she'd rather destroy Manderley than see us happy here," and the film ends with its wicked witch meeting the traditional fate of witches, being burned alive. The direct threat to the heroine is particularly interesting because in popular gothic romances, as Joanna Russ points out, "the culminations of the books' plots almost always involve attempted murder" of the heroine. Such romances routinely "advertise themselves as 'in the Du Maurier tradition,' 'in the Gothic tradition of *Rebecca*,' and so on" (35, 31). But in this threat to its heroine, as well as in its "happy ending" embrace, it is actually the film, rather than the novel, that more clearly anticipates the conventions of the popular genre

These changes at the beginning and the end of the film both follow from the exoneration of Maxim: the first, obviously enough, because if there is no crime, there is no need for punishment, no need for the purgatorial exile; the second, because making the burning of Manderley unambiguously the act of a vindictive madwoman has the effect of reducing the implications of retributive justice central to the novel; Maxim's guilt and his punishment are both, in effect, transferred to Danvers. However faithful to Du Maurier's novel the film may be in characterization, dialogue, and scenic detail, then, it is fundamentally and radically different in narrative event and thematic implication. So if its director was right in his insistence that "it's not really a Hitchcock picture," this is clearly not because of any excessive fidelity to its source.

But was he right? If the demonstrable contributions of Du Maurier, Selznick, and Breen to the film make it difficult, indeed impossible, to regard the director as its only begetter, does that necessarily make it any the less "Hitchcockian"? Or do those contributions perhaps actually contribute to the "Hitchcockiness" of the film? After all, does it really sit all that oddly (narratively, generically, stylistically, thematically) within the Hitchcock oeuvre, a sort of cuckoo in the nest? Was the source material he inherited from Du Maurier, for instance, really as uncongenial as he suggested in interviews? "The story is old-fashioned," he complained to Truffaut. "There was a whole school of feminine literature at the period, and though I'm not against it, the fact is that the story is lacking in humor" (127). Nevertheless, Hitchcock himself considered optioning the screen rights to the novel after reading it in galley proofs in 1938, before he had yet signed on with Selznick, and it was not its lack of humor that ultimately deterred him but only the asking price. In any case, however willingly or unwillingly he accepted the assignment, the plain fact is that Hitchcock was to return to the basic narrative situation of *Rebecca* again and again, most obviously in his films of the forties. There had been elements of the female gothic in his earlier films, admittedly, in *The Lodger* and *Blackmail*, but it was clearly *Rebecca* that provided the template for *Suspicion* (in many ways virtually a remake of *Rebecca*), *Shadow of a Doubt*, and *Notorious*. And the claustrophobic anxieties of the woman entrapped would figure fully as prominently in Hitchcock's films for the remainder of his career as the agoraphobic anxieties of the man on the run. It is perhaps no accident, then, that Daphne du Maurier was the only author to whom Hitchcock was drawn more than once.

Similarly, however infuriating Hitchcock found Selznick's endless interfering, the producer also had a lasting and, on balance, a benign influence on his work. "Selznick served his new director well by forcing him to play closer heed to character," as Leonard Leff convincingly argues, "for Hitchcock too often matched his cleverly reasoned visual logic with pallid characterization" (46). The relative merits of Hitchcock's British and Hollywood films can be debated, and their discontinuities can easily be overstated, but *Rebecca* clearly does mark the beginning of a different approach to character on Hitchcock's part. And in purely stylistic terms, although it is difficult to know just how much should be attributed to Selznick's objections to Hitchcock's "cutty" editing style, Maxim's confession scene, with its extended subjective long take, clearly marked the beginning of an increased interest on Hitchcock's part in the formal possibilities of the long take, one that would extend through his films of the forties, culminating in *Rope*, and a heightened fascination with the possibilities of point-of-view editing that would extend to the end of his career.

Unexpectedly, though, it was arguably the interference of that least welcome of collaborators, Joseph Breen, that did the most, albeit unwittingly, to make *Rebecca* into what turned out to be, the director's disclaimers notwithstanding, "really a Hitchcock picture." Presumably, Hitchcock found Breen's insistence on transforming "the story of a man who has murdered his wife" into "the story of a man who has buried a wife who was killed accidentally" as absurd as Selznick and Du Maurier did. But Maxim is only one of a series of murderers in Hitchcock's sources—along with Mr. Sleuth in Marie Belloc Lowndes's *Lodger*, Johnny Aysgarth in Francis Iles's *Before the Fact*, and Guy Haines in Patricia Highsmith's *Strangers on a Train*—who found themselves exonerated on their way to the screen. None of these changes was Hitchcock's doing; indeed, he never tired of complaining in interviews of the decisions forced upon him either by the censors, as with *Rebecca*, or by studio executives, as with *The Lodger* and *Suspicion* (based on *Before the Fact*), who found it unthinkable that matinee idols such as Ivor Novello and Cary Grant should play murderers. But it is precisely these exonerations that permit the protagonists of these films to join those of *The 39 Steps, Young and Innocent, Saboteur, Spellbound, To Catch a Thief, The Wrong Man, North by Northwest,* and *Frenzy* as examples of that most familiar of Hitchcockian motifs, the falsely accused man.

In all these cases, though, what is most characteristically Hitchcockian is not the innocence of the protagonists as much as the ambiguous nature, in many different ways, of their innocence. In the case of *Rebecca*, it was not Joseph Breen's intention, of course, that there should be anything in the least ambiguous about Maxim's innocence. But the staging and shooting of the confession scene manage to introduce the shadow of a very significant doubt. The obvious way of handling the scene would have been with a flashback, to which Hitchcock apparently objected mainly on the grounds that he wanted something more original, less hackneyed. But a flashback would also have had the effect of authenticating Maxim's story for most viewers, who tend to assume the objective truth of flashbacks even when subjectively introduced (a tendency of which Hitchcock must have been well aware since he would later cunningly exploit it in *Stage Fright*). No doubt most viewers accept Maxim's version of Rebecca's death even in the absence of any authentification, but it is perfectly reasonable for Raymond Durgnat, for instance, to insist that "it is not quite clear whether he did in fact kill her in rage, thus being morally and legally guilty of murder as she of suicide, or whether he meant to kill her in rage but she died accidentally" (167). And as Karen Hollinger points out, spectators who had read the novel would, of course, presumably be particularly likely to doubt his claims of innocence (25). It is not the ambiguity concerning Maxim's literal or legal innocence that is most characteristically Hitchcockian, however, but rather the question of his moral innocence. We know, for instance, that Guy Haines in *Strangers on a Train* did not kill his wife, but we also know that he wanted to—and so did Maxim. We know that Richard Blaney in *Frenzy* did not kill his ex-wife, but we also know that he was capable of doing so—and so was Maxim. And it is precisely this conjunction of literal innocence and moral guilt that is one of the things most quintessentially Hitchcockian about *Rebecca*.

This moral guilt on Maxim's part might seem at first to go unpunished. He not only gets off "scot free," after all, but also, like Guy Haines, rid of the first wife he detested and united with the second whom he loves, with the film's penultimate image "the happy heterosexual couple," as Karen Hollinger describes them, "united with Jasper [the dog] as a child-substitute, foreshadowing the children who will enhance the de Winters' future marital bliss" (although surely Jasper might as easily foreshadow their future childlessness, as in the novel) (26). But that future bliss is less secure than many viewers apparently assume. For the final image of the film is not, as we might expect, the embracing couple, but rather Rebecca's monogram in flames, a reminder of the dark secret the couple shares. Other Hitchcock films end with the construction (or reconstruction) of a couple similarly subverted by reminders of shared homicidal secrets: the accusing painting of the joker in *Blackmail*, for instance, or the funeral oration eulogizing a serial killer in the background in *Shadow of a Doubt*.

The longer and more closely we consider *Rebecca*, the more similarities to other Hitchcock films emerge from its shadows. For most viewers, whether or not a film is "really a Hitchcock picture" ultimately has very little to do with privileged information about who was responsible for what during the production process. Our sense of "the Hitchcockian" emerges, rather, from our familiarity with his films in their totality. That sense is something that inevitably changed and evolved over the course of his career. In 1960, to viewers most immediately familiar with films such as *Rear Window* and *North by Northwest*, *Psycho* understandably seemed radically uncharacteristic. And in 1939, to viewers accustomed to films such as *The 39 Steps* and *The Lady Vanishes*, *Rebecca* might well have seemed "not really a Hitchcock film." But viewed retrospectively in the context of Hitchcock's career as a whole, it is clear that it really is, and not despite the contributions of Du Maurier, Selznick, and Breen, but very largely because of them.

Notes

1. "Survey of Patrons of UA Theatre, San Francisco, CA, 31 March and 1 April 1940," Selznick Collection, folder 172 8, Harry Ransom Humanities Research Center, University of Texas at Austin, cited by Edwards, 44–45.

Works Cited

Berenstein, Rhoda. "Adaptation, Censorship, and Audiences of a Questionable Type: Lesbian Sightings in *Rebecca* (1940) and *The Uninvited* (1944)." *Cinema Journal* 37, no. 3 (1998): 16–37.

Brown, Kay. Memo to David O. Selznick. 19 June 1939. *Hitchcock and Selznick: The Rich and Strange Collaboration of Alfred Hitchcock and David O. Selznick in Hollywood.* Ed. Leonard J. Leff. Los Angeles: University of California Press, 1987.

Durgnat, Raymond. *The Strange Case of Alfred Hitchcock, or The Plain Man's Hitchcock.* London: Faber, 1974.

Du Maurier, Daphne. *Rebecca*. 1938. London: Arrow Books, 1992.

Edwards, Kyle Dawson. "Brand-Name Literature: Film Adaptation and Selznick International Pictures' *Rebecca* (1940), *Cinema Journal* 45 no. 3 (Spring 2006), 32–58.

Hollinger, Karen. "The Female Oedipal Drama of *Rebecca* from Novel to Film." *Quarterly Review of Film and Video* 14, no. 4 (1993): 17–30.

Leff, Leonard J. *Hitchcock and Selznick: The Rich and Strange Collaboration of Alfred Hitchcock and David O. Selznick in Hollywood.* London: Weidenfield & Nicolson, 1987.

McGilligan, Patrick. *Alfred Hitchcock: A Life in Darkness and Light.* New York: HarperCollins, 2003.

Russ, Joanna. "Somebody's Trying to Kill Me and I Think It's My Husband." In *The Female Gothic*, ed. Juliann E. Fleenor. London: Eden, 1983.

Schickel, Richard. *The Men Who Made the Movies.* New York: Atheneum, 1975.

Selznick, David O. *Memo from David O. Selznick.* Ed. Rudy Behlmer. New York: Avon Books, 1973.

Truffaut, François, and Helen G. Scott. *Hitchcock.* New York: Simon & Schuster, 1983.

9

ALAN WOOLFOLK

Depth Psychology on the Surface

Hitchcock's *Spellbound*

In many respects, of course, Freud's ideas have established themselves very firmly in our culture. It is not only that the modern practice of psychiatry is chiefly based upon them. They have had a decisive influence upon our theories of education and child rearing. They are of prime importance to anthropology, to sociology, to literary criticism; even theology must take account of them. We may say that they have become an integral part of our modern intellectual apparatus.

Yet no one who speaks of the establishment of Freud's ideas can fail to be aware of the fact that they are still very new ideas. If they have become part of what we might call the "slang of our culture," it is also true of them that they are ideas that, taken at firsthand, seem very startling, very radical, calling for instinctive resistance. How seldom they are taken at firsthand, from Freud's own exposition of them! How easily they are misunderstood—how *strategically* they are misunderstood! There is scarcely a play on Broadway that does not make use of some version of some Freudian idea that the audience can be counted on to comprehend. Yet when we go back to the works in which Freud sets forth his ideas, we are confronted again by their original force and difficulty, by their aggressive novelty. We know that we have not yet begun to comprehend what they have discovered.

—Trilling, *Freud and the Crisis of Our Culture*

☙

A LFRED HITCHCOCK'S *SPELLBOUND* (1945), as acknowledged in the opening credits of the movie, was "suggested" (a word with clear psychoanalytic implications) by Francis Beeding's *House of Doctor Edwardes* (1927), which was retitled *Spellbound* in the same year that the movie was released. As a loose adaptation of the English novel to film, *Spellbound* is notable for its amplification of psychoanalytic motifs, especially the development of Freudian conceptions of "the unconscious" and "guilt," which are briefly but significantly referred to in the novel, as well as its elimination of the novel's explicit heritage of gothic horror. But where Beeding's novel (which will henceforth be referred to by its original title of *The House of Doctor Edwardes*) presents a psychologically informed criminal, who displays familiarity with the work of Sigmund Freud and his circle, Hitchcock's film informs the investigation of a crime with popularized Freudian psychology. Where the novel probes the depths of criminal transgression and antinomianism within the context of a failing Victorian Christian culture and a parochial French folk culture, the film interprets criminality within the context of an American culture increasingly under the influence of psychology, Freudian and otherwise. That neither the novel nor the film gets Freud right is perhaps at first glance beside the point, but the centrality of psychology is nonetheless important for understanding cultural influences upon both the novel and Hitchcock's loose film adaptation.

Both works reflect the dissemination of Freudian theory and practice at the time of their respective public releases. At the time of the publication of *The House of Doctor Edwardes* in 1927, the influence of Freudian psychology was still mostly limited even in England and Europe to an esoteric network of intellectuals and educated professionals. By late 1945 when *Spellbound* was released, Freud's influence was growing in the United States among the larger populace, especially the middle classes, and would continue to do so for the next few decades. More important, both works illuminate profound cultural and moral shifts in the representation and understanding of criminal transgression during the twentieth century, depicting contrasting and yet closely related moments in what Philip Rieff would call by the late 1950s the emergence of "psychological man" in Europe and America and the eventual "triumph of the therapeutic" in the 1960s.[1]

I

The House of Doctor Edwardes and *Spellbound* are similar in that both explore the themes of criminal transgression and romantic love through the modern authority figure of the scientific psychologist. In the novel, Dr. Edwardes is an absent director formerly in charge of the asylum at Chateau Landry who has been replaced by the authority figure of an insane and criminal patient (thus closely linking insanity and criminality), Geoffrey Godstone, who in turn has taken on the guise of being Doctor Murchison, a newly arrived doctor at the asylum. In the film, in contrast, Dr. Edwardes, who is scheduled to become the new head of the Green Manors asylum, has been killed by the outgoing director, Dr. Murchison (Leo G. Carroll), and replaced by an amnesia patient, Dr. John Ballantine (Gregory Peck), who temporarily assumes the identity of Dr. Edwardes. In both cases, a mental asylum falls under the control of a false authority figure representing himself to be a scientific psychologist charged with what used to be called the "cure of souls"—one figure is evil (Godstone), and one figure is benign (Peck as Ballantine). In the film, however, the real scientific authority figure, Murchison, is himself the criminal and regains control of the asylum until he is exposed, thus making him the true parallel to the false Dr. Murchison (Godstone) in the novel, who also displays a masterly knowledge of psychology turned to wrong ends. Hitchcock's Murchison thus retains some of the sinister connotations of Beeding's false Murchison/Godstone, although the latter is a much greater transgressive figure whom Beeding represents in explicitly demonic terms.

Both works also explore the complications of romantic love when confronted with the analytic attitude and the intellectual detachment of the modern scientist, primarily through the authority figure of the female scientist—Dr. Constance Sedgwick in *The House of Doctor Edwardes* and Dr. Constance Peterson (Ingrid Bergman) in *Spellbound*. In the case of the former, the female scientist, who is of questionable competence, falls under the spell of the false Dr. Murchison; in the case of the latter, she falls in love with the amnesia patient, Ballantine, whom she initially believes to be her professional superior and later takes on as her patient. In both works, the female scientist becomes romantically attached to a male whom she believes to be her professional superior; in the film, moreover, the romantic attachment is further complicated by the fact that the supposed superior falls in love also and then becomes the patient, the subordinate, whom she cures without breaking the transference. In the case of Dr. Sedgwick, her romantic attachment clouds her scientific judgment with disastrous consequences. In the case of Dr. Peterson, her romantic attachment leads to the eventual triumph of scientific insight: she not only cures Ballantine, but she also eventually solves the crime and exposes the criminal scientist, Dr. Murchison, thus succeeding as both a psychologist probing the psyche and as a detective solving a perplexing murder. Indeed, the work of the psychoanalyst is assimilated to the model of a detective solving a mystery. Consequently, the depiction of modern psychology *on the whole* is much more sympathetic and approving in *Spellbound* than in *The House of Doctor Edwardes*. But it is also less complicated and less profound than in the novel.

II

To wit, *Spellbound* opens with a hopelessly naïve statement about psychoanalysis that can only be described as antiquated and humorous to the contemporary viewer:

> This movie deals with psychoanalysis, the method by which modern science treats the emotional problems of the sane.
> The psychoanalyst seeks only to induce the patient to talk about his hidden problems, to open the hidden doors of his mind.
> Once the complexes that have been disturbing the patient are uncovered and interpreted, the illness and confusion disappear . . . and the evils of unreason are driven from the human soul.

As Jonathan Freedman has argued, "the addition of these introductory words reminds us that the film that follows was both a product of and a participant in a specific historical event: the full integration of psychoanalysis into American cultural life." As Freedman goes on to explain, until the 1940s psychoanalysis was a "coterie concern," especially among "eastern intellectuals." During the 1930s and early 1940s, the limited number of films that dealt with the topic associated the psychoanalyst with foreignness, fraudulence, and criminality; only a few represented psychoanalysis sympathetically. "It was not until *Spellbound* that psychoanalysis was most fully purified of its aura of fraudulence and criminality, for it was in *Spellbound* that psychoanalysis first became, for Hollywood cinema, the means of solving a crime, not a means of committing one" (Freedman 80–83). Indeed, the elevation of psychology in *Spellbound* parallels the elevation of psychology not only in American cultural life but also in its institutionalization in the modern American state. Can it be a coincidence that in 1946 Connecticut was the first state to pass legislation regulating the licensing of psychologists? Connecticut was followed by three additional states in the late 1940s, twelve states in the 1950s, and twenty-five states in the 1960s. Although one cannot establish neat cause-and-effect relations among cultural acceptance, state licensing, and the appearance of psychologists in courts of law, the use of psychologists as expert witnesses in courts also began, albeit more slowly, in the 1940s and continued to spread to increasing numbers of states for the next few decades (Nolan 68–72).

The normalization and institutionalization of psychology in American public life were not, however, without their complications and contradictions. In the case of psychoanalysis, these complications and contradictions are reflected in *Spellbound*. As Freedman has pointed out, "neither psychological nor epistemological depths are evident in *Spellbound*; the symptoms of mental distress—the amnesia that afflicts the film's hero, John Ballantine . . . disappear with the greatest of ease as soon as the traumatic event occasioning these manifestations is brought to consciousness." As suggested above, throughout the film the psychoanalytic process of discovering the meaning of a past event is assimilated to a detective narrative with the result that psychoanalysis is "defanged." The famous doors in one of the film's well-known dream scenes are opened rather too easily. Psychoanalytic theory and practice are popularized, vulgarized, for easy absorption, the psychoanalytic cure routinized beyond recognition. Nonetheless, *Spellbound* "does not disavow the criminality that thoroughly infects the early Hollywood notion of psychoanalysis." While Dr. Peterson succeeds in curing Ballantine and eventually proving his innocence, she does so at the expense of discovering the criminality of Dr. Murchison. According to Freedman, the discovery of Dr. Murchison's criminality has the effect of ascribing "to psychoanalysis itself a faint afterimage of its earlier sinister, criminal, transgressive identity" (83–87).

III

The image of a "sinister, criminal, transgressive identity" associated with psychology, and psychoanalysis in particular, is much stronger in *The House of Doctor Edwardes* than in *Spellbound*. In Beeding's novel, the false Dr. Murchison/Godstone is explicitly represented as a transgressive figure of some magnitude, who has taken Napoleon as his personal hero and practices demonic rituals and rites. He is characterized as "a man possessed" who describes himself as "different" and as having "a mission to fulfill," and through the course of the novel, his preternatural powers of persuasion and cunning are repeatedly exhibited with both the inmates and the staff of Chateau Landry (143–45). The "spell" that Godstone casts is much more powerful and threatening than that of Dr. Murchison of Hitchcock's *Spellbound*, who is unmasked as a villain late in the narrative and only briefly before his suicide. Furthermore, Hitchcock's Murchison relies upon his influence as a psychoanalyst, the powers of

his official position, where Godstone's power is personal and inseparable from his transgressive personality. The real spell of Hitchcock's
Spellbound is double and has nothing to do with Murchison: it is the
spell of Ballantine's so-called guilt complex that lies at the root of his
amnesia, which is in turn broken by the spell of love between Ballantine
and Peterson because it permits the good doctor to persevere and cure
the patient, as well as to solve the case.

Both types of spells—the spell of the mentally disturbed and the
spell of love—are much more problematic in *The House of Doctor Edwardes*
because they can and do easily merge and turn demonic. Indeed, mental
disturbance is equated with the demonic, an indication of the cultural
residues of Christianity present in the novel. In *Spellbound*, the spell of
Ballantine's guilt complex is broken when he remembers that he was
accidentally responsible for the death of his brother when he was a child.
In classic Freudian terms, his "sense of guilt" is revealed to be irrational
and compulsive and thus not an accurate index of criminality. *The House
of Doctor Edwardes*, in contrast, picks up some of the more dangerous and
sinister implications of the Freudian penchant for resolving "guilt" into
a "sense of guilt," of relaxing the demands of the superego.

In an early discussion with Sedgwick, Godstone openly discusses
the less than benign implications of loosening the restrictions of the
superego and probing the depths of the unconscious, although she fails
to recognize (or more accurately does not want to recognize) what he
is really saying. Sedgwick refers to (the false) Dr. Murchison's discussion
of "in the curious language of Freud and the later school of Zurich the
secret forces which lie beneath the threshold of consciousness." Sedgwick
continues:

> Doctor Murchison had discussed at length the *Zensur* of Freud,
> describing it as the Warder who stood perpetually on guard at the
> gate which separated the unconscious self from the intelligent and
> regulated activities of the mind. Beyond the gate, blindly dynamic,
> moved and worked, insentient and with no knowledge of good and
> evil, the primitive will of the human creature to persist, to develop,
> to fulfill an unknown purpose, a darkness that stirred with primeval
> memories.
>
> He had talked much of the Warder and his office, for it
> was in his attitude to the *Zensur* that he differed from Doctor
> Edwardes. Doctor Edwardes had set his face against the method
> of Freud, which sought to lure the Warder from his post so that
> the secrets of the unconscious mind might come into the open
> and there be destroyed. Doctor Edwardes argued that this process
> of introspection and analysis merely encouraged the madman in

his delusions . . . Doctor Murchison had admitted that for most practitioners this was undoubtedly the safer way; but there were others, he had said, who might claim to have special powers. And at this point he had used a simile which had deeply impressed her. She could see him still, sitting in his chair, gazing in front of him, a confident, proud smile on his lips.

"You remember," he had said, "the legend of the sorcerer's apprentice. He stole the spells of his master and raised a horde of demons whom he was unable to control."

He had gone on to tell her of a case in which a doctor, who was endeavoring to effect a cure by the Freudian method, and who had thereby concentrated upon himself all the dormant evil of the sufferer, had been murdered by his patient in an access of dementia. He had added that those who raise the whirlwind must be prepared to ride it. Personally, he had no misgivings (76–77).

What Godstone presents clearly draws misleading implications from Freud and is actually closer to the views of C. J. Jung, as indicated by his reference to the Zurich School. Howard Kaye aptly summarizes the differing views of Freud and Jung that eventually led to their break in 1914: "Jung longed for an antinomian rebellion led by psychoanalysis, a 'drunken feast of joy' in which 'ecstatic forces' would be reawakened and a new myth, or a new religion, would be born. 'Must we not love evil,' he asked Freud, 'if we are to break away from the obsession with virtue that makes us sick and forbids us the joys of life?'" (122).

As a putative secular guide to the conduct of life in the twentieth century, the psychoanalyst retains a bivalent image both in theory and in practice—one focused on a limited and apparently benign therapy of healing and the other focused on a powerful sorcery that claims that the only path to genuine health is complete liberation from all civilized restraints. In Hitchcock's *Spellbound*, the image of the benign therapist clearly dominates, and the image of the psychoanalyst as sorcerer is carefully demarcated, muted, and suppressed in the figure of Dr. Murchison. In Beeding's *The House of Doctor Edwardes*, the image of the psychoanalyst as sorcerer embodied in Godstone surfaces in such a powerful manner that it continues to haunt the imagination even after the sorcerer is defeated.

IV

This haunting of the imagination is most obvious in the case of Constance Sedgwick, who falls in love with the false Dr. Murchison/Godstone. In the moments after she discovers his transgressive depths, she reflects with

shock that "he had made love to her. That was the bitterest thought
of all. This madman, whom she had admired from the very first for
the splendor of his mind, the tenacity of his purpose, for the beauty of
his soul, had made love to her . . . Horror of horrors" (147)! And yet
Godstone had more than hinted at his fascination with raw power and
the chaos of the unconscious on more than one occasion with Sedgwick.
Consequently, there is far more than a mere suggestion in the novel that
the good doctor secretly longs for the abject submission to transgressive
power that Godstone has planned. That is, Dr. Sedgwick is, in classic
Freudian terms, ambivalent—she is both attracted and repulsed by the
sorcery of Godstone, although she cannot consciously acknowledge her
attraction. None of this ambivalence remains in Hitchcock's *Spellbound*.
Constance Peterson's love may be read as either stable and true to the
point that ambivalence is controlled or, perhaps unfairly, as a shallow
rendition of Constance Sedgwick's more complicated infatuation in *The
House of Doctor Edwardes*.

The novel is a psychological art form that by and large has drawn
its energy and subject matter from the exploration of the inner life of
the individual, especially the tension between the deepest desires of the
self and the conventional demands of society. Beeding's *The House of
Doctor Edwardes* is no exception. As a work of art, the novel simply
makes the rise of psychology more explicit. The discipline and practice
of psychology become a means of exploring the conflicting desires of
the self, employing a version of Jungian depth psychology, while at the
same time depicting the incorporation of a more benign version of depth
psychology into conventional society, represented by the institution of
Chateau Landry.

It is no accident that *The House of Doctor Edwardes* ends with the
real Dr. Murchison and the hapless Dr. Sedgwick falling in love with one
another and marrying after the false Dr. Murchison has been exposed and
leaps to his death. Conventional psychology and conventional love triumph; the orderly love of marriage prevails over the chaotic and demonic
god of eros. Indeed, the narrative ends with the death of the demonic
erotic, Godstone, and the reassertion of what may be called "orderly
bourgeois" sexual relations, if not Christian agape. Once conventional
order returns to personal and professional life, there is no more story
to tell. The narrative is played out.

Both stories unfold within emergent post-Christian cultures.
However, *The House of Doctor Edwardes* is set within a failing Victorian
culture in which the power of evil clearly dominates the imaginations
and actions of individuals, even if they are unaware of its influence, as in
the case of Dr. Sedgwick. Demonic possession is represented in explicit

anti-Christian images, most notably in the case of the dead faith of the Reverend Mark Hickett, who inverts his crucifix and hangs it upside down in his room (101–03). But the power and attraction of evil still depend upon their Christian context to give them meaning and a point of reference. Psychology has not yet displaced religion and morality as an explanation of human motives.

Hitchcock's story also takes place within the context of an emergent post-Christian culture but in this case a postwar America in which the demonic has been trivialized and a psychological worldview is in the process of being widely accepted. Evil is now no longer located in an erotic figure, but rather in a bureaucrat, a self-serving professional psychologist out to protect his own self-interest. There is no demonic rebellion. Nor is there the temptation of a forbidden knowledge that carries the power of sorcery—only what Hannah Arendt calls the "banality of evil." Consequently, evil casts no shadows; it cannot haunt the imagination, because there are no clearly functioning symbols of evil. Evil has disappeared from the post-Freudian world not because it does not exist. Rather, evil has disappeared because of a massive failure of the collective imagination in which modern psychology is clearly implicated. Of that disappearance, Hitchcock's *Spellbound*, viewed as an adaptation, provides an intriguing glimpse.

Notes

1. See Philip Rieff, *Freud: The Mind of the Moralist*, and *The Triumph of the Therapeutic*.

Works Cited

Beeding, Francis. *Spellbound*. Cleveland: World, 1945.

Freedman, Jonathan. "Alfred Hitchcock and Therapeutic Culture in America." In *Hitchcock's America*, ed. Jonathan Freedman and Richard Millington. New York: Oxford University Press, 1999, 80–83.

Kaye, Howard L. "Why Freud Hated America," *Wilson Quarterly* 17, no. 2 (1993): 118–25.

Nolan, James L. *The Therapeutic State*. New York: New York University Press, 1998.

Rieff, Philip. *Freud: The Mind of the Moralist*. Chicago: University of Chicago Press, 1979.

———. *The Triumph of the Therapeutic: Uses of Faith after Freud*, with an introduction by Elisabeth Lasch-Quinn. Wilmington, Delaware: ISI Books, 2006.

Trilling, Lionel. *Freud and the Crisis of Our Culture*. Boston: Beacon, 1955.

10

MATTHEW H. BERNSTEIN

Unrecognizable Origins

"The Song of the Dragon" and *Notorious*

THE UNCREDITED STORY SOURCE for *Notorious* is John Taintor Foote's November 1921 two-part *Saturday Evening Post* short story, illustrated by George E. Wolfe, "The Song of the Dragon," originally purchased as a possible vehicle for Vivien Leigh around 1940. Most Hitchcock scholars dismiss it out of hand as a factor in the realization of the film—Leonard J. Leff barely mentions it at all in his detailed account of how the film was written and edited (177), and Bill Krohn's essential and meticulous production history of the film comments that this source "could not have been less promising" for what Truffaut would call "the very quintessence of Hitchcock" (82).

According to Leonard Leff, David O. Selznick's story editor Margaret McDonell told her boss in early August 1944 that Hitchcock was interested in making a film with Ingrid Bergman "about confidence tricks" on a grand scale in which Ingrid could play the woman "who is carefully trained and coached into a gigantic confidence trick which might involve her marrying some man. He is fascinated with the elaborateness with which these things are planned and rehearsed, and the idea would be to have the major part of the picture with the planning and training and the denouement more or less as the tag" (297).

As biographer Donald Spoto notes, Hitchcock would realize this scenario quite fully, and without espionage, in 1958's *Vertigo* (297). In September 1944, however, Hitchcock pitched a variant of this story—in Spoto's words, "a woman sold for political purposes into sexual enslavement"—to eagerly interested RKO executive William Dozier (298).

Biographer Patrick McGilligan, by contrast, mentions "a few basic elements" of Foote's story in the finished script—"its lead female character is an amateur Mata Hari recruited into the pretense of romance with a German agent." But McGilligan also goes on to explain that the use of Foote's story "was mainly an excuse for Selznick to use a property he owned, and for Hitchcock and Hecht to lull the producer into complacency while they went about changing the story so radically that its origins were unrecognizable" (366). As anyone familiar with Selznick's amortization-obsessed working methods knows, this is extremely likely. If so, it would make the connection between Foote's story and *Notorious* a fluke.

Moreover, McGilligan tells us that "the real inspiration" for the story came from nonprinted sources: from the romantic intelligence activities of members (including Charles Bennett and Reginald Gardner) of Hollywood's English set on behalf of England's Ministry of Information; from Ben Hecht's ardent Zionism and his and Hitchcock's obsession with the possibilities that the Nazis could regroup after the war—further cemented by the writers' December 1944 visit to Washington D.C. to discuss making a short film about postwar worldwide unity and the need to guard against future aggressor nations for the U.S. State Department and Office of War Information; from Hitchcock's March 1945 talk, recounted in the Truffaut interview, with Cal Tech scientist Dr. Robert Millikan, about the role of uranium ore in the creation of a nuclear bomb. Even the notion of uranium in the wine cellar arose from Hitchcock's love of wine and his fascination with bombs evident in earlier films (367–74).

So the John Taintor Foote story was one of the more obscure sources for an American Hitchcock film (Leitch, 237, 239), and here, once again, Hitchcock would seem to have followed the process he usually brought to adaptation, which he described to François Truffaut: "What I do is to read a story only once, and if I like the basic idea, I just forget all about the book and start to create cinema" (Truffaut, 71; quoted in Leitch, 238). More specifically, Hitchcock told Truffaut that "after talking it over with Ben Hecht, we decided that the idea we'll retain from this story is that the girl is to sleep with a spy in order to get some secret information" (168). Oddly enough, Hitchcock remembered Foote's tale in detail when he recounted it to Truffaut, who, as Krohn notes, found it quite amusing (82).

So even if Hecht and Hitchcock used "The Song of the Dragon" as a starting point, it is worth asking if this is even a case of adaptation at all. More precisely, what can we learn about Hitchcock's approach to adaptations by looking at Foote's story? In the broadest sense, Hecht and Hitchcock basically turned the Foote story inside out to craft what we now recognize as one of Hitchcock's most emotionally compelling works, and one that offers a surprising critique of the ways in which women are treated in a male-dominated society. Looking closely at Foote's story is worth the time and trouble. Doing so enables us to consider certain aspects of their achievement that might otherwise go unremarked.

For the record, it is worth knowing that John Taintor Foote (1881–1950) was a playwright and short story writer, who specialized in two kinds of stories. One set concerned fly fishing, centering specifically on the not always happily married couple, the Baldwins (George is a fly-fishing fanatic, and Isabelle is not). Foote also favored stories about horses and horse racing, and his expertise therein led him to write several Hollywood screenplays: *Kentucky* in 1938 and *The Story of Seabiscuit* and *The Great Dan Patch in 1949*, notable in their day for being the first biopics about race horses. Though Foote also wrote screenplays for two musicals in 1939—the Stephen Foster biopic *Swanee River* and the Jeanette McDonald vehicle *Broadway Serenade*—his best-remembered film work is probably the 1940 classic swashbuckler *Mark of Zorro*, starring Tyrone Power.

Zorro's double identity aside, the theatrical setting and espionage plot in "The Song of the Dragon" are far removed from any of these stories and screenplays. Foote became familiar with the New York theater scene during World War I by having a play, *Toby's Bow*, produced in New York in 1918 (adapted, incidentally, into a film the following year). He published "The Song of the Dragon" in late 1921. Perhaps it was inspired by actual situations he had observed.

Foote's tale is narrated by veteran stage producer William Kinder, who begins the story pondering the impossibility of casting for an ingénue in a new play: experienced actresses are too old to be plausible in the part, and new actresses are too inexperienced to pull it off. He is interrupted by a visit from federal Agent Smith, who asks Kinder to ask an accomplished stage star with whom Kinder worked and was in love to sleep with the German head of a ring of saboteurs, who currently pretends to be a British playboy living the high life on Fifth Avenue. Meanwhile, Kinder grants an audition to an unknown actress on whom he takes pity when she is knocked out in his office.

Kinder's former paramour rejects the idea angrily and stomps out; the ingénue, Sylvia Dodge, auditions and turns out to be an astonishing performer; and as Kinder is making plans with her for their box office success, Agent Smith turns up again to follow up on his request. Though Kinder gives him the bad news, both men witness Dodge's spontaneous expression of her intense desire to do something to help the young American recruits marching through Manhattan before going off to fight in World War I. Before Kinder can stop him, Smith has whisked Dodge away for the assignment. Part 1 of the story ends here.

Part 2, published a week later, picks up with Kinder angry that Dodge, having accomplished her espionage mission, has not returned as she had promised to his office to resume her incipient career. He chews out Agent Smith because she has chosen to entertain the troops instead. A scene follows between Dodge and her new beau, Captain Eugene Weyeth. The son of a wealthy New York family, Weyeth proposes to Dodge; she holds him off with the promise of eventual marriage and shows up in Kinder's office to ask his help. She rightly suspects that the captain's parents will be suspicious of her and will reject her when they learn, as they will, of her sleeping with the enemy. Kinder accompanies Dodge to the Weyeths' apartment, where she tearfully explains her past service to her country, producing a letter of commendation from the president as proof. The Weyeths accept her with enthusiasm, and the story ends.

Krohn further notes that in 1921, when Foote's story was published, "Hitchcock was writing parodies of just this kind of corny popular fiction in a magazine published by the employees of the advertising company where he worked" (82). But Foote's spy melodrama featured generic plot elements and characters familiar to Hitchcock and Hitchcock fans by 1944. The man-about-town German saboteur whom Sylvia Dodge must bed in "The Song of the Dragon" could easily become the wealthy, well-spoken Charles Tobin (Otto Kruger), the debonair (if admittedly fatherly) leader of the saboteurs in Hitchcock's 1942 film of that title, who plan much of the same destruction against America's war efforts. Foote's government Agent Smith, who recruits the actress for her unpleasant work, is physically unimpressive and somewhat bumbling but nonetheless effective; he could be a sketch for the bureaucratic professor (Leo G. Carroll) in *North by Northwest* (1959). "Sexual enslavement" aside, Agent Smith's first choice for the assignment, the established stage star and former paramour of Kinder, reacts as angrily and with the same logic when he describes it to her as Alicia Huberman does when Devlin does likewise: both women accuse the men of knowing this was to be the assignment all along and of even recommending their lovers for it (46).

Yet another affinity between Hitchcock and Foote's story is self-reflexivity, expressed through the thoughts of producer Kinder. In part

1, he characterizes Kaiser Wilhelm as an inept actor (3); when Agent Smith describes the government's plan to use an actress to seduce the German spy, Kinder thinks to himself that it "seemed more like a plot for a moving-picture scenario or a tale by Oppenheim [espionage and mystery author E. Phillips Oppenheim] than vital facts as real as the pictures on the walls, the rugs on the floor, the sunshine streaming in through the window" (4). In other words, Foote's story was not so far removed from Hitchcock's espionage story affinities as we might otherwise assume, a fact that explains why Hitchcock would have chosen this story from Selznick's unused property files. No wonder Selznick commented to Daniel O'Shea in June 1940 that "Hitchcock is the ideal director for this subject" (Selznick).

Still, it is undeniable that Hecht and Hitchcock radically altered Foote's story. Patrick McGilligan notes, most obviously, that Hecht and Hitchcock shifted Foote's tale from the early days of America's involvement in World War I to just after World War II (367). (With few exceptions—most notably *Jamaica Inn* (1939) and *Under Capricorn* (1949)—Hitchcock did not make period films.) They also shifted the story's locale from Manhattan to Rio de Janeiro. Germans are still the enemy, but now the concern is with what they might do after World War II rather than their plans to disrupt the American home front's mobilization and munitions build-up during World War I.

To this fundamental shift, we should add the fact that Hecht and Hitchcock rearranged the romantic plot of Foote's story. In "The Song of the Dragon," the heroine, young actress Sylvia Dodge, beds the German—a total stranger to her—exposes him, and then falls in love with Captain Eugene Weyeth. Dodge then seeks approval of their marriage from Weyeth's parents. The seduction of Alex Sebastian occurs after Alicia and Devlin have fallen in love. It is as if Sylvia Dodge fell in love first with Weyeth and then did her espionage work. In focusing first on Devlin and Alicia, Hecht and Hitchcock achieved the film's artful melding of espionage and romance, doubling the narrative lines that generate suspense. Richard Allen has described this well: the viewer's hope that the hero will emerge safely from espionage work combines with the desire for a happy romantic ending between the lovers, providing an intensified "emotional investment in the narrative outcome" (48–49).

We might add that *Notorious* plays with our desires to see Alicia and Devlin reunited, not only by staging the steamy—by 1946 standards and still today—extended kissing and walking scene, but also by having Alex comment constantly on what a handsome couple they make, an observation that plays upon the viewer's recognition that the two leads in any film should wind up together and that these are perhaps the most popular and glamorous Hollywood stars of 1946. In any case, Hecht and Hitchcock's shifts—in time, setting, and romantic plot—have major consequences for the adaptation of Foote's story. For one thing, they inspire Hitchcock, with the considerable help of Claude Rains and Cary Grant, to create his most powerful depictions of sexual and romantic jealousy since *The Ring* (1927) and *The Manxman* (1929).

But these changes also facilitate Hecht and Hitchcock's delineation of more complex romantic lovers than in Foote's story, the perverse lovers who generate the romantic ironies that Allen singles out. We can best appreciate what the filmmakers took from Foote's story if we consider their approach to point of view in narrating the tale, a shift that gives rise to the film's compelling emotional itinerary. Simply put, Hecht and Hitchcock brought what was "offscreen" in the Foote story onscreen in the film—and this makes all the difference. A great deal of the suspense arises from our witnessing of every phase of Alicia's ordeal. Through cutting, close-ups, and Bergman's performance, we experience Alicia's distasteful first date with Sebastian at a restaurant—seeing her unhappy reaction shots when Sebastian looks away, especially her moment of resigned despair at the end of the scene as he prepares to order dinner from offscreen. We see her harrowing first visit to the Sebastian home, focused on Alicia's point-of-view as each of Alex's associates is introduced to her, comes up to the camera, and kisses her hand; as Hitchcock told Charles Thomas Samuels, "I wanted to say visually, 'Here is Ingrid in the lions' den; now look at each lion!'" (233). Moreover, we realize Alicia is doing her mortally dangerous work with only the most minimal training: Devlin's boss Paul Prescott (Louis Calhern) judges her skill "at making friends with gentlemen" as being adequate to the task. Prescott's instructions to her before dinner at Alex's are simply: "[T]ry to remember the names of all the people you see there tonight—the men, I mean, and get their nationalities . . . and I suggest that you don't ask any questions, just use your eyes and ears. They're a pretty keen and desperate bunch, don't underestimate them." We understand Alicia's unverbalized plea to Devlin to prevent her from marrying Sebastian when she comes to the American embassy office. The film's romantic drama thrives on the ironies of Alicia's married life when she is abandoned by Devlin to do "the job"—most of all when she pretends to suffer a hangover while she is being poisoned. In other words, as Robin Wood puts it, it is "clear" that "Alicia is from a very early point (arguably from her first appearance on camera) its emotional center, the magnet that draws our sympathy the most powerfully" (306–07). This is *her* story.

Moreover, our close identification with Alicia also trades upon our familiarity with film noir (she is film noir's femme fatale, whom both Devlin and Sebastian must investigate) and the woman's gothic (she is the victim of a cold lover and a murderous husband—and his mother). Many critics have commented on the film's generic hybridity. As Richard Allen has put it, "The achievement of Hitchcock and screenwriter Ben Hecht is . . . a tour de force of plot construction and illustrates the way in which the ambiguity and irony in Hitchcock's plots are sustained by the hybrid combination of these different plot archetypes" (100).

None of this is in the Foote story. This is true, fundamentally, because the Foote story is narrated by the New York theatrical producer William Kinder, who auditions Sylvia Dodge early on. With the exception of one scene—when she puts off Captain Weyeth's marriage proposal—we only read about Sylvia through Kinder's eyes. Part 1 of "The Song of the Dragon" ends when Sylvia voluntarily leaves Kinder's office and goes off with Agent Smith to start her mission. Part 2 begins with Kinder lambasting Smith in outrage because Sylvia has done her dirty work, the saboteurs have been arrested, and yet Sylvia still has not returned to Kinder's office to begin rehearsals for the play; she instead is lingering to entertain the troops by singing them Irish airs. Foote's story ends after Kinder accompanies Sylvia Dodge to meet—she hopes—her future in-laws, and they embrace her. In other words, Dodge does her patriotic duty "off-screen." Unlike Hecht and Hitchcock, Foote has left out the most suspenseful, compelling part of the story. Instead, we have the suspense of what Captain Eugene Weyeth's mother and father will say when Sylvia informs them of her unsavory wartime duties. There is simply no comparison.

The discrete tastes of *Saturday Evening Post* editors, as well as that of the popular readership of 1921, was likely a strong factor in Foote's treatment of Sylvia's espionage work.[1] Foote prudently leaves her mission off the page but does his best to emphasize how horrible it actually is: the recruiting agent Smith describes the job as "going to hell" for the country, something tougher than dying for America. Smith goes on: "The woman who tackles this job . . . can't bother with the usual concealments. She'll have no time to cover up. She's got to forget reputation, family, friends, everything that a woman values" (12 November, 4). In part 2, Sylvia describes the job to her beloved's parents as she seeks their approval: "I was given six weeks to get the papers. I found where they were in five—five weeks and a day from the night I was introduced to the man at a dinner that had been arranged. I got the papers in the only way possible. It was all very horrible, but necessary—oh, so necessary! And I kept telling myself that I was only one girl, and it was for America. I must give, as the boys would have to give . . . So I gave" (51).

The narrator comments in part 2, "It had been harder than anyone could ever know to do what she had done" (42). It was Hecht and Hitchcock's decision, inspired by the determination to create a vehicle for Ingrid Bergman, to make sure their audience knew how hard, how agonizing, how full of anguish, the assignment is for Alicia.

This entailed making "the job" itself even harder for Alicia than it is for Sylvia Dodge. We have already noted one difference: Alicia falls in love with Devlin while awaiting her assignment. Dodge has no romantic attachments going into the espionage. She does not even have a living father. She is an orphan and like Alicia the daughter of an immigrant—in Dodge's case, an immigrant Irish Shakespearean actor well respected in the theater world who has trained his daughter well. We understand that Sylvia's devotion to America arises in part out of her gratitude for her father's refuge and opportunities here. Like her prototype, Alicia loves "this country." Unlike her prototype, Alicia also loves Devlin.

Moreover, unlike Alicia, Sylvia Dodge has a definite assignment with a limited time frame—six weeks. The apparently British bon vivant living on Fifth Avenue, Smith explains, is actually a German agent. He would "presently order in action a small army of bomb planters and incendiaries located at well-chosen points in various parts of the country." He needs to be arrested, but the government needs to learn the names of his associates to put them all in prison. Agent Smith describes the solution: "This man has a weakness—the usual one . . . A woman might find out where he keeps his papers. He'd never fall for a cheap woman—not enough to tell her secrets at any rate; but a woman of class might throw him off his guard. It's worth a chance, we think" (4).

Recall how vague Alicia's assignment is. Something is going on in the Sebastian house. The OSS agents think it is something big, and Alicia has to "land" Alex and find out what is going on—and keep at it until she does. True, the discovery of uranium ore reveals the magnitude of what the Sebastians and their associates are planning. But no one knows this when they describe the assignment to Alicia or when she accepts it. At this early point in the film, sleeping with the enemy to prevent a vague threat of resurgence of the defeated Nazis is far less urgent than helping to save the lives of young soldiers marching off to their training camp and World War I.

Hecht and Hitchcock's Alicia agrees to fly to Rio because she is intrigued with Devlin, she despises her father and feels guilty for his traitorous actions, and she is unhappy with the life she leads. Foote's Sylvia is inspired by the sights and sounds of young recruits marching through Manhattan. More than halfway through part 1 of Foote's story, the spy recruiter Smith comes back to Kinder's office just after Sylvia Dodge has astonished Kinder with her considerable acting abilities—one of those "remarkable coincidences" that occur in fiction. Kinder has just decided to cast Sylvia in the lead of his next play and is confident he will make a fortune "in one season" from doing so. This matter of Sylvia Dodge's casting settled, Kinder reports to agent Smith while she is in his office that he has failed to recruit two seasoned actresses for Smith's assignment. Kinder is interrupted as "Over There" and cheers waft through his office window, arising from a draft regiment of young, inexperienced soldiers as they make their way in the streets below (50).

At this point, Sylvia Dodge is transported by the singing to the window, where she watches the young recruits and cries out that she cannot "go on with silly plays. They were so young . . . so young. I never realized how young they were. I've got to help." Smith can't resist giving her a chance to help. He describes the job. She thinks it over for a few minutes, looking out the window of Kinder's office: "When she turned to them again her face had changed. It was rapt, ethereal and very lovely. Her eyes suggested that she had seen a vision." She refuses any pay scale above that of the recruits, thirty dollars a month, identifying with them completely, and she goes off with Smith, leaving Kinder apoplectic as part 1 concludes (50).

Sylvia Dodge willingly embraces her duty. The men do not coerce her. Compare this with the perverse form of emotional blackmail Devlin and his colleagues apply to Alicia by asking her, in Devlin's words, "to make up for some of your daddy's peculiarities." In the Hitchcock film, fathers are a burdensome source of guilt and self-destruction, and father figures (Prescott, his men, Devlin, and eventually Alex) are disapproving; in Foote's story, they are an enormous source of pride and gifts—specifically, Sylvia Dodge's acting gifts, which have landed her the lead in Kinder's next play and which allow her to succeed in exposing the ring of German saboteurs. Every man besides Captain Weyeth that Sylvia encounters is also a supportive father figure: Kinder, Agent Smith, and even Captain Weyeth's father.

That Sylvia Dodge would embrace the job thus illustrates one more fundamental difference between Foote's story and Hitchcock's film: its treatment of patriotism. Indeed, Bill Krohn in *Hitchcock at Work* informs us that Ingrid Bergman first rejected "The Song of the Dragon" when Selznick offered it to her in the early 1940s "because of the story's crude flag waving" (82). Alicia likewise rejects the notion of patriotism when Devlin proposes it as a rationale for why she would accept the job. Alicia denounces the p-word as a cynical ploy ("waving the flag with one hand and picking pockets with the other") until the recordings of her argument with her father prove she is bluffing. She changes her mind about working for "Uncle Sam" just as Bergman changed her mind about the Foote story in 1945. By contrast, Foote's story takes diehard patriotism for granted. Early on, Kinder shares with agent Smith his belief that "the average American woman would die for her country" (4). The refusal of two seasoned actresses to accept Smith's assignment suggests otherwise.

Alicia's initial cynicism about helping the United States is entirely justified in Hecht and Hitchcock's script because they make absolutely blatant the hypocrisy of the men who recruited Alicia. In the brief scene before Alicia comes to the embassy to ask "permission" to marry Alex Sebastian, Beardsley (Moroni Olsen) objects to "a woman of that sort" coming to their offices. Devlin in response sticks up for her in a way that he earlier refused to do when the job was first proposed and when Alicia asked him if she should take the job. When Mr. Beardsley dismisses Alicia so peremptorily and comments that "none of us have any illusions about her character," Devlin retorts, "Miss Huberman is first, last and always not a lady. She may be risking her life, but when it comes to being a lady, she doesn't hold a candle to your wife, sir, sitting in Washington and playing bridge with three other ladies of great honor and virtue."

The power of Devlin's comments arise in part from the fact that Devlin himself has been similarly hypocritical in his judgmental attitude toward Alicia, and his remarks signal his growing awareness of his own error and the impossible position he and his colleagues have put her in. But Devlin is alone in this realization among the men in the office. When Devlin visits Prescott late in the film to tell his boss he believes something is seriously wrong with Alicia, and he asks permission to visit the Sebastian home, Prescott lies in bed eating cheese and crackers nonchalantly—his main concern is that Devlin not mess up their set up as they begin to make arrests. The agency's callous regard for Alicia—even as Prescott knows of her and Devlin's love for each other—is unmistakable (and Prescott was even less admirable in earlier script drafts). The *Motion Picture Daily* reviewer put it well: "The American agents begin to look pretty seedy, morally speaking, at this point in the tale, but the German agent saves their face somewhat by proposing marriage to the girl."

In Foote's story, certainly Kinder and Smith put Sylvia Dodge to work, as the agents do Alicia. But Sylvia feels certain her boyfriend, Captain Eugene Weyeth, whom she has met at a training camp, will take her "backstory" in stride because "he's so young. He doesn't know what gossip means. When I tell him he'll just brush it aside. He'll say it's only between us" (46). Weyeth is apparently (we never find out for sure) not so judgmental as Devlin or as jealous as Devlin and Sebastian. No man in Foote's story judges Sylvia Dodge harshly; in fact, Kinder, Smith, and Weyeth's father fiercely admire her.

Instead, in Foote's story, the voice of social disapproval is a society matron, Captain Eugene Weyeth's mother, Clara, who immediately suspects Sylvia of golddigging after her only child. Clara feels this so strongly that she visits her husband's Manhattan office to complain about it and asks him to arrange for Sylvia to be transferred to another camp. Her husband waves her off. Sylvia, though not aware of the extent of Clara Weyeth's disapproval, is determined to earn the Weyeths' blessing before accepting his marriage proposal. She is rather like Sidney Poitier's Dr. John Prentice in *Guess Who's Coming to Dinner* (1967), who tells his fiancé's parents, behind her back, that if they don't approve of his marriage to their daughter, he will not go through with it. (Devlin has no parents, of course.)

Sylvia insists on visiting her possible in-laws to gain their approval because she has great personal integrity. She seeks to spare the Weyeths any social embarrassment and is willing to sacrifice her personal happiness to theirs. As she explains to them, her marriage to Eugene would make her an object of fascination and talk, and her previous association with the spy would come up: "[T]he trouble was," she tells Kinder, "that others knew what I was doing, and they didn't know why. They can never know, of course. I've met the man's [i.e., the spy's] valet on the street once since, and he leered at me and said something familiar. He's only one—others know, and a lot suspect" (51). Had Sylvia Dodge, like Alicia, done her duty in a foreign country, she could have come home and married without explanations. Instead, she must face the music. And, of course, Alicia has to face social disapproval by the entire corps of American spies in Rio—enough to make up for any imposing, dignified, member of Manhattan's social register.

So in Foote's story, Kinder accompanies Sylvia to meet Eugene Weyeth's parents, and they explain everything. When they are done, Sylvia is certain that the elder Weyeths could not accept her after all she has done. She breaks into tears while reading her special commendation from the president of the United States "for extraordinary services rendered her country in time of war" (51).

The suspense of this final scene resides in what the parents will say. They remain silent for a while, long enough for Kinder to wonder to himself, "Are they made of stone?" Readers might wonder, will the Weyeths prove as hypocritical as Beardsley and, as implied in Devlin's comments, Beardsley's bridge-playing wife in Washington?

Mr. Weyeth speaks first, looking at his wife while he speaks to Sylvia and Kinder. "From the time he [Eugene] was a little boy we've thought more or less about what kind of a girl we wanted for his wife and our daughter. We dreamed about a pretty fine girl . . . planned her, so to speak. But . . . we never planned anything as fine as this, did we Clara? We weren't equal to it." After a pause, Mrs. Weyeth slowly gets out of her chair and opens her arms to Sylvia. "You wonderful child!" she exclaims. "Come here, come here" (51).

The next two paragraphs of this scene—the last two brief paragraphs of the entire story—describe how the father approaches his wife and Sylvia Dodge as they embrace. Mr. Weyeth pats his wife "almost roughly on the back" and says, "Good girl, Clara." He has, in effect, been waiting for his wife to give up her preconceptions, her social snobbery, and recognize Sylvia's amazing integrity and respond as the story conceives a true American patriot would. Men like Smith may have assigned Sylvia her distasteful job, but Smith, Kinder, and Mr. Weyeth, even President Woodrow Wilson, appreciate and applaud her sacrifice. In this final scene, in other words, it is the mother who is being tested, not Sylvia. We are waiting for this matron to catch up with the enlightened men, both of them father figures, in accepting and praising this true patriot.

Unlike Alicia Huberman, Sylvia Dodge comes through her ordeal unscathed, physically or psychologically. She remains devoted to supporting the war, giving up stardom on Broadway to lift up the recruits' spirits in the training camps, and then planning to marry. When he first sees Sylvia after she's done her duty, Kinder measures the impact of her assignment by her appearance: she was "as lovely as ever . . . not quite so fresh, not quite so girlish, but with an added something—a tenderness, an understanding. They were expressed by the faintest of shadows under the eyes, a slightly deeper line at the nostrils. The lips no longer had a tendency to pout" (46). She is a fantastic figure, almost inhuman, doing her bit in a society ruled by benign if patronizing men. She is, at least on her own terms, decidedly not a victim.

Hecht and Hitchcock's trademark questioning of government malfeasance or ineffectuality is nowhere to be found in Foote's story. Conversely, the unabashed patriotism of Foote's characters would not have worked in 1946 Hollywood. This contrast is likely, and in part, evidence of the gulf between popular sensibilities in 1921, an era of comparative innocence and idealism, however tarnished by the senseless destruction of World War I, and the period two decades later in which film noir and Hollywood's woman's gothic film could flourish—the latter thanks in no small part to Hitchcock's films such as *Rebecca* (1940), *Suspicion*, and even *Shadow of a Doubt* (1943).

What is truly astonishing is that Hecht and Hitchcock hit upon the story outline, as well as the title, from the very start of their first three-week writing conference in New York from December 1944 to January 1945. The conception of Alicia as sexually promiscuous, her father as a Nazi traitor, her assignment to bed the Sebastian character "to shoot

down tomorrow's Luftwaffe," in the words of Boone (the Devlin character), her discovery and poisoning at the behest of Sebastian's mother,
and Boone's last minute rescue of her—all of this was in place. Leonard
Leff describes the treatment's conclusion: "Armed with a presidential
citation for her work, Alicia returns to America and the home of Boone's
parents to await Walt's return from the war" (180). Leff comments, "Even
in this rudimentary treatment, the moral implications of male-female
relationships enriched what might otherwise have been a routine Latin
American thriller," a quality even the highly critical David O. Selznick
could see (181–82).

Hecht and Hitchcock's work on the script would undergo many
more changes and variations, as they figured out the action, responded
to and/or ignored Selznick's criticisms, and experimented with story and
character elements. Leff describes their "somber" second draft (184), in
which Alicia became a café singer who narrates her story of falling in
love with flyer Wallace Fancher in Brazil; spies on Sebastian; and survives
Sebastian and Fancher, who fall to their deaths under Rio's giant statue
of Christ in a fight over her. She still receives a presidential citation and
comments to Prescott that "some of me is still alive—and I'm luckier
than those others who helped—much luckier." A third draft discarded the
frame tale in the bar and the fight and fatal fall of Devlin and Sebastian
but added the opening trial scene, reduced Devlin's role, had him killed
in his attempt to rescue Alicia at the end, and added a more fraught,
fetishistic, and masochistic element to both Alicia and Devlin (185).

More revisions of their treatment provided more variations: Devlin
rescuing Alicia in a gunfight at the Sebastian house during a party and
most importantly, by April 1945, having Alicia find the MacGuffin of
uranium ore in the wine cellar by herself. As Leff points out, the writers devised this just weeks before the American armed forces made
preparations for dropping two atomic bombs on Japan (194). By June
1945, under Selznick's browbeating over dialogue and his exhortations
to keep Devlin onscreen as much as possible, their latest script version
got Devlin into the basement, had Devlin and Alicia kiss to cover up
their spying activities, and included the climactic descent of the Sebastian
staircase (201–03). Playwright Clifford Odets' experiments with the script
in September and October proved useless. They were removed when
Hecht returned to work (207–10), and Hitchcock commenced shooting
later that fall. It is fair to say that Hecht and Hitchcock worked slowly
toward their definite conception of the story from the very start.

The Production Code Administration's input was, I would argue,
crucial to the film's final form and emotional appeal. Joseph I. Breen
had rejected outright Hecht and Hitchcock's "Temporary Screenplay"

of 9 May 1945 as "unacceptable under the provisions of the Production Code" principally because of "the characterization of your lead, Alicia, as a grossly immoral woman, whose immorality is accepted 'in stride' in the development of the story and who, eventually, is portrayed as dying a glorious heroine." Breen and his colleagues recognized that the "frequent references throughout the story to Alicia's gross immorality" could be intended "to point up and emphasize her attempts at regeneration," but there were also no compensating moral values for her sexual promiscuity (Breen). Yet Breen in this missive made a crucial suggestion: "It might be indicated that motivation for [Alicia's] characterization is prompted by her total loss of faith in her father, which leads her to sour on society in general, and, instead of becoming a kept woman of loose morals, such souring process might be evidenced by her determination to get what she can out of life, without paying any personal price for it." Breen planted the seed for Alicia's crucial, revealing speech about her father on the plane to Rio, even as Hecht and Hitchcock revised it to a terse and pithy polish.

Hecht and Hitchcock assured Breen's assistant Geoffrey Shurlock within weeks of Breen's initial rejection of the script that they "agreed that the characterization of the female lead would be changed in such a way as to avoid any direct inference that she is a woman of loose sex morals" (Shurlock). Here, as with Selznick, the writers told the authority in question what he wanted to hear and went their own way. The problem of Alicia's immorality persisted as Hecht and Hitchcock revised the script and the production moved to RKO. A July 1945 letter to RKO's William Gordon referred to the frequent characterizations of Alicia as a "tramp" and pleaded for dialogue in which male characters stick up for her—perhaps the Brazilian agents (who "defend Alicia's character, indicating that they are satisfied she is not an immoral woman") or Devlin at the film's conclusion, who could deliver "a definite statement" "that he has misjudged Alicia" (Breen); here again, one can see a suggestion that led to Devlin's "first, last and always not a lady" speech in Alicia's defense. Devlin's retort to Beardsley in the 16 September 1945 script draft had included Devlin characterizing her as "A tramp, ready to die for her country," yet another line of dialogue the writers ultimately removed at the Breen office's request.

Still, Hecht and Hitchcock proved stubborn on the subject of Alicia's immorality: Breen had to warn them against an early scene they shot and included in the film's initial cut, which was to occur between the courtroom sentencing of Alicia's father and her evening party, which Devlin crashes: here, Alicia's lover Ernest abandons her out of fear, and Breen pointed out that the scene had "the inescapable flavor . . . that she and Ernest are living together" (Breen; Gordon). Had this scene remained, Devlin's suspicions and ill-treatment of Alicia would have been easier for viewers to accept. As we have it in the film, her sexual availability is still broadcast in the party scene ("I like party crashers," she says, looking at the eye-candy Devlin), but, in light of her change after her father's suicide, the overseas service men and Devlin's judgment of her seems unfair.

Of course, a scene between Sylvia Dodge and a live-in lover would have been unthinkable in a *Saturday Evening Post* story such as Foote's; Sylvia Dodge is clearly a virgin before her espionage assignment. But the difference between a 1921 ingénue and a 1946 woman, and between 1921 flag-waving and 1946 depiction of patriotic duty performed at the directive of those who hold you in contempt is above all a contrast between sensibilities and artistic talents. It would be easy to exaggerate the effects of the passage of time. Yet it should be remembered that Hollywood had on occasion produced "sleeping with the enemy" scenarios before 1946. One key example predates even the 1931 Greta Garbo *Mata Hari*. United Artists released *The Woman Disputed*, based on the play by Denison Clift, in which Natalie Talmadge plays Mary Ann Wagner, an Austrian reformed prostitute forced to sleep with an occupying Russian officer to save the life of an Austrian spy. *The Woman Disputed* resembles *Notorious* in other ways: the Russian lieutenant insists on Mary Ann's sexual favors because he acts out of jealousy, since Wagner has promised to marry his erstwhile friend, the Austrian officer Paul Hartman (Gilbert Roland). Her sleeping with the enemy enables Austria to retake her town; her fiancé refuses to accept her, but then relents as ten thousand Austrians kneel before her in gratitude. Clift's play was produced on Broadway just five years after the publication of "The Song of the Dragon"; the film version premiered two years later.

Then there is the matter of Foote himself. A *New York Times* review of *The Great Dan Patch*, for which Foote wrote the screenplay, commented that Foote "writes with more feeling when he is dealing with [the horse] Dan Patch and the people who train and love him than when he is simply concerned with the domestic affairs of Dan's owner, and the snobbery and ruthless ambition of his socially climbing wife" ("T.M.P."). Foote's reliance on the stereotype of the socially obsessed wife (Clara Weyeth in "The Song of the Dragon") may have been a mainstay of his writing. But more significantly, Foote simply does not display in the short story the complex sense of character, morality, society, and irony that informs Hitchcock and Hecht's script.

Thus, *Notorious* was developed from such an "unpromising" source into Truffaut's "quintessential" Hitchcock film. One of its most distinctive features is the often analyzed perverse quality of the film's romantic plot, whereby the obstacles to the central couple's formation are as much Devlin's suspicious, emotional, and sadistic coolness as the nature of the assignment for which he recruits Alicia; and her confused decision to take it. *Notorious* is a key example of what Richard Allen has described as Hitchcock's tendency to imbricate a romantic ideal of heterosexual romance with "its opposite—human perversity," "a profound anxiety" about the woman's possible infidelity and the man's possibly lethal desires "that threaten to destroy them both (11–12).

If *Notorious* is exhibit A of this dynamic in Hitchcock's work, the characterizations and plot of the film are likewise familiar. Indeed, there are antecedents and successors to the central characters in *Notorious*. The most obvious successor to Alicia is Eve Kendall (Eva Marie Saint) in *North by Northwest*, as she arouses fierce sexual jealousy in Roger O. Thornhill (Cary Grant) after seducing him because of her espionage pose as the lover of villainous spy Philip Vandamm (James Mason); and it is easy to see *North by Northwest* as a reworking of *Notorious's* romantic triangle (with Cary Grant in effect repeating his role as the right, jealous man for the compromised female spy). Another instance would be Alex Sebastian, a mother-dependent prototype for the later villains Bruno Anthony (Robert Walker) of *Strangers on a Train* (1951) and Norman Bates (Anthony Perkins) in *Psycho* (1960). However, the most obvious prototype for Alicia as the daughter of a traitor, as Patrick McGilligan has pointed out, would be Carol Fisher (Laraine Day) in *Foreign Correspondent* (1940), who belatedly discovers with the audience that her father, Stephen (Herbert Marshall), the head of an international world peace organization, is actually a Nazi agent (367). More generally, as Tania Modleski has noted, fathers have a huge impact on several Hitchcock heroines; but whereas Alicia's promiscuity and alcoholism are motivated by her father's traitorous affiliations, the repression of *Suspicion* (1941) heroine Lina (Joan Fontaine) is inspired by her father's status as an "upstanding military officer" (57, 58).

Yet for all these commonalities and echoes across films, the character configurations are more deeply felt than in any preceding or succeeding Hitchcock work. It may well be that the lengthy gestation period during which scriptwriter Ben Hecht and Hitchcock worked on the script resulted in a scenario that captures its characters' sensibilities and motivations with greater complexity than ever before. To take one example, Alex Sebastian becomes the gothic murderous husband once he learns that Alicia is a spy, but up until that point, he is the most sympathetic villain in all of Hitchcock's work. Sebastian's attentiveness to Alicia and his demonstrated affection (sending flowers, complimenting Alicia left and right) seem to arise from his insecurities. But they also make him a better romantic partner than Devlin, who—as Alicia points out—can never bring himself to tell her he loves her ("actions speak louder than words," he tells her, adding curtly, "When I don't love you I'll let you know"). Alex even makes an "honest woman" of Alicia, in the moral framework of 1946, by marrying her—something Devlin is not ready to do when they get the assignment.

To take another example, Alicia's disgust at her father's traitorous actions drives her into self-destructive behavior that never occurs to Carol Fisher in *Foreign Correspondent* when she discovers her father has been secretly undermining their work for world peace. Carol does not feel disgust, only deep disappointment and sadness, especially at her loss when her father sacrifices himself after the plane crash—understandable, since we have seen the two of them interact with mutual affection and humor. Though we never see Alicia and her father onscreen (we only hear them argue on a surveillance recording), when she learns en route to Rio of her father's suicide in prison, she offers unselfconsciously a clear and plausible explanation for why she is a "notorious" woman: "I don't know why I should feel so bad. When he told me a few years ago what he was, everything went to pot. I didn't care what happened to me. But now I remember how nice he once was—how nice we both were. Very nice. It's a very curious feeling. As if something had happened to me and not to him. You see, I don't have to hate him anymore—or myself." If we remember this brief monologue, we can believe that Alicia is, as she claims in Rio, "a new woman."

One reason that Devlin fails to trust Alicia is that this statement of hers does not register with him at all (he is too busy staring out the plane at Rio). But the other is the characterization of Devlin himself that Hecht, Hitchcock, and Cary Grant devised. Devlin is a consummate spy—unperturbed when he accidentally shatters a wine bottle in the Sebastian cellar during the big party and joking about pretending he is a janitor while Alicia is "terrified" that someone will discover them; thinking on his feet when confronted with new circumstances—acting quickly to embrace Alicia when Alex has found them in the cellar, and immediately discerning Alex's vulnerability among his Nazi associates when Devlin escorts Alicia down the stairs of the Sebastian house and into the safety of his car. Alex, by contrast, cannot be so glib with his emotions in this film. He is paralyzed with fear and cannot speak, despite Devlin's and his mother's exhortations to do so. Devlin is so skilled that it is easy to overlook the fact that it is Devlin's late arrival at the Sebastian's party that creates the problem of Alex running out of champagne and needing to visit the wine cellar while Devlin and Alicia poke around there—leading to Alex's discovery of them in a fake but authentic embrace. (We never even find out why Devlin was late. Was he so reluctant to see Alicia in the Sebastians' house?) Even Devlin's discovery of the uranium in the bottles is a happy accident, but one that has unhappy consequences for Alicia. We might forget these details because Devlin arrives "just in time" the second time he comes to the Sebastian home—to rescue Alicia for good.

Devlin breaks his fealty to the OSS only in that final sequence, a loyalty that in part prevented him from asking Alicia not to take "the job." As Richard Allen has noted, Devlin is a typical Hitchcock detective hero in that he works within the agency of the law to expose spy secrets; he is atypical because "though not a wrong man, he is a victim of the forces of social authority in the form of his employers, the U.S. intelligence service (OSS), as much as the heroine, Alicia Huberman, is a victim" (99). The "love vs. duty" theme Hitchcock used here as in his other films certainly operates for both lovers in *Notorious*, but it agitates Devlin most forcefully.

Moreover, the very skill Devlin possesses—controlling his emotions for espionage work—is what prevents him from allowing himself to admit he loves Alicia—to her and to himself. One keynote of Hitchcock's most accomplished films is the way his male characters in particular can embody a consistency that ties their work to their personal life. The most obvious example of this is L. B. Jefferies' (James Stewart) much discussed voyeurism in *Rear Window* (1954); he is an accomplished photographer, but this skill combined with his emotional immaturity makes him disinterested in Lisa Fremont (Grace Kelly). It is not just his job but the way he performs it that comes to dominate Jefferies' entire personality.

Similarly, Devlin's nature as what we today call a "control freak" is one reason he has always been "afraid of women" and why he is quick to accuse Alicia of making fun of him when she encourages him to hold her hand in the outdoor Rio café. Devlin sadistically punishes Alicia and himself by treating her coldly, refusing to declare his love, then pushing her into a (for her) repulsive sexual and nearly fatal relationship with Alex. He is so caught up in controlling his emotions, as the conventional "emotional brick" of romantic melodrama, that he cannot recognize what is so clear to the audience via Hitchcock's close-ups and editing, Bergman's performance, and especially her speech on the plane: the death of her father does make Alicia a "new woman," and not someone going on the wagon as a fad because as Devlin has it, "change is fun."

None of this emotional anguish and moral complexity transpires in "The Song of the Dragon." Foote took his title from a mininarrative epigraph to his story which is credited to "an old fairy tale": "And the elders took council, lest the fields and villages be destroyed by the dragon, and a maiden was chosen to be delivered up to him." Agent Smith, with the approval of Kinder, Mr. Weyeth, and the American president offers Sylvia Dodge to the German dragon. It is in fact Foote's story itself that resembles a fairy tale when we compare it with *Notorious*. This is why Bill Krohn can say that "The Song of the Dragon" "could not have been less promising as source material for the film." Foote's story gave Hecht and Hitchcock no basis for their sympathetic, ardently lovelorn villain, Alex Sebastian, their cool but jealously enraged "good guy" in Devlin, and the tormented Alicia, endlessly fated to play roles she does not believe in.

Yet considering in greater detail what Hecht and Hitchcock actually took from Foote's story can only encourage us to admire their skills in story and character construction all the more. They created more human, complex characters; they made Alicia the central consciousness of their story; they compelled the audience to acknowledge how terrible her assignment was even as they raised the stakes of her work in both national and personal terms.

For all these reasons—including the powerful performances of Bergman, Grant, Rains and an array of excellent character actors, including several stage veterans who were exiles from Hitler's Germany and portrayed Alex Sebastian's "friends" and "family"—the resulting film remains one of Hitchcock's most exciting and profoundly moving works. François Truffaut called it "truly my favorite Hitchcock picture . . . in the black-and-white group" (167). More recently, in December 2006, the National Film Preservation Board named *Notorious* to the Library of Congress's National Film Registry.

Among its other virtues, studying adaptation helps the critic to understand artistic choices made in a production context, even in the unusual case presented by so many Hitchcock films. *Notorious* does indeed have its basis in a low-brow literary piece with a Victorian sensibility. Yet, Hecht and Hitchcock performed what we might call a surgical adaptation and sophisticated elaboration: of a compelling narrative scenario, one encapsulated in Margaret McDonell's memo to Selznick as much as Foote's fairy tale epigram, and filtered through Hitchcock's own story interests.

Notes

I thank Patrick McGilligan for his comments on an early version of this chapter.
1. See Lea Jacobs, *The Decline of Sentiment: American Film in the 1920s*, for an account of shifting sensibilities and tastes in movie audiences from sentimental "hokum" to what came to be called "sophistication," a shift heavily influenced by contemporary literature.

Works Cited

Abel, Richard. "*Notorious*: Perversion Par Excellence." In *A Hitchcock Reader*, ed. Marshall Deutelbaum and Leland Poague. Ames: Iowa State University Press, 1986, 162–69.

Allen, Richard. *Hitchcock's Romantic Irony*. New York: Columbia University Press, 2007.

Breen, Joseph I. Letter to David O. Selznick, 25 May 1945, "*Notorious*" File, Motion Picture Producers and Distributors Association Collection, Margaret Herrick Library, Academy of Motion Picture Arts and Sciences, Los Angeles, California (hereafter MPPDA).

———. Letter to Mr. William Gordon, 25 July 1945, MPPDA.

———. Letter to Mr. William Gordon, 21 September 1945, MPPDA.

———. Letter to Mr. William Gordon, 26 June 1946, MPPDA.

Foote, John Taintor. "The Song of the Dragon." *The Saturday Evening Post*, 12 November 1921: 3–5; 19 November 1921: 18–19.

Gordon, William. Letter to Joseph I. Breen. 28 June 1946, "*Notorious*" File, MPPDA.

Jacobs, Lea. *The Decline of Sentiment: American Film in the 1920s*. Berkeley: University of California Press, 2008.

Krohn, Bill. "Writing with the Camera: *Notorious*," in *Hitchcock at Work*. New York: Phaedon, 2003, 80–103.

Leff, Leonard J. "Notorious" in *Hitchcock and Selznick: The Rich and Strange Collaboration of Alfred Hitchcock and David O. Selznick in Hollywood*. New York: Weidenfeld & Nicolson, 1987, 174–223.

Leitch, Thomas. *Adaptation and Its Discontents: From* Gone with the Wind *to* The Passion of the Christ. Baltimore: Johns Hopkins University Press, 2007.

McGilligan, Patrick. *Alfred Hitchcock: A Life in Darkness and Light*. New York: Regan Books, 2003.

Modleski, Tania. "The Woman Who Was Known Too Much: *Notorious*." In *The Women Who Knew Too Much: Hitchcock and Feminist Theory*. New York: Methuen, 1988, 57–72.

"*Notorious*." *Motion Picture Daily*, 24 July, 1946.

Samuels, Charles Thomas. "Alfred Hitchcock." In *Encountering Directors*. New York: Capricorn Books, 1972, 231–50.

Selznick, David O. Memo to Daniel O'Shea, 4 June 1940. On Notorious, Criterion Collection DVD Edition, Extras.

Shurlock, Geoffrey. "Memo for the Files: Re Notorious," 15 June 1945, "*Notorious*" File, MPPDA.

Spoto, Donald. *The Dark Side of Genius: The Life of Alfred Hitchcock*. New York: Ballantine Books, 1983.

"T.M.P." "All Over Town" (review of *The Great Dan Patch*). *The New York Times*. 9 November, 1949: 37.

Truffaut, François. *Hitchcock/Truffaut* (rev. ed.). New York: Touchstone Books, 1983.

Wood, Robin. "Star and Auteur: Hitchcock's Films with Bergman," In *Hitchcock's Films Revisited*. New York: Columbia University Press, 1989, 303–35.

11

DAVID STERRITT

Morbid Psychologies and So Forth

The Fine Art of *Rope*

. . . in a murder of pure voluptuousness, entirely disinterested, where no hostile witness was to be removed, no extra booty to be gained, and no revenge to be gratified, it is clear that to hurry would be altogether to ruin.

—Thomas De Quincey, "On Murder Considered
as One of the Fine Arts"

I've always wished for more artistic talent. Well, murder can be an art too. The power to kill can be just as satisfying as the power to create.

—Brandon Shaw in Hitchcock's *Rope*

"DELIGHTFUL" WAS ALFRED HITCHCOCK'S word (Spoto 528) for "On Murder Considered as One of the Fine Arts," the satirical essay published by Thomas De Quincey in 1827, exactly a century before Hitchcock directed *The Lodger: A Story of the London*

Fog, which the director later dubbed "the first true 'Hitchcock movie'"
(Truffaut 43). *Rope: A Play*, published by Patrick Hamilton in 1929, was
intended as "a De Quinceyish essay in the macabre," according to the
English author who wrote it,[1] and it too delighted Hitchcock when he
saw its West End premiere (Spoto 302). Although the story and tone of
Rope areconsiderably darker than those of De Quincey's essay—the play is
no satire, Swiftian or otherwise—it has the quality of outlandish pleasure
at outrageous crime that Hitchcock savored. One can say with only mild
exaggeration that his filmmaking career was an extended exercise in what
De Quincy sardonically proposed: considering (imaginary) murder as a
source of aesthetic satisfaction.

The more immediate model for Hamilton's drama, although he
steadily refused to acknowledge it, was another text in which Hitchcock
had taken keen interest: press coverage of the famous 1924 murder case
centering on Nathan Leopold and Richard Loeb, two wealthy and intelligent Chicago youths who kidnapped and murdered a fourteen-year-old
neighbor, simply "for the thrill of it," a legal scholar writes, "and to prove
their perverse misunderstanding of Friedrich Nietzsche's philosophy of
the 'superman,' who was above all law so long as he made no mistake"
(Dershowitz 256–57). The part of Nietzsche they left out was the "no
mistake" proviso: the victim's body, meant to remain hidden indefinitely,
was promptly found near one of Leopold's bird-watching sites; ditto for
a pair of Leopold's glasses, which had a distinctive hinge that was easily
traced; when questioned about the fatal night, the two said they had
been picking up women in Leopold's car, but the police learned that
the family chauffeur was repairing it that evening; and both murderers
fell apart when arrested, each blaming the killing on the other. At the
court hearing that followed their guilty pleas, legendary defense attorney
Clarence Darrow used the widely publicized case to argue vigorously
against capital punishment, touching on various other topics along the
way. "Is there any blame attached because somebody took Nietzsche's
philosophy seriously and fashioned his life upon it?" he thundered at
one point, adding, "It does not meet my ideas of justice and fairness to
visit upon [nineteen-year-old boys] the philosophy that has been taught
by university men for 25 years" (Shermer 776). Darrow's oration saved
the killers from the death penalty, but both were sentenced to life in
prison for the murder, plus ninety-nine years for the kidnapping that
preceded it.

Taking fundamentals of the Leopold and Loeb case as his raw
material—the narcissistic wrongdoers, their homosexual relationship,
their shallow engagement with Nietzsche's concept of the *Übermensch*,
the incriminating clue that contradicted their denials of guilt—Hamilton

wove them into a chamber play set immediately after the murder in a room of the London house shared by the killers Wyndham Brandon and Charles Granillo, during a party they hold to celebrate their secret crime.[2] Among those invited are the father and aunt of the victim, Ronald Kentley, and the murderers serve refreshments to their guests from the trunk containing Ronald's unsuspected corpse. Their ghastly festivity goes smoothly until suspicions of wrongdoing start nagging at a guest named Rupert Cadell, whose cynical view of life, nourished by his experiences in the recent war, have been a major influence on the two young men. Returning to their home after the party, Rupert exposes the crime and summons the police, holding the killers at bay with a sword that was concealed in his walking stick.

Rope was staged twice in 1929, first with Anthony Ireland and Sebastian Shaw as the murderous housemates, then with Ireland and Brian Aherne in the roles. Hitchcock had spoken of it to screenwriter Peter Viertel when they were working on *Saboteur* in the early 1940s (McGilligan 400), saying it might be an appropriate vehicle for an experimental technique he was considering, whereby scenes would be filmed in "real time," as opposed to cinematic time, by means of lengthy moving-camera shots lasting as long as the camera's film capacity allowed.[3] He tried out this method when he shot his courtroom drama *The Paradine Case* in 1947, but producer David O. Selznick, one of Hollywood's most notoriously hands-on executives, hated the "torturous and unnatural camera movement" and proceeded to recut, reshoot, or excise the long, languorous takes of which Hitchcock was so proud (Leff 258).

Now, however, Hitchcock and his longtime friend Sidney Bernstein were forming their own production company, Transatlantic Pictures, for the very purpose of gaining independence from meddlesome producers and officious studio bosses. Unauthorized press reports unveiled the venture in spring of 1946, stating that the first Transatlantic movie would be an adaptation of *Under Capricorn*, a 1937 novel by Helen Simpson, followed by a contemporary *Hamlet* with Cary Grant as the melancholy prince. It is unlikely that the latter had a chance of getting off the drawing board, but *Under Capricorn* became the frontrunner as Transatlantic's debut production, only to falter when Hitchcock's dream star for the picture, Ingrid Bergman, proved unavailable because of other commitments. (*Under Capricorn* became Transatlantic's second release in 1949.)

Stuck for a project, Hitchcock turned his thoughts again to *Rope* and to the novel method he would use to film it. Bernstein liked the play as well—he had seen it with Hitchcock in London—and he helped to focus Hitchcock's thinking when he made the chance remark that since significant theatrical productions are important events in British culture, they should perhaps be filmed exactly the way they were presented on the stage (McGilligan 400). Hitchcock had no known interest in preserving England's theatrical legacy, but putting motion-picture techniques into dialogue with an inherently theatrical subject (and vice versa) awakened the same enthusiasm for technical challenges that had motivated his more unorthodox projects in the past, as when he pioneered synch-sound filming in the 1929 thriller *Blackmail* or set the 1944 drama *Lifeboat* in a single isolated location. Acquiring, developing, and filming Hamilton's play became Transatlantic's first official undertaking, and Hitchcock looked forward to signing Cary Grant for the role of Rupert, the murderers' friend, mentor, and unexpected nemesis.

Hitchcock and Hamilton had different but overlapping sensibilities. Hamilton was born to "a strange and unhappy family" in 1904 (Mepham), became a successful writer early in life—he wrote *Rope*, his first theatrical success, when he was only twenty-four—but was permanently disfigured after being run over by a car in 1932. Subsequently, he turned increasingly to alcohol in his private life and as a subject for his novels, which are peopled by hopeless characters and preoccupied with "the perils and pleasures of drinking" (Drabble and Stringer). His works include the 1941 novel *Hangover Square: A Story of Darkest Earl's Court*, the much-altered source of John Brahm's 1945 melodrama *Hangover Square*, about an insane composer who is driven to kill women when he hears unsettling noises, and the popular 1938 play *Gas Light: A Victorian Thriller in Three Acts*, which was seen by royalty during its West End run in 1939, ran on Broadway with the title *Angel Street* from 1941 to 1944, and inspired two respected films about a criminally insane man who tries to drive his wife mad in order to get hold of hidden jewels.[4] One gathers from these works that Hamilton had an almost clinical interest in insanity, especially the criminal kind, and that his interest in crime was, conversely, rooted in a fascination with psychological deviance.

Hitchcock was equally drawn to narratives of crime and criminal psychology. In the 1940s alone, his pre-*Rope* pictures include at least five that share the atmosphere of morbidly inclined domesticity found at the core of *Gas Light* and like-minded melodramas: *Rebecca*, about a household dominated by a malign presence; *Suspicion* (1941), about a paranoid marriage; *Shadow of a Doubt* (1943), about an insane killer cloaked as a loving family member; *Spellbound* (1945), a psychoanalytical murder mystery; and *Notorious* (1946), another household story of paranoid marriage and dissimulated evil. As a filmmaker seeking the largest possible audience, though, Hitchcock cultivated the ability to embed the malign and the morbid within stylish, accessible stories that were widely accepted as mass-audience entertainments. However steadily he probed the shadow side of human experience, one could never write of Hitchcock what a critic wrote of Hamilton, that his work is "full of bitter, anguished brooding" organized around "a desperate sense of isolation and failure to cohere" (Taylor). Hitchcock and Bernstein were genuinely intrigued by Hamilton's play, but their decision to inaugurate Transatlantic by filming it reflected the expectation that Hitchcock and his creative partners could transform its creepier elements—the notion of party food served from a de facto coffin, for instance—into the stuff of popular Hitchcockian suspense.

The choice of *Rope* was not dictated any great popularity of the play itself. To keep up with the majors at this time, Hitchcock might have considered ideas that would "challenge the studio system," film historian Leonard J. Leff observes, by being "so radical in content that only an independent could produce them" (268). Transfixed by his inner vision of the film, Hitchcock evidently believed this is exactly what he was doing—that the "shocking" story, shot with moving cameras in Technicolor hues, "would show everyone how modern he could be" (Spoto 303). Yet while *Rope* had been novel and daring in 1929, it now seemed "stagy and dated" to most eyes; indeed, all three finalists for Transatlantic's first production—in addition to *Rope* and *Under Capricorn*, the churchy *I Confess* (filmed for Warner Bros. five years later) was also under consideration—were known in Hollywood as "weak properties that the major companies, using their better judgment, had passed over" (Leff 268). The irony was compounded when Hitchcock, who believed *The Paradine Case* had failed because Selznick's approach was formulaic and passé, set about reproducing Hamilton's aging play with striking fidelity, in overall style if not in strict detail. Bernstein had a say in these matters, of course—the final say, as he understood his arrangement with Hitchcock—but, he told a colleague, "the moment I exercise it, it's the end of our partnership" (Moorhead 178).

On the other side of the equation, Hitchcock had understandable reasons for wanting to film *Rope*. One was its suitability for filming with real-time techniques, which may have been suggested to him by Hamilton's own use of continuous action, with no time elapsing between the play's three acts. Two decades later, Hitchcock spoke slightingly of this film, as he often did with his box-office disappointments, telling François Truffaut that he "undertook *Rope* as a stunt" and that the long-take method seemed "crazy" and "nonsensical" in retrospect; yet he discussed the production with Truffaut in considerable technical detail, still clearly fascinated by this aspect of the picture (179–84). More broadly, Hitchcock had a general interest in adapting plays—fourteen of his fifty-three features are derived from stage works, from *Downhill* in 1927 through *Dial M for Murder* in 1954. This reflects his longtime preoccupation with the blurry lines between reality and illusion, manifested in some pictures (the 1930 thriller *Murder!* and the 1950 whodunit *Stage Fright* are the most vivid examples) by the filmed "realities" of cinema and the stylized "illusions" of theater. Hamilton's play is a theater piece *about* a theater piece—the latter is the highly stage-managed party that the villains throw after their murder—and Hitchcock must have found this doubly alluring.

On a practical level, Hitchcock also saw *Rope* as a showcase for the economic possibilities of long-take techniques, which could (he hoped) shorten the schedule for principal photography to about half of the normal ten-to-twelve-week period. After the box-office failure of *The Paradine Case*, and at a time when Hollywood was challenged by higher production expenses, falling domestic earnings, blocked foreign markets, and the looming threat of antitrust actions, such a dramatic cut in the film's schedule and budget would have reaffirmed Hitchcock's reputation as a bankable filmmaker in solid touch with economic realities (Leff 269). The method worked out less well in practice than in theory, however. The lengthy moving-camera shots were difficult to pull off, especially with bulky Technicolor rigs; the actors bristled at having to repeat long, complicated scenes because someone muffed a line or a piece of scenery was out of place; and Hitchcock felt compelled to reshoot the last five reels when the sunset outside the set's large window came out a bright orange hue that reminded him of a "lurid postcard" (Truffaut 182).

Alongside his practical and technical reasons for gravitating to Hamilton's play, Hitchcock felt it tapped into areas of human pathology that he could explore and embellish with tactical contributions of his own. After commissioning his actor friend Hume Cronyn to write a motion-picture treatment (transplanting the action from a London house to a Manhattan apartment) and hiring the young playwright Arthur Laurents to compose the screenplay, Hitchcock made changes that tended to increase the ghoulishness of the story, as if there were not already enough ghoulishness in the play, which outdoes Leopold and Loeb with its macabre merrymaking over the murder victim's corpse. Engaging in macabre merrymaking of his own, Hitchcock played up jokes in the dialogue, especially double entendres along the lines of "Knock 'em dead!" and "These hands will bring you great fame," anent Phillip's piano-playing skills, and this exchange:

BRANDON [to the maid]: Mrs. Wilson, [bring] champagne!

KENNETH [a party guest]: Oh, it isn't someone's birthday, is it?

BRANDON: Don't look so worried, Kenneth. It's r-really almost the opposite.

The casting also throws revealing light on Hitchcock's approach. In addition to Cary Grant as Rupert, he hoped to have Montgomery Clift as Brandon, the more self-confident of the killers, and Farley Granger as the weaker-willed Phillip, as the Granillo character was now called.[5] These are sensible choices, but there is a semi-hidden agenda behind them, relating to the implied homosexuality of the main characters. Laurents believed that Hitchcock had hired him as screenwriter because *Rope* was "to be filmed as a play and I was a playwright, and because its central characters were homosexual and I might be homosexual." Laurents was indeed homosexual, as Hitchcock knew from Hollywood gossip, and he was having an affair with Granger, although they were not living together yet. "It was very Hitchcock," wrote Laurents in his memoir: "it tickled him that Farley was playing a homosexual in a movie written by me, another homosexual; that we were lovers; that we had a secret he knew; that I knew he knew . . . All titillating to him, not out of malice or a feeling of power but because they added a slightly kinky touch" for a director who "lived in the land of kink" (124–30).

As for the other first-choice actors, in Laurents's words, "Cary Grant was at best bisexual and Monty was gay," but both turned the picture down because, as Hitchcock understood it, "each felt his own sexuality made him too vulnerable to public attack." The role of Brandon went to John Dall, a gay actor who *was* willing to undertake it, and the role of Rupert—who was once Brandon's lover, as Laurents conceived things (McGilligan 404, 406)—went to James Stewart, "which meant not a whiff of sex of any kind . . . I don't know whether it ever occurred to Jimmy Stewart that Rupert was a homosexual. Hitchcock didn't say anything but it wouldn't have mattered if he had" (Laurents 131). Stewart was a romantic leading man whose grim experiences in World War II, where he flew numerous combat missions over Europe, had made him question the rightness of continuing in a profession as insubstantial as acting. When he did decide to continue, he turned to darker and more psychologically complex roles, of which Rupert in *Rope* was one of the first. It was also the first of four Hitchcock films—the others are *Rear Window* (1954), *The Man Who Knew Too Much* (1956), and *Vertigo* (1958)—that stand with the richest achievements of Stewart's career.

As adapted and filmed, the movie version of *Rope* is a palimpsest in which Hamilton's unorthodox, quasimisanthropic play remains distinctly visible beneath the overlays of meaning, mood, and mass-audience enticement provided by Hitchcock's additions, subtractions, and alterations, which provide instructive clues to his predilections and priorities. The most important changes merit individual analysis.

- Hitchcock changes Granillo's name to Phillip and his national-ity to American rather than Spanish, making him less "exotic" and "foreign" in the film than in the play. Hitchcock was well acquainted with the United States by the late 1940s, and his decision to give *Rope* a more homogeneously American flavor bears out his wish to have the characters call forth particularly American kinds of paranoia—not only fears of crime and violence but also resentment of such "sins" as intellectuality, effeminacy, egotism, and perhaps even the guilt-free enjoyment of upper-crust creature comforts.

- Hamilton's play begins in nighttime gloom as the murderers complete their crime: "The room is completely darkened save for the pallid gleam from lamplight in the street below, which comes through the window. Against this are silhouetted the figures of Granillo and Brandon . . . [They] are bending over [a] chest, intent, working at something—exactly what, we cannot discern." Brandon then draws the window curtains so that even this light is eliminated as they "continue whatever they are doing" (1–2), and when he switches on a light immediately afterward, he instantly turns it off again on Granillo's order. Only gradually do they become visible in dim illumination from the fireplace, and only well into the first act do they turn on normal lighting that gives the audience a satisfactory view of the setting. By contrast, the film opens on an amply lit close-up of the strangled victim with the rope still tight around his neck, marking a clear difference between the approaches of the playwright and filmmaker: The former uses darkness as a metaphor for death, while the latter plunges us without warning into explicit visual horror.

- In keeping with the interest in theatricality that I discussed above, Hitchcock adds a scene wherein Brandon and Phillip create a key part of the "set" for their "production." In the play, it is understood from the outset that the party's food will be served from the trunk containing the corpse. In the film, the food is ready to be served in the dining room until Brandon is seized with his fiendish idea of moving everything onto the chest in the living room. We then watch the killers move candelabras onto the chest—an unmistakably funereal touch—and order their maid to place other items there too, thus creating the set before our eyes and demonstrating Hitchcock's vision of the dinner party as, like the film itself, a self-consciously theatrical experience. Hitchcock's long-take/real-time filming heightens this theatricality, moreover, allowing his camera to "attend" the party just as the guests of Brandon and Phillip do. This takes on additional resonance when we remember how much Hitchcock enjoyed putting his audience into complicity with his villains. Here he makes *himself* the accomplice of the criminals by being present as a silent witness via the continuously rolling camera, which—unlike the intermittently rolling camera of montage-based films—mimics an immanent human eye that stands in for his own.

• Hitchcock, like Clarence Darrow, was strongly opposed to capital punishment. Yet an ideological contradiction built into Hamilton's play turns upon that very issue: if Rupert turns the killers in after uncovering their crime, he will be killing *them*. Hamilton acknowledges this difficulty, and disposes of it, thus:

> BRANDON: . . . you can't give us up. Two lives can't recall one. It'd just be triple murder. You would never allow that . . . [O]ur lives are in your hands. You can't kill us. You can't kill. If you have us up now, it'd be killing us as much as if you were to run us through with that sword in your hand. You're not a murderer, Rupert.

> . . .

> RUPERT: You have brought up my own words in my face, and a man should stand by his own words. I shall never trust in logic again. You have said that I hold life cheap. You're right. I do. Your own included.

> . . .

> BRANDON: (*pale and frozen*) What are you saying? What are you doing?

> RUPERT: It is not what *I* am doing, Brandon. It is what society is going to do . . . That's its own business. But I can give you a pretty good guess, I think . . . You are going to hang, you swine! Hang! Both of you! (64–65)

- Hitchcock abbreviates this exchange, evidently because he considered it too cynical for acceptance by Production Code and Legion of Decency censors, and perhaps by audiences as well. This is a rare instance where Hitchcock weakens the drama instead of strengthening it; the film is at its murkiest and least persuasive in the final scene.

- While neither the play nor the film states explicitly that the main characters are homosexual, Hamilton implies this more strongly than Hitchcock does. Male characters put their arms around each other more than once in the play, never in the film; in the play Brandon and Kenneth lurch into a bizarre wrestling bout that's absent from the movie; and at least one bit of Hamilton's dialogue is more suggestive of an intimate marriagelike relationship than any words in the film: making excuses for Granillo's overwrought emotionalism in the third act, Brandon says to Rupert, "Granno and I have a certain trouble between us which concerns no one else. Will you kindly oblige us by going at once and leaving us to it?" Hamilton also makes Rupert a poet who gives long, florid speeches now and then, whereas Hitchcock makes him a publisher, a more "masculine" pursuit by the codes of postwar America, since it transforms language into business rather than creative art. The film also specifies that in his schoolteaching years Rupert was the housemaster of Brandon, Phillip, David, and Kenneth, providing an "innocent" rationale for his close, avuncular relationship with them.

Rope did not distinguish itself at the box office. Yet it has achieved a lasting reputation among critics and scholars in the years since its release, partly for its technical ingenuity, and perhaps more for its portrayal of gay characters at a time when even implied homosexuality was taboo in American entertainment. Accomplishing this necessitated a good deal of diplomacy, indirection, and tact on Hitchcock's part, as well as compromises and half measures that diluted the film's impact in this regard. Although the film was "obviously about homosexuals," Laurents says in *Rope Unleashed*, a 2000 documentary about the production, "the word was never mentioned—not by Hitch, not by anyone at Warner's where it was filmed. It was referred to as *it*. They were going to do a picture about *it*. And the actors [Granger and Dall] were *it*. The picture was much more successful in Europe, because I suppose in Europe they were used to *it*." The play's insinuation that Rupert had once indulged in an affair with one of the killers sank out of sight with the casting of

Stewart, a "Boy Scout" who "never had an affair with anyone." As a result, Laurents concludes, "the picture is curiously off focus and [lacks] the sexual center that it should have." Far from opening up cinematic discourse about homosexuality in the late 1940s, "it simply didn't make much of a stir one way or the other. The culture at that time was trying to deny that homosexuality even existed, and here they had well-known Hollywood players involved in it, so they didn't want to see what was there." The prevailing attitude became, "Let's not talk about this picture about *it*." With the passage of time, however, the film came to look very different to Laurents, who now finds it "one of the most sophisticated movies ever made" about homosexuality.[6]

In addition to being the first Transatlantic picture, *Rope* inaugurated Hitchcock's new Warner Bros. contract, which called for Warner's to distribute Transatlantic pictures. Not surprisingly, perhaps, *Rope* made the studio nervous about this. It appears that no one there took notice of the film's homosexual subtext or its resemblance to the Leopold and Loeb case—something else nobody wanted to talk about, according to Laurents—until it was screened as a completed picture. "Hitchcock had pulled it off," McGilligan writes; "with all his talk about technique, he'd distracted them . . . long enough to make the film *his* way, right under their noses." Urged by Paramount Pictures president Barney Balaban to cut himself off from further association with the disreputable product, Jack Warner defensively replied that Hitchcock emphatically denied any link between *Rope* and the Leopold-Loeb case, and anyway, the film takes place in New York and has no Jewish characters. Still and all, Warner added confidentially, "had [someone] called my attention to the resemblance between the case and this picture before the picture was made, Warner Bros. would not have made any deal" to release it (McGilligan 420).

The studio did release it, of course, launching a $450,000 marketing blitz in support. Initial earnings were good, thanks partly to Hitchcock's coming-attractions trailer, in which the about-to-be-murdered David Kentley banters with his girlfriend, Janet, on a park bench and leaves with a promise to see her at the party that evening; then Jimmy Stewart takes the screen and speaks straight into the camera, declaring that neither Janet nor we moviegoers will *ever see him alive again*. Ticket sales quickly diminished, though, as did the studio's publicity campaign.

Critics were divided on the picture. On the favorable end, the unsigned *Time* review called it "a rattling good melodrama" (*New Pictures*). In the middle of the spectrum, the trade paper *Variety* wished Hitchcock had "chosen a more entertaining subject" but praised the performers and the camera style (*Rope*). On the low end, Bosley Crowther wrote in *The*

New York Times that "the picture takes on a dull tone as it goes and finally ends in a fizzle which is forecast almost from the start" (Crowther). On the European front, French critics Jean-Charles Tacchella and Roger Thérond got the production history wrong in *L'Écran français,* calling *Rope* a "pre-fab" foisted on Hitchcock by the Hollywood system, but used it as evidence of the director's increasing boldness and maturity (Neupert 129). A disgruntled Lindsay Anderson wrote in the British film magazine *Sequence* that the "debilitated version of Patrick Hamilton's play" joins *The Paradine Case* and *Notorious* as "the worst of [Hitchcock's] career" (57). France and Italy banned the film; Chicago and Seattle tried to; and Canada expurgated it.

The lukewarm reception of *Rope* did not launch Transatlantic with the flourish that Hitchcock had hoped for, but the undismayed director pressed forward with plans to shoot *Under Capricorn* in the same long-take style, this time on a more expansive and complicated set. Cronyn again wrote the treatment, but this time Laurents refused to sign on for the screenplay. "What Hitchcock and Ingrid [Bergman] saw in [Simpson's novel] was a mystery to me," he remarked later. "I felt it was wrong for *all* of us" (Chandler 176). Its awful box-office performance in 1949 was a substantial factor in Transatlantic's subsequent demise, and Hitchcock quickly abandoned the real-time technique, repledging his allegiance to the time-honored tradition of montage. Gone were the near-impossible logistics of recording sound and image simultaneously, the need for lengthy retakes when the smallest thing went wrong, the lengthy rehearsals that were supposed to prepare the actors but caused Stewart to complain, "The only thing that's been rehearsed around here is the camera" (McGilligan 412). Emphatically not gone, however, was the bold inventiveness in story and style that made Hitchcock's pictures ever more Hitchcockian in time to come. Moving to Paramount in 1954, he directed and produced *Rear Window* and entered the greatest period of his career.

"I have gone all out," wrote Hamilton in the preface to his drama, "to write a horror play and make your flesh creep . . . When *Rope* is accused of delving into morbid psychologies and so forth, of being anything but a sheer thriller . . . I am at a wretched loss" (Hamilton "Foreword"). Hitchcock transmuted those morbid psychologies into something richer and stranger than Hamilton probably expected, and when the playwright saw the picture in London, he "felt bamboozled" and denounced the director on the sly (McGilligan 408). He might have consoled himself with the reflection that Hitchcock had indubitably made a horror film and that it would continue to make flesh creep many decades after its darksome concept sprang from his uneasy imagination.

Notes

1. Patrick Hamilton, "Forward," in *Rope: A Play*; Sean French, "Sean French on the roller-coaster life of Patrick Hamilton: Playwright, novelist, alcoholic." *DSpace* http://dspace. dial.pipex.com/town/parade/abj76/PG/works/notes/patrick_hamilton.shtml (accessed 5 May 2009).

2. The Repertory Players opened their production on 3 March 1929 at the Strand Theatre in London; in addition to Ireland and Shaw the cast consisted of Frederick Burtwell, Hugh Dempster, Betty Schuster, Daniel Roe, Ruth Taylor, and Robert Holmes. The production in London's West End, directed by Reginald Denham, to whom Hamilton dedicated the play, opened at the Ambassadors' Theatre on 25 April 1929; besides Ireland and Aherne the cast included Stafford Hilliard, Patrick Waddington, Lilian Oldland, Paul Gill, Alix Frizell, and Ernest Milton. It ran on Broadway with the title *Rope's End* for a hundred performances in 1929.

3. Bill Krohn and Donald Spoto are among the commentators who have misdescribed *Rope* as consisting of ten-minute takes. In fact the shots vary between four minutes thirty-seven seconds and ten minutes six seconds, and no two are the same length.

4. One was the British version (also with the title *Angel Street* in the U.S. market) starring Anton Walbrook and Diana Wynyard, directed by Thorold Dickinson, released in 1939; the other was the MGM remake, starring Ingrid Bergman and Charles Boyer, directed by George Cukor, released in 1944.

5. The film's killers are named Brandon Shaw and Phillip Morgan, while those in the play are named Wyndham Brandon and Charles Granillo, identified in the character list as "young" and "a Spaniard, young," respectively. The film substitutes Mrs. Wilson, a maid, for the play's Sabot, a French manservant. The murder victim is David Kentley in the film and Ronald Kentley in the play, and in the play he is never seen by the audience. Other names are changed as well.

6. *Rope Unleashed*, directed and produced by Laurent Bouzereau (Universal, 2000). An extra on the DVD of *Rope* from Universal.

Works Cited

Anderson, Lindsay. "Alfred Hitchcock." *Sequence* 9 (Autumn 1949). In Albert J. LaValley, ed., *Focus on Hitchcock* (Englewood Cliffs, NJ: Prentice-Hall, 1972), 48–59.

Bouzereau, Laurent, dir. *Rope Unleashed*. 2000. Rope. Dir. Laurent Bouzereau. Universal, 2000.

Chandler, Charlotte. *It's Only a Movie—Alfred Hitchcock: A Personal Biography*. New York: Simon & Schuster, 2005.

Crowther, Bosley. "*Rope*, an Exercise in Suspense Directed by Alfred Hitchcock, Is New Bill at the Globe." *The New York Times*. 27 August 1948. *NYTimes.com*. 4 May 2009 <http://movies.nytimes.com/movie/review?res=980DE3D81630E03B BC4F51DFBE668383659EDE>.

De Quincy, Thomas. "On Murder Considered as One of the Fine Arts." *Thomas De Quincey Electronic Library* 2009 <http://supervert.com/elibrary/ thomas de_quincey> (accessed 8 May 2009).

Dershowitz, Alan M. *America on Trial: Inside the Legal Battles That Transformed Our Nation*. New York: Warner Books, 2004.

Drabble, Margaret, and Jenny Stringer. "Hamilton, Anthony Walter Patrick." *The Oxford Companion to English Literature*, ed. Margaret Drabble. Oxford: Oxford University Press, 1998.

French, Sean. "On the roller-coaster life of Patrick Hamilton: playwright, novelist, alcoholic." *DSpacehttp*//dspace.dialpipe.com/town/parade/abj76/PG/works/notes/patrick_hamilton.shtml (accessed 5 May 2009).

Hamilton, Patrick. *Rope: A Play*. London: French, 2003.

Laurents, Arthur. *Original Story By: A Memoir of Broadway and Hollywood*. New York: Applause, 2001.

Leff, Leonard, J. *Hitchcock and Selznick: The Rich and Strange Collaboration of Alfred Hitchcock and David O. Selznick in Hollywood*. New York: Weidenfeld & Nicolson, 1987.

McGilligan, Patrick. *Alfred Hitchcock: A Life in Darkness and Light*. New York: ReganBooks, 2003.

Mepham, John. "Patrick Hamilton." In *The Literary Encyclopedia*. 12 November 2001 <http://www.litencyc.com/php/speople.php?rec=true&UID= 1959 (accessed 16 April 2009).

Moorhead, Caroline. *Sidney Bernstein: A Biography*. London: Cape, 1984.

Neupert, Richard. "Red Blood on White Bread: Hitchcock, Chabrol, and French Cinema." In *After Hitchcock: Influence, Imitation, and Intertextuality*, ed. David Boyd and R. Barton Palmer. Austin: University of Texas Press, 2006, 127–43.

"New Pictures, The." *Time* 13 September 1948. 4 May 2009 <http://www.time.com/time/ printout/0,8816,888513,00.html>. (accessed 4 May 2009).

"Rope." *Variety* 1 January 1948. 4 May 2009 <http://www.variety.com/review/VE1117794569.html?categoryid=31&cs=1&p=0>. (accessed 4 May 2009).

Shermer, Michael. "Creationism." *The Skeptic Encyclopedia of Pseudoscience*. Ed. Michael Shermer. Vol. 2. Santa Barbara: ABC-CLIO, 2002. 776.

Spoto, Donald. *The Dark Side of Genius: The Life of Alfred Hitchcock*. Boston: Little, Brown, 1983.

Taylor, D. J. "The Lost Worlds of Patrick Hamilton." *TLS: Times Online* 16 May 2007. 24 March 2009 < http://tls.timesonline.co.uk/article/0,,25338-2644199,00.html>. (accessed 24 March 2009).

Truffaut, François, with Helen G. Scott. Revised edition. *Hitchcock*. New York: Simon & Schuster, 1984.

12

CONSTANTINE VEREVIS

Under a Distemperate Star

Under Capricorn

TOWARD THE END OF THE FORTIES and following a decade of working in Hollywood, Alfred Hitchcock teamed up with Sidney
Bernstein to found the independent production company
Transatlantic Pictures and announced his intention to direct three films:
Rope (1948), *Under Capricorn* (1949), and *I Confess* (1953), the third
produced by Warner Bros. after the short-lived Transatlantic closed
its operations. The middle film—*Under Capricorn*—was adapted from
Helen Simpson's 1937 novel, a period piece set in New South Wales
in 1830, which tells the story of the governor's cousin, Charles Adare,
newly arrived in the colony, and the relationship he establishes with
Sam Flusky, an emancipist landowner and his aristocratic wife, the Lady
Henrietta (née) Considine. Hitchcock's version of *Under Capricorn* was
a critical and commercial failure,[1] and (despite the reevaluation of other
Hitchcock works) there exist only a small number of critical pieces (in
English) devoted to it, and even fewer that take an interest in Simpson's
novel. Rather than examine the book as a source of Hitchcock's version,
available accounts typically understand *Under Capricorn* in relation to
Hitchcock's other film work, discussing it in terms of either the director's
distinctive use of the long take or in relation to a body of gothic melodrama and/or the historical romance (Wood 326–27).[2] This chapter seeks

to extend these existing approaches, returning to Helen Simpson's *Under Capricorn* to consider Hitchcock's decision to focus mostly on the first third of the story, in particular the class and gender divisions expressed through its principal characters: Adare, Flusky, and Henrietta.

* * *

"It is extraordinary that this director [Alfred Hitchcock], responsible for some of the most brilliant British films of the 'thirties—lively, fast, and full of incident—should return to this country from Hollywood for the sake of a ponderous novelette [*Under Capricorn*], which even more than *Rope* shows a preoccupation with complicated camera movements of no dramatic value whatsoever" (G. L. 179).

These words—typical of the notices attracted by *Under Capricorn* at the time of its initial theatrical release—not only draw attention to Helen Simpson's "ponderous novelette" as a literary source (evidently one of negligible interest or value) but also to the textual and dramaturgical terms that have dominated critical accounts of the film. The first of these approaches seeks to understand Hitchcock's work as a *formal* gesture and interprets *Under Capricorn*—an almost two-hour-long feature that consists of fewer than 170 shots—stylistically (and largely *apolitically*) in relation to the more deliberate aesthetic exercise of *Rope*, a film made up of just nine shots and designed (with "invisible" edits) to appear as a single, eighty-one-minute take (Belton 367). In this approach, *Under Capricorn* is read as both a challenge to and an affirmation of Hitchcock's other work, a film that instead of *alternating* between the director's earlier use of montage and mise-en-scène (choosing one *or* the other) fuses these two modes in single, shot sequences (Belton 367–68). In the second approach, *Under Capricorn* is read as a genre film, one that recalls the gothic melodrama of *Rebecca* (1940) and anticipates—in terms of its depiction of a dysfunctional relationship—later films such as *Vertigo* (1958) and *Marnie* (1964). This approach is best represented by Lesley Brill's "Bygones Be Bygones" chapter of *The Hitchcock Romance*, a piece of writing that understands *Under Capricorn*—along with *Spellbound* (1945) and *Marnie*—as a film constructed largely within dramatic traditions of romantic love and characterized by protagonists who set out to restore or resolve past (or bygone) events (239). The distinguishing feature of Brill's chapter is that it attends to both dramatic *and* formal aspects, to see *Under Capricorn* as a complex response to social, and (some would argue) colonial and nationalist, issues. More specifically, Brill refers to Hitchcock's "obtrusively unrealistic mode"—most evident in the film's highly choreographed sequence shots—to insist that *Under Capricorn's* "dissimilarity to ordinary reality" works to uncover or depict a more urgent social reality or truth (241–51).

The tension between reality and artifice—the way Hitchcock brings an unexpected (and, in the opinion of critics and audiences of the day, *unmotivated*) level of fabrication to the historical romance—is equally evident in the first of the three "books" that make up Simpson's romantic novel. Simpson begins *Under Capricorn* with documentarylike reportage, the novel's opening lines—shadowed in the initial establishing shots and voice-over narration of Hitchcock's version—declaring: "The year, eighteen hundred and thirty-one. The place, Sydney; a city whose streets were first laid by men in chains for the easier progress of the soldiers who guarded them . . . Maps show where the habitations were gathered; they were not many, though diarists and letter-writers of the period agree they were tasteful, and showed up cleanly against the dark universal background of trees" (3). But within a few paragraphs, Simpson moves to boldly assert the story's dramatic invention: "So much for maps and for prose," she writes, "It will be seen that Sydney, in the year 1831, may very well serve as setting for a highly-colored, improbable, and yet simple story" (3–5). This mixture of fact and fancy continues into book 1's second chapter, which depicts the arrival at Sydney Cove of a government vessel conveying the incoming governor, Sir Richard Bourke. The only historical figure in Simpson's novel,[3] Bourke is accompanied by his sixth cousin, the young Irish gentleman Charles Adare. As the governor and Adare wait at South Head (in the wings, as it were) for the December calm to lift and facilitate *HMS Foxhound*'s entry to harbor (and the dramatic action to begin), Simpson contrasts Bourke's stated ambition to build a nation out of the convict "scum of England" to Adare's interest in benefiting not from employment, inheritance, marriage, or even modest ability to write poetry but rather through the social privilege afforded by his installment as cousin to the governor of the colony (8–9).

The first panel of *Under Capricorn* follows young Charles Adare's first few weeks in the New South Wales colony, including his introduction to an embittered former convict and wealthy landowner Samson Flusky and his aristocratic (but hopelessly alcoholic) wife, Henrietta. Invited to dine at Flusky's Woolloomooloo mansion, curiously named Minyago Yugilla, Adare recognizes Flusky's wife to be Lady Henrietta ("Hattie") Considine, an old friend of his elder sister, Alethea, back in Queen's County. It happened that Henrietta and Flusky, a former groom in her father's stables, eloped many years before in their native Ireland. Pursued by Hattie's enraged brother, James (renamed Dermot in the film), to a neighboring county, a struggle ensued, and Flusky was convicted of James's murder. Deported in turn to the Australian penal settlement, Flusky was followed by Hattie who turned to drink during the many years of waiting for his emancipation. Following a disagreement with the governor (and at Flusky's encouragement), Adare moves into the mansion where he discovers that it is Flusky's long-tenured and self-righteous housekeeper, Milly, who provides Henrietta with a supply of spirits in the hope that Flusky will tire of his tarnished wife and take up with her instead. Confronted by Adare, Milly resigns, whereupon Adare proceeds to restore Henrietta to her proper place in the household, and in the process becomes increasingly attached to her. The beginning of book 2 takes up the story—some three months after Adare's arrival—on the occasion of the St. Patrick's Day dance, the event Adare chooses to present the restored Lady Henrietta to social life.

Hitchcock's filmed version closely follows the narrative units of the first part of Simpson's novel, and (retrospectively) one can imagine Hitchcock's interest in the *Vertigo*-like reconstruction of Henrietta's earlier incarnation and image. At the same time, the Irish dance becomes Hitchcock's point of departure, setting up Henrietta's emergence at the ball (as Adare's first artistic creation) as the occasion of Flusky's public reclamation of his wife. This event provokes—in the film's celebrated 9.5-minute sequence shot—Henrietta's confession to Adare that it was she (not Flusky) who killed Dermot in self-defense and sets up a number of confrontations that lead (ultimately) to the restoration of the married couple, Flusky and Henrietta. In order to effect this, Hitchcock excises from the novel Adare's encounter at the dance with a young working-class woman much nearer his age—the locally born Susan Quaife—to whom he takes an immediate and strong liking, and (around the same time) Adare's enlistment of the help of "Ketch," an aboriginal who lives at the foot of Flusky's house, to undertake a risky expedition to the interior in search of gold. These deletions in turn have the effect of emptying Hitchcock's film of much of the book's local specificity. The expatriate Simpson (who resided, from her late teens, in Europe)[4] researched *Under Capricorn* during a 1937 visit to Australia, and gave the novel a sense of local flavor and accent. This she achieved, for instance, in the map of the geography of the new colony provided by Adare's first walk from the Government Domain, past a convict chain-gang shuffling and chinking its way along an "unpaved and damn dirty" King Street, to his destination, the premises of the Bank of New South Wales on George Street (15–18). More generally, such factors as Simpson's interest in (sometimes exaggerated) patterns of local dialect and depiction of indigenous peoples contributed to the novel's colorful engagement with antipodean attitudes (and issues of colonialism and race).

Simpson sets up *Under Capricorn* as a novel of fresh opportunities and (in further anticipation of Hitchcock's *Vertigo*) second chances,
but prospects in the new colony are mediated by the expectations and
prejudices of the old country. At the very outset Adare is warned that
"out here [in New South Wales] we don't talk of the past . . . [T]his is a
country of the future" (20), but at the same time Simpson makes it clear
that "life in this newest of worlds was patterned in circles upon much
the same plan as life in the old" (28). She goes on to describe a social
hierarchy that extends from the "outer darkness" of the convict world
and the "twilight existence of emancipated men," through the ranks of
tradesmen and landowners who "become visible at certain periods, like
the remoter stars," and on to "the innermost circle [of uniformed men]
which accepted the full light of His Excellency's countenance" (28).
Despite the governor's insistence that "you can't mix society, it gives
too much offence" (30), Adare quickly grows weary of the governor's
table and accepts (against Bourke's advice) an invitation from Flusky's
secretary, the gentleman-convict William Winter, to dine at the Flusky
mansion. As described by Simpson, the letter is conventional and civil
but for "the astonishing address": Minyago Yugilla, Woolloomooloo.
It is soon revealed that Flusky adopted the phrase upon hearing (but
not understanding) the words—meaning "Why weepest thou?"—used
to describe the house "by [the] blacks perpetually encamped in his garden" (31–32). Alongside the celestial metaphor of light and dark (and
by extension, "civilized" and "primitive"), the name of the mansion links
Flusky—already marginalized due to his class and ethnic origins—to the
new world and its aboriginal peoples, so disenfranchised that they do not
even figure in Simpson's stratified social model.[5]

Adare's acceptance of the dinner invitation sets in motion a flurry
of activity at the Flusky house orchestrated by the housekeeper, Milly,
who is described as "a large woman in carpet slippers, upon whom the
domestic authority of the establishment devolved; Miss Milly, surname
forgotten long ago, who could slap up a dinner, kill a rat, or . . . deliver
an excellent impromptu prayer" (32–33). Flusky spares no expense to
put on a handsome dinner for Adare and other dignitaries but is forced
to make excuses for his wife, Henrietta: "[M]y wife [who] isn't any too
good," he says "can't be with us" (38). At the dinner—separated from
Mr. Banks, a "student of aboriginal tongues and Colonial conditions"
by Henrietta's empty chair—Adare asks after Flusky's absent wife. Banks
replies by lifting an empty glass with meaningful intent. Soon after, as a
fine dessert of walnuts imported from England is being served, Henrietta
makes her first startling appearance: "[Henrietta] appeared framed in the

long window. She wore the leaf-green skirt of a ball-dress, with a cambric bodice which did not cover the rising points of her stays; red hair hung free on her magnificent shoulders, and her bare feet were shod with ancient red cloth slippers that flapped as she moved. She looked like a goddess careless of human clothing, or some heroine of antiquity run nobly mad" (39). Taking her place at the table (and even though quite drunk), Henrietta immediately recognizes Adare from her home county, and later the same evening (after Henrietta retreats to her upstairs bedroom) Flusky takes Adare into his confidence, telling him the story of the elopement and the circumstances leading to the present.

Within days of the dinner, Adare accepts Flusky's invitation to take up residence at Minyago Yugilla, a move that puts in place the romantic triangles (and tensions) that structure the opening half of *Under Capricorn*: Flusky, Henrietta, and Adare, on the one hand; and Flusky, Henrietta, and Milly, on the other hand. Adare immediately sets about his Pygmalionlike task of restoring Henrietta's noble (maiden) image, something he quite literally achieves at one early point by holding his dark green coat behind a French window to create a "mirror impromptu" for Henrietta's reflection, upon which he observes: "Henrietta Considine was the loveliest thing" (59). Throughout his residence, Adare is careful to insist (and reassure himself) that his devotion to Henrietta is nothing more than altruistic: "I am no more in love with you than with Britannia on the penny," he tells Henrietta. "I treasure you . . . Perhaps because I've never been able to write poetry . . . You're the only chance I'll ever have to make a lovely thing . . . Darling woman, you're a beauty and a queer one . . . [but] I don't go blind with you." Henrietta, too, makes her feelings (and devotion to Flusky) clear: "I am obliged to you, I like you very dearly. It is beautiful what you have been trying to do for me . . . I can say things to you that he [Flusky] would not understand. But for him I'd die . . ." (115–17). Despite these reassurances, Adare's presence destabilizes the already fragile ecology of the household. One evening, when Henrietta has taken to drink, Adare scales a trellis to her upstairs bedroom, leaving (in a spatialized metaphor exploited further in Hitchcock's version) the working-class Flusky below. Adare's brazen act so offends the righteous (and scheming) Milly that she tenders her (temporary) resignation in protest.

* * *

Hitchcock's version of *Under Capricorn* covers the narrative events of book 1 of Simpson's novel in sixteen sequences (some seventy minutes of screen time), amplifying the unrealistic elements of the novel.[6] Following the opening credits—which unfold with dramatic overture against an early map of Australia—the first of these sequences consists of a series of patently artificial establishing shots of the Sydney penal settlement over which an authoritative voice narrates significant details in the history of the colony: "In seventeen hundred and seventy, Captain Cook discovered Australia. Sixty years later the city of Sydney, capital of New South Wales, had grown on the edge of three million square miles of unknown land. The colony exported raw materials. It imported material even more raw: prisoners, many of them unjustly convicted who were to be shaped into the pioneers of a great dominion. In eighteen hundred and thirty one, King William has sent a new governor to rule the colony. And now our story begins."

As in Simpson's book, the preamble is followed by expository sequences—Governor Bourke's (Cecil Parker's) reply to a dignitary's welcome at Sydney Cove, and Adare's (Michael Wilding's) chance encounter with Flusky (Joseph Cotton) at the Bank of New South Wales—but the drama does not begin in earnest until Adare (vain and slightly bored) accepts Flusky's invitation to take dinner at his Woolloomooloo mansion. The sequence commences with Adare arriving by buggy at the gate of Flusky's property where he reads the name—Minyago Yugilla—for which the driver provides a translation: "Why weepest thou?"[7] The question posed by the mansion's mysterious title is not answered until late in the film (when a single, silver tear streaks Henrietta's face), but along with the coachman's warning (that there is "something queer" about the place), it sets up an expectation of a gothic house of terrible secrets. Adare's initial uneasy movement toward the mansion is captured (by Hitchcock, in signature style) in a series of shots alternating between a subjective view of the approaching object (mansion) and an objective view of the subject (Adare) in motion. As Adare nears the entrance of the mansion—"a storehouse of past sorrows," as Brill describes it (270)—Hitchcock begins an elaborately choreographed sequence shot. Adare hesitates at the open door and rather than ring the bell, he walks along the porch, past French doors that open to the dining room (where he catches his first glimpse of Milly [Margaret Leighton] taking instructions from Flusky) and then around to the kitchen where he makes his unannounced entrance.

Adare's movement from outside to inside is disguised by an invisible edit (of the type used in *Rope*), the camera continuing its horizontal movement through the kitchen door, into the dining room, and beyond to the hall where Flusky receives his dinner guests, the Reverend Smiley and the engineer Rigg. To Adare's mild amusement, both gentlemen proceed to explain that their wives have taken ill and convey their apologies. The men enter the parlor where Adare takes up conversation with Rigg, while Flusky moves to the hall to receive further guests.[8] Hitchcock covers the action by pulling focus back and forth between Adare and the new arrivals—Major Wilkins and Dr. McCallister—taking care to register the young Irishman's amused reaction to more apologies extended on behalf of absent wives. The light-hearted mood of the sequence—which makes abundantly clear the stigma associated not only with Flusky's dubious past and social standing but also his Irish origins—is further assisted by a brief exchange between Adare and Wilkins. The latter asks that Adare communicate to his cousin, the governor, the deplorable state of the prison, saying that he "wouldn't keep a pig in his quarters." Asked if he is a "connoisseur of pigs," Wilkins replies that keeping swine is something he would "leave to the Irish." Immediately realizing his mistake, he hurriedly adds: "Oh I beg your pardon, sir. You're an Irishman yourself . . . And so is the Governor . . . A great race. Fine body of men. Great gentlemen. Great soldiers."

With the arrival of the final caller, Attorney General Corrigan, Flusky and his guests make their way to the dining room. Flusky's hushed instruction to Milly—"[D]on't let her come down [to dinner]"—followed by Dr. McAllister's discreet inquiry into the "health" of his patient, only adds further to the mystery surrounding the house, its secrets, and Flusky's wife, Henrietta. Once the men take their places, the camera begins to track along the length of the table, pausing to frame McAllister and Rigg in medium close-up. Some small conversation begins, but the table suddenly falls silent, McAllister and Rigg looking to their left, past where Flusky is seated at the head of the table, to something off-screen. The camera resumes its track, moving to Flusky and pausing there as he slowly turns to look over his shoulder in search of that which has distracted his guests. With this cue (it should be remembered that Hitchcock had made much of his triumphant return to London with the biggest star of the day, Ingrid Bergman) and some eight minutes into the sequence (twenty-five into the film), Hitchcock cuts to a startling close-up shot of the bare feet of Lady Henrietta/Ingrid Bergman. She moves forward (face still unseen) to place her hands on Flusky's shoulders and announces in Irish lilt: "Please be seated gentlemen. I hope I'm not too late to take a glass of wine with you." As Flusky says, "My wife, gentlemen. Lady Henrietta Flusky," the camera tilts up to show Henrietta's face, in close-up, for the first time.

Following the departure of the other guests, Flusky and Adare walk together along the porch, during which time Flusky provides a partial account (one that will be completed by Henrietta's confession after the ball) of his elopement and marriage as a way of explaining their present situation. Hitchcock covers the conversation, tracking laterally to accompany the men walking along the porch, in two symmetrical long takes, each of which ends with the camera craning up to Henrietta's bedroom window. As in the previous sequence, the fluidity of the camera movement—its presentation of time as "an endless, seamless ribbon" (Rappaport 43)—contributes to a sense of inertia and to an understanding of a house haunted by traumatic memories and bygone events. Flusky talks of the young Henrietta with great love and admiration but also recalls the difficult times that followed his deportation: "We weren't the same people, the two of us, after all those years. There was nothing to talk about we wanted to talk about. What is it they say in the Bible? A great gulf fixed . . . I had my work of course, but she had nothing. You see, sh-she missed her own sort." The spatialized metaphor—the "great gulf"—that describes the couple's estrangement, along with Flusky's obvious and ongoing insecurity regarding his class difference, is given further expression in the inviolable thresholds and vertical camera movements that counterpoint the film's lateral tracks.

Essential to Hitchcock's realization of mise-en-scène of the Flusky mansion is the curved staircase that leads to Henrietta's bedroom. Hitchcock dramatizes the staircase (significantly, the site of Flusky and Henrietta's eventual reconciliation) and other spaces of the mansion, with Henrietta spending most of her time in the upstairs room and Flusky restricted to the parlor downstairs (not venturing upward until near the film's conclusion). By contrast, Adare (like Milly) traverses the divide that separates the couple. At the earlier dinner scene, when the drunken Henrietta retreats to the sanctuary of her bedroom and beckons Adare to come quickly (saying there is something in her bed), his ascent is emphasized by the camera craning up to the room with him. Upon finding nothing there, Adare humors Henrietta, pretending to shoot whatever it was that frightened her by discharging his pistol (in a sexually explicit metaphor) into the fireplace (Walker 366). In a later scene, when Henrietta reacts to Milly's humiliation of her (in the kitchen, in front of the servants) by taking to drink and refusing to come down for dinner, Adare responds by again crossing the divide, scaling a sturdy vine to Henrietta's balcony. In this case (and in a departure from anything so bold in Simpson's novel) Adare finds Henrietta in her bed and proceeds to forcibly kiss her despite her insistence that "this is all wrong, this is not the way of it."

Adare persists with his (class) rehabilitation of Henrietta, Hitchcock developing from Simpson's novel two mirror sequences in which Adare gives back her image ideal. The first (described above) is that in which Adare persuades Henrietta ("sister Hattie," he calls her) to look at her reflection in a "glass" that he has improvised by holding his jacket up behind the French door to darken the background; the second (immediately following) is that where Adare unwraps a gift of a new mirror and in the process returns "Lady Henrietta Considine" to her true (and maiden) self. This culminates in the sequence leading to the governor's ball in which Adare and Flusky wait at the foot of the staircase for (the restored) Henrietta to appear. When Henrietta descends, radiantly gowned and coiffured (in sharp contrast to her first, disheveled appearance), she asks Flusky, "How do I look, Sam?" When he replies, in typically modest fashion, "Alright," Adare is quick to seize the opportunity to underline Flusky's social awkwardness. "Alright" exclaims Adare, "the lakes of Killarney are alright. Sunrise over the Pyramids is alright. The Taj Mahal is alright. Oh, come Sam you must do better than that." When Flusky goes on offer Henrietta jewelry—a collar of rubies, concealed all the while behind his back—Adare mocks Flusky's lower-class sensibility: "Rubies with that Dress. Do you want your wife to look like a Christmas tree?" With this Adare hurries the Lady Henrietta to the coach and away to the governor's ball.

* * *

Book 2 of Simpson's *Under Capricorn* takes up the story—three months after Adare's arrival—on the occasion of the St. Patrick's Day dance at Sydney's Temperance Hall. Adare chooses the event to present the Lady Henrietta to his cousin, the governor, and to social life in the colony. At the dance, Adare meets a young working-class woman—the "currency" lass, Susan Quaife—whom Simpson describes as "a young girl, short, frail, [with] dark hair atrociously sown with gum flowers . . . She had a small pointed face like an animal, much too wide between the eyes, the mouth much too large" (135). Adare proceeds to court Susan, visiting her at her father's barbershop on George Street. Around the same time, Adare enlists the help of "Ketch," the aboriginal leader introduced (none too sympathetically) following Adare's first dinner with Flusky, to embark upon a treacherous journey north to Port Macquarie and then inland to unknown territory in search of gold. Milly has spread vile rumors that Adare and Henrietta are lovers, and Flusky (mildly suspicious of Adare) is quick to agree to fund the expedition. Convinced that Flusky has effectively delivered Adare (in a repetition of her brother's fate) to his death, Henrietta becomes despondent and turns to drink.

Book 3 thus begins with Henrietta again fighting her demons. Five months have passed with no word of Adare. Milly returns to assume control of the household, and this time it is Winter, the gentleman servant, who challenges Milly's authority. Winter is soon expelled (given his ticket back to the convict prison), but before leaving he passes to Henrietta a message left by Adare prior to his departure. The letter asks Henrietta to look up Susan Quaife, and upon doing so she invites Susan for an extended stay at the Flusky mansion, where Henrietta proceeds to groom the illiterate colonial girl in manner and appearance. Around the same time, Flusky is told that Adare has been found close to death but that he is recovering and is expected back in Sydney in December. After some weeks, Adare returns, declaring his love for Susan and desire to stay and work honestly in the colony. This, along with Susan's exposure of Milly's attempt to usurp Henrietta's place, conclusively disrupts the romantic triangles and paves the way for a restored relationship between Henrietta and Flusky.

The shorter, second book of *Under Capricorn* functions as a bridge to book 3, the latter repeating—and ultimately resolving—the tensions introduced in the first. Simpson achieves this by substituting the character of Susan Quaife for that of Charles Adare, whose search for gold happens (in keeping with the determined interiority and theatricality of the novel) entirely off-stage.[9] Upon relocating to Minyago Yugilla, Susan not only proves herself an able match for the wily Milly, but also comes to function as a surrogate daughter to the childless Henrietta. Adare returns from the expedition matured (and, like Flusky, indigenized) by his experience on the land (the Irish functioning in the novel as a third, mediating term between the colonizing British and subaltern aboriginal people). At this point, Adare asks for Susan's hand in marriage and declares his dedication to the new continent: "Susan . . . you've never put your nose out of George Street. Sydney's nothing . . . But the country's great and exciting . . . It's country that could feed the world and that you can be quiet in . . . It's got me; I can never leave it now" (276). With this, Simpson sets up the working-class Susan and nobleman Adare as a parallel (cross-class) couple to Henrietta and Flusky, the latter stating (in anticipation of the young folks' union), "It would be like us, only t'other way round," to which Henrietta replies: "With a better chance. Better hope. Both free" (283). Finally, of Adare's triumph, Henrietta concludes: "[Charles] can only work in flesh and blood. He made something of me for a while, only I was not young enough; and then, I didn't love him. She, though, Susan. He may turn her out an ode or, I don't know, a sonnet to Australia Felix" (284).

Hitchcock's decision to eliminate the character of Susan Quaife (and to a lesser extent, or less directly, that of "Ketch") has the effect of intensifying the relationship between the four remaining (principal) characters: Flusky and Henrietta, Adare and Milly. This move galvanizes the dramatic (and generic) focus of *Under Capricorn* and sets up a series of oppositional structures—past and present, love and hate, innocence and guilt (Belton 378)—and a more elaborate set of rhyming effects, specifically the way that Adare's re-creation of Henrietta Considine sets in train a series of events that closely reenact the drama of Henrietta and Flusky's elopement and the shooting of Dermot at Gretna Green many years prior. More specifically, the Hitchcock version is organized around two "couples"—Flusky and Henrietta, Adare and Milly (Wood 334)[10]—and the latter pair moves to open up social divisions in the household, with both Milly and Adare working in particular on Flusky's feelings of social inferiority. As Brill describes it, Adare and Milly form an *inverted* parallel couple to that of Flusky and Henrietta, contrasting the "mutual devotion" of the central married couple to the more "selfish, possessive desires" of the other two (261). Hitchcock in turn develops (from the literary source) these antinomies—the opposition between "true love and grace" and "false love and damnation" (262)—and works this along two axes: *temporally* through the fluidity of the sequence shot (and aforementioned emphasis on the unbroken connections between past and present) (273) and *spatially* through the camera's vertical and horizontal movements (and ideas of accessible and inaccessible space in the mansion) (Gallafent 72). Ultimately, the film resolves itself (and underscores its political dimension), not through the remaking of Henrietta in a more socially acceptable form but through the restoration of a partnership—the couple Flusky and Henrietta—"founded on a negation of social protocol and a declaration of passion and mutual respect" (Jacobowitz 21).

As previously stated, the governor's ball is the point at which Hitchcock begins his substantial revision of Simpson's novel. Adare triumphantly presents Henrietta to Bourke, but the occasion is interrupted by Flusky who arrives (driven by Milly's insinuations and his own feelings of class resentment) to reclaim his wife. Humiliated, Henrietta flees, followed by Adare. Back at the mansion—in the film's longest single take—Henrietta completes Flusky's earlier account of past events, telling Adare of her elopement, the shooting of her vengeful brother Dermot, Flusky's assumption of her guilt, his sentence and deportation, the difficult years spent waiting for his release, and their eventual reunion in the colony. Henrietta's monologue demonstrates her deep and unwavering commitment to Flusky, but Adare continues to insist that she leave with him for Ireland. Flusky's sudden arrival interrupts the intimate scene and (in a reenactment of the events described in Henrietta's confession) a pistol goes off, the lower-class Flusky again involved in the critical wounding of a nobleman (Adare). Flusky is arrested, and Henrietta's attempt to save him from prison—by publicly confessing (to Bourke and Corrigan) her initial crime—only results in talk of her extradition to Ireland to face criminal charges.

The disaster of the Irish society ball and the subsequent shooting leads to Henrietta's relapse and to Milly's return to the household. A lesser player in Simpson's novel, the scheming Milly—with her repeated and calculated attempts to play upon Flusky's sense of social inferiority and endeavor to drive his resentment of upper-class values—is the structural (darker) counterpart to Hitchcock's version of Adare. When Flusky says that (in a reversal of Henrietta's passage to New South Wales) he will sell everything and return to Ireland to be with Henrietta, Milly (who is already terrorizing Henrietta with a shrunken head) responds in desperation, undertaking to poison Henrietta. A storm breaks, and a shot of Henrietta's bedroom window streaked with rain dissolves to a close-up of Henrietta awakening, a single tear rolling down her cheek, to find Milly emptying a vial of sleeping draught into a glass of wine. Henrietta frantically calls to Flusky, whereupon Milly's plot is exposed, and she is finally expelled, down the staircase and out of their lives. Flusky and Henrietta's reconciliation takes place on the staircase (they ascend it, together, at the end of the segment), but Flusky's freedom depends on Adare's corroboration of events following the ball. For this, Henrietta goes to Government House to appeal to Adare: "You've helped me, more than anybody knows," she says. "Help me now . . . Tell them what happened . . . Give [Sam] back to me." With this, Adare recounts a limited version of the events of the evening, enabling—in a final selfless act—all charges to be dropped.

At the end of *Under Capricorn*, Hitchcock returns (in classical rhyming fashion) to the artificial, establishing shot of the harbor with which the film began. Simpson resolved her story—restored the couple, Flusky and Henrietta, to each other and their former innocence—by expelling Milly and shifting Adare's attentions to Susan, but Hitchcock's version requires the departure of both Milly and Adare. In the final sequence, Adare says his goodbyes to Flusky and Henrietta: "Don't forget me," says Henrietta (failing to register the depth of Adare's feelings for her), to which Adare replies, "I won't ever forget you." Descending a set of stone steps to a waiting rowboat, Adare tells Winter he is sorry to be leaving: "Not a bad place . . . They say there's some future for it. There must be. It's a big country." He pauses to look back over his shoulder toward Flusky and Henrietta and adds: "[but] not quite big enough." As Adare's skiff moves out of frame to the ship bound for home, the final shot settles on the couple—Flusky and Henrietta—together (again) at the top of the stairs.

Reflecting on *Under Capricorn*, Hitchcock told François Truffaut that "he had no special admiration for the [Simpson] novel" (185). Yet— as this chapter demonstrates—Hitchcock's filmed version follows the contours—especially of the first book of Simpson's work—with remarkable precision. Hitchcock not only shadows the key narrative units of the first part of the novel but also finds inspiration for some of the film's best remembered visual motifs and moments—the shrunken head, the collar of rubies, the reflection of Henrietta's image in the glass, and her first, startling appearance at the dinner—in Simpson's book. More than this, the theatricality—the staginess—of Simpson's novel inspires and enables the diagrammatic structure of Hitchcock's film: its fluid horizontal passages through time, and its craning vertical movements through space. Hitchcock's strategy is not only to remake the Simpson novel according to filters of genre convention, star image, and authorial signature but also to intensify the principal structural relationships and repetitions of the book. This effectively empties the work of much of its local specificity (and something of the associated antinomies: colonizer-colonized, primitive-civilized), but it also enhances and extends the universal themes (love-hate, innocence-guilt) of its source material. A little commented upon novel, Helen Simpson's *Under Capricorn* proves itself a valuable point of reference for Hitchcock's own "highly-colored and improbable" tale of love, sacrifice, and second chance in colonial Australia.

Notes

1. There is the notable exception of French reviewers, such as Eric Rohmer and Claude Chabrol, who considered *Under Capricorn* a great and undervalued work. See Rappaport 64 n.1.

2. Robin Wood rightly points out that the "richness" of Hitchcock's *Under Capricorn* is the result of its *multiple* sources and intertextual references: not just Simpson's novel but also the period film, melodrama, long take technique, and other Hitchcock films.

3. Historical record shows that the Irish-born Bourke, a former governor of Britain's Cape Colony (1826–28), arrived with his family in the New South Wales colony in December 1831. His governorship extended through to his resignation in January 1837.

4. Simpson was born in Sydney in 1897. As a young woman (aged 17) she went to France to continue her studies and (when war broke out) moved to England where she resided until her untimely death in 1940.

5. Simpson's depiction of the aborigines—shadowy figures at the margins of the novel—is always problematic. "Ketch" is introduced during Adare's first visit to the mansion: "On a shadowy verandah some blacks and their wives had

gathered unnoticed. When the [dining room] door closed they ran forward and began to stuff nuts into their clothes, and like so many monkeys, into the pouches of their cheeks. They sampled the wine, spitting out claret, sour stuff, but gulping brandy down . . . Suddenly their leader, a man wearing a brass half-disc engraved with the name 'Ketch,' signalled for quiet" (42–43).

6. The first sixteen sequences are (1) Introduction, (2) Governor Bourke and Adare arrive in the Colony, (3) Adare meets Flusky during a visit to the Bank of NSW, (4) Adare and Flusky walk to the Labour office, (5) Flusky engages the services of the gentleman-convict, Winter, (6) Charles tells the governor he has accepted an invitation to Flusky's mansion, (7) Charles takes dinner at the Flusky mansion and meets Hattie, (8) Flusky tells Adare about his life with Hattie, (9) Adare moves from government house to the Flusky mansion, (10) Adare tells Hattie of his determination to rehabilitate her, (11) Milly humiliates Hattie before the servants, (12) Charles climbs into Hattie's bedroom, (13) Milly resigns, (14) Milly leaves, and Hattie takes charge of the kitchen, (15) Sam, Hattie, and Charles take breakfast, (16) Charles and Hattie prepare for the ball.

7. Hitchcock would have been aware that Simpson takes the name-question "Why weepest thou?" from the New Testament story of Christ's resurrection.

8. Rigg is Hitchcock's token gesture to the "Australianness" of the piece. Rigg speaks in a broad local accent, and when he inquires as to what Adare thinks of Sydney, the Irishman's amused reply is: "I like it very much. I admire in particular the bandicoot, the rock wallaby and the duck-billed platypus . . . the spiny anteater, the cockatoo [and the] frilled lizard . . . [and] there's always the kangaroo, Mr. Rigg, always the kangaroo."

9. The 1983 Australian mini-series remake of *Under Capricorn* (dir. Rod Hardy) provides a counterpoint, making some attempt to open up the "staginess" of Simpson's novel (and cover all of its key narrative events).

10. Wood presents this in a simple chart of character and class relations: the upper-class Henrietta and Adare to one side; the lower-class Flusky and Milly to the other.

Works Cited

Belton, John. "Alfred Hitchcock's *Under Capricorn*: Montage Enhanced by Mise-en-Scène." *Quarterly Review of Film Studies* 6, no. 4 (October 1981): 365–83.

Brill, Lesley. *The Hitchcock Romance: Love and Irony in Hitchcock's Films*. Princeton: Princeton University Press, 1988.

Gallafent, Ed. "The Dandy and the Magdalen: Interpreting the Long Take in Hitchcock's *Under Capricorn* (1949)." In *Style and Meaning: Studies in the Detailed Analysis of Film*, ed. John Gibbs and Douglas Pye. Manchester: Manchester University Press, 2005, 68–84.

G. L. Rev. of *Under Capricorn*. *Monthly Film Bulletin* 16, no. 196 (October 31, 1949): 178–79.

Jacobowitz, Florence. "*Under Capricorn*: Hitchcock in Transition." *Cineaction!* 52 (2000): 18–27.

Morrison, James. "Hitchcock's Ireland: The Performance of Irish Identity in *Juno and the Paycock* and *Under Capricorn.*" In *Hitchcock: Past and Future*, ed. Richard Allen and Sam Ishii-Gonzáles. London: Routledge, 2004, 193–208.

Rappaport, Mark. "*Under Capricorn* Revisited." *Hitchcock Annual* 12 (2003–04): 42–66.

Simpson, Helen. *Under Capricorn*. London: Heinemann, 1937.

Truffaut, François. *Hitchcock*. New York: Simon & Schuster, 1983.

Walker, Michael. *Hitchcock's Motifs*. Amsterdam: Amsterdam University Press, 2005.

Wood, Robin. *Hitchcock's Films Revisited*. New York: Columbia University Press, 1989.

13

Douglas McFarland

Bruno's Game, or the Case of the Sardonic Psychopath

"As I see it," asserted Truffaut in his interviews with Hitchcock, "your approach is anti-literary and purely cinematic." "That's about the size of it," replied the director, "I am wary of literature" (319–20, 335). Hitchcock could be as dismissive toward his sources as he was at times toward his actors and even the parts they were called upon to play. He admits to Truffaut that he has a problem with strong parts: "I'm like the old lady with the Boy Scouts who're trying to help her across the street: 'But that's not where I want to go!'" (319) And so it is with his source material. Hitchcock claimed that he liked to read a work once, perhaps quickly or even haphazardly, extract a gripping situation, and then place that situation into the context of "pure cinema."

Patricia Highsmith's 1951 noir fiction *Strangers on a Train* provided Hitchcock with source material to which he responded best: a literary property that would not threaten his own imaginative control of the project. Highsmith was at the time relatively unknown, and *Strangers on a Train* was her first published novel. She was dismissed as insignificant by many working on the film version and has suffered the same fate from many contemporary film scholars. The novel has been damned as both a "breathlessly florid melodrama" (Spoto 321) and a "blatantly homophobic novel" (Corber 110). Patrick McGilligan, Hitchcock's most careful biographer, argues that the director was attracted to the "springboard situation . . . [T]he rest of the story was pretty expendable." Moreover, as McGilligan points out, Highsmith was an "unknown commodity," and thus "the screen rights wouldn't be very expensive" (442). Raymond Chandler, hired to write the screenplay, accused Highsmith of concocting a story that could not have happened in real life and hence would be of little use. But Chandler's opposition was ignored (he was eventually fired from the project). And, McGilligan argues, Hitchcock went ahead with the film because it could be done in black and white, without major stars, and would require an overall modest budget (442).

The adaptation process did not go smoothly, and this seems to have further distanced the film from its source material. After a quick read by the Hitchcocks in transit from New York to Los Angeles, the novel was handed over to Whitfield Cook to develop an initial treatment. From this Chandler produced a working script, but his contributions were mostly discarded. A young and largely unknown writer, Cenzi Ormonde, was called in to complete the work. The final version of the script included significant contributions from Barbara Keon, Alma Reville, and Hitchcock himself.

Given Chandler's dismissive attitude and the troubled process of adaptation, one might rightly question the value of conducting a source study of *Strangers on a Train*. In his analysis of Shakespeare's use of Holinshed in *Henry IV Part I*, A. R. Humphreys points out that the dramatist's "alterations [to his source material] suggest his shaping spirit of imagination" (xxiv). A similar case can be made for changes made to Highsmith's novel, all eventually approved, of course, by Hitchcock. A comparison of the film with its sources will thus highlight the "shaping spirit of imagination," in this case a collective and ultimately individual artistic phenomenon.

I

For both novel and film, the initial encounter between Bruno and Guy on the train establishes the imaginative paths that they will respectively take. The novel begins with Guy musing over his troubled relationship with his estranged wife as the train on which he rides hurtles across Texas. Given access to his silent musings, readers immediately learn of his sordid past. Miriam has cheated on him, is now pregnant with another man's baby, and had previously aborted Guy's own child. These memories cause Guy to be "nettled" (10) by shame and failure. Thoughts of Anne, the woman he now loves, dispel this painful fixation. But moments later, Guy feels uneasy over his dependence on her. It is at this unsettling moment, seemingly something more than a mere accident, that he shifts his leg and bumps Bruno's foot, initiating the growing connection between the two. With her account of Guy's troubled thoughts, Highsmith has already signaled her intention to probe beneath the surface of agitated states of mind, and this pattern takes an even more dramatic and unusual turn with the introduction of Bruno, whose psychology is explored in greater depth.

Highsmith's portrait differs considerably from the version of Bruno (played by the charismatic and good-looking Robert Walker) offered by Hitchcock. Bruno is no smoothly handsome charmer but rather something of a grotesque: "pallid undersized face . . . grey, blood shot eyes . . . poor teeth . . . odd feet . . . a shy stare . . . hair darkened brown from sweat . . . puffy eye lids . . . drunk and then drunker . . . stiff shaking hands . . . nails bitten below the quick" (11–13). Bruno's salient physical characteristic seems to be a large pimple festering at the center of his forehead, a sign perhaps of some disease or dissatisfaction working its way outward. The precise meaning of the pimple is soon confirmed. Speaking of his "agony of self-torture" (21), Bruno tells Guy that his skin is unusually smooth, even girlish because all the masculine impurities have gathered themselves in that pimple, which becomes the reflex of an arrested development. Bruno seems stuck in adolescence, suffering from acne but also from a troubled sense of his own sexuality.

Once settled in Bruno's compartment, Guy condescendingly listens to his new acquaintance's confession of Oedipal angst. Speaking of his desire to "cut in" (17) on his father, Bruno begins to breathe harder and harder, his voice turning into a shriek as he picks convulsively at his nails. In an attempt to create a conspiratorial intimacy with Guy, Bruno brags about a dare devil burglary he committed, confessing, perhaps deliberately, an inability to make his actions align with motive: "I didn't want what I took," and, "especially took what I didn't want" (22). At first unresponsive, Guy himself begins to unravel when Bruno cleverly changes the subject and asks, "You married?" (23). Almost inexplicably Guy feels his own need to confess to Bruno of that day he found Miriam with another man. If Guy, now in love with a "good" woman, has projected all his loathing of women onto his trampish wife, thereby constructing a clean dichotomy between angel and whore, Bruno refuses his erstwhile companion such easy comfort. All women, he taunts, are deceitful, promiscuous, or both. Guy, protesting little, follows Bruno down into this psychological "whirlpool." The two men share such deep rage and feelings of impotency that the compartment becomes, the narrator suggests, "a little hell" (35). Bruno goes too far, however, when he suggests that they swap murders so that they can attain their desires and keep their freedom: Guy is to eliminate the father who stands between Bruno and the fulfillment of incestuous desire, while Bruno is to rid

Guy of the troublesome wife who stands in the way of his marriage to
Anne. Guy quickly regains his composure and sneers at Bruno, "Pick up
someone else" (31), recognizing Bruno's scheme as, among other things,
a seduction. The underlying homoerotic tension has now become pal-
pable. But when Bruno reacts strongly to this rejection and degenerates
further, Guy explodes with a "burst of companionship" and links "his
arm through Bruno's" (36). Thus the strangers find themselves bound
together less by a plan for criss-crossing murders than by a Dostoyevskian
intimacy of psychological ruin. They are complicit not in plotting but
in their envy, resentment, and self-loathing.

In the remainder of the novel, the scenario of this "tiny hell" of
mutual self-destruction is played out. Bruno murders Miriam not so that
Guy will kill his father but to bind Guy to him through the intimacy
of crime. When Guy learns what Bruno has done, he is overcome with
guilt not for his complicity in the murder, but because of his emotional
and psychological one night stand with Bruno. Although Guy decides to
kill the father so as to cut Bruno off as if he were a "malignant growth"
(140), in the aftermath of the murder he no longer feels enmity toward
Bruno and recognizes that he "was like Bruno . . . he loved Bruno"
(148). Bruno himself feels no relief with the elimination of his father.
He longs "for Guy to be with him . . . He would clasp Guy's hand and to
hell with the rest of the world" (167). Bruno drowns accidentally, despite
Guy's desperate attempt to save him, and the investigation of his father's
death is officially closed. Nevertheless, Guy deteriorates rapidly, unable
to bear it alone without his "friend, his brother" (263). He is driven
eventually to confess his crime by his need for intimacy, by his inability
to live with himself, or as René Girard describes this existential state,
by "an insuperable revulsion for one's own substance"(54). The novel
asks to be read as a portrait of modern man's intense need for intimacy
and the crushing failure to locate that intimacy in anything other than
mutual self-destruction, a joint fall into an existential abyss.

II

The film version incorporates two fundamental and interrelated changes. First, the familiar Hitchcockian alibi plot has been substituted for
Highsmith's portrait of psychological degeneration. In the novel, Guy is
at a hotel in Mexico with Anne's family at the time Bruno kills Miriam
and hence has an ironclad alibi. In the film, Guy cannot account for
his whereabouts at the time of the murder, and the narrative thus
can be oriented around his need to prove himself innocent, as well as
the attempt of Bruno, who feels jilted by his friend's indifference and
betrayed by his failure to do "his murder," to incriminate him. The

celebrated cross-cutting (or perhaps criss-cross cutting) between Guy and Bruno that provides the film's climax is driven by this dynamic. Suspense depends not on psychological entanglement, so pronounced in the novel, but simply on one character's need to clear himself and the other's vengeful desire to implicate him, a variant of the "wrong man plot" that Hitchcock found so compelling. Will Bruno plant the lighter before Guy can prevent him from so doing?

Second, as suggested earlier, there is virtually no chemistry generated, homoerotic or otherwise, between the two male protagonists. The weight of the film rests not on the couple, but instead on Bruno, a "very clever fellow," and as Robert Walker portrays him, a sardonic psychopath. Guy's role thus recedes, taking with it Hitchcock's customary interest in transference of guilt. This may, in fact, result from the casting of Farley Granger in the role of Guy Haines. Hitchcock had originally wanted William Holden for the part but was forced by the studio to use Granger. One can imagine a very different relationship between the two principles if Holden had been used. At very best, transference is relegated to the periphery of the film, in the largely unexplored intimacy between Bruno and Anne's sister. In short, and as analysis of several key scenes will substantiate, Hitchcock is concerned less with Highsmith's portrait of two victims of modernity, figures for whom intimacy can be nothing other than destructive, than, to use a phrase of Tom Gunning, a "demon of modernity"(104), a figure intent upon manipulating the lives of others.

As in the novel, the opening scenes on the train establish the relationship between the characters and the direction of the narrative. Most strikingly reconfigured is Bruno. Rather than Highsmith's dissipated, pimpled creature, Hitchcock's Bruno is dapper, sophisticated, witty, and seemingly more at ease in the 1950s modernist décor of chrome and glass than is the stiff and upright Guy. After the purely accidental kick leads Bruno to recognize the tennis star, he moves fluidly across the car to sit alongside him and make his acquaintance. Although Bruno's body language might initially be suggestive of an overfriendly, even flirtatious manner, he rather quickly becomes a tease, jabbing Guy with references to Anne and Miriam, weddings and divorces, infidelities and deceits. This is the first instance in what will become Bruno's chief trait throughout the remainder of the film: he is, right up until the final frame, relentlessly sardonic. As for homoerotic tension, there is very little of it. Let us concede that Bruno has done this sort of thing before, has picked up strangers in public places. But surely his previous experiences, his expertise in these matters, would quickly tell him that Guy is not a prospect.

The remainder of the initial encounter takes place in Bruno's compartment. Unlike the corresponding space in the novel, which is a "labyrinth" of material and psychological possessions, the compartment of the film is neat and well ordered. There is nothing here to suggest the degenerative, overcrowded mental state of Highsmith's Bruno. Against this uncluttered backdrop, one object, which belongs to Guy and not to Bruno, does stand out: the lighter Anne had given Guy, appropriately engraved from A to G. Once taken out of his pocket, it sits foregrounded on the table separating Bruno and Guy, thereby literally forming a triangle with the two figures and suggesting a multiple set of psychological triangulations of desire: Guy/Anne/Bruno; Guy/Miriam/Anne; Guy/Bruno/Miriam; Bruno/Father/Mother; and Guy/Bruno/Mother. Only at this point does the room, which contains something belonging to Guy, begin to resemble a labyrinth of criss-crossing desire. A critical commonplace is that the lighter is a marker of homoerotic desire. Robert Corber, for example, suggests that the lighter "functions as a signifier of the instability of Guy's sexual identity" (113), while Michael Walker observes that Bruno "handles the lighter with a fetishistic pleasure which makes it seem like a lover's gift" (27). Robin Wood goes so far as to conclude that by leaving the lighter behind, Guy "connives at the murder of his wife" (87).

But no matter how compelling it might be that Guy has either purposefully or unconsciously left behind the lighter as a signal to Bruno of his interest in sex, murder, or both, this reading does not bear up under scrutiny. After he has proposed his criss-cross scheme, and Guy is about to leave the compartment, Bruno seeks confirmation from Guy: "We do understand one another, don't we Guy?" Guy's response is dismissive and condescending. He clearly believes he has met a strange, eccentric, and perhaps unbalanced passenger. He intends never to see Bruno again and clearly thinks that there is no reason to expect he ever will. His words, the inflection of his voice, his posture, and his facial expression all suggest a thoroughgoing dismissal of this encounter. To argue, as Corber does, that the Motion Picture Code made it necessary for Hitchcock to disguise Guy's interest in Bruno is to use the Code to justify interpretive license.

At any rate, as soon as Guy leaves, Bruno discovers that he has left the lighter. After making a move to call Guy back, he thinks better of it, sensing an opportunity. With a sardonic chuckle, he flips the lighter in the air, already plotting how he might use it. Guy has come under Bruno's power, not his spell. By the conclusion of the scene, the lighter as a signifier of desire has evaporated and has instead become a tool by which Bruno might play with the destiny of his new acquaintance. In this regard the earliest critical assessment of the film, the 1955 analysis of Borde and Chaumeton still rings true. They write, "Only eroticism is missing, although the hypothesis might be envisioned of Bruno's obscure affection for Haines" (103). While Highsmith relentlessly probes the destructive chemistry between her protagonists, Hitchcock is by and large disinterested in either establishing or exploring that chemistry. The pleasure of Hitchcock's version flows from the way it chronicles the sport of a very clever and sardonic fellow as he torments his victim. Bruno, as I said, is a demon of modernity, a victim of his era only in the sense that his game might be born out of the boredom of modern life. Hitchcock's cleverly turns depth psychology and transference of guilt into MacGuffins.[1]

Let me consider four critical set pieces that follow from this initial encounter. The first is the killing of Miriam on the island at the amusement park. The episode is framed by two examples of Bruno's sardonic wit. As he enters the park, he uses his cigarette to pop the balloon of a boy who aims a toy gun at him. As he leaves the park, after strangling Miriam, he helps a blind man across the road, his good deed for the day. Between these two instances of cool wit, he follows Miriam and her two playful friends onto the island where he murders her. It is on the way to the island in the tunnel of love where Hitchcock startlingly reveals the essentially demonic nature of Bruno's persona. The scene is shot so that the shadows of Miriam and her new friend, as he grapples her body and she flirtatiously resists, reach the point at which the shadow of Bruno begins to envelop them. It appears as if the maw of Bruno opens wide to consume his two victims. There is no sense here of triangulation of desire or that Bruno is responding to a primal scene. There is only the sense of a demon about to consume his prey.

Once on the island, Bruno carries out the murder with dispatch. The act itself is committed with a cool and passionless expediency. The celebrated shot of Bruno strangling Miriam reflected in one lens of her glasses is, contrary to the opinions of many critics, deeroticized. There is an eerie calmness as Bruno slowly and effortlessly takes Miriam to the ground, into an otherworldly, distorted space almost as if Miriam were being abducted. And in a shot even more startling than the earlier scene in the cave, we momentarily see the shape of Bruno's darkened hands as he lifts them from Miriam's throat. In the distortion of the lens, they become elongated and hooked, the claws not of a sexual pervert but of an otherworldly demon. At this moment Bruno's hands eerily resemble those of Murnau's Nosferatu, a vampire, as Gilberto Perez argues, who is feared "not for the threat of sexuality but for the threat of death (146). Adding to the spectral tone is the muted carnival music playing in the background. The moment captures a demonic display of power and control, certainly not passion or redirected sexual energy. To claim, as Robin Wood does, that the murder is a "sexual culmination for both killer and victim" (90) misses the almost antiexpressionist quality of the surreal distortion reflected in the lens of Miriam's glasses. Not even in murder is there any suggestion of intimacy.[2]

The scene in the bedroom of Bruno's father where Guy has come to expose his tormentor's plan, not to commit murder, reveals neither Bruno's expectation nor any overture to Guy to join him in bed. That said, the most blatantly erotic shot in the film does occur when Guy turns to leave. Bruno stretches back on the bed, his legs slightly spread with the gun at his hip, and the camera staring suggestively below waist level. But he is not so much attempting to seduce Guy as he is mocking him. His sexual orientation becomes a mark of sexual sophistication. Bruno opens his legs in order to rattle Guy with his perversity. One can't help but compare this to the scene in *Double Indemnity* (1944) when Barbara Stanwyck spreads her legs at an angle so that only Walter can see as he sells an insurance policy to her husband. In *Strangers*, however, there is no third party present either literally or figuratively. There is no noir triangulation; nor is Bruno, as John Orr describes him, an *homme fatal* (164). Bruno's clear intent is to unsettle and discomfort Guy by this sardonic display of sexuality.

Much has been made of the change of locale to Washington D.C. Corber, for example, unconvincingly claims that the change signifies Hitchcock's interest in "the cold-war construction of 'the homosexual' as a national security risk" (Corber 103). In this scenario, Guy finds himself vulnerable to the government's attempt to cleanse itself of dangerous "perverts." McGilligan surmises that in his initial treatment Whitfield Cook may have brought these issues into play: "The politically left-leaning Cook was . . . drafted by Hitchcock expressly because he was comfortable with sexually ambiguous characters" (McGilligan 442). This makes sense, but this radical change from the novel had to survive the subsequent series of transformations that the script went through. Ormonde, who was responsible in large measure for the final working script, claimed to be unaware of any homoerotic subtext associated with Washington D.C. or otherwise in the script or the film (McGilligan 449).

The film itself offers the best evidence of what the Washington setting signifies. The most startling use of the official city is in the shot of Bruno on the steps of the Jefferson Memorial, where he is shown looking down on Guy and Hennessey. Guy has just revealed his plans to go into politics when all this is over. A point of view shot from Guy's perspective then reveals Bruno menacingly looking down. The meaning of this sequence seems to be that Bruno now stands between Guy and a career in Washington; he seems poised to expose Guy not as a lover, but as someone complicit in murder. Robert Corber has argued that Bruno stands alongside the monument as an "emotionally unstable homosexual who threatens national security" (Corber 111). But the shot itself is far different in its visceral impact. It is not simply Bruno that appears menacing, but the memorial itself with its massive vertical columns and dark interior that symmetrically balances the dark figure of Bruno. Bruno thus seems less an impediment to politics than a part of it. And indeed, throughout much of the film, Bruno is more at home in Washington and its upper-class social circles than is Guy, whose social origins are more humble. In this scene, he seems to be mocking Guy, stripping away the façade of political power to suggest that Guy is in over his head.

The climax of the film comes with a return to the amusement park and Bruno's attempt to plant the lighter. The final shot is of Bruno entangled amidst the wreckage of the merry-go-round, symbolic perhaps of the damage he has wrought upon middle America. Although the carnival employee tells the police that Bruno, not Guy, is the killer, they are not convinced. Guy demands that Bruno provide a death bed confession to exculpate him. Instead we are treated to a final display of the unwavering sardonic persona of Bruno. His voice drips with irony: "They got you at last, huh Guy . . . I'm sorry Guy, I want to help you, but I don't know what to do." Only death extinguishes what is essential to Bruno's identity. Even the self-incriminating revelation of the lighter, coming at the moment of death, speaks to Bruno's game, not his psychosis. The image of the lighter cupped in his palm does not suggest an eroticized object. It is emblematic instead of the sardonic machinations of someone who, as Guy then tells the police, was a "very clever fellow."

In Hitchcock's film, transference of guilt is minimized, depth-psychology is avoided, and a political subtext is evoked to deepen the portrait of the villain as a "demon of modernity," not to make some larger point about American society. Like many of her subsequent works, Highsmith's novel foregrounds the destructive nature of the failed modernist desire for intimacy. Hitchcock's version is notable for its lack of interest in intimacy, sexual or otherwise. His *Strangers* is not about the menace within but about the menace of everyday life. With its multiplicity of criss-crossings and cross cuttings, its play of the arbitrary and random, its uncanny and powerful coincidences, and its web of dreadful ironies, the modernist world of Hitchcock is fundamentally sardonic. It is an existential landscape ideal for the irony Hitchcock characteristically deploys. Bruno, unlike his fictional counterpart, is a demon of modernity, not its victim; a perpetrator of dread, not its casualty. He lives according to the philosophy of Dr. Mabuse, who believes, as Gunning puts it, that "there is only one thing that is interesting anymore, playing with people and the destinies of people" (107). Need it be said that Hitchcock himself, rather than Guy, fills the role as Bruno's double? Who, after all, has popped more balloons of the unsuspecting than Hitchcock? For his alter ego to have the personality of a psychopath is in itself an example of the director's mordant and sardonic wit.

Notes

1. With respect to Bruno's Oedipal attraction to his mother and hatred of his father, the casting of Marion Lorne in the part of his mother effectively turned this very real dynamic in Highsmith's novel into something that one has difficulty taking seriously. In the novel, Bruno travels with his physically attractive mother, discusses her latest lovers, and upon one occasion is present when she dresses: "He watched his mother's legs flex as she tightened her stockings. The slim line of her legs always gave him a lift" (63). Lorne brings something almost comic to the role. We are left with a cartoon version of an unresolved Oedipal complex.

2. The killing of Miriam differs in tone and psychological resonance from the scene at the party in which Bruno almost strangles a dowager to death while staring at Anne's sister. It is obvious because of the music and the physical resemblance of Pat Hitchcock, who plays the sister, to Miriam that Bruno is reliving the murder of Miriam. Unlike the killing on the island, in this instance he does become aroused to the point of swooning. I think this has less to do with Miriam than with the sister. As I stated earlier, there does seem to be some intimacy between them. The sister flirts with Bruno at the club and has an overdeveloped interest in sex and murder. But again, this has been relegated to the periphery of the film and remains undeveloped.

Works Cited:

Borde, Raymond, and Etienne Chaumeton. *A Panorama of Film Noir*. Trans. Paul Hammond. San Francisco: City Lights Books, 2002.

Corber, Robert J. "Hitchcock's Washington." In *Hitchcock's America*, ed. Jonathan Freedman and Richard Millington. New York: Oxford University Press, 1999, 439–472.

Girard, René. *Deceit, Desire, and the Novel*. Baltimore: Johns Hopkins University Press, 1976.

Gunning, Tom. *The Films of Fritz Lang*. London: BFI, 2000.

Highsmith, Patricia. *Strangers on a Train*. New York: Norton, 2001.

Humphreys, A. R. "Introduction," *King Henry IV Part 1*. London: Methuen, 1960.

McGilligan, Patrick. *Alfred Hitchcock: A Life in Darkness and Light*. New York: Regan Books, 2003.

Orr, John. *Hitchcock and the Twentieth Century*. London: Wallflower, 2005.

Perez, Gilberto. *The Material Ghost*. Baltimore: Johns Hopkins Press, 1998.

Spoto, Donald. *The Dark Side of Genius: The Life of Alfred Hitchcock*. New York: Da Capo, 1988, rpr. ed. 1999.

Truffaut, François. *Hitchcock*. New York: Simon & Schuster, 1984.

Walker, Michael. *Hitchcock's Motifs*. Amsterdam: Amsterdam University Press, 2005.

Wood, Robin. *Hitchcock's Films Revisited: Revised Edition*. New York: Columbia University Press, 2002.

14

Ina Rae Hark

Alfred Hitchcock Presents
Dial M for Murder

The Submerged Televisuality of a Stage-to-Screen Adaptation

.

O NE OF THE MOST ORIGINAL AND INSIGHTFUL minds in my film studies classes over the years belonged to an exchange student from the American studies program at the University of Hull in the UK. Favoring spiky hair and black leather jackets—it was the early eighties—he produced sophisticated Marxist readings of the various films viewed in common for the course. For the final paper, students could choose any film they wanted, and I was initially surprised when he selected Hitchcock's *Dial M for Murder*. Upon further consideration, I concluded that the parasitical Cambridge man who uses nonproductive tennis skills to latch onto a wealthy woman and is prepared to murder her when his meal ticket appears imperiled would appeal to my student's class-conscious preoccupations. Imagine my surprise when the completed paper (brilliant as usual) turned out to focus not on class struggle but on *lamps*. They were so prominently and obtrusively displayed in the mise en scène and frame compositions, he argued, that they must have extreme thematic importance. In my comments, I was careful to praise the ingenuity of his interpretation of these light fixtures in terms of their indicia of truth and deception and their illumination of the mind of protagonist Tony Wendice before dropping the bombshell: that *Dial M for Murder* had been shot in 3-D "NaturalVision," and the lamps were not signifiers of meaning but markers of spatial relations.

The relatively scant scholarly work on *Dial M* does not replicate my student's ignorance of the film's vexed origins as a studio-mandated participation in a fad whose day would be over by the time the film was ready for release. Indeed, were it not for this novelty in its production history, one wonders if it would be written about at all. While I would agree that how Hitchcock represented Frederick Knott's serviceable clockwork plot on film is of more interest than any deep themes or subtle characterizations within that plot, the dual focus of most analysis on the 3-D effects on the one hand and the conservative retention of and limitation to most of the play's stage-bound mechanics on the other has overlooked a crucial element of the adaptation. Alternately excised and unspoken, there is a discourse about television in the play's origins and dialogue that the film disavows, much as 3-D was one of several ploys the film industry adopted in the early 1950s to combat this upstart living room medium. However, the film Hitchcock shot in multiplane format was doomed to be viewed predominantly in its "flat" configuration, and that configuration partakes to a considerable degree in the aesthetics of early television drama. Perhaps it is not purely coincidental that a year and a half after its release, Hitchcock associated himself with just that sort of television drama when *Alfred Hitchcock Presents* premiered on CBS.

Staging Three-Dimensional Space

In choosing to film *Dial M*, Hitchcock was not initially thinking to add anything new and different to his repertoire. Biographies and memoirs present varying degrees of linkage between his decision to adapt a stage play for his next project and Warners' desire that the film be shot in 3-D. Bill Krohn writes that Hitchcock flew to Chicago to see a stage production "at the suggestion of Warners executives" (130). Charlotte Chandler reports that Jack Cardiff claimed to have been the first to alert Hitchcock to *Dial M* when it was broadcast on the BBC months prior to its stage debut (207). Donald Spoto more vaguely asserts that the director "began poring over recent plays in an effort to find something he could film" (342). In retrospect Hitchcock confided to Chandler that adapting a stage play served both his own purposes and those of the studio: "If one is going to make a 3-D movie, the most convenient medium to adapt it from is the stage. A play is seen in 3-D normally, and within the confines of a stage set it's much easier to control the added complications of shooting in 3-D. When I made *Dial M*, I was running for cover while waiting for the muse. A play is a safety net picture" (Chandler 207).

These remarks, combined with the hiring of Frederick Knott to write the adapted screenplay of his own dramatic text, indicate that there was nothing in the events or characters of *Dial M* that called forth his muse. The complex backstory that precedes the rising of the curtain, and which is later recounted in painfully long exposition, could easily have been used to open up the proceedings. One can imagine a film commencing with the troubled Wendice marriage and taking Margot's point of view through the affair with Mark, the decision to end it, and the reconciliation with Tony. Then we would follow the subsequent mystery of the stolen handbag and love letter and the blackmail notes—asking for a payoff that was never retrieved. Only when Tony began his negotiations with Swann would the surprising explanation be revealed. Alternately we could follow Tony's plotting from its inception. But Hitchcock was clearly committed to the "safety net" of having a very controlled environment in which to grapple with the challenges of 3-D photography. Only in modifying the lackluster depiction of the murder attempt in Knott's playtext did the director indulge his mastery of suspense by having Tony delayed in making the call that will bring his wife within the assailant's grasp, putting the audience in the uncomfortable position of hoping that Swann will not leave before the phone begins its fatal ringing. And he spent take after take making sure that the gleam on the blade of the descending scissors was just right.

For the rest, he accepted the challenge of making nonstop exposition gripping. As many commentators on *Dial M* have noted, Hitchcock in the decade 1944–54 became enamored of the challenge of restricting the space in which a film's events would take place or to which the camera had access, with *Dial M* joining *Lifeboat, Rope* (another stage play), and the film that followed it, *Rear Window*. But the director was stymied and frustrated by the bulk of the 3-D double camera. Grace Kelly recalled that "with this camera it was like having to go into a boxing ring with your hands tied. . . . the frustrations and the things he wanted to do and the technicians said, 'Oh no, with the camera we can't do this and we can't do that' " (Spoto 343). However, in previous experiments with shooting in limited settings, he had been free to compensate with ingenious technical solutions, for instance the " 'collapsible' apartment in *Rope*" (Conrad 213). Most 3-D pictures were shot outside on spacious back lots, so the unwieldy mechanism was less of a handicap. Having decided to stay in the Wendices' flat—the play's one location—as much as possible, he found himself in a bind.

One solution was to exploit the mise en scène fully. Spoto reports that Hitchcock personally selected the set dressings (344). Their distinguishing features were their multiplicity and their textures and patterns. The desk and an armoire are fashioned from wood with complex inlaid designs. The couch and matching chair are done in a floral pattern, flowers being one dominant in the overall art direction. Lamp bases are ceramics with raised decorations or painted scenes. Two medieval-style wooden chairs flank the table by the entryway, their high backs displaying intricate carvings. The walls are crowded with paintings, drawings, and photographs, many in large, ornate frames. The finishings of the interior architecture of the flat are also the opposite of simple, suggesting the interior of a Greek temple. A classical design is etched into the chair rails; the mantel rises above the fireplace on three oversize pediments; the lintel above the door so central to the plot echoes the shape of this mantel; and twin lions' heads are carved just below it on the upper ends of the two door jambs. The built-in bookcase and the other door frames pick up this architecture as well. Various chinoiserie, decorative boxes, liquor decanters, and Tony's tennis trophies crowd an already cluttered décor. It comes as quite a relief to the viewer when a character is framed against the lower, blank half of a door or Tony sinks into a somewhat worn, plain brown plush armchair.

This riot of textures allows Hitchcock to utilize three-dimensional space without constantly invoking the frontal assaults on the camera so stereotypical of 3-D films. By situating "his actors behind a fussy clutter of monumentalized bric-a-brac" (Hoberman), he reinforces the idea of the flat being a maze where Tony expertly navigates obstacles to force other characters to play the parts he has scripted for them. As B. Kite astutely observes, echoing my student, in a review of a 3-D screening of the film in 2003: "Alfred Hitchcock's only excursion into 3-D, *Dial M for Murder* stars Ray Milland, Grace Kelly, and a bilge green ceramic lamp . . . No preening prima donna (and wisely not, since it is not an attractive lamp), it is a loyal corps member in the object ballet for keys, stockings, telephone, and corpse that underlies the plot. Nothing if not pliable, it also serves as an anchor in the squalls and eddies of space unleashed by the 3-D process" (Kite). (Kite, I'm afraid, slights the great work in support of the desk lamp with the bright yellow china base overlaid by a colorful Oriental design. Knocked to the ground during the struggle between Margot and Swann, it assumes its framing duties undamaged after the intermission.)

Kite's remarks make clear that the focal points of the narrative are not in fact people but objects: the three keys that pass from hand to hand; the purloined letter; the scissors that allow Margot to fend off

Swann; her handbag; the identical raincoats that figure in Hubbard's ruse; the banknotes in the blue attaché case. *Dial M* contains far fewer close-ups than a typical film, partly because the massive double-camera was difficult to focus in such shots.[1] Most of the ones it does contain focus on these objects rather than human faces, and the few "coming at you!" 3-D effects feature them as well, when Margot seems to reach out into the audience for the scissors or the keys that are heading for locks appear poised to open up the spectator's eyeball. The director always had a fondness for significant objects that carried meaning beyond their pragmatic uses: "Things, yes, forged signatures of all things Hitchcock. As Godard noted in the *Histoire(s) du Cinéma*, we forget the stories of Hitchcock's films, 'but we remember a row of bottles, a pair of spectacles, a sheet of music, a bunch of keys.'" Perhaps it was the importance of so many objects to the structure of Knott's plot that led him to select it in the first place.

Presented in a theater, *Dial M*'s signifying props present a problem, in that there are no such things as close-ups. Elaborate stage business has to be devised to make sure that audiences notice the various key transfers; the acting edition contains detailed advice about how to stage Swann's attack on Margot with real and with collapsible scissors and offers hints to avoid injury to the back of the actress portraying her (4, 37). Similarly, stage productions must employ creative blocking to make sure that a spectator's attention focuses on the most important actions and speeches when that immobile audience member has the entire stage in view and may choose to look anywhere he or she pleases. Although many reviewers found Hitchcock's film "stagey," *Dial M* in fact shows how the camera can do the work of limiting the audience's perspective to the optimum view of what is played out onstage, a view the stage director can only hope to achieve, and even to perspectives no stage production could achieve. (Sheldon Hall notes that the shot of Margot and Mark taken from behind the bar table could only be achieved if the camera were embedded in one of the walls of the apartment [248].)

While most filmed plays do not restrict themselves to the perspective of a member of the audience, they do occasionally pull back for a long shot that replicates the entire view available through the invisible fourth wall. Hitchcock studiously avoids access to such a view, even at the climactic moment when Tony opens the entry door with the key only Swann's accomplice could have found, and we would expect the camera to pull back and reveal his spatial relationship to Hubbard, Mark, and Margot as he is hoist on his own petard. Indeed, the director reconfigures the mise en scène so that entering and exiting that door—the central axis of the stage setting—is replaced by the opposition to the desk and windows of the bedroom and fireplace. The bedroom is Margot's space; we never see Tony in it, and after her conviction he even moves his bed into the living room. The mantel holds his tennis trophies, and he destroys Swann's scarf in its grate—a change from the play, in which he simply puts it into his pocket for later disposal. The apex of all his scheming is the desk with its sinister telephone, the instrument that summons Swann to be the agent of Margot's doom and that draws her into that trap, only to have her be the one to deal out death to Swann. Moreover, Tony's being summoned to the phone by Margot calling during the theatrical intermission while Swann rehearses the murder plan signals us that the final victim of Tony's plotting will be Tony himself. And he does nonchalantly concede victory to a Hubbard who stands behind that desk ready to phone Scotland Yard, placing the incriminating latch key on its surface. As Peter Bordonaro observes, Hitchcock "turned the set ninety degrees"; the audience is effectively positioned in the wings instead of the auditorium much of the time, and "the least frequent [camera view] is the one the play used consistently" (176).

There are other examples of Hitchcock preserving the play's theatricality yet turning it on its head. His use of a camera situated in a pit for a number of shots and the foregrounding of objects between the camera and the actors have been remarked upon as efforts to give a view from the stalls (Almeireda 33). Yet at key moments the camera ascends to an impossible balcony directly above the stage; rather than a proscenium arch, which distances the audience with a demarcation between the top and sides of the stage, the director places his barriers either across the bottom of the frame (the row of liquor bottles, the headboard of Tony's bed) or on either of its bottom corners (usually a chair or a table with a lamp).

If *Dial M*'s mise en scène is theatrical with a twist, then his camerawork is cinematic with a theatrical purpose. More so than in most of Hitchcock's films, the camera eschews both subjectivity and independent agency. It instead focuses on or follows exactly the character(s) or objects a stage director would want the spectator to concentrate on at any given moment. If a character it is involved with moves, the camera follows. Dolly-in shots within the flat are restricted to instances when Hitchcock wants to increase the emotional intensity, as in the case of Swann realizing that Tony intends for him to murder Margot or Hubbard's suspicions of Margot coming to the fore. (In the latter shot, as Hubbard and Margot speak in profile two-shot behind the table with the green bisque lamp, the movement forward of the huge 3-D camera causes the shade of that sturdy performer to quiver in perfect sympathy with Margot's growing distress and confusion.) Cross-cutting and shot-reverse shot sequences bear some of the usual cinematic meanings of parallelism and opposition but also do not often stray from holding on the character who is speaking; rare cuts to reaction shots are thus pointed up to a pronounced degree, as when we cut to Tony with his back turned, freezing in place when Mark and Margot joke about planning the perfect murder.

Frequent critiques of *Dial M* as "stagey" underestimate the skill with which the director transforms the language of theatrical blocking, which seeks to draw the attention of a stationary spectator to the most important elements within the proscenium, to a cinematic language in which the camera becomes a mobile spectator, always getting the view it needs to have. Companion critiques of the film as "talky" are, however, much more valid. Plays, to be sure, favor dialogue over action when compared to films or novels. And the dramatic action they stage often presents the culmination of a much more complicated chain of circumstances that have to be conveyed to the audience through exposition. But most plays, even serviceable thriller-mysteries, also use dialogue to allow characters to enunciate the deeper significance of their relationships to each other, to express emotional states, to debate issues and ideas. *Dial M*, subtitled *A Collage for Voices*, is, by contrast, almost entirely narrational. The playscript or the film's soundtrack could be broadcast unchanged as an installment of Margot's favorite radio program, ·*Saturday Night Theatre*, and the only onstage action that would not be made perfectly clear is Tony's hunt for the key in Swann's pockets after the murder and his substitution of the stocking for the scarf.

The four predominant modes of speech are to explicate, to interrogate, to manipulate, and to improvise. Explication dominates up through the murder attempt. Margot fills Mark in on the strange blackmail attempt and her reconciliation with Tony. In the long colloquy with Swann, Tony manages to relate his discovery of the affair, reveal himself as the figure behind the theft of the letter and the blackmail notes, provide the history of Swann's life since leaving Cambridge, and explain his elaborate plan to have Swann murder his wife. Rightly described as a director or stage manager of the action by reviewers, Tony is equally a stand-in for the playwright, explicating the play's premise in minute detail before blocking the proposed murder for Swann while the camera gives a bird's eye view of the geography of the flat in which it will take place. There is no higher praise of Hitchcock's direction and Ray Milland's performance than to note that they make this massive "info dump" mesmerizing.

If explicators speak for the playwright/screenwriter, interrogators represent the skeptical audience member who might question the logic of his plot construction. Since the vital role of Margot's key passing from hand to hand would be irrelevant if gaining entry to the street door required a key, Tony twice responds to an inquiry about this point with, "The street door is never locked." And since the audience might find it rather convenient that Margot walks all the way around the desk to answer the phone, thus making it possible for a man hiding behind the curtains to attack her unawares, Hubbard asks that very question. Margot replies that it is her habit, because it enables her to have pen and paper handy, should she need to write anything down. In the play's first act, Swann fulfills the interrogator function, bringing up many reasons why the plan might fail and then challenging Tony to cope with his simply telling the police of the murder-for-hire plot in which he has been asked to participate. After Swann's death, interrogation naturally falls to Hubbard, who exposes the contradictions in both Margot's lies and truthful statements and then catches Tony out on his rationale for spending large sums of cash. Even Tony gets a turn, however, as he tries to show up the holes in Mark's fabricated scenario of Tony having set up Margot's murder, a scenario that is of course not fabricated at all and that he himself has implemented, with modifications forced on him by circumstances. It is telling that Mark, presented as a shameless hack writer, figures out that Swann must have left the key outside the department before entering it, the one fact not previously available to the audience because it, like Tony, thinks that Margot's missing key is back in her handbag after being transferred from Swann's pocket. Only Hubbard eventually realizes that we are dealing with *three* keys, including Swann's own latch key. The audience and the criminal, in possession of knowledge concealed from all the other characters, outsmart themselves through overconfidence in their privileged epistemological access.

Interrogation is not Tony's forte, however; he is an explicator par excellence, equally assured when putting forth a plan that has been months in the making or improvising lie after lie to launch an alternate plan to be rid of his wife when it goes disastrously wrong. (We have a preview of his improvisational skills when he must deal with Margot's unexpected decision to go to the movies instead of staying home on Saturday night.) He is unflappable and unstoppable as long as he is talking. It is only the action of recovering the key under the stair carpet that establishes his guilt. Nevertheless, as interrogation takes on a greater significance as the play proceeds, Tony talks less and thus commands the camera less.[2] His dominance is linked to the night, while Hubbard, committed to bringing truth to light rather than concealing it, only appears in scenes set during the daytime, which constitute the last half of the film.

Margot, the only woman in the cast, suffers from being the subject of narration rather that the subject who narrates, especially after the murder attempt. Tony at first will not let her tell her story to the police and then scripts an alternative version for her to relate when she does talk to them. Hubbard constructs a damning version of the events of the fateful night that convinces a jury of her guilt. In Hitchcock's surrealistic representation of the trial, Margot looks straight into the camera, unable to utter a word, while various colors flash across a plain background as male voices question and condemn her. She does get to interrogate Hubbard's account of how he cracked the case by his discovery that the key in her handbag wouldn't open the door to the Wendices' flat, but she shares this task with Mark. She does at least get to see Tony reduced to her status as narrated subject. That the screenplay adds dialogue in which Hubbard explains to Mark and Margot what Tony is doing as he discovers that Margot's key won't open the door, while at the same time the camera shows these actions clearly to the audience, makes clear how far Tony has fallen from his status as narrator par excellence.[3]

"Television—for My Sins"

Because of the constraints of working with the 3-D camera, *Dial M* is a stylistic hybrid, neither completely theatrical nor cinematic in its aesthetic. Setting aside the manipulations of the mise en scène to achieve a three-dimensional effect, the camera work, editing, and composition do, however, strikingly resemble a third aesthetic: that of television. A preponderance of medium to full shots, framing that follows the main actor in a scene, and dialogue trumping action characterize that medium, especially those studio-bound dramas that were current in the fifties. And it is no wonder that *Dial M* as a drama should particularly call forth a televisual style. Its very first production had been for television. Knott initially failed to convince any theatrical management in London to stage the play (his first), so he submitted it to the BBC, which broadcast it live as an installment of *BBC Sunday Night Theatre* on 23 March 1952. No kinescopes were made, so we can have no idea how it was photographed, and it is doubtful Hitchcock, in the United States at the time, could ever have seen it.

One wonders whether the joking about Max Halliday's travails as an overworked writer of television mysteries was already in the play or was added after its broadcast led to a successful West End theatrical engagement. At any rate, the play's dialogue is scathing about the rock-bottom quality of television writing. Max apparently has to crank out a teleplay a week, and he describes a system in which he has three hats for murderer, victim, and motive, pulling out one from each when inspiration wanes, as if he were dramatizing a game of *Clue*. He confesses to Margot that it is about as artistic as sorting the week's washing "but better paid. It's no more frustrating than writing plays that aren't produced or novels that aren't published . . . And don't forget: It all goes to prove that WITO makes teeth bright—white and *bite*" (Knott 7).

Warner Bros. had no interest in reminding audiences of the availability of television programming, even if portrayed sarcastically as hack work, so this dialogue is all gone from the film, although the exchange remains in which Tony asks if Mark (as Max is called in the film) writes for the radio, and Mark replies, "Television—for my sins." The sins here were rather the studio's, driving the consummate preplanner Hitchcock to cope with obstacles created by a technology that most working on the project knew would be passé before the film was even released. The director must have sympathized with Tony's desperate improvisations when his carefully scripted murder plan goes off the rails. Even more ironic is the fact that what the director improvised looked amazingly like the hated televisual competition, only in color, with glossier production values and no commercial interruptions.[4]

Different obstacles confronted Hitchcock when he directed episodes of *Alfred Hitchcock Presents*. They included, as enumerated by Thomas Leitch, "accelerated television production schedules and diminished television budgets, which prescribed limited camera set-ups, mostly on rudimentary indoor sets, over a three-day production allowance" (60). Yet, viewing a Hitchcock-directed episode such as "The Case of Mr. Pelham," produced during the first season in 1955, one sees parallels to *Dial M* at once. The camera moves with the actors, and shots are mostly medium to full. There are more interior locations than one apartment, but none of them is particularly spacious. A great amount of the dialogue is expository, as Pelham explains to a psychiatrist the existence of an apparent double who is taking over his life. One significant clue to the mystery is a latch key, which receives a privileged close-up. Another close-up shows Pelham's finger dialing home on his office phone. When emotions become intense, the camera dollies in from medium close-up to close-up. And there is a unique and unsettling swish pan, when the double, whom Pelham and the audience suspect may be a figment of his imagination, enters through a doorway in the presence of a neutral witness. Of course, every episode of *Alfred Hitchcock Presents* foregrounds the connection between television and narrativity, by providing the droll director-as-narrator to bookend the episode and lead into the advertisements for the WITOs of the day.

One might speculate that Hitchcock's curiosity about filming in restricted spaces and the various aesthetic experiments he made in that vein over a ten-year period was answered when he discovered how one coped with the restrictions of television drama. It is a fact that he never made one of these films again once he became involved with *Alfred Hitchcock Presents*; when he used his television crew to make a movie, they came up with the ultracinematic *Psycho*. Perhaps the director after 1955 better appreciated the opportunities *not* to have to film in close quarters that the cinema offered. And perhaps also the first step to this realization was the arduous task of filming a play meant to distinguish itself visually from television that turned out to reflect what one could achieve with the expert deployment of televisuality.

Notes

1. This was the reason Hitchcock had to construct a giant telephone and wooden finger to get his desired extreme close-up of Tony dialing the "M" for the Maida Vale exchange.

2. It is probably because of the inextricability of plot and dialogue that Hitchcock most of the time subordinates the camera to whomever is speaking. The flashy camera movement generally appears when there is momentary lack of conversation: the circling shots of Margot kissing Mark and menaced by Swann; the swish pan when Tony tosses the bundle of cash Swann's way, the tracking shots approaching the apartment building from the outside.

3. Tony does, even in defeat, retake control of conversation and camera when he reassumes the duties of charming host as if he were buying drinks for a successful tennis rival. This dialogue, also, was an addition not in the play.

4. My first encounters with Hitchcock's 1950s films came when they were broadcast on network television in the 1960s. *Dial M* was an early favorite, preferred over such greater works as *Vertigo* and *North by Northwest*. Looking back, this may have happened because the small screen diminishes those other films' visual brilliance, while *Dial M* with its talking heads is a perfect match for the medium that evolved from radio rather than silent pictures.

Works Cited

Almeireda, Michael. "Double Take: Hitchcock." *Sight and Sound* 52 (1982): 33.

Bordonaro, Peter. "*Dial M for Murder*: A Play by Frederick Knott/a Film by Alfred Hitchcock." *Sight and Sound* (1976): 176.

Chandler, Charlotte. *It's Only a Movie: Alfred Hitchcock, a Personal Biography*. New York: Simon & Schuster, 2005.

Conrad, Peter. *The Hitchcock Murders*. London: Faber & Faber, 2000.

Hall, Sheldon. "*Dial M for Murder*." *Film History* 16 (2004): 248.

Hoberman, J. "The Stunt Men." *The Village Voice*. <http://www.villagevoice.com/film/9914,hoberman,4777,20.html> (accessed 7–13 April 1999).

Kite, B. "Staged Fright, Dial E for Experiment: Hitch crafts a master's maze in his sole foray into 3-D filmmaking." *The Village Voice*. 31 December 2003–06 January 2004. http://www.villagevoice.com/film/0353,kite,49910,20.html.

Knott, Frederick. *Dial "M" for Murder.* New York: Dramatists Play Service, 1982.

Krohn, Bill. *Hitchcock at Work.* London: Phaidon, 2000.

Leitch, Thomas. "The Outer Circle: Hitchcock on Television." *Alfred Hitchcock: Centenary Essays.* Ed. Richard Allen and S. Ishii Gonzales. London: BFI, 1999, 59–71.

Spoto, Donald. *The Dark Side of Genius:The Life of Alfred Hitchcock.* Boston: Little, Brown, 1983.

15

PAMELA ROBERTSON WOJCIK

The Author of This Claptrap

Cornell Woolrich, Alfred Hitchcock, and *Rear Window*

The author of this claptrap is Cornell Woolrich, a popular drugstore author, and Hollywood's affinity for him is easily understandable. What isn't understandable, however, is Alfred Hitchcock's association with this.

—McCarten, *The New Yorker*

ᖃ

MOST OF THE CRITICAL DISCOURSE AROUND *Rear Window* celebrates it as an auteurist film with technical and thematic links to other Hitchcock works. In auteurist accounts, *Rear Window* stands as an exemplar of Hitchcock's manipulation of point-of-view and sound; it contains numerous Hitchcock motifs, including his famous cameos, his use of handbags and jewelry, and a fall from a high place; it is one of his single-set films, along with *Lifeboat*, *Rope*, and *Dial M for Murder*; it is one of the Jimmy Stewart films, along with *Rope*,

213

The Man Who Knew Too Much, and *Vertigo*; and it is one of the Grace Kelly films, sandwiched between *Dial M for Murder* and *To Catch a Thief.* Most notably, *Rear Window* has been dissected and debated as a film about voyeurism, in discussions that link the film to stylistic and thematic voyeurism in other Hitchcock films but that also claim the film as the consummate example of cinematic and patriarchal voyeurism.[1]

The quote above, however, taken from John McCarten's 1954 review of *Rear Window* in *The New Yorker*, reminds us that the film's current acclaim and canonical status as the quintessential Hitchcock film were by no means obvious to all from the start. McCarten not only dismissed the film's plot as implausible but also cast aspersion on some of the features most venerated in the film today—Jeff's voyeurism, the delineation of the neighbors, and, especially, the limited mise-en-scène of the film. For McCarten, the single set reflected not Hitchcock's genius but his "footless ambition to make a movie that stands absolutely still." In McCarten's view, the film was "claptrap," easily aligned with Cornell Woolrich's "drugstore" writing, but unworthy of Hitchcock, who "used to" make "satisfactory" films.

McCarten differs from most critics who attribute little of the film's power to its original source, Woolrich's short story "Rear Window." They view the film as, at most, a "makeover" of the story (Renzi 151). Nonetheless, McCarten's view of Woolrich as "author of this claptrap" has support in a key copyright decision, *Stewart vs. Abend* 495 U.S. 207 (1990). The case stems from a claim by Sheldon Abend, a literary agent, that the film infringed on his copyright when it was shown on television and rereleased in theaters and on videocassette in the 1970s. Abend had acquired the rights to the story "Rear Window," for $650 from Chase Manhattan Bank, which administered Woolrich's estate. Although Woolrich had promised to renew the movie rights when the copyright expired, he died in 1968 before he could do so, and Abend refused to honor his prior agreement to renew. In a decision written by Justice Sandra Day O'Connor, upholding a 1988 ruling by the United States Court of Appeals for the Ninth Circuit, *Stewart vs. Abend* argues that the owner of the copyright to the original source, in this case, "Rear Window," in essence, trumps the copyright to the "derivative" work, in this case, the film *Rear Window*. Therefore, according to *Stewart vs. Abend*, control of the original work snaps back to the author, or author's successors, when renewal comes up. Accordingly, authors are protected from being deprived of the "surprising" value of their work. And, thus, the writer of the source material can be viewed, legally, as author, in some significant sense, of the adapted work.

While *Stewart vs. Abend* has far-reaching implications for many classic films (so many stories from so many forgotten underpaid authors), the case also acknowledges the complexities of film authorship and the relationship between source and adaptation. In his opinion for the Court of Appeals, Justice Pregerson awarded damages and royalties to Abend but refused to impose an injunction on the film, arguing that it would cause "great injustice" to the owners of the film (James Stewart, Hitchcock, and MCA). In part, Pregerson appraised the significant work and money behind the "derivative" work: "Defendants invested substantial money, effort, and talent in creating the "Rear Window" film." For Pregerson, "The "Rear Window" film resulted from the collaborative efforts of many talented individuals other than Cornell Woolrich, the author of the underlying story. The success of the movie resulted in large part from factors completely unrelated to the underlying story." In particular, Pregerson argued, the "tremendous success" of the film "initially and upon its re-release is attributable in significant measure to, inter alia, the outstanding performance of its stars—Grace Kelly and James Stewart—and the brilliant directing of Alfred Hitchcock." At the same time, Pregerson pointed to the impossibility of clearly separating source from adaptation. He distinguished between quotation and adaptation when he argued that it would be impossible for the owners of the film *Rear Window* to separate out the "new matter" in the derivative work and simply renew the copyright for that material. He further acknowledged that, while it is clear that the film was based on the story, it is not at all clear how much of the story was used in the film.

While *Stewart vs. Abend* points to how complicated is the film's relationship to the underlying story, the relationship becomes even more complex when we trace the genesis of the story and its route to the screen.[2] Woolrich first submitted the story under the title "Murder from a Fixed Viewpoint" in September 1941. It was published with the title "It Had to Be Murder" in the February 1942 issue of *Dime Detective Magazine* and reprinted under that name in *The Saint Mystery Magazine* a year later. Then, in 1944, it was included in an anthology, *After-Dinner Story*, under a new title, "Rear Window," and using Woolrich's frequent pseudonym William Irish. Thus, before the story was even optioned, it had three different names, two different "authors," and could be categorized as a detective story, a mystery or an "after dinner" thriller.

The first-person story, in brief, involves a man, whom we discover, only in the last line, has broken his leg and who consequently spends his time watching the neighbors outside his window. After noticing some changes in the habits of one neighbor, he begins to suspect that he has killed his wife. Unable to convince the police, the narrator seeks to prove it himself. He is aided by his black "houseman," Sam. Without being told of the narrator's suspicions, Sam finds the man's address and name, Thorwald; delivers an ominous note to him; and messes up Thorwald's apartment to scare him. The narrator finally confirms his suspicions when he notices a "hitch" in his view: as Thorwald and a prospective tenant stand at the same moment in the exact spot in their respective kitchens, the prospective tenant is raised higher than Thorwald. The narrator realizes that the woman is buried in the newly remodeled kitchen of the unrented apartment. As the narrator figures out the mystery, he also draws the killer to his apartment but is saved at the last minute by the police, who have also come to believe in Thorwald's guilt.

The inspiration for the story, according to Woolrich's autobiography, *Blues of a Lifetime*, can be traced to an instance when Woolrich was typing near a window in his undershirt and realized, after hearing some muffled giggling outside, that he was being spied on by two teenage girls (21–22).[3] Whatever the fascination, the experience of spying through a window, or being spied on, made its way into several Woolrich stories, both before and after *Rear Window*. For instance, in "Wake Up with Death" from 1937, Woolrich has a character wake up in a hotel room to find a dead woman on the floor by his bed. The man then receives a call from someone claiming to have witnessed him murder the woman from a window opposite. "Silhouette" from 1939 has a couple witness what appears to be a man strangling a woman behind the shade of a window. "The Boy Cried Murder" from 1947, later retitled "Fire Escape" and made into the movie *The Window*, places a young boy sleeping on a fire escape to witness a murder through an open window. Yet, despite Woolrich's clear interest in window voyeurism, Steven DeRosa argues, "It Had to Be Murder" likely had its origin in a story by H. G. Wells called "Through a Window" (13).

Published in 1895, it concerns a man confined to his couch in London overlooking the Thames who passes time during his illness watching passersby and activities outside. Eventually, he spies a madman being pursued by armed men. As he sits helplessly watching, the madman enters his flat through the window. The main character, Bailey, throws medicine bottles at the madman until he is shot and killed by one of the pursuers.

Woolrich's story began its progress to the screen in May 1945 when Paramount Pictures acquired the rights to "Rear Window" along with five other Woolrich stories. None were made at the time. In 1950, the producer and agent Leland Hayward bought "Rear Window" for his company, Orange Productions. In 1951, Heyward tried unsuccessfully to interest his former client Hitchcock in the property. In 1952, still hoping to entice Hitchcock, Heyward asked playwright and director Joshua Logan to write a treatment. Hayward sent Logan's treatment to Lew Wasserman, then president of MCA, and within a month contracts were drawn to make the film at Paramount.

Logan's treatment was presumably shown to Hitchcock, along with Woolrich's story, and it already contains some key elements of what will become *Rear Window*. Logan makes Jeff something of a playboy, with a cast full of lipstick marks and women's signatures. He adds a love interest, Trink, who seeks to marry Jeff. She wins his respect when she (rather than Sam) crosses over to Thorwald's apartment to "muss it up" and then "acts" her way out of danger.

When Hitchcock agreed to make "Rear Window," he selected the writer John Michael Hayes, a fellow MCA client. Prior to this, Hayes was known primarily as a radio writer, though he was recognized as having potential for the movies. In DeRosa's account, Hayes wrote a treatment, while Hitchcock was still busy in postproduction for *Dial M for Murder*. According to Hayes, he and Hitchcock had conversations, but Hitchcock "gave me my head and let me go ahead and write the screenplay" (DeRosa, 30). Hayes' treatment added more detailed accounts of the neighbors and made Jeff a photographer, to give him a reason to have broken his leg and to provide a contrast to his temporary sedentary lifestyle. Hayes kept the love interest, but named her Lisa. He made Lisa a model, giving her his own wife's profession. As casting was settled, Lisa and Jeff were shaped to fit the qualities of Grace Kelly and James Stewart, respectively. Hayes also replaced Sam with Stella, an insurance company nurse, viewing her as the film's comic relief, something he felt strongly necessary and something he had appreciated in earlier Hitchcock films. He switched the mode of discovery from the "hitch" in the kitchen to mismatched photos of the garden, showing that something had been buried in the zinnias. And he added a key detail of suspense by having Jeff be asleep when Thorwald exits the apartment with a woman. His treatment also included material that does not make it to the final script, involving Thorwald's telling reaction to a crime magazine headline at a newsstand, and Lisa spying on Thorwald at a construction site, both incidents taking place well beyond the bounds of the *Rear Window* view.

Hayes turned in this treatment on 11 September 1953 and had a first draft script done by October 14. This draft differed little from the treatment. At that point, Hayes and Hitchcock began working on a shooting script, which was complete by the end of November. This shooting script became the final screenplay and differed in a few significant points from Hayes' draft. In particular, Hitchcock changed a neighbor portrayed as a cheating husband in the Hayes script to the couple with the dog, allowing the dog to pinpoint the discrepancy in the garden. He also referred Hayes to two of his favorite real-life British murder cases for some key inspiration. The first case, that of Patrick Mahon's unsuccessful dismemberment of his wife, focused attention on the problem of how to dispose of Mrs. Thorwald's head. The second case, that of Dr. Crippen, involved a man who poisoned his wife, cut her up, and buried her in his basement. He then pawned her jewelry and gave some to his mistress, which became incriminating evidence leading to his arrest. Thus, where Hayes had Lisa seek a crime magazine as evidence in Thorwald's flat, Hitchcock suggested the more evocative wedding ring.

There is some dispute as to how much of the screenplay was written by Hayes and how much by Hitchcock. In his deposition for *Stewart vs. Abend*, Hitchcock claimed to have "dictated" the entire script.[4] Asked about the process of writing the film, Hitchcock says that he "engaged a writer," named

> John Michael Hayes, and the writing was done in my office, with his typewriter, in my office, and there are many witnesses if you need them. In other words, I dictate the picture. I did not hand the book to the writer and say, "Make a screenplay of this," which is a custom of the business. But it doesn't apply to me, because I make a specific type of film, and I dictate to him what I want to go into the story, and just as a matter of interest, the reason that is done is because I want it my way, in my style, and I would say that in the process there is twenty percent Cornell Woolrich and eighty percent Hitchcock.

Hitchcock's deposition never mentions Logan's treatment and discounts both Hayes' contribution and Woolrich's. Pressed to explain what he means by "dictate," Hitchcock explains that he talked with Hayes and ultimately told him what to write. In Hitchcock's account, not only the matter of the head, the ring, and the dog, but also the love interest, the addition of the neighbors, the invention of Stella, and Jeff's profession as a photographer were all "dictated" by him. Allotting Hayes no percentage of the content, Hitchcock claims that Hayes only wrote dialogue. With reference to Woolrich, Hitchcock says that after reading "Rear Window" in 1952, he threw it away and never reread it. And, according to Woolrich, Hitchcock never acknowledged his debt to the author and refused even to send him a ticket to the New York premiere (Nevins 383).

Hitchcock's account firmly inhabits the myth of the auteur as sole and primary author of a film: "I am actually a writer, producer, and director. But I never take credit for it." However, as even this brief report indicates, the writing of a film is not something that happens once, in an office. It takes place in stages, with the help of numerous personnel, and involves multiple formulations, recastings, and reshapings. At a minimum, here, we have to recognize Woolrich, Logan, Hayes, and Hitchcock as each contributing to the overall script. Each of their contributions is fed by personal influences and inspirations, ranging from personal experience, to true crime stories, to stories by H. G. Wells. They are fostered and enabled by editors, agents, producers, and studios. Beyond that, of course, the film reflects the contributions of its stars, set designers, sound designer, editor, composer, cameraman, and more. At the same time, "Rear Window," in all its permutations, circulates in a world of other texts—other stories, other films, star texts, gossip, and more. And it is marked by the historical context in which it is produced, a context shaped by world-historical events, everyday occurrences, and artistic production.[5]

New Matter

In considering the relationship between "Rear Window," and *Rear Window*, it is not a question of whether they are different. They are. But, are they different in kind? To what degree does the "new matter" of the "derivative" text alter, fundamentally, the "underlying story?" The basic premise of the text and its eventual outcome are little changed at all. Each version shows "murder from a fixed viewpoint." Crucially, the story's setting in a Greenwich Village courtyard is unchanged from story to film. If not texts "that stand absolutely still," they are both texts that are rooted in one place. Certainly, though, the text is Hollywood-ized. The first-person narration is dropped. The "new matter" stitches the murder investigation to a love story; adds characters and a richly detailed mise-en-scène to flesh out the scenario; gives the characters depth and traits that determine their actions; and ensures that all added material contributes to the plot, forming a tight cause-and-effect narrative.

Many of these changes occur in tandem with the deletion of Sam from the original text. Where Sam serves simultaneously as caretaker to the wounded Jeff and as aid to his investigation, the film divides his role between the romantic interest, Lisa, and the comedic relief, Stella. This may be the most significant change in the text. In what follows, I discuss Sam, Lisa, and Stella to suggest ways in which the "new matter" both represses and reflects the queer erotics of the original story.

Sam

In order to fully understand the effect of Sam's removal from the text, it is useful to review his role. In part, Sam's entrances and exits serve as punctuation in the story, marking the days and nights. He enters the first morning just after the narrator notices that Mrs. Thorwald's shade hasn't been raised. He carries out a tray just before Thorwald returns home at the end of the day and says goodbye as the narrator ponders why Thorwald doesn't go to the bedroom to see his wife. He returns the next morning after Jeff observes Thorwald's insomnia and at noon the third and final day.

Sam also serves a somewhat stereotypical role as the authenticating black man. Before he goes home on the first full day, he pauses, "head down," and then shakes his head "slightly as if at something he didn't like":

"You know what that means? My old mammy told it to me, and she never told me a lie in her life. I never once seen it to miss, either."

"What, the cricket?"

"Any time you hear one of them things, that's a sign of death—some-place close around . . . It's somewhere close by, though. Somewhere not very far off. Got to be."

While the narrator deduces the fact of Mrs. Thorwald's death slowly and carefully, compiling evidence to back up his intuition, Sam's superstition leads him straight to the truth. However, Sam does not apply his knowledge to the situation at hand. He merely asserts the truth, that the cricket indicates death and is unaware of the narrator's worries about Mrs. Thorwald.

Primarily, Sam serves the narrator as an adjunct to investigate out-side the confines of the house. Three times, Sam goes to Thorwald's—once, to get his name and address, once to deliver a note reading "What have you done with her?" and once to "disturb" Thorwald's room and show someone's been in there" (28). Despite being Jeff's helper, Sam is not his confidant. Jeff never tells Sam of his suspicions and refuses to answer any questions. Nonetheless, Sam performs his work, saying, " 'I'm just an easy mark for you" (28).

The racially charged hierarchical homosocial relationship between Sam and Jeff also underscores a queer erotics in the story. Nancy Steffen-Fluhr has posited a queer reading of "Rear Window," interpreting the exchange of glances between Thorwald and Jeff in view of Woolrich's own closeted homosexuality" (69–90).[6] My use of the word *queer*, here, signifies partially, with Steffen-Fluhr, that there are gay elements and gay references in these texts; but, more importantly, I would suggest, along with Alexander Doty, that "basically heterocentrist texts can contain queer elements" and that there are a "wide range of positions within culture that are 'queer' or non-, anti-, or contra-straight" Whether Jeff is "really" queer, the text plays with the narrator's "closeted" desire and knowledge, the desire for concealment and disclosure. Observing Thorwald's reaction to the anonymous note, Jeff describes himself and Thorwald as caught in a double-bind desire: "Two minds with but one thought, turned inside-out in my case. How to keep it hidden, how to see that it wasn't kept hidden" (24). Jeff wishes to bring the murder "out of the closet," to makes its secret known. At the same time, Jeff frequently fails to recognize clear signs of disclosure, failing to read the codes of murder. He calls this "delayed action": a "formless uneasiness, a disembodied suspicion" until his suspicions finally "land" into "certainty" (12). "Coming out," according to Eve Kosofksy Sedgwick, often involves retrospective recognition: "Coming out is a matter of crystallizing intuitions or convictions that had been in the air for a while already and had already established their own power-circuits of silent contempt, silent blackmail, silent glamorization, silent complicity" (79–80). The text as a whole participates in the logic of the "delayed action," or "coming out," as readers discover only in the last line that Jeff has a cast on his leg, ultimately an anticlimactic disclosure.

Along with these other elements, Sam's relationship with Jeff supports a queer reading. On the one hand, their relationship seems hierarchical and determined by Sam's status, as "houseman," and his race. On the other hand, Sam and Jeff seem to have an intimacy. They have "been together ten years" (28). At one point, Jeff calls Sam and asks, "Whatever became of that spyglass we used to have, when we were bumming around on that cabin-cruiser that season" (23)? The use of "we" and "bumming around" here both seem to indicate a more intimate relationship that master and servant. Further, if Jeff "cruises" Thorwald, Sam triangulates and enables Jeff's relationship with Thorwald. Sam mediates between Jeff and Thorwald, moving between the two men's interior spaces—both spaces intended to be hidden from each other, frequently dark—provoking Thorwald out of his apartment so that he enters Jeff's. Sam doubles for Jeff, doing his bidding. He also doubles for Thorwald—he enters his apartment while Jeff watches him through his rear window, and, at the end, Jeff experiences a "delayed action" as he mistakenly thinks he hears Sam return to the house when, in fact, it is Thorwald, coming to kill him.

Lisa and Stella

In dividing Sam's role between Lisa and Stella, the film alters and expands the roles. Where Sam is kept in the dark about the narrator's suspicions, Lisa and Stella are both drawn in. As they become more convinced of

Jeff's theories, and more complicit with his gaze, so do we. In sharing his gaze, and serving as his accomplices, Lisa and Stella also remove whatever traces of gay cruising might be in the gaze. Instead, Laura Mulvey famously positions the film as a paradigmatic instance of the "male gaze" in her essay "Visual Pleasure and Narrative Cinema." In *Rear Window*, according to Mulvey, Hitchcock "takes scopophilic eroticism as the subject of the film . . . [T]he look is central to the plot, oscillating between voyeurism and fetishistic fascination" (36). For Mulvey, the moment at which Lisa crosses over to Thorwald's room is particularly significant: "When she crosses the barrier between his room and the block opposite, their relationship is reborn erotically. He does not merely watch her through his lens, a distant meaningful image, he also sees her as a guilty intruder exposed by a dangerous man threatening her with punishment, and thus finally saves her" (37). In this reading, Jeff's voyeurism and the concomitant point-of-view shots are particularly directed at images of women—the Bathing Beauties, Miss Torso—and also entail a sadistic component, insofar as Lisa is most endangered when she becomes the object of Jeff's gaze.[7]

While the addition of Lisa, especially, can be read as heterosexualizing the text, Jeff's resistance to marrying Lisa also raises the specter of homosexuality. On the one hand, Jeff's desire to remain a bachelor suits a 1950s playboy ideology. But the confirmed bachelor, however, is always suspect in fifties ideology. Stella, especially, voices concern about Jeff's desires. She pathologizes him, remarking, "You got a hormone deficiency . . . Those Bathing Beauties you've been watching haven't raised your temperature one degree in a month." When Jeff tells her that Lisa wants to get married, she responds, "That's normal." When he says he does not, she tells him, "That's abnormal." Then, when he claims that Lisa lacks what he wants, Stella asks, "Is what you want something you can discuss?" Like Stella, Lisa also suggests that Jeff's bachelorhood may conceal secret desires: "If you're saying all this because you don't want to tell me the truth, because you're hiding something from me, then maybe I can understand."

Jeff's fear of marriage gets mapped onto class discourse. When Jeff complains to his editor, Gunnison, that he will end up married to a nagging wife, Gunnison reminds him, "Wives don't nag anymore. They discuss." Jeff counters, "Maybe in the high-rent district they discuss. In my neighborhood, they still nag." He later describes Lisa as "too sophisticated": "She belongs to that rarified atmosphere of Park Avenue. You know, expensive restaurants, literary cocktail parties." Jeff identifies Lisa with her Upper East Side neighborhood, where, we learn, she lives on E. Sixty-Third Street, and declaims, "If she was only ordinary." Here Jeff produces a theory of what sociologists refer to as residential differentiation, or the idea that similar people live close to each other; or, in other words, that residential areas differ from one another and are internally homogenous (Harvey 108–24).

By "ordinary," Jeff partly means "not rich." In his categorization of apartments, John Hancock lists three different kinds of "high-rent" apartments, any of which might appear in Lisa's Park Avenue neighborhood. These are "palatial" apartments (those with their own private entrance), "luxury" apartments (generally high-rise), and "owner occupied" apartments (overlapping with the other two previous categories). Against these, Hancock notes that "by far the largest number of multi-family dwellings" are "efficiency" apartments, compact one-to-five room units in small walk-up buildings several stories high (160–71). Unlike the Park Avenue world of expansive "high rent" apartments, Jeff's courtyard neighborhood consists of small efficiency apartments—studios, one bedrooms, railroad flats, and Jeff's own two-room apartment in an "old fashioned stoop house," according to Woolrich (33). Within a modest income level, the tenants in Jeff's courtyard represent the lower rung on what Constance Perrin refers to as "the ladder of life: from renter to owner." Renters, who tend to be less socially esteemed than owners, tend to be young, single, or in small households (Hancock 157–58). In *Rear Window*, many, but not all, are single—Miss Lonelyhearts, the Composer, Miss Torso, the Bathing Beauties, and Jeff. Married tenants include the Thorwalds, the middle-aged Childless Couple, the Newlyweds, and the family on the private balcony. The latter are the only ones with children, and they live in the seemingly larger and possibly more expensive apartment with the private balcony. As numerous critics have pointed out, they have a negligible presence in the film. Missing from this "ordinary" array of tenants are nonwhites, the elderly, and—surprising for the Village location—gays.

Along with the lack of wealth, "ordinary," in Jeff's terms, signals bohemian and unconventional. To a large degree, the tenants are artists—Miss Torso, who is a dancer; the Composer; the Sculptress; and Jeff, the photographer. Many of these tenants are home during the day—rehearsing, composing, sculpting. Their apartments function as combined live-work spaces and show traces of work—the Composer's piano; the Sculptress' work-in-progress, titled "Hunger"; Jeff's cameras, negatives, flashbulbs, lenses, and photographs. Although nobody is explicitly homosexual, the Greenwich Village setting, as well as the bohemianism of the tenants, all evoke the Village's most famously bohemian residents, gays and lesbians. Thus, in marking Lisa as too "ordinary," Jeff also marks her as too "straight."

Of course, Jeff is wrong about Lisa or wrong to think that her sophistication blocks her from fitting into his world. As Stella advises, "people with sense belong wherever they're put." Lisa supports Stella's view when she queries, "What is so different about it here from over there? Or any place, that one person couldn't live in both places just as easily?" Part of Lisa's transformation in Jeff's eyes will occur not just through her transformation into spectacle, or victim, or adventuress, but through her entrance into the courtyard and into the "ordinary" apartment across the way. Rather than simply the victory of heterosexist ideals, or Jeff's capitulation to Lisa's desires, the promised marriage at the end can also be read queerly, as Lisa is masculinized, in pants, and secreting her true feminine identity and desires by concealing her fashion magazine.

Stella also contributes to a queer reading. In her discussion of character actors, Patricia White notes how often supporting characters embody marginal identities mean to support "the imbricated ideologies of heterosexual romance and white American hegemony. They prop up a very particular representational order" (93). According to White, character actors not only serve as the repository for sexual and ethnic difference in classical Hollywood cinema but also support the dominant by providing a measure of difference against which the dominant can assert itself. Thus it is not merely the case that queer encoded characters are relegated to minor roles but also that the dominant requires reinforcement from these marginal identities; and, therefore, minor roles are necessarily rife with queer encoded characters who serve to buttress the main character's heterosexuality.

In part, in line with the film's mapping of identity onto place, Stella's marginal status is highlighted through the logic of residential differentiation. Ritter's thick Brooklyn accent signifies not only ethnicity and class but also place. This place, Brooklyn, signals a certain kind of authenticity at the same time that it relegates her to the margins. Just as the "queer" characters are rarely explicitly identified as such, Stella's residence is never mentioned but nonetheless transparent. As a Brooklyn native, Stella serves to "prop up" a "representational order" in which Manhattan is the representational dominant, and the boroughs are the marginalized communities. In addition, as White notes, Thelma Ritter, like Eve Arden, is one of many female character actresses whose sardonic persona has made her a favorite for lesbian viewers. And her role as insurance company nurse furthers a queer reading. White claims, "Nurses, secretaries, career women, nuns, companions, and housekeepers connote, not lesbian identity, but a deviation from heterosexualized femininity."

The "new matter" of *Rear Window* can be seen as sublimating the queer erotics of the original story. In replacing Sam with Lisa and Stella, the film transforms a potentially gay story into a determinedly heterosexual one. Instead of a confirmed bachelor with a black male companion, Jeff is a would-be playboy, moved, by film's end, to heterosexual marriage. However, aspects of the original story's queer erotics linger. Queer elements manifest in elements of plot, casting, and dialogue, as well as, subtly, in the film's sense of place and residential differentiation. If Woolrich's ultimate contribution to the film is something generally ignored or suppressed in discussions of the film, it nonetheless surfaces, bubbling through the text, in those queer elements. Adapting "Rear Window," then, can be seen as a game of concealment and disclosure: "How to keep it hidden, how to see that it wasn't kept hidden."

Notes

1. The following are some of the more prominent books and essays reflecting these views: Elisabeth Weis, *The Silent Scream: Alfred Hitchcock's Sound Track* (Toronto: Associated University Presses, 1982); John Fawell, *Hitchcock's Rear Window: The Well-Made Film* (Carbondale: Southern Illinois University Press, 2001); Michael Walker, *Hitchcock's Motifs* (Amsterdam: Amsterdam University Press, 2005); Eric Rohmer and Claude Chabrol, *Hitchcock: The First Forty-Four Films*, trans. Stanley Hochman (New York: Ungar, 1979); Robin Wood, *Hitchcock's Films Revisited*, revised edition (New York: Columbia University Press, 2002); Robert Stam and Roberta Pearson, "Hitchcock's *Rear Window*: Reflexivity and the Critique of Voyeurism," in *A Hitchcock Reader*, ed. Marshall Deutelbaum and Leland Pogue (Ames: Iowa State University Press, 1986), 193–206; Laura Mulvey, "Visual Pleasure and Narrative Cinema," in *Issues in Feminist Film Criticism*, ed. Patricia Erens (Bloomington: Indiana University Press, 1990), 28–40.

2. My understanding of the various treatments and scripts leading to the film is drawn from Steven DeRosa, *Writing with Hitchcock: The Collaboration of Alfred Hitchcock and John Michael Hayes*, and Renzi, 143–50.

3. See also Francis M. Nevins, *Cornell Woolrich: First You Dream, Then You Die*, 24.

4. Excerpts from the deposition can be found at DeRosa's website, http://stevenderosa.com/writingwithhitchcock/ontherecord.html.

5. If we consider the context for the film's production, we could read the film in relation to Cold War politics. See, for instance, Robert J. Corber, "Resisting History: *Rear Window* and the Limits of Postwar Settlement." Or, we might consider the way in which the characters are shaped to adhere to the actors' star images and performance style. For an excellent discussion of star persona and performance in *Rear Window*, see James Naremore, *Acting in the Cinema*. Or we might consider resemblances between the film's characters and

those in the real world. Lisa, especially, has been interpreted as having real-life counterparts. Hayes said he based Lisa on his own wife. Hitchcock supposedly admitted that Lisa was based on Anita Colby, a one-time fashion model and beauty expert who became a top account executive in the advertising department at *Harper's Bazaar* and then "Feminine Director" at the Selznick Studio. Others have argued that Lisa and Jeff's relationship was modeled on the affair between Ingrid Bergman and photographer Robert Capa. See DeRosa, 20; and Steve Cohen, "*Rear Window*: The Untold Story."

    6. See also Nevins, 76.

    7. In the story, this dynamic plays between Jeff and Sam: "I watched him at it. There wasn't any way I could protect him, now that he was in there . . . He must have been tense doing it. I was twice as tense, watching him do it." Woolrich, "Rear Window," 29.

Works Cited

Cohen, Steve. "*Rear Window*: The Untold Story." *Columbia Film View* 8, no. 1 (Winter/Spring 1990): 2–7.

Corber, Robert J. "Resisting History: *Rear Window* and the Limits of Postwar Settlement." In *In the Name of National Security: Hitchcock, Homophobia, and the Political Construction of Gender in Postwar America*. Durham, NC: Duke University Press, 1993. 83–110

DeRosa, Steven. *Writing with Hitchcock: The Collaboration of Alfred Hitchcock and John Michael Hayes*. New York: Faber & Faber, 2001.

Doty, Alexander. *Making Things Perfectly Queer: Interpreting Mass Culture*. Minneapolis: University of Minnesota Press, 1993.

Hancock, John. "The Apartment House in Urban America." In *Buildings and Society: Essay on the Social Development of the Built Environment*, ed. Anthony King. Boston: Routledge, Kegan & Paul, 1980, 151–189.

Harvey, David. *The Urban Experience*. Baltimore, MD: The Johns Hopkins University Press, 1989.

McCarten, John. "Hitchcock Confined Again." *The New Yorker*, 7 August 1954, 50–51.

Naremore, James. *Acting in the Cinema*. Berkeley: University of California Press, 1988.

Nevins, Francis M. *Cornell Woolrich: First You Dream, Then You Die*. New York: The Mysterious Press, 1988.

Perrin, Constance. *Everything in Its Place: Social Order and Land Use in America*. Princeton, NJ: Princeton University Press, 1977.

Renzi, Thomas C. *Cornell Woolrich: From Pulp Noir to Film Noir* (Jefferson, NC: McFarland, 2006.

Sedgwick, Eve Kosofsky. *Epistemology of the Closet*. Berkeley: University of California Press, 1990.

Steffen-Fluhr, Nancy. "Disabled by Desire: Body Doubles in 'Rear Window' (1942), *Rear Window* (1954), and *Rear Window* (1998)." *Post Script* 22, no. 3 (Summer 2003): 69–90.

White, Patricia. "Supporting Character: The Queer Career of Agnes Moorehead."
     In *Out in Culture: Gay, Lesbian, and Queer Essays on Popular Cultur,*. ed.
     Corey Creekmur and Alexander Doty. Durham, NC: Duke University
     Press, 1995, 91–114.
Woolrich, Cornell. *Blues of a Lifetime: The Autobiography of Cornell Woolrich.* Ed.
     Mark T. Bassett. Bowling Green, OH: Bowling Green State University
     Press, 1991.
Woolrich, Cornell. "Rear Window" and Four Short Novels. New York: Ballantine
     Books, 1984.

16

HILARY RADNER

To Catch a Thief

Light Reading on a Dark Topic

I N DAVID DODGE'S *TO CATCH A THIEF* (1952), the protagonist, John Robie, finds himself listening to a young woman, who clearly has set her sights on him: "He realized, with great surprise, that he had · forgotten the leash he wore and the danger Francie represented to him. He was genuinely enjoying her company" (87).

The leash is metaphorical, but the danger is real enough for John Robie, best known to cinephiles and film scholars as the character played by Cary Grant in Alfred Hitchcock's *To Catch a Thief* (1955). Dodge's creation shares with his Hitchcockian avatar a deep ambivalence about heterosexuality and marriage. Not unlike his cinematic prototype, Robie begins the novel as a contented bachelor and concludes it as a member of a belated and vexed, if ultimately enthusiastic, couple. A comparison between Dodge's novel and Hitchcock's film highlights, on the one hand, the extent to which Hitchcock's preoccupations were a product of his times and, on the other, the personal inflections that he brought to what is generally considered to be "the crisis of post-war masculinity" (Berry 104). By emphasizing the erotic dimension of the tale, articulating the leading couple through a series of triangles, and replacing a fascination with the body by a certain sexual perversity, Hitchcock makes the story his own.

229

David Dodge was a mystery and travel writer who enjoyed a degree of success in the postwar years. His most popular book, reprinted in both *Cosmopolitan Magazine* and *Readers' Digest*, by most accounts was *To Catch a Thief*, in which he combines his flair for the description of scenery with a mildly exhilarating, if somewhat convoluted caper plot (Brandt).[1] The novel recounts the adventures of a retired thief, John Robie, wrongly accused of perpetuating as series of jewel heists on the Côte d'Azur, who must catch the real criminal in order to exonerate himself. In the process, Robie finds himself caught in turn by an attractive American heiress, Frances or Francie Stevens. Hitchcock purchased the rights to the novel before it was published possibly because it fell into the category "thriller/romance" (a genre with which he had long been associated) in a setting that lent itself to postwar culture's thirst for exotic imagery (Weiler). Tourism was already a significant force in the public imaginary, a fact of which Dodge was well aware, for he routinely wrote for travel magazines such as *Holiday* (Brandt).

Concomitantly with the flourishing of leisure culture, women's consumer culture was a significant economic force, a fact that neither Hitchcock nor Dodge ignored. Dodge imbues the novel with the elements of woman's culture propagated by women's magazines of the day, creating a fantasy of exotic affluence for the middle-class housewife confined to the routines of suburbia. For example, Danielle, the female thief of the novel's title, who is ultimately apprehended by Robie, wears, as a rule, elegant contemporary beachwear. The bikini was considered such an extreme fashion statement at the time that Danielle's task at her place of employment often consisted of "simply standing around ornamentally in a Bikini so gentlemen could admire her figure and possibly patronize the *plage*" (41, 50).[2] At the other end of the social spectrum, The Carlton, at which Frances Stevens, her mother Mrs. Stevens and Robie in his guise as Conrad Burns were guests, continues to welcome travelers to its luxurious premises.[3] Francie herself often seems to have stepped off the pages of *Vogue*:

> She wore a black, strapless evening gown; very plain in the way that only Dior or Schiaparelli could make plain black dresses. She had done her hair so as to expose her ears, with sapphire earrings at the ear lobes. The blue of the stones at her throat and ears, matching and emphasizing the blue of her eyes, produced an effect that could not have been accidental. It was as if she had chosen deliberately to display the necklace and earrings, not as ornaments but as they might be displayed on a model for themselves. (78)

Similarly, Mrs. Stevens' jewelry is often described in detail, including prices, as in the case of a small pin, which the novel carefully notes was purchased at "Cartier's" (37): "It was a small diamond dog with emerald eyes and a diamond leash ending in an emerald safety clasp . . . Even at a snap guess, it represented an investment of five or six thousand dollars" (36–37). The novel participates in the creation of a context that encourages the cultivation of consumer culture and the association of consumer culture with femininity, invoking the icons of high fashion by name as well as offering details such as designer names that lend a sense of authenticity to these descriptions. The novel's descriptions of Danielle presage the explosion of youth culture later in the decade with such stars as Brigitte Bardot, also associated with the Riviera, and the development of a new kind of disposable, cheap fashion, represented by the bikini that was directed at very young women (and not at their mothers).

While Hitchcock (perhaps constrained by Hollywood protocol) did not embrace this new youth culture that emphasized the body and relatively inexpensive body-revealing fashions,[4] he was attuned to the female audience.[5] This affinity is most obviously manifested in his collaboration with Edith Head, who is credited with popularizing Dior's New Look by dressing actresses such as Grace Kelly in films such as *To Catch a Thief*. Importantly, Head was nominated for an Academy Award for her work on this film. Hitchcock himself confides to François Truffaut in his discussion of *To Catch a Thief* that: "I'd like point out that it's generally the woman who has the final say on which picture a couple is going to see. In fact, it's generally the woman who will decide, later on, whether it was a good or bad picture" (226). Thus both Hitchcock and Dodge are mindful of their women viewers and readers in terms of creating a milieu that is attractive and inviting to them. Similarly, in terms of plot, the film, preserving the premise and the location, reprises much of its material from the novel often, however, condensing and redistributing it. For example, Robie as played by Cary Grant presents a very brief version of his life early in the film to the insurance agent with whom he enters into an alliance. In the novel, Robie presents a much longer version of his life to Francie, near the middle of the novel, emphasizing the pathos of his plight (116–17). Grant's Robie is cynical and unrepentant; Dodge's protagonist is prey to existential angst and regret regarding his profession, a product of a difficult childhood and an indifferent society.

These changes shift the tone of the narrative from one that attempts a kind of psychological depth to a lighter, comic discourse dependent on irony and double entendre. But this tonal transformation is not perhaps crucial in marking the film as a Hitchcock film. A number of other shifts have a greater impact. These include the fact that Hitchcock does not follow Dodge in highlighting the body as an object and an extension of identity; that he emphasizes romantic and sexual dimensions, which are underplayed by Dodge; and that in the film the two couples depicted in the novel become a triangle of one man and two women.

If the fundamental plot of the novel is preserved, with Robie serving as the primary focalizer in a third-person narrative, the novel and the film diverge in representing his motivations and appearance. In both narratives, Robie had been arrested in 1939 for thievery. Set free by the Germans, he redeems himself by joining the Resistance. In the novel, his fellow members of the Underground remain loyal to Robie. In the film, he realizes only near the end that they are his primary antagonists, a change that reflects perhaps the shifting political alliances of Europe at the time, but also Hitchcock's greater cynicism. For Hitchcock, there is no loyalty among thieves, or between man and woman. Robie's most trusted ally is an insurance agent (played by John Williams) with whom he makes a deal, agreeing to return the jewels in return for his freedom; he is completely self-serving. In the novel, Robie's primary motivation is to protect his fellow *maquisards*, who are all escaped criminals enjoying an unofficial reprieve and, as a result, vulnerable to pressure from the police. To achieve his goals, unlike the debonair Cary Grant, Robie is transformed into a middle-aged man, ten years his senior (he is only thirty-four in the novel), wearing an elaborate harness that thickens his youthful and muscular body, described in detail (Dodge 33).

Though Cary Grant, born in 1904, was still a fine figure of a man when the film was shot, even in his bathing suit, he was far from thirty-four. Even in his youth, he did not evoke the kind of physicality attributed to his counterpart in the novel.[6] In the film, Robie's mastery as a thief is largely intellectual, expressed through his charm and charisma; Grace Kelly as Francie is a frosty, ethereal, yet spunky, clotheshorse, almost bloodless. In contrast, the culture of the body pervades the novel, focusing for example on the bikini worn by Danielle, the female thief, as noted above.

Unlike Grant's character in the film, who figures out who the real thief is and then *sees* her, the novel's Robie discovers the identity of the thief by *touch*: "He turned instantly to seize and hold the figure beside him, and knew in the immediate moment of contact, unmistakably, that he had caught a woman" (180). For Robie, this is a "shock." He must "attempt to think, bring his mind to accept the stunning fact of the discovery." He considered the thief's identity, in particular her sexual identity as a woman, "a reality he still could not grasp (181). Ultimately, however, he moves beyond the fact of her difference and accepts her as a thief, like himself, assisting her to escape. "She was a thief, he was a thief" (181).

Sexual difference is overtaken by an identity determined by class and experience—as outside the law. Not coincidentally, both are orphans. The narrator comments: "Her story was so much like John's own that he knew, as she went on, what was to follow" (185). This affinity cannot be expressed sexually, at least between Robie and Danielle. The resolution depends upon a chiasmic structure rather than a triangular set of relations (as in the film). In the novel, Danielle is safely paired with Paul, the French count who has befriended John, while Francie, a wealthy American won over to John's cause (and who has him on a "leash), proposes to whisk him off to America, leaving Mother behind (199).

The two thieves, Danielle and John are parted and appropriately paired with partners who will bring them back into the law as well into their proper nationality. John will return home with Francie, to become the American he almost forgot he was; having found a man to provide for her, Danielle will become the proper French housewife she always wanted to be. This coupling suggests other therapeutic advantages: Francie separates herself from her demanding mother, and Paul recovers from the untimely death of his first wife, who, interestingly enough, resembled Danielle. While marriage may be a "leash"—it is a happy one that brings harmony to the social group, lending an almost Shakespearean dimension to the novel's conclusion, in which law and order are restored, with each member of the couple finding his or her rightful place. At the same time, the novel testifies to a certain trouble inherent in definitions of gender and identity and, perhaps even, to a deeply rooted instability.

Both Danielle, as a thief, and Francie, as a more typical heroine, are initially out of place, aggressive and independent women. Francie knows too much—she divines the fact that Jack Burns[7] is really John Robie very early in the novel, and as such, remains dangerous to him until the identity of the real thief is discovered. At the heart of her attachment to him is her fascination with his "thievery," his outlaw nature that she perceives his (faux) middle-aged exterior, which she manipulates for her own gratification, not without a certain sadistic satisfaction. She is looking for her *"raison d'être"* (198), which she finds in John; however, it is John who must bring into realization this *raison d'être*—reasserting in the final analysis, a triumphant masculine mode. Francie is incapable of acting for herself—of transforming her potentially pathological fascination with criminality into correct heterosexuality: "[I]t did not discourage him that she had put up another of her protective barriers between them, because he was a good thief and he knew how to surmount barriers between him and something he wanted as badly as he found he wanted Francie Stevens. But he was clumsier than usual. The chair that he had been sitting in went over with a bang before he reached her" (200).

And so the novel concludes, with a kind of protocinematic fade to black, presaging the narrative's first amorous embrace. The novel's characters are seemingly asexual—they have "one-track minds" as noted in the novel (199). They are obsessed by the act of thievery and its apprehension, by crime and punishment. It is only with the resolution of the mystery surrounding the thief's identity that Francie and John can turn to romance. Romance is left open as a happy future possibility; romance also excuses what might otherwise seem an unhealthy obsession on Francie's part.

The novel does not conclude with the identification and apprehension of the thief. Danielle is never turned over to the police, with marriage to Paul apparently a more reliable way of putting an end to her criminal career. Rather it is the return of the jewels, which buys both John's and Danielle's freedom, that permits each character to move out of one state (isolation) and into another (happy coupling). In this way, they can proceed down the path of prescribed heterosexuality, which, while not entirely idyllic, offers at least an improvement on the characters' previous state. In this sense the novel is caught up in the crisis of postwar masculinity, entailing among other issues an increasing skepticism about marriage, while nevertheless confirming marriage as the best of all possible solutions. Being caught in a marriage is after all better than serving a prison term. Hitchcock's cinematic version follows similar lines but raises far more questions about marriage than it can resolve. By replacing the two couples with a triangle, Hitchcock emphasizes the general instability of relations without calling into play the problem of sexual difference as manifested through the body.

Indeed, the presence of a series of triangles in Hitchcock's *To Catch a Thief* serves to mark the film as Hitchcockian.[8] A primary triangle created Danielle and Francie in their competition over John provides one of the driving erotic themes of the film in which John himself, rather than the jewels, constitutes the prize.[9] Similarly, Robie and the insurance agent cooperate together at some points against the thief, but also the police. Robie satisfies the police and the insurance agent when he offers up Danielle, forcing her to reveal the location of the jewels. Seemingly, he also eliminates Danielle in her competition with Francie at the film's conclusion; however, "Mother" or "Jessie" threatens to take Danielle's place in the all-too-proximate future. While John and Francie kiss in the film's final scene in John's hideaway (where he began), Francie happily remarks that "Mother will love it up here" to her lover's visible dismay. Hitchcock comments: "Since *To Catch a Thief* is in a rather nostalgic mood, I didn't want to wind up with a completely happy ending. That's why I put in that scene by the tree, when Cary Grant agrees to marry Grace Kelly. It turns out that the mother-in law will come and live with them, so the final note is pretty grim" (Truffaut 226). This ambiguity in Jessie's relation to John was clearly marked from their first encounter, the film sketching out a very powerful Oedipal triangle.[10] Jessie upon meeting John, as Conrad Burns, remarks: "If I were Francie's age, you'd sound too good to be true." Jessie pushes John into Francie's arms, later admonishing her daughter for her lack of enthusiasm for a real man unlike "the milksops" to whom she usually attaches herself. Jessie also initially protects John from the police when her jewelry is stolen because, perhaps, as she explains to Francie, "You father was a swindler." Francie may have acquired, then, her fascination with transgressive men honestly, so to speak, from her mother. It is undoubtedly the case that Jessie likes and approves of John, perhaps too much so for John's comfort—who, thus, finds himself at the film's conclusion with a mother and a lover—at which point he may feel that "leash" once more. Hitchcock, then, unlike Dodge is unwilling even to offer up the possibility of an untrammeled happy heterosexuality—on the contrary, it is in his own words, "pretty grim." Here then Hitchcock differs significantly from Dodge and from the postwar era more generally, which, though it had its doubts about marriage, was not, by and large, ready to condemn it as "pretty grim."[11]

At the same time, Hitchcock infused Francie's infatuation with a highly erotic charge. The couple kiss four times in the film, including the conclusion with appropriate romantic framing and often music. They in fact engage in heavy petting, at the very least, represented by a display of fireworks to which the film conveniently cuts. While Francie is the initiator—explaining to John "I kissed *you*"—John, bantering with her, is not loath to take up the challenge:

JOHN: Give me a woman who knows her own mind.

FRANCIE: No one gives you a woman like that. You have to capture her.

JOHN: Any particular method?

FRANCIE: Yes. But it's no good unless you discover it yourself.

John subsequently evokes the film's finale, coming up with a retort to which Francie can furnish no reply:

JOHN: You need something I haven't the time or inclination to give you.

FRANCIE: And what is that?

JOHN: Two weeks with a good man at Niagara Falls.

One can hope that John and Francie get their two weeks of that nonstop newlywed sex for which Niagara is infamous before "Mother" moves in.

While his more or less explicit sexuality distinguishes the film from the novel, Hitchcock pushes this eroticism further, into the realm of fetishism and perversity. Within the novel, once sex becomes legitimate through the prospect of marriage, the characters' "kinkiness" is resolved. Francie is not really kinky, for example; she is in love with John but unable to express it in more conventional terms because of her deep suspicion of men. By way of contrast, Hitchcock posits the eroticism of both Francie and John as irrevocably intertwined with their perversity, suggesting, perhaps, that this is the nature of desire itself. Within the film, Francie finds John's profession a definite turn-on: "I never caught a jewel thief before. It's stimulating." In a later scene, John refers to her indirectly as in the class of "women who need weird excitement" and asks her if she has "been to a psychiatrist"—observations that in no way seem to daunt his own ardor." Sarah Berry comments that *To Catch a Thief* is concerned with "the desire for transgressive or elusive objects," a dynamic in which both principle characters find themselves ineluctably caught and that yet again distinguishes the film from the novel (95).

In conclusion, then, certain dimensions of the film, such as Grace Kelly's and Brigitte Auber's portrayals of what Sarah Berry calls "strong-willed and financially independent women whose self-assurance results in relationship problems" (79), are also present in Hitchcock's source, David Dodge's *To Catch a Thief*; however, Hitchcock transforms other elements, such as, for example, the meaning and the implication of the woman's independence, to suggest a dark and perverse sexuality that is not explicitly present in the novel but that is widely associated with Hitchcock's oeuvre.[12] Unlike certain other films such as *Rear Window*, this dark vision is only partially realized. In Hitchcock words, "[i]t was a lightweight story," explaining, perhaps, why the film remains relatively neglected (Truffaut 223).

The lightness of the story is reflected in Bosley Crowther's review of *To Catch a Thief* for *The New York Times* upon its release in 1955. While he praises the film and its stars, the majority of his positive comments are reserved for the scenery (14). In a later review, he couples the film with *Love Is a Many-Splendored Thing* (1955), encouraging "travel minded filmgoers . . . to lend an eye" (97). He continues: "[W]e are happy to report that the scenery is a decided excitement in both films. It lends an air of distinction and authenticity to average tales." Considering that Hitchcock purchased Dodge's novel before it was published, it is possible that one of the most significant resources that the novel offered him was a pretext to film the Riviera coastline in Vista Vision.

In truth, many but not all of Hitchcock's films offer only "average tales"; his genius emerges through the ways in which he highlights certain thematic possibilities such as contemporary anxiety about marriage and the woman's place, translating them into a personal iconography. To this story, Hitchcock brings a dramatization of the perverse and triangular nature of erotic relations. The intellectual rather than physical embodiment of the characters is what he chooses to emphasize. Granted, *To Catch a Thief* remains very much "caught" by its source; like Dodge's novel it is a "lightweight story" whose intent is to reach and satisfy women viewers. More generally, *To Catch a Thief* issues an appeal to general audiences through its deployment of technical innovations. In many ways, as we have seen, it nonetheless remains a Hitchcock film.

Notes

1. *Publisher's Weekly* described the novel as "Dodge's most famous book," 14 August 2006: 185.

2. Indeed it is "Danielle" in a bikini that graces the cover of the paperback edition of the novel. David Dodge, *To Catch a Thief*, Dell 658.

3. *The Economist* reports: "The Carlton Hotel in Cannes is the scene of crucial parts of Alfred Hitchcock's *To Catch a Thief*. Staying there is a thrill, says a Hollywood executive," 18 October 2003, 6.

4. The casting of the young, sexy Brigitte Auber as "Danielle" was a nod in this direction. She remains for the most part overshadowed by Grace Kelly in the role of "Francie."

5. For a discussion Hitchcock's affinity with women, see Berry, " 'She's Too Everything' " and John Fawcett, "Torturing Women and Mocking Men: Hitchcock's *Rear Window*," 88–104.

6. Ironically, Grant did begin his career as an acrobat. See John M. Smith and Tim Cawkwell, *The World Encyclopedia of Film*, 111.

7. John Robie goes by the pseudonym of Jack Burns in the novel and Conrad Burns in the film.

8. The Oedipal triangle as significant structuring device in Hitchcock's films has been discussed at length by a number of scholars. See for example Raymond Bellour, *The Analysis of Film*.

9. It is impossible not to be reminded here of the mildly vulgar aphorism "the family jewels," as a term used to describe male genitalia.

10. This triangle is re-played, as it were, in *North by Northwest*, when the same actress (Jessie Royce Landis) portrays Grant's character's (Roger Thornhill's) actual mother (Clara Thornhill).

11. For a fuller discussion of the post-war crisis of masculinity, see Barbara
Ehrenreich, *The Hearts of Men: American Dreams and the Flight from Commitment*.
12. See for example Daniel Spoto, *The Dark Side of Genius: The Life of
Alfred Hitchcock*.

Works Cited

Bellour, Raymond. *The Analysis of Film*. Bloomington, Indiana: University of
  Indiana Press, 2000.
Berry, Sarah. " 'She's Too Everything': Marriage and Masquerade in *Rear Window*
  and *To Catch a Thief*." *The Hitchcock Annual* (2001–2002): 79–107.
Brandt, Randal. "A David Dodge Companion." http://www.david-dodge.com, 16
  March 2010.
Crowther, Bosley. "Screen: Cat Man Out 'To Catch a Thief.' " *New York Times*,
  5 August 1955: 14.
———. "On Places and Faces." *New York Times*, 21 August 1955: 97.
Dodge, David. *To Catch a Thief*, Dell 658. New York: Dell Publishing Company,
  1953.
Dodge, David. *To Catch a Thief*. 1952. London: Dent and Sons, 1988.
Ehrenreich, Barbara. *The Hearts of Men: American Dreams and the Flight from
  Commitment*. Garden City, N.Y.: Anchor, 1984.
Fawcett, John. "Torturing Women and Mocking Men: Hitchcock's *Rear Window*."
  Midwest Quarterly 44, n. 1 (2002): 88–104.
Smith, John M., and Tim Cawkwell. *The World Encyclopedia of Film*. New York:
  Galahad Book, 1972.
Spoto, Daniel. *The Dark Side of Genius: The Life of Alfred Hitchcock*. Boston: Little,
  Brown and Company, 1983.
Truffaut, François. *Hitchcock*, Revised Edition. New York: Simon and Schuster,
  1985.
Weiler, A. H. "By Way of Report." *New York Times*, 23 December 1951: X5.

17

BARBARA CREED

Woman as Death

Vertigo as Source

I was intrigued by the hero's attempts to re-create the image of a
dead woman through another one who's alive.

—Hitchcock, *Hitchcock by Truffaut*

VERTIGO (1958) IS CONSIDERED TO BE one of Hitchcock's greatest
films, a classic of modernist cinema and one of the most discussed films of all time. In paying tribute to *Vertigo*, Martin
Scorsese has said that as with all "truly great films, no matter how much
has been said and written . . . the dialogue about it will always continue" (qtd. in Auiler x). The same is true of discussions about *Vertigo's*
sources. A substantial volume of work already exists on this topic in
which different scholars have argued for the influence of many sources,
from the writings of Edgar Allan Poe and Pre-Raphaelite art to Felix
De Boeck's abstract painting, *Vertigo* of 1920, and Man Ray's *Rotoreliefs*
of 1935 (Païni and Cogeval). There is also evidence of the influence of

Freudian theories on *Vertigo*, particularly those of melancholia, necrophilia, and the compulsion to repeat. Hitchcock himself was, at the time,
interested in Freud, and this interest is reflected in a number of his other
classics, such as *Psycho* (1960) and *Marnie* (1964), in which he explored
incestuous desire and female sexual frigidity, respectively. A close study of
Hitchcock's films reveals that he was very responsive to a diverse range
of nineteenth-century influences (Symbolism, pre-Raphaelite painting,
Wagner's operas, Poe's fiction), as well as those from the modernist
period (surrealism, pop culture, the horror film).

Despite the influence of such powerful sources and metanarratives,
Vertigo remains a very personal film; it reveals Hitchcock's own fascination with psychoanalysis, the power of illusion and myths of the femme
fatale, *amour fou*, and the falling man. Hitchcock's literary source for
Vertigo was the 1955 French psychological novel *D'entre les morts* (From
among the Dead) by Pierre Boileau and Thomas Narcejac. The film has
much in common with the Boileau-Narcejac novel, although some critics
have played down this influence. Robin Wood, who described *Vertigo* as
"one of the . . . most profound and beautiful films the cinema has yet
given us" argues that "Hitchcock took very little from *D'entre les Morts*
apart from the basic plot-line" (71). Ken Mogg, in his comprehensive
essay on *Vertigo*'s sources, argues that this is simply not the case (Mogg),
as I will demonstrate in this chapter.

Hitchcock himself acknowledged that he was drawn to the novel:
"I was intrigued by the hero's attempts to re-create the image of a dead
woman through another one who's alive" (Truffaut 369). *Vertigo* is a
quintessentially Hitchcockian film that—along with other Hitchcock
texts—owes much to mythic, literary, and artistic sources. This chapter will explore in depth a number of these influences, particularly the
Boileau-Narcejac novel, while also analyzing the ways in which Hitchcock
transformed the original by introducing his own personal obsessions, values, and aesthetic concerns, rendering these through the stylistic prism
of surrealism. This chapter will argue that Hitchcock also focuses on
the mythic association between woman as the source of both life and
death in order to offer some observations about the meaning of concepts
such as source, origin, and copy. Hitchcock does so through an extended
use of the surrealist symbol of the vortex. In conclusion, this essay will
draw upon Lacan's theory of the sinthome, as distinct from symptom, to
explore the related themes of adaptation, creativity and pleasure.

Although Hitchcock has made important changes to characterization and the narrative trajectory, *Vertigo* is surprisingly faithful to the
novel's main events. The setting, of course, is different: the events of the
novel take place in Paris, during World War II, and later in Versailles

after the war has ended, whereas *Vertigo* is set in San Francisco in the late 1950s. The novel tells the story of an ex-detective (Flavières/Scottie) who left the force because he suffers from vertigo. He is hired by an old acquaintance (Gévigne/Elster) to follow his wife (Madeleine, in both novel and film)—a mysterious figure, fatally obsessed with her great-grandmother (Pauline Lagerlac/Carlotta Valdes), who committed suicide as a young woman. In both texts, the heroine fixes her hair in a bun at the back of her neck and carries a bouquet identical to those in the portrait of her dead ancestor. The hero falls passionately in love with Madeleine, who appears to commit suicide by leaping from a church bell tower. Flavières and Scottie are both devastated by Madeleine's death.

In the novel, Flavières descends into melancholia but remains relatively sane, whereas Scottie has a complete mental breakdown and is institutionalized for a time. In both texts, the hero meets another woman (Renée/Judy), who bears an uncanny resemblance to Madeleine, commences a relationship with her, and then tries to persuade her to change her appearance to look just like the "dead" Madeleine. In the novel, Flavières, who believes that Renée is the reincarnation of Madeleine, hopes that by forcing her to become Madeleine she might then remember her true identity. In the film, Scottie is obsessively in love with an image—the fantasy figure of "Madeleine" created by Elster and Judy and inspired by mythic associations of woman with death. Deep down he knows he will not be able to make love to Judy until she "becomes" Madeleine. So deep is his obsession, at one point, that he even calls Judy by the dead woman's name.

In the end, Flavières/Scottie discovers that Renée/Judy is Madeleine and that Gévigne/Elster hired her to impersonate his own wife, so he could stage her suicide from the bell tower in order to inherit her wealth. On discovering the truth, Flavières strangles Madeleine while also declaring his love for her. The fate of Scottie, and his Madeleine, is much more ironic. Scottie drives Judy/Madeleine back to the tower. Scottie tells Judy this is his "second chance." "I want to stop being haunted," he says. Perhaps he believes if he can reenact the scene and make it to the top of the bell tower with Judy/Madeleine it will feel as if he has saved her. Perhaps he will also overcome his obsession with Madeleine. They stop at the point where Scottie, on the previous occasion, could climb no further. He explains to Judy that he realized the truth the minute he saw the necklace. He accuses her of not being Elster's "real wife" but the "copy," the "counterfeit." He says that Elster made her over, just as he did but that Elster did a better job. "Not only the clothes and the hair but the looks and the manner and the words. And those beautiful phony trances." He forces Judy, who is struggling to escape, to go up the stairs, and although he experiences vertigo when he looks down, he is able to overcome his fear. He then drags Judy up into the bell tower where the huge bell hangs motionless, framed by an arch.

Scottie berates Madeleine for the terrible deception she has played upon him. He tells her she should not "keep souvenirs of a killing," that she should not be so "sentimental." Momentarily overcome and once again in thrall to his creation, Scottie says: "I loved you so Madeleine." Judy pleads with him to believe that she too loved him—still loves him. This is why—against her better instincts—she let him back into her life, even agreeing to become Madeleine for him. Scottie then tells her it is too late, but at the same time he kisses her passionately. At this very moment a nun, cast in shadows, suddenly ascends the steps into the bell tower. Terrified, Judy/Madeleine steps back, loses her footing, and this time "Madeleine," the object of Scottie's desire, falls to her death. Thus Scottie inadvertently brings about the death of "Madeleine" for a second time. This time, however, he has conquered his vertigo. His cure appears to be brought about by the unraveling of Madeleine's mystery, that is, the truth of her masquerade. This does not alter the fact, however, that Scottie was in love with a woman who was married to another man and who appeared to be possessed by the persona of a dead woman. Scottie becomes psychotic when he loses Madeleine the first time and coldly vengeful when he discovers that she was not herself from the very beginning, but at the same time he is still obsessed with the image, the possibility of Madeleine. At the end, Scottie stands alone on the balcony of the bell tower, looking down at her body, his vertigo gone, his empty hands stretched outward; he appears completely overcome and desolate. Unlike Flavières, his counterpart in the novel, Scottie is not directly responsible for her death. Nor does he kiss her and promise to wait for her. Hitchcock's focus is on a man who has cured his vertigo (his symptom) and yet may not be healed.

In his famous book-length interview with François Truffaut, Hitchcock discusses the changes he made in adapting the novel to the screen in relation to the narrative trajectory and the hero's character. He distinguishes between the first and second parts of the novel, explaining that *Vertigo* follows the main plot line of *D'entre les morts* very closely in relation to the first part of the novel, which ends with what the hero falsely believes is the death of Madeleine. The second part of the story commences when the hero meets the woman who closely resembles Madeleine. In the novel, Boileau and Narcejac focus on the hero's attempts to persuade the woman to change her appearance so that she will look just like Madeleine. Only at the end of the novel do the hero and the reader discover that the two women are one and the same, an intriguing twist and substantial surprise, but one that Hitchcock discards.

Instead, Hitchcock uses a flashback, narrated by Judy, to inform the viewer that Judy had been impersonating Madeleine all along and that Elster threw his wife's body from the bell tower. "Everyone around me was against this change," Hitchcock tells Truffaut (369). Hitchcock, however, was interested in what Scottie would do next when he discovered the truth. If viewers knew the truth about Madeleine, they could focus on Scottie's reactions: "[S]uspense will hinge around the question of how Stewart is going to react when he discovers that Judy and Madeleine are actually the same person" (370).

A closer examination of the two texts reveals the different relationship of each of the men to Madeleine's death. Before Flavières strangles Madeleine, he explains the reason he loves her was because she was already living in the other world—the land of the dead. "I've always loved you—right from the start—because of Pauline, because of the cemetery, because of your dreamy eyes" (169). His words recall a number of earlier scenes in which he discussed his attraction to death and his association of Madeleine with death. After watching Madeleine in the cemetery, where he first studied her carefully, he reflects: "Madeleine dreaming in front of Pauline's tomb . . . Homesick! For the grave!" (32). Madeleine's perfume reminds him of the "rich earth and dead flowers" (33) and the deep caves of Saumur near the Loire, which as a boy he loved to explore despite the fear they aroused in him. "Flavières experienced once again the fearful attraction of the shades, and he understood why, at the first glance, Madeleine had touched him" (34). To Flavières Madeleine signifies the eternal, mythical feminine: When he first sets eyes on her, she reminds him of "those unknown beauties admired in the Louvre, the Mona Lisa, La Belle Ferronière" (21). Later, she reminds him of another "well-known picture—La Femme á l'Eventail" (22). When he first sees her wearing her severely cut "grey suit, very tight at the waist," he recalls another portrait: "La Femme au Loup" (24–25). Later she is "La Femme à la Tulipe" (32).

She tells Flavières that she too dreams of "the other country" (55) and that "It doesn't hurt to die" (77). After Madeleine's death, he suffers a "hideous agony" (89), nursing his melancholia "like a convalescent lifting the bandage to have a peep at his wound" (89). He lives with "death in his soul" (90). At night he suffers nightmares, "losing himself . . . in a labyrinth of corridors crawling with vermin" (94). But even before he met Madeleine, Flavières, then suffering from vertigo, was drawn to death, "trembling on the edge of a slope at the bottom of which was the abyss" (22). In the end, he murders Renée rather than have her destroy his memory of "Madeleine," whom he believed was already a shade, a ghost returned from the world of the dead. After she is dead, he kisses her forehead and says: "I shall wait for you" (170), suggesting that no one else could ever take her place.

In the novel, we see that the hero, obsessed with death, is drawn to Madeleine's darker side and is attuned to the lure of the underworld symbolized for him by the cave-dwellings near the Loire. Obsessed with Madeleine, he is filled with a melancholy love (Nicholls). After saving her from drowning, he calls her his "little Eurydice" because like Eurydice she also traveled back from the underworld. The hero's obsession with death and the idea of woman-as-death belongs to the romantic tradition as Keats tells us in his poem "Ode To a Nightingale": "I have been half in love with easeful Death."

Scottie too is drawn to Madeleine because of her alignment with death and the belief that she is possibly possessed by her dead relative, Carlotta. Hitchcock goes to greater lengths than Boileau and Narcejac to represent Scottie's obsession as a form of necrophilia. As he explains to Truffaut, he shot the scene where Judy finally emerges from the bathroom as an exact replica of Madeleine in a green light to give her a "ghostlike quality" (371). Scottie remains deeply in love with the dead woman—the eternal femme fatale—and is unable to love anyone else. The fact that Scottie cannot experience desire for an ordinary, everyday woman is clear from his relationship with Midge (Barbara Bel Geddes), his former fiancée. Hitchcock created the Midge character for the film; she is the opposite of Madeleine in every respect—sensible, rational, mothering. When Scottie falls from the step ladder in her apartment, Midge rushes to his rescue and catches him in her capable arms. Scottie, however, does not want a "real" woman, rejecting both Midge and later Judy, who is a relatively pragmatic, working-class shop assistant. Her performance as Madeleine, however, is so convincing that the viewer cannot help but conclude that the security of the masquerade enables her to speak at times from her own heart, a point made by Robin Wood (93). She does make it clear that she, like Madeleine, has been hurt by men who never valued her for herself.

Scottie, like Flavières, is in love with a mythic image of woman—woman as femme fatale, a beautiful but doomed, fateful figure. However, Scottie's desire, as Hitchcock has stated, is a form of necrophilia; he is sexually aroused by the idea of woman as a harbinger of death, woman as the dark abyss that he both desires and fears. As Scottie follows Madeleine around San Francisco, he finds himself in places associated with death: the graveyard, the art gallery and its portrait of the dead

Carlotta, the waters of San Francisco Bay, the Spanish church and its bell tower. The most significant of these is possibly their trip to the forest where Madeleine is drawn to the ancient sequoia tree: "the oldest living things" she says. "I don't like it . . . Knowing I have to die." As she touches a cross-section of a felled tree on display, she remarks portentously: "Somewhere here I was born, and there I died. It was only a moment for you, you took no notice" (79). Madeleine is able to articulate, to express in words and through her actions, what Scottie most fears.

Hitchcock expresses the nightmares that Scottie experiences after her death though powerful visual imagery. In one nightmare, Scottie finds himself walking into the open grave of Carlotta/Madeleine, where he falls screaming. Scottie's terrifying dream recalls an earlier scene where Madeleine describes a nightmarish scenario to Scottie in which she was "walking down a long corridor . . . When I came to the end there's nothing but darkness and a grave—an open grave. It's my grave." So powerful is Madeleine's association with death in *Vertigo*, that Scottie in a sense lets himself become feminized; he becomes Madeleine in order to experience death through her. Her terror of an empty grave becomes his nightmare, as he assumes the role of the falling man of mythology. After Madeleine dies the first time, Scottie becomes just like the dead Carlotta, searching the streets of San Francisco in vain for the one he has loved and lost. Scottie suffers from a nexus of Freudian maladies— vertigo, melancholia, necrophilia. In this context, he is both a modernist and a romantic hero—a man of sentiment and pathology.

It is Scottie's attempt to transform Judy into Madeleine that most clearly reveals his unconscious and perverse desires. Scottie never sees Judy for herself; he is only interested in the masquerade, in her ability to "become" the image of Madeleine, in the power of her image and her portrayal of woman as an unobtainable ideal and mythic harbinger of death. In a sense, Scottie also creates Madeleine, brings her back to life, remodels the image of Judy into Madeleine. He is a complete perfectionist. The lady in the clothes shop comments: "The gentleman seems to know what he wants." When Judy, having changed everything else about her appearance, finally agrees to put her hair up, just as Madeleine had worn hers, she effectively becomes a living embodiment of Scottie's dream world and a dead woman—a dream made concrete. Hitchcock says of her transformation: "Cinematically, all of Stewart's efforts to re-create the dead woman are shown in such a way that he seems to be trying to undress her, instead of the other way around" (Truffaut 370). According to Hitchcock, when Judy puts her hair up into a bun, she is signaling to Scottie that she is "totally naked" and "ready for love"—that she has finally become Madeleine (371). The bun is a key signifier in the film;

it represents Madeleine and also signifies female sexuality. As Hitchcock explained to Truffaut: "To put it plainly, the man wants to go to bed with a woman who's dead; he is indulging in a form of necrophilia" (370). The figure of a naked woman also suggests a body laid out for burial.

Only at this moment is Scottie at last able to kiss her, and to signify the importance of this kiss, Hitchcock has the camera enact a 360 degree circular movement around the couple as images from the Spanish mission, where Madeleine died, appear in the background causing Scottie momentary anxiety. Although Hitchcock originally planned to indicate clearly that the couple then have sex, by focusing on the bed, he ends the scene on the kiss (followed by a black screen), whose intensity is so powerful it is perfectly clear that sex follows. Scottie's fear of heights, or rather his experience of paralysis at the thought of heights (a metaphor for sexual impotence), is finally overcome, and he is able to make love to the "dead" woman.

Although the ending of the novel is not as bleak and desolate as the ending of *Vertigo*, it contains a scene that in a sense anticipates the film's powerful alignment of woman, death, and the cinema—a scene that must have exerted a strong impact on Hitchcock, although it is rarely discussed by critics. In discussing the origin of the novel, Thomas Narcejac explained that he was inspired by the idea of a character in a cinema recognizing in a newsreel he had thought dead, an experience he had himself after the war, as he recalls: "I began to think about the possibilities of recognizing someone like this. Maybe someone who was thought dead . . . and this is where *D'entre les morts* began to take shape" (Auiler 28). This is exactly how Flavières first sees Madeleine again. Still unable to accept her death, he had been to visit his psychiatrist and then to a cinema to kill time. Flavières is watching the events unfold when suddenly he sees "[a] woman who turned slowly round and faced the camera. The eyes were pale, and the delicate features recalled some portrait by Lawrence. The camera moved on, but Flavières had had time to recognize her . . ." (107). He feels as if his chest will burst from lack of air. In this way, the novel draws a direct and powerful connection: woman/death/cinema. In the cinema, those dead, and those forgotten, are brought to life. Flavières sees the face of his dead beloved on the cinema screen—woman and cinema are thus linked inextricably to death, in a parallel to his earlier musing about the associations among woman/death/cave.

Hitchcock does not include the novel's cinema scene in *Vertigo*; instead he emphasizes these associations visually. Not only does he express Scottie's necrophiliac desires through the settings to which the narrative delivers him, but Hitchcock also suggests that woman has the power to draw man into the abyss of her very being through his evocation of the surrealist image of the vortex, which is associated with the female face (and its desiring eye) in the famous opening credit sequence designed by Saul Bass and John Whitney and based on the Lissajous spiral[1] and several of René Magritte's surrealist paintings. The sequence commences with the left side of a young woman's face, which references Magritte's *Eye* (1935), moves down to her lips, and then eventually moves in to a close-up of her right eye. The title, *Vertigo*, emerges from the eye, followed by the revolving spirals with their central black hole, which draws on Magritte's *False Mirror* (1928). The image of the abyss later reappears, more threateningly in Scottie's nightmare. There the vortex becomes an unmistakable signifier of woman, the grave, and death.

In his short essay, "Why I am Afraid of the Dark," published in June 1960 (just two years after the release of *Vertigo*), Hitchcock talked about the influences of Edgar Allan Poe and the French surrealists on his own work: "It's because I liked Edgar Allan Poe's stories so much that I began to make suspense films. Without wanting to seem immodest, I can't help but compare what I try to put in my films with what Poe put in his stories: a perfectly unbelievable story recounted to readers with such a hallucinatory logic that one has the impression that this same story can happen to you tomorrow" (143). Hitchcock's interest in creating films that work through the structures of "a hallucinatory logic" is clearly evident in *Vertigo*, particularly the film's ending, which creates for the viewer a sense of "eternal return" combined with Freudian themes of the uncanny (the familiar yet unfamiliar reenactment of Madeleine's fall), the death drive (Madeleine's desire for stasis and oblivion), and a compulsion to repeat (Scottie's unintended re-creation of Madeleine's death scene). Hitchcock also recognized the surrealists' influence on his own work. "And surrealism? Surrealism certainly has exerted a great influence on the cinema, especially between 1926 and 1930, when it was transposed onto the screen by Buñuel with *L'Age d'Or* and *Un Chien Andalou*, by René Clair with *Entr'acte*, by Jean Epstein with *The Fall of the House of Usher*, and by . . . Jean Cocteau with *The Blood of A Poet* . . . an influence that I experienced myself, if only in the dream sequences and the sequences of the unreal in a certain number of my films" (144).

The influence of surrealism is especially pervasive in *Vertigo*, with the entire film partaking of the qualities of dream, or rather of nightmare. Key surrealist themes are emphasized: falling, loss of balance, death, and the lure of the abyss. Scottie's malady, his vertigo, becomes the psychological reflex of these themes, his destabilizing fear of, yet fascination with, the vortex defined by Hitchcock's famously expressive dolly back/ zoom in, a self-canceling movement toward, but also away from, his object of desire, the woman who is love, madness, self-destruction, and death.

Marcel Duchamp's *Rotoreliefs of 1935* clearly inspired the spirals of the opening credits sequence where the film's title and the lines of a spiraling movement arise from the interior of a woman's eye only at the end to collapse back into that eye. Duchamp, it should be noted, was a contemporary of Hitchcock. Dominique Païni argues that this was indeed significant and suggests that Duchamp, whose "work contains more Symbolist elements—and is also more conceptual—than that of any other 20th century artist," may have influenced Hitchcock quite profoundly, particularly in the way he draws "the viewer's gaze into descending spirals, thus undermining our concept of reality" (381). Throughout the narrative Hitchcock reinforces this spiraling movement through a series of forward tracking shots and an array of images that draw us further into the depths of the Scottie's nightmare world. Hitchcock represents Scottie's fear of *Vertigo* and woman-as-death in and through the spiral and its many manifestations in the film: the whorl of Madeleine's bun, her circular bouquet, the shots of the bell tower's descending stairs, the swirling waters of the Bay, the coiling cross-section of the giant Sequoia tree, and Scottie's nightmare of falling into an open grave. Scottie, and perhaps Hitchcock as well, suffers from an *idée fixe* that must lead to acts of recreation—as Scottie remakes Judy and as Hitchcock remakes *Vertigo*—following the artistic path described by Cocteau: "But having an idea is not enough: the idea must have us, haunt us, obsess us, become unbearable to us" (157).

As an adaptation, it seems fitting that *Vertigo* draws our attention to remaking. Of all Hitchcock's films, *Vertigo* most consistently focuses on the problems associated with distinguishing between original and copy. Hitchcock explores this issue through the figure of his female actress, Kim Novak, who is associated throughout with three women: Madeleine, Carlotta, and Judy. But who is Woman? *Vertigo* dramatizes the difficulties involved in reaching the source, defining what is the original and thus grasping the meaning of creation. Judy's "Madeleine" is a copy of the real Madeleine Elster, and "Madeleine" is obsessed with her belief that the dead Carlotta is remaking her in her own image. A symptom of Scottie's madness seems to be his inability to distinguish between originals and copies or, rather, to accept the original (Judy) as herself; once he realizes that Judy is simply Judy, that "Madeleine" is a copy, he forces Judy to recapitulate the death of the original. Yet it is the original Madeleine, herself a copy, with whom he is in love. In his desperation to uncover the source, the starting point or origin, he descends even further into the vortex. Such bottomlessness (or perhaps depthlessness) is also the madness of the cinema, which represents reality exactly, seeming to offer an authentic image of the world, in which the spectator "believes" for the duration of the narrative but actually contains nothing outside its own frames of reference (Fuery). Through its fascination with both masquerade and madness, *Vertigo* offers an allegory of the problems that surface in cinematic adaptation, of searching for the presence of the "original" in that second version that is, and yet cannot be, the same. This desire for the presence of the original—for the real Madeleine—similarly oppresses both Scottie and *Vertigo's* spectators. "Madeleine" does not exist (she is Judy's performance), yet Scottie forces her back to life, at which point, inevitably perhaps, she is revealed as a copy. Scottie needs Madeleine, or the image of Madeleine, in order to feel whole, to experience pleasure—and so too does the spectator, whose desire for conventional romantic closure is energized by Judy's determination, which cannot succeed, in making Scottie love her "for herself."

In the end, Scottie has apparently overcome his vertigo. But is he cured? Will he, in other words, continue to desire Madeleine, a woman who does not exist? One way of understanding what Madeleine represents for Scottie is through Lacan's theory of the sinthome (symptom).[2] The sinthome, which is the Old French spelling of the term, is radically different from the symptom. In Lacan's earlier writings a symptom functions as a message that can be interpreted through reference to the unconscious: the sinthome is very different. Lacan stated in his lecture at Yale: "To explain art with the unconscious seems to me most dubious, yet it is what analysts do. To explain art with the symptom [or the sinthome?] seems to me more serious" (Harari 24).

We could argue that vertigo constitutes Scottie's symptom but that Madeleine represents his sinthome. Lacan introduced the term *sinthome* in his 1975–76 seminar on James Joyce, in which he interpreted Joyce's writing as an extended sinthome that enabled Joyce to organize his own experience of enjoyment. "In the last years of his teaching, Jacques Lacan established the difference between symptom, and sinthom: in contrast to symptom which is a cipher of some repressed meaning, sinthom has no determinate meaning; it just gives body, in its repetitive pattern, to some elementary matrix of jouissance, of excessive enjoyment" (Žižek, *Symptom* 199).Jouissance is interpreted in this context by Jacques-Alain Miller, as "*sens joui* [enjoyed sense]" (6). The symptom is something that can be interpreted: "To treat the symptom within the framework of the analytic experience means deciphering it. As Freud demonstrated, neurotic symptoms have a sense" (Solano-Suárez 96). If the concept of jouissance is introduced in relation to the symptom, we are talking of the sinthome. The sinthome offers a "kernel of enjoyment immune to the efficacy of the symbolic" (*No Subject* website). The sinthome is "what 'allows one to live' by providing a unique organization of *jouissance*" (*No Subject* website). The sinthome confers a degree of consistency upon the subject: "The subject of the symptom, by contrast, is a barred or divided subject, one who says: "I do not wish to be like this," "I do not wish to have that," or, indeed, "I cannot go on living like this." Conversely, one is sure that "one cannot live without" the *sinthome*" (Harari 358–59). If woman is the sinthome of man this is because woman confers consistency on man. According to Harari, Lacan in his later writings argued that man could similarly be a sinthome for woman. The relation, however, is "*intersinthomal*" (209): "If the relation were supported by the symptom, they would begin to fall together, opening a space for a pathology of mutual stimulation, of falling. If, by contrast, it were *intersinthomal*, it might be considered a relation that does not 'fall,' or fade away" 209). The crucial aspect of the sinthome is that it is bound up with the creative act. In his analysis of Joyce, Lacan argued that he created his own sinthome in his writings through the deployment of the epiphany. "Thus, an *élan* or buzz is generated, which becomes indispensable and which works in a way quite unlike the symptom. The suffering entailed by the symptom is certainly not at work in the same way in the *u*, linked as it is to the epiphanic quality of inventing something" (Harari 70).

In a sense, Scottie is an artist, a man who creates or recreates woman as sinthome in two quite distinct ways. In the first part of the film (ending with Madeleine's supposed death), Scottie creates her through the workings of narrative; that is, he knits together the threads of her strange (and fictitious) story, involving her dead ancestor Carlotta Valdes and in so doing brings her to life for himself; in the second part Scottie finds Judy, a stranger, whom he recreates as Madeleine, right down to the last detail. Scottie approaches his task as an artist, obsessed with every facet of her appearance. The woman becomes his sinthome—a "repetitive pattern" (a severe grey suit, blonde hair, bun at the nape of her neck, antique necklace), which cannot be interpreted but which offers him (and he alone) a special arrangement of jouissance that has the potential to save him from madness. It is only when Scottie loses her that he falls into a psychotic state. In recreating Judy as an exact copy of Madeleine, he gradually regains his sanity and a sense of enjoyment. Her presence confirms a certain consistency on his being as well as pleasure, although at times an unbearable pleasure. In recreating Madeleine, Scottie appears to heal himself in the fashion traced out by Žižek, who argues that the

> symptom conceived as *sinthome*, is literally our only substance,
> the only positive support of our being, the only point that gives

consistency to the subject. In other words, symptom is the way
we—the subjects—"avoid madness," the way we "choose something
(the symptom-formation) instead of nothing (radical psychotic autism,
the destruction of the symbolic universe)" through the binding of
our enjoyment to a certain signifying, symbolic formation which
assures a minimum of consistency to our being-in-the-world.' (Žižek
Sublime Object, 75)

When Scottie loses Judy/Madeleine for a second time, a question
remains: Will he attempt to recreate her image again, perhaps in a different form? After Scottie saves Madeleine from drowning, he tells her
that the Chinese have a saying that if you save someone's life you are
responsible for them forever. She replies: "And you'll go on saving me?
Again and again?"

Hitchcock knew that the cinema, with its power to transform the
"original" (play/novel/script), is able to endlessly valorize and vampirize
sources that are thus both present (because referenced) and absent (having been transformed). In *Vertigo*, Hitchcock does much the same to (and
for) Judy. In a sense, he never allows her to come fully to life: she remains
the raw material for the hero's dreams, then dies as herself but reconfigured as a copy. Judy's reluctant willingness to be remade suggests the
malleability of the source—its potential for endless visual and narrative
transformations. Woman's malleability offers itself a source of perverse
enjoyment for filmmakers and spectators alike, as indeed malleability
seems a key element in the enjoyment of an adaptation as an adaptation.
The pull of attraction and repulsion, deriving from such endless destabilization, is emphasized in films such as *Vertigo*, which explore abject
themes such as madness, *l'amour fou*, and necrophilia. Viewers enjoying
adaptations as endless displacements of an undiscoverable source can
thus find their textual double in the figure of Scottie, who in the short
term appears to find a degree of pleasure from his success in recreating
Madeleine but who ultimately appears unable to overcome a desire for
that which always eludes his grasp. Yet, for Scottie and Hitchcock, there
is presumably an experience of pleasure that occurs during the creative
process of remaking.

The concept of the "sinthome" invites us to reconsider various
aspects of *Vertigo*: the role of creativity in Scotty's remaking of Madeleine;
the film itself as representing, in its formal elements, and in its choice
of heroine, a sinthome for Hitchcock; and Hitchcock's role as the author
of the remake. In a sense Scottie stands in for Hitchcock in that he
the obsessive lover (like Hitchcock the obsessive director) is assigned
the role of the artist—the one who must struggle to create his ideal

woman. Hitchcock too struggled to find a perfect heroine.[3] This woman of course also held a special meaning for the director. As with all Hitchcock heroines, she signifies a series of formal qualities—beautiful, sophisticated, blonde, and unobtainable—which meant something specific to Hitchcock. For the spectator there is always a touch of the uncanny about the Hitchcock heroine: she is familiar yet strange. The problem for Scottie is that his desire is to create an *exact* copy of a woman who is his sinthome, a copy that he will eventually destroy. This amounts also to destroying that which confers a certain consistency on his being and a specific form of enjoyment. Hitchcock too was famous for the way in which he created his heroines—selected their clothes, detailed their appearance, and molded their personae.[4] Like Scottie, he is also caught up in a sinthomatic process of creating, destroying, and recreating the object of his desire. (Similarly, Norman Bates murdered the mother he loved, recreated her as a mother/mummy, and then recreated himself as his mother). In this context Scottie becomes Hitchcock's textual double, enabling Hitchcock to explore his own obsessions and his own desire for woman as sinthome through a series of female figures: Kim Novak, Madeleine, Carlotta; Midge-as-Carlotta; and Judy.[5] In a sense, the process of the transformation of Madeleine into Carlotta and Judy into Madeleine parallels the process of the adaptation of novel into film—what to include, omit, reject, reinterpret, rename, invent, alter, and copy. *Vertigo* offers a metaphor for the process of adaptation itself. In choosing repeatedly throughout his career to direct films which were adaptations, to transform the written word into the cinematic sound and image, Hitchcock created for himself a sinthome through which he fashioned his own unique form of resistance and jouissance. In so doing Hitchcock reinvented himself as author, artist, and origin.

Notes

1. A French mathematician designed the Lissajous spiral in the nineteenth century in order to signify mathematical formulae. See Auiler 155.

2. Lacan includes the sinthome in his topology of the borromean knot, which is a group of three rings that he used to demonstrate the interdependence of the three orders of the imaginary, symbolic, and real. If any one of the rings in the borromean knot is cut, all three separate. The sinthome becomes the fourth ring, tying together a knot that constantly threatens to come undone (*No Subject* website).

3. Dan Auiler discusses Hitchcock's attempts to re-create Grace Kelly after she left Hollywood—to find another actress whom he could fashion after Grace Kelly (xviii) of whom it is said she was Hitchcock's ideal woman (16).

4. According to Kim Novak: "It was almost as if Hitchcock was Elster, the man who was telling me to play a role . . . [H]ere's what I had to do, and wear, and it was so much of me playing Madeleine . . . but I really appreciated it" (Auiler 179).

5. In *Enjoy Your Symptom*, Žižek argues that various *motifs* represent sinthomes for Hitchcock in many of his films. He discusses the sinthome of the spiral in *Vertigo* in some detail (198–200).

Works Cited

Auiler, Dan. Vertigo: *The Making of a Hitchcock Classic*. New York. St. Martin's Griffin, 2000.

Boileau, Pierre, and Thomas Narcejac. *Vertigo*. Trans. Geoffrey Sainsbury. London, Bloomsbury Film Classics, 1997.

Cocteau, Jean. *The Art of Cinema*. Trans. Robin Buss, London and New York: Boyars, 2001.

Foster, Hal. *Compulsive Beauty*. London: MIT, 1993.

Fuery, Patrick. *Madness and Cinema*. New York: Palgrave Macmillan, 2004.

Harari, Roberto. *How James Joyce Made His Name: A Reading of the Final Lacan*. New York: Other, 2002.

Hitchcock, Alfred. "Why I Am Afraid of the Dark." In *Hitchcock on Hitchcock*, ed. Sidney Gottlieb, London: Faber & Faber, 1997.

Keats, John. "Ode to a Nightingale." In *English Romantic Poetry*, vol. 2, ed. Harold Bloom, New York: Doubleday.

Miller, Jacques-Alain. "Interpretation in Reverse." In *The Later Lacan*, ed. Véronique Voruz and Bogdan Wolf. New York: State University of New York Press, 2007, 3–9.

Mogg, Ken. "The Fragments of the Mirror: *Vertigo* and Its Sources." In *New Publications*; http://www.labyrinth.net.au/muffin/*Vertigo*_sources_c.html m1998.

Nicholls, Mark. *Scorsese's Men: Melancholia & the Mob*. Melbourne: Pluto, 2004.

Païni, Dominique, and Cogeval, Guy. *Hitchcock and Art: Fatal; Coincidences*. Montreal. The Montreal Museum of Fine Arts. Mazzotta, 2001.

Thurston, Luke. Editor. *Re-Inventing the Symptom*. New York: Other, 2002.

Solano-Suárez, Esthela. "Identification with the Symptom at the end of Analysis." In *The Later Lacan*, ed. Véronique Voruz and Bogdan Wolf. New York: State University of New York Press, 2007, 95–104.

Truffaut, François. *Hitchcock by Truffaut*. Revised ed. London: Paladin Grafton Books, 1986.

Wood, Robin. *Hitchcock's Films*. 2nd ed. London. A. Zwemmer Limited & New York, A. S. Barnes, 1969.

Žižek, Slavoj. *The Sublime Object of Ideology*, London and New York: Verso, 1989.

———. *Enjoy Your Symptom!* New York and London: Routledge, 2001.

18

Brian McFarlane

Psycho

Trust the Tale

The cinema has its own methods and its own scope. We must beware
of missing the significance of a shot or a sequence by applying to it
assumptions brought from the experience of the other arts.

—Wood, *Hitchcock's Films Revisited*

[Hitchcock's] readiness to claim full authorship of the films at the
expense of his collaborators, can be seen as an unattractive egotism
or as an astute marketing ploy, or as a mixture of both, but there is
no reason for critics to go along with it unquestioningly.

—Barr, *English Hitchcock*

THESE TWO DISTINGUISHED HITCHCOCK scholars suggest complementary approaches to reading *Psycho*, indeed, to Hitchcock's
oeuvre at large. Famously ungenerous in acknowledging indebtedness to his sources, especially to his screenwriters and to the works on

which his films have drawn, Hitchcock lays down a challenge to those
of us who value the written word on a par with the audio-visual moving
images that constitute the semiotic system of film. It is not a matter of
undermining the cinematic genius that informs a run of titles almost
unique in film history; rather, one wants to investigate what the great
director owed to the antecedent texts and also to other influences that
helped to shape their remarkable contours.

In 1966, in his book-length interview with François Truffaut,
Hitchcock declared: "What I do is read a story once, and, if I like the
basic idea, I just forget all about the book and start to create cinema"
(49). In considering *Psycho*, one is forced to find this statement disingenu-
ous and/or mendacious. It is not that anyone would lightly characterize
Hitchcock as a "literary" filmmaker: he is by no means the Merchant/
Ivory of murderous mayhem. Equally, though, he has never paid his
dues, except in the most minimal terms, to the texts from which he
took his inspiration—and then converted into something, as it were,
rich and strange.

When Peter Bogdanovich asked him "why he had chosen to have
Janet Leigh stabbed to death in the shower," he answered "reasonably":
"Well, that's what life is like . . . Things happen out of the blue" (27).
He might easily have replied with something like: "Well, the film was
based on a novel by Robert Bloch, and that's how it happens at the end
of chapter 3." Look at the last paragraphs of that chapter: "The roar
[of the shower] was deafening, and the room was beginning to steam
up. That's why she didn't hear the door open or the sound of footsteps.
And at first, when the shower curtains parted, the steam obscured the
face . . . It was the face of a crazy old woman. Mary started to scream,
and then the curtains parted further and a hand appeared, holding a
butcher's knife. It was the knife that, a moment later, cut off her scream.
And her head" (31).

One recalls in this respect Charles Barr's comment about an account
of *Murder!* (1930) that attributed complex reasons to Hitchcock's use of
a theatrical setting: "The reason for the theatrical setting of *Murder!* is
precisely the same as the reason for the Dublin setting of Hitchcock's
previous film, *Juno and the Paycock*: it is taken from the original text that
is being adapted" (8–9). It is as though it would detract from the director's achievement as auteur if acknowledgment were to be made of the
precursor text as at least a starting point. And while acknowledging the
soundness of Wood's warning quoted in the epigraph, it is also worth
noting that his account of *Psycho*, like many others, fails to mention
Bloch's name.

I do not want this piece to be yet another "adaptation study," nor do I aim to offer a new, let alone definitive, interpretation of Hitchcock's most celebrated thriller. My modest aim is to suggest that its brilliance as cinema does not arise fully formed, like Aphrodite from the sea, fully formed and owing nothing to several important sources, most obviously Bloch's novel, which, it is worth noting, went through a dozen reprints before 1983, the year of my edition. But there are other sources too that one should have in mind, though there is not space here to look at these in detail: there is an apparent understanding of (or grappling with) Freudian psychology; the movement of 1950s Hollywood melodrama toward a more overt grappling with its psychological underpinnings; and the whole concept of 'genre' as it relates to popular American cinema. The fingerprints of such intertextual influences, as well as the wholesale borrowings from Bloch, ensure that *Psycho*, brilliant achievement as it is, is not the product of a vacuum-sealed auteur at work.

Who was Robert Bloch? The short answer is that he was an immensely prolific novelist and screenwriter for both film and television. No doubt best remembered now for *Psycho*, he also wrote twenty-four other novels (including two sequels to *Psycho*), over three dozen short story collections, and a dozen screenplays, among the most notable being a series of enjoyable horror films in Britain for director Freddie Francis and the Amicus production company, in the late 1960s. These latter titles included *The Deadly Bees* (1966) and *The House That Dripped Blood* (1970), but probably his most successful screen involvement was as original author and screenwriter of the five short stories comprising Roy Ward Baker's horror compendium, *Asylum* (1972). This latter had the advantage of an excellent British cast (Peter Cushing, Charlotte Rampling, Sylvia Syms, Herbert Lom, et al.) and Baker's experienced direction. In his autobiography, Baker pays tribute to Bloch's "cracking good script" (136), claiming that "*Asylum* is one of my favourite films. There is no point in describing the stories . . . : they were all excellent" (37). Geoff Mayer, in his study of Baker's work, notes that the third story in *Asylum*, "Lucy Comes to Stay," has "basic similarities" with *Psycho*, dealing as both do with murder and obsessiveness within the family. Ultimately, when the institutionalized Barbara (Rampling) "looks into a mirror she does not see herself, only [her friend] 'Lucy,'" noting the "variation on the final [sic] scene in *Psycho*, when 'mother' assumes total control of Norman Bates" (177).

Amicus specialized in portmanteau films, and Bloch's short stories provided the basis for several of their most successful productions, Bloch himself allegedly claiming that *Asylum* was "the best adaptation of his stories."[1] In Hollywood, his best-known work included *The Cabinet of Dr Caligari* (Roger Kay, 1962), tenuously connected with its great German predecessor; *Strait-Jacket* (William Castle, 1963), a melodrama about a woman committed to an asylum after killing her husband and his mistress with an axe (another echo of *Psycho?*), and *The Night Walker* (William Castle, 1964), a frightening enough shocker, starring Barbara Stanwyck and Robert Taylor. The British work is arguably more imaginative. My point is that Bloch's career, with its early influences coming from Edgar Allen Poe and, especially, H. P. Lovecraft, is not so negligible as to have been all but obliterated from many of the multiplying exegeses on *Psycho*.

It is not my aim to make unsustainable claims for Bloch in general or for his *Psycho* in particular. Nevertheless, I want to draw attention to accounts of the film that fail to mention the novel or give any idea of what Hitchcock might have found in it and to examine the extent to which he appears to have made use of his source novel. Wood's comment quoted in my epigraph seems to me to be incontestably true, and, as I have noted elsewhere, those trained in literature are often oblivious of how little their training equips them for recognizing virtues such as subtlety or complexity when these arise from cinematic usages as distinct from the purely verbal (McFarlane, 2000, 163–69). Wood very aptly refers to "the moment in *Psycho* when Norman Bates carries his mother down to the fruit cellar. In literary terms there is almost nothing there: a young man carrying a limp body out of a room and down some stairs. Yet in the film the overhead shot with its complicated camera movement communicates to us precisely that sense of metaphysical vertigo that Hitchcock's subject requires at that moment: a sense of sinking into a quicksand of uncertainties, or into a bottomless pit; communicates it by placing us in a certain position in relation to the action and controlling our movements in relation to the movements of the actors" (56–57). That is an admirable account of how the viewer's response is manipulated by cinema-specific codes, and Wood's whole analysis of how "the greatness of *Psycho* lies in its ability not merely to *tell* us [that we share in a common guilt], but to make us experience it" is charged with understanding of how film works *as* film. However, this highly regarded analysis of the film at no point so much as mentions Bloch as a point of departure. Nor does David Sterritt in his chapter on *Psycho* as an articulation of anal-compulsive behavior, nor does Bogdanovich, quoted above. John Russell Taylor at least mentions it, if dismissively: "[I]t had little to recommend it, but there was the germ of something there, something Hitchcock thought he could work on" (252). It is not clear from Taylor's brief reference to Bloch whether he read the novel; it is not even clear what was "the germ" that Hitchcock recognized and got screenwriter Joseph Stefano to work on. As Taylor goes on to add erroneously that "the book begins with her arrival at the motel" (253), one's confidence in his assessment of Hitchcock's literary source, and how much he took from it, is further diminished. Donald Spoto, in his long, Freudian account of the film, refers only three times (and briefly) to Bloch. He speculates about the "title of the picture . . . presumably, an abbreviation for 'psychopath' or 'psychopathic killer.' This, at least, seems to have been the intention of novelist Robert Bloch" (356). In parentheses he assures us that "(he [Hitchcock] and scenarist Joseph Stefano improved Bloch's novel considerably)" (356). He at no stage elaborates on this claim—and presumably he means "improved *on*," since there is no record of the filmmakers actually touching up the novel itself. Later he draws attention to the film's change of Mary's name to Marion (360). In the famous interview, Truffaut asks: "What was it that attracted you to the novel?" and Hitchcock replies: "[T]he suddenness of the murder in the shower" (205).

Three more recent works go some distance to acknowledging Bloch's importance to the ensuing film. In 1985, Janet Leigh, Hitchcock's Marion, collaborated with Christopher Nickens to give her version of the making of the film. They provide an ampler sense of Bloch's career and how he became involved with filmmaking. Bloch finally secured nine thousand dollars for the film rights to his novel ("He got screwed royally," said his friend, writer Harlan Ellison [Leigh 8]), which he in turn had based on a grisly series of crimes committed by Ed Gein, a solitary Wisconsin handyman. Bloch's Norman Bates shares some key characteristics with Gein (both lonely, middle-aged men with domineering mothers who have, in various ways, distorted their sons' sexual development). Gein's favorite reading had to do with Nazi atrocities, which is interesting to note in relation to a point Wood made about the kind of horror represented by *Psycho* (see later reference). Hitchcock's Norman, of course, is much less unprepossessing in the personable form of Anthony Perkins. Leigh recalled her reaction to reading the novel as follows: "I read the novel in one sitting. Mesmerised. It was not a pretty picture Mr. Bloch had word-painted. In fact, it was downright ugly and frightening" (30).

Then in 1998 Stephen Rebello's book-length study of the film devoted a short but useful chapter to the novel and to Bloch's fascination with Gein's crimes and how a small town had "only suddenly discovered" that a mass murderer lived there (8). He goes on to quote Bloch as saying: "I decided to develop the story along Freudian lines. The big Freudian concept was the Oedipus fixation, so I thought, 'Let's say he had a thing about his mother,' based strictly on the kind of inverted personality he was" (9). Somewhat worryingly, Rebello offers no footnotes so that one cannot guarantee the provenance of this remark. However, if one accepts the account Rebello quotes at some length, including the idea that "a person is never more defenseless than when taking a shower," then it is clear Hitchcock owed much more to the original than has been commonly allowed. Obviously smarting from the way reviewers dismissed his novel when the film was released, as did later critics, Bloch allegedly still objected decades later to the "inference . . . that [Hitchcock] introduced all the things that seemed to make the film work—killing the heroine early in the story, killing her off in the shower, taxidermy—when, of course, they're all in the book" (Rebello 170). Peter Conrad's *Hitchcock Murders* (2000) sprinkles a dozen fairly respectful references to "Bloch's *Psycho*" in his idiosyncratic approach to the films. This is no academic account, but an often fiercely intelligent one, with neat locutions such as how Bloch "treats the Bates house as a combination of the Black Museum and the Chamber of Horrors" (334). Conrad then goes on to detail the kind of response to this one finds in the film. One of the few earlier critics who does more than merely name Bloch as the antecedent author is Ivan Butler. He believes, "The book . . . is crudely and luridly written. Hitchcock and Stefano have skillfully raised the film script above this rather squalid level" (100). His general sense is that the filmmakers have lifted "*Psycho* far out of the framework of sensationalism in which its bare story is moulded" (100).

I want now to turn to the "bare story" from which Hitchcock extracted the "germ" and then went on "to create cinema." Perhaps many, even most, people coming to the film will not be familiar with Bloch's *Psycho*: it is not a novel weighed down with immense cultural prestige.[2] Nevertheless, it was popular over several decades, and a knowledge of it will influence one's viewing of the film. Whereas the film deals linearly with Marion's story up to the point of her murder, the novel begins with Norman, who is presented as "a big fat Mamma's boy" (12), about forty years old, whose reading includes works on Incan preservation rites and the psychology of the Oedipus complex. The tormented relationship between mother and son is established in the opening chapter: he can no longer break away from her or leave the motel. The "conversations" between Norman and his mother have been described by Truffaut as evidence of how Bloch "cheats" his readers: "I've read the novel . . . and one of the things that bothered me is that it cheats. For instance, there are passages like this: 'Norman sat down beside his mother and they began a conversation.' Now, since she doesn't exist, that's obviously misleading, whereas the film narration is rigorously worked out to eliminate these discrepancies" (205).

One might add that Norman believes in the conversations. Not to dispute the superior subtlety with which Hitchcock renders the "presence" of Mrs. Bates, there is surely no question but that he is "obviously misleading" the viewer in his own way, using cinema's powers to mislead, to give certain bits of information while concealing others. Again, for Hitchcock to have implied that he took little from the novel apart from "the suddenness of the murder" is clearly at odds with the whole appropriation of "Mrs. Bates," however crudely Truffaut believes Bloch handles this. In this, as in so many of Hitchcock's quoted statements about the film (how he thought of it as a "comedy," as "fun," etc.), one is reminded of D. H. Lawrence's famous dictum: "Never trust the artist, trust the tale" (14). The "tale" of the filmed *Psycho* hews much closer to Bloch than any of Hitchcock's accounts would allow. What distinguishes the film is not so much the events that make up the narrative as the narrational mode in which these are retold. They are retold in a different semiotic system, the practitioner of which in the field of film is assuredly a master.

I do not want to undertake an exhaustive comparative study of the events of the novel with those of the film. It is enough to say that, in terms of Roland Barthes' taxonomy of narrative functions, in which he defines "cardinal functions" as those that "constitute real hinge-points of the narrative" (93), it could be said that Stefano and Hitchcock offer a virtual palimpsest of Bloch's novel. The film may rearrange the order, as in the decision to open with Marion's frustrating liaison, and the temptation to which it gives rise and to which she succumbs, instead of with Norman's sense of entrapment with "mother" and motel. However, the causal chain linking Marion's arrival at the Bates motel is transferred from novel to film: the possible alternative outcomes opened up by the cardinal functions are resolved along the same narrative lines. The novel's second chapter, which begins with Mary driving in the rain and the night, makes us privy to those events that have brought her this far: she recalls Sam's financial problems, the delaying of their prospect of marriage, her theft and running away, the switching of cars to confuse her trail, and making a wrong turnoff from the main highway. This chapter ends with finding the motel and "a big dark shadow [that] emerged out of the other shadows and opened her car door." "Looking for a room?" a soft, hesitant voice asks at the start of the next chapter.

There is no need to make one's way painstakingly through the rest of the novel and film in this way to establish that the cardinal functions, or, to use Seymour Chatman's concept, "kernels ('narrative moments that give rise to cruces in the direction taken by events')" (53) are essentially those established in Bloch's novel. In my own work on adaptation, I have argued that these functions or kernels are amenable to "transfer" from novel to film and that one of the hallmarks of the so-called faithful adaptation is the preserving of these key events (McFarlane, 1996, 14). This is not to imply the slightest merit in such an enterprise, and my purpose in referring to it here is simply to say that, in the case of *Psycho*, this narrative skeleton is retained throughout with a congruence that makes nonsense of Hitchcock's refuting the importance of his source. Oddly, in 1969, he claimed, rather late in the day, that "*Psycho* all came from Robert Bloch's book," but his purpose in this uncharacteristic touch of magnanimity seems to have been to put Stefano in his place as having "contributed dialogue mostly, no ideas" (Higham and Greenberg 99).

This is not the end of what the film has derived from—or, at least, has in common with—Bloch's novel. The latter changes its perspective disconcertingly almost from chapter to chapter. For instance, the first chapter is from Norman's point of view, the prose enacting his responses to the confinements and obsessions of his life; the second, takes us into Mary's mind as she drives and considers what has led her there; the third is divided between them, Mary's perceptions taking over when Norman leaves; chapters 4 and 5 are from Norman's; 6, 7, and 8 are from Sam's; 15 is from Lila's; and there are several that read as more or less neutral third-person reporting. My only point in adducing this is to highlight Hitchcock's own (more rigorously pursued) agenda in this respect: the audience is encouraged to align itself sympathetically with Marion until the moment of her death, and thereafter with Norman, sympathy in conflict with horror—and horror at *feeling* sympathy. Neither Bloch nor Hitchcock, that is, maintains a steady detachment from the material of the narrative; nor does either manipulate the reader/viewer into unilateral alignment with a single Jamesian "central reflector" for the limitation of narrative perspective.

But the "sources" of Hitchcock's *Psycho* go beyond the events and shifting viewpoints of Bloch's efficient thriller, though it is worth maintaining that, yes, it is efficient for the most part. The novel's function is to maintain suspense, mystery, and horror, and it generally achieves this, without being a prime example of its genre: there are some awkward time transitions that film would handle more adroitly, as when the action of chapter 9 predates Arbogast's phone call in the previous chapter, and there is conventional sloppiness about Lila's finding one of Mary's earrings in the motel room. (Is this, though, so much more conventional than finding a scrap of Marion's calculations in the lavatory bowl in the film, "daring" as the latter was in its time?) What is perhaps more surprising is the extent to which that other apparent Hitchcockian source—the elements of Freudian psychoanalysis that have (rightly) so preoccupied the film's commentators—is also to be found in the novel. The Oedipal scenario is quite explicitly articulated in the novel's opening chapter when Norman rebuts his mother's charge of "those filthy things" he reads and hides in his room with, "But I was only trying to explain something. It's what they call the Oedipus situation" (11). This leads to her taunt of "Mamma's Boy. That's what they called you, and that's what you always were. Were, are, and always will be. A big, fat, overgrown Mamma's Boy!" (12).

Film melodrama of the 1950s was often posited on Freudian concepts and patternings; one has only to think, almost at random, of Elia Kazan's *East of Eden* (1954), Nicholas Ray's *Rebel without a Cause* (1955), Douglas Sirk's *All That Heaven Allows* (1955), Robert Aldrich's *Autumn Leaves* (1956), or Vincente Minnelli's *The Cobweb* (1955). This genre, the melodrama of relationships, family and otherwise, forms one strand in the sources of Hitchcock's film. He had contributed to the genre himself in such films as *Shadow of a Doubt* (1943), *Spellbound* (1945), *Under Capricorn* (1949), *Rear Window* (1954), and *Vertigo* (1958) and would do so memorably again, but the overt Freudianism of *Psycho*, leading to the psychiatrist's analysis at the end, takes him and the genre considerably further than any of those earlier mainstream melodramas. Again, the film's penultimate sequence in which the psychiatrist (Simon Oakland) explains to Sam and Lila how Norman "tried to be his mother . . . and now he is" echoes the account Bloch has Sam pass on to Lila from Dr Steiner: "Norman wanted to be like his mother, and in a way he wanted his mother to become part of himself." This sequence attracted some criticism as being unduly explicit. Indeed, one respectable reviewer at the time dismissed the story as "the sheerest rubbish," referring to "a final 'revelation' which will disconcert only the infinitely credulous" (Houston 126). Among later critics, Spoto claimed that its "attempt to provide neat psychoanalytic maps to the contours of Norman's twisted mind seems jejune" and that, in the final moments when the car is raised from the swamp, "Hitchcock mocks the insufficiency of the psychiatrist's cant" (379, 380). Wood, however, defends the psychiatrist's "explanation" by asserting, "It crystallises for us our tendency to evade the implications of the film, by converting Norman into a mere 'case,' hence something we can easily put from us" (149). For Wood, "*Psycho* is one of the key works of our age. Its themes are of course not new . . . but the intensity and horror of their treatment and the fact that they are grounded here in sex belong to the age that has witnessed on the one hand the discoveries of Freudian psychology and on the other the Nazi concentration camps" (150). In film, *Psycho* represents an extension of the

Freudian preoccupation with explicitness and also with the horror arm
of melodrama, in which family would increasingly become the monster
far-from-*sacré*.

Having quoted D. H. Lawrence above, I find it instructive to recreate the context of his famous *mot*. It is preceded by: "An artist is usually
a damned liar, but his art, if it be art, will tell you the truth of his day.
And that is all that matters." If *Psycho* doesn't quite do this, it at least suggests how far the artist was prepared or able to go in his day, disturbing
without alienating his audience. Lawrence went on to say: "The proper
function of the critic is to save the tale from the artist who created it."
In regard to *Psycho*, and to most of Hitchcock's comments on how he
meant it to be understood, the critics have, on the whole, done as they
ought. They might, however, have shown more overt awareness of those
aspects of this masterly film that owed their origins elsewhere. *Psycho* is
not really a work sui generis; it is not just the "comedy" its maker suggested; it is not merely a brilliant technical exercise, though it is that at
almost every moment: it is a film with an intertextuality, with an array
of sources that deserve an acknowledgment that would not detract from
its achievement.

Notes

1. All further page references to *Psycho* refer to this edition.
2. http://www.kirjasto.sci.fi/rbloch.htm

Works Cited

Bogdanovich, Peter. *Pieces of Time: Peter Bogdanovich on the Movies*. New York:
    Dell, 1973.
Baker, Roy Ward. *The Director's Cut*. Richmond, Surrey: Reynolds & Hearn,
    2000.
Barr, Charles. *English Hitchcock*. Moffat, Dumfriesshire: Cameron & Hollis, 1999.
Barthes, Roland. "Structural Analysis of Narratives" (1966). In *Image-Music-Text*,
    trans. Stephen Heath. Glasgow: Fontana, 1977, 79–124.
Bloch, Robert. *Psycho*. London: Corgi Books, 1959.
Butler, Ivan. *The Horror Film*. London: Tantivy, 1967.
Chatman, Seymour. *Story and Discourse: Narrative Structure in Fiction and Film*.
    Ithaca, NY: Cornell University Press, 1978.
Conrad, Peter. *The Hitchcock Murders*. London: Faber & Faber, 2000.
Higham, Charles, and Joel Greenberg. *The Celluloid Muse: Hollywood Directors
    Speak*. London: Angus & Robertson, 1969.
Houston, Penelope. *Monthly Film Bulletin* 27, no. 320, September 1960.
Lawrence, D. H. "The Spirit of the Place." In *Studies in Classic American Literature*
    (1923). Cambridge: Cambridge University Press, 2003.

Leigh, Janet, with Christopher Nickens. *Psycho: Behind the Scenes of the Classic Thriller*. London: Pavilion Books, 1983.

Mayer, Geoff. *Roy Ward Baker*. Manchester: Manchester University Press, 2004.

McFarlane, Brian. *Novel to Film: An Introduction to the Theory of Adaptation*. Oxford: Clarendon, 1996.

———. "It Wasn't Like That in the Book." *Literature/Film Quarterly* 28, no. 3 (2000), 164–169.

Rebello, Stephen. *Alfred Hitchcock and the Making of Psycho*. London and New York: Boyars, 1998.

Spoto, Donald. *The Art of Alfred Hitchcock: Fitly Years of His Motion Pictures*. New York: Dolphin Books, Doubleday, 1976.

Sterritt, David. *The Films of Alfred Hitchcock*. Cambridge and New York: Cambridge University Press, 1993.

Taylor, John Russell. *Hitch: The Life and Work of Alfred Hitchcock*. London: Faber & Faber, 1978.

Truffaut, François. *Hitchcock*. New York: Simon & Schuster, 1966.

Wood, Robin. *Hitchcock's Films Revisited*. New York: Cambridge University Press, 2002.

19

MURRAY POMERANCE

Thirteen Ways of Looking at *The Birds*

Why do birds suddenly appear ev'ry time you are near?
Just like me, they long to be close to you.

—Hal David, "Close to You," © 1963

1. Hollow

PLEASE DO NOT BE TAKEN IN BY that exceedingly *ersatz* look of the crows and seagulls swooping into the hair of those mortified children scampering down the road away from Annie Hayworth's (Suzanne Pleshette's) schoolroom in Bodega Bay. Yes, one can literally see how they have been matted into the shot, these arrogant attackers from the air, how the shot looks flat, even pasted over, clearly the work of some inventive madmen who had an apocalyptic vision—Robert Boyle, Albert Whitlock, Harold Michelson; Richard Edlund, engaged in looking back upon it, were "struck by the sheer weight of [their] project" (Krohn

38)—but at the same time the children can't see, and on their faces it
could not be more evident that they are fully convinced they have become
prey to creatures never before envisioned as predators. The balance of
nature has shifted, perhaps. The masses have revolted. But the patent
falseness! Think of the repleteness, the depth, the range of attention
that has been paid in the critical and popular literature to the artifice:

> The panicked children were shot running on treadmills, the images
> sandwiched with the school in the background several kilometers
> away, all against the slope of Taylor Avenue . . . papier-mâché
> ravens were placed everywhere ("This Town" H2)—and to the way
> Ray Berwick wrangled, taught, managed flocks of birds to work
> in this film, how the seagulls that in the finale attack Melanie
> Daniels (Tippi Hedren) were attached to long rubber bands, how
> beaks were wired shut and when one little bird was lost he spent
> the afternoon roaming the countryside to find it lest it die of star-
> vation, how Tippi Hedren was so exhausted after shooting some
> scenes she could hardly move—Hedren called it "the worst week of
> my life" . . . Periodically, shooting would halt while makeup artist
> Howard Smit applied latex strips and stage blood to simulate cuts
> and scratches on Hedren's face and arms . . . The gull that she
> whacks with her torch was a dummy, and the real one that bites
> her hand had a rubber cap fitted over its beak. But the terrorization
> of Melanie was also the terrorization of Tippi, who recalled of the
> grueling, day-long operations for the scene's final seconds: ". . . I
> just sat and cried. It was an incredible physical ordeal" (Paglia 16)

The scholarship reads like a studio press release dedicated to the
relief of viewers' panic, in the event they fail to interpret the signals
sent so overtly in the imagery that these are not really birds, or at least
not vicious birds, or at least not birds truly engaged in warfare against
the human species in this quaint little town, or at least not actual inter-
positions of the sharpnesses of birds into the softnesses of human flesh.
A sort of culmination is reached by Richard Allen, who proclaims it
"right" that scholarship has found in this motion picture, essentially, a
melodrama "with the attacks of the birds that temporarily interrupt that
thread" and who decides that a "power of any hysterical femininity that
requires containment" has a way of generating "the Hitchcockian universe as whole" and that "[i]n *The Birds*, the social world of human interaction, embodied in the microcosm of the American family, is restored by
containing feminine agency" (Allen 281, 288). The attacks of the birds
interrupt something greater, wholer, more provocative, more central than

themselves, which is the human family and its vicissitudes. We should not, then, even pay too much attention to the birds themselves; not worry about the birds; not even *see* the birds, ideally. Slavoj Žižek wonders about the possibility of *The Birds* "without any birds" (104–06). Our focus turns toward poor, grieving Lydia Brenner (Jessica Tandy), her need to dominate by love, the rejected Annie who could never triumph over this matriarch, the son whose filial duty is recognized and accepted by the stranger who through this recognition gains passage into the family life, the little sister's coy little lovebirds symbolizing what? the love of one bird for another?—no, the love that Mitch should ideally be able to consummate with Melanie, the love Lydia seems never fully to have had herself with the man who is no longer by her side and that, therefore, she extends to her son. What, then, imagined from this humanistic perspective, must we take the birds to be in their violent movements—their plastic, superficial, simplistic, artificial movements—but symbols of this familial agon of blood and passion? Yet even as I can grasp the logic of this argument, see it as geometrically pure and fascinating in its structure considered independently of this or any particular work of art, this film does not strike me as a metaphor upon humanism when I watch it, and, fool that I am, the birds always and inevitably do seem real, their visitations—call them "attacks"—entirely actual. Let us say, following Thomas and Znaniecki, the birds are real when, and as long as, we are watching them as real (*Peasant*), projections and artifices only in our deconstruction. Dan Fawcett's face would be convincing enough, except that even the first visit—that gull dropping onto Melanie in her dinghy—has all the ring of reality I need, the ring, that is, that Melanie herself has for me, coiffed and furred and rowing across that inlet as though the oars are natural extensions of her arms. The birds are real *enough*, and their attacks have a logic that seems to me to emanate from some invisible source of organization and intelligence, a bird mind, that is to say, a species mind, all this to the extent that they appear, these birds, to have a view of the human condition (a view Hitchcock even depicts explicitly) of, as Allen has it, the "social world of human interaction," which world is certainly not simply "embodied in the microcosm of the American family" anymore than in a gas station, a restaurant, a scholarly career such as ornithology, a tiny general store-cum-post office, a school, a newspaper owned or partly owned by somebody's father, a musical composition. When with the hovering gulls we gaze down at Bodega Bay burning (that is, at Albert Whitlock's stunning six-foot-square matte painting, which I gazed upon, one hazy afternoon in the 1970s at New York's Hammer Gallery), we see much more than the American family, more than melodrama, and we note, almost without thinking, how quaint and vulnerable it all is from the right point of vantage. The birds see this, too. Allen argues about the birds, "If their beady eyes suggest an inside, it is a hollow interior" (289), which is to say, having no agency they constitute a human projection, the vibrant excrescence of a wound produced by mothers and sons, and yet with his camera, which now makes our eyes the birds' eyes, our perspective from on high their perspective, Hitchcock has given the lie to this kind of argument. One cannot fly forever. The land looks so appealing. Why should we not go down and stand upon it, perch on a jungle gym, squat on a roof?

2. Control

The birds in their attacks are surprising, and we say that surprises come out of thin air. The shot of the seagulls hovering over the burning town: does it not reveal that for these creatures, equipped as they are with the one appendage of which mankind has eternally been jealous, the air is not altogether thin, at least not so fashioned by the creative spirit hovering above all that it might prove as insubstantial as to our lowly human eyes it persists in appearing? These birds *are* standing in thin air, in fact, or even sitting, in defiance of gravity, gaining through this feat an aura of extreme potency, even a divine glow as though by moving in proximity to the heavens some capacity has been imbued in, and some force has worn off on, them. When they mass together in flight and then descend to meet their tidily organized human neighbors, they seem to transport and invoke powers of which we can only stand in wonder and fear. (Hitchcock was fond enough of airplanes, yet in this film of the air not a touch of aeronautical engineering is to be found.) The birds are thus not simply signs for Nature in general (nature that includes lowly insects, rivers that we dam for electricity, trees that we fell); they reference what they are, living powers that supersede us in at least one vital dimension. How eagerly we would like to believe, the scene at the diner shows, that in deft analysis, in articulate language, in emotion, in resilience, in the investment of capital we easily dominate all things and gain a prospect from which to look down upon even the birds. They cannot have a plan, we tell ourselves; they cannot be acting with intentionality, and in this way we deny them as objects of value. When we are impotent, writes Max Scheler, "the oppressive sense of inferiority which always goes with the 'common' attitude cannot lead to active behaviour. Yet the painful tension demands relief," so "the common man seeks a feeling of superiority or equality, and he attains his purpose by an illusory *devaluation* of the [other's] qualities or by a specific 'blindness' to these qualities" (Scheler 34). And if, particularly, the genteel little cages we manufacture to house them contain and curtail the birds' impulse and extension, more broadly our intellect and communication form a cage in which birds are trapped and bounded in the world at large so that their perching and their soaring are measurable for us and, through our ability to define and describe, leashed (as though our thought were the rubber band holding the gull from Hedren's face). Repeatedly the alarm is sounded when the birds transgress their cages. In the pet shop, the degree of Melanie's discomfort when the tiny bird is flying free and its counterpart, a seemingly effortless domination displayed by Mitch in putting this secret of the air under his hat, reflect upon the social importance of maintaining a belief in the unchallenged efficacy of techniques and technologies of control. In the jungle gym scene the birds, who are copresent with the filmmaker, exercise nothing less than a methodical step-by-step interrogation of our ability to sustain that belief. The cage, an elaborate system of manners and attitudes, not to say walls and surfaces, is offered in smug independence by all those who take the liberty of configuring avian life; and in the sequence at Dan Fawcett's farm we see not only that the cagey civilization we have erected for constraint is inadequate but also that it is mocked and reviled in its hopeless inutility as a token of our superabundant arrogance: see how the delicate teacups, one by one, have been shattered as they hang so sweetly upon their pegs.

3. Tireisias

Dan Fawcett's eyes are replaced, it would seem, not by pearls, evidencing a sea change, but by portals to the dark abyss. Yet the twin black vacancies, shown those three times in the celebrated triple jump cut, are surely not indicative of the absence of vision, surely do not denote the twin fields from which soaring raptors, ravenous and rapacious, have in a jerky unmeditated frenzy plucked out as food his spectacular organ. Vivian Sobchack recognizes that when we see "what is believed to be a real corpse" onscreen, "we respond to it always as other than we are and as an object," and then, "The corpse as a body-object is physically passive, semiotically impassive" (236–37). I take this to mean not only that we do not feel ourselves to be things in the way that we regard a corpse to be, but also that the body as corpse cannot do, but can be done to; and if it speaks—if it is or has language—it expresses the fact of itself, but not feeling, presence but not experience. It is in this semiological impassivity that finally Fawcett is mobilized for us, however, and as we confront it, suddenly he is not *only* other than we are; and we note that he does see, that the dark orbs are eyes of darkness seeing past the

limits of what we can limn and define. He sees beyond what our bodies, seeing and knowing that they see, can see. The dead Fawcett, then,
"sees" the birds for what they are and credits them with an identity that
Melanie Daniels only fears and suspects, only tends toward acknowledging. For surely there are two shocks waiting for the audience in that
triple cut: first that the farmer is not only dead, but dead with his eyes
eaten out, quite as though his organ of vision is nothing but a meal, his
seeing and understanding (our seeing and understanding) only a protein
to satisfy some gelid alien hunger; but secondly that eyeless, he finally
really does see, and see what we have been blinded to all along. This
because our *sense* of him as he lies there in his gaping emptiness, utterly
belying our intelligence and deduction, is that in this condition he has
indeed seen, *and persists in seeing*, a truth we might call "horrific" if we
did not comprehend its sweeping magnificence and simplicity. In the
story that is the origin of this film, "The Birds," by Daphne du Maurier
(1952), there is no indication of such an eyeless victim, such a Tireisias.
The farmer there is dead, but his eyes are in his head, so he sees
nothing.

4. Hysteria

Nor does Du Maurier provide us with a model for Melanie Daniels,
her story being focused upon a Cornish estate farmer, Nat Hocken,
whose eye is rather naturally attuned to changes in the weather (since
he has crops to be concerned about). He has a family to protect, and,
like Mitch Brenner, he ultimately sets himself to the assiduous board-
ing up of a little house; and he does find his neighbors slain, in a way
that is described rather circumlocutionally; but, his wife's persisting, and
persistently intelligent, concerns aside, there is no central female who
comes slowly unhinged as the birds attack, except, perhaps—and she
makes a clear show of maintaining the greatest poise during what may
be terrifying her—the author herself:

> "Won't America do something?" said his wife. "They've always
> been our allies, haven't they? Surely America will do something?"
>   Nat did not answer. The boards were strong against the
> windows, and on the chimneys too. The cottage was filled with
> stores, with fuel, with all they needed for the next few days. When
> he had finished dinner he would put the stuff away, stack it neatly,
> get everything shipshape, handy-like. His wife could help him, and
> the children too. They'd tire themselves out. (38)

Before leaping, however, to the conclusion that *The Birds* revolves around the hysterical female, and drawing whatever theoretical link between female and avian experience, notwithstanding the obviously discomfited presence of Melanie in Bodega Bay once the attacks have commenced and the similarly discomposed behavior of the diner owner's wife, the ornithologist, and the mother who has gone out of control in fear for the safety of her children, it pays to consider the relatively tranquil demeanor of Lydia Brenner and Annie Hayworth, both of whom seem acutely aware of what is happening around them even as they fail significantly to react with spasms of withdrawal. Melanie, indeed, becomes more and more like Annie and Lydia as the narrative progresses, protective and sober—

589 FULL SHOT—THE LIVING ROOM

A kerosene lamp is burning. Melanie is awake, watching the fire. Lydia has fallen into a semi-recumbent position asleep on the couch. Cathy is curled up in one of the easy chairs. Mitch is asleep by the fire. The fire is burning brightly and steadily. The house is almost still. There is no longer the sound of the clawing and pecking, but there is another SOUND now: the sound of SOMETHING FALLING, or dropping in a steady dribbling, difficult to place.

590 CLOSE SHOT—MELANIE

listening to the curious sound, trying to fathom its meaning.

MELANIE: (whispering) Mitch?

591 MED. SHOT—MELANIE

as she turns toward him.

MELANIE: (still whispering) Mitch?

592 CLOSE SHOT—MITCH

asleep.

593 CLOSE SHOT—MELANIE

> seeing this, making her decision. The SOUND is still coming
> from somewhere in the house. She decides to let Mitch sleep and
> investigate it herself. She rises, goes to the table, picks up a very
> long flashlight. (Script, 164)

—and is thus finally able to withstand the awful attack in the attic (SHOT
615: "Melanie is overwhelmed by the birds") and embrace the family as
they exit the scene. Perhaps it is sufficient to say that it is not femininity
per se that flails under the unyielding scrutiny of the birds—unyielding but not unhesitating, because in both the story and the film there
are distinct periods when the creatures retreat to mass up again with
new force, periods in which the humans can take a breath and realign
their defenses—but a certain style of enacting the female performance,
one influenced by the near and controlling presence of powerful men,
the men of Melanie's life, for example, who are only mentioned in the
film but about whose easy dominance we can glean much. (Mitch shows
capacity in the presence of his mother but does not control her.) The
ordeal of the bird ravaging frees Melanie completely from the brittle and
conventional role she has been having to play all her urban life. "This
seems to me the function of the birds," writes Robin Wood: "they are
a concrete embodiment of the arbitrary and unpredictable, of whatever
makes human life and human relationships precarious, a reminder of
fragility and instability that cannot be ignored or evaded and, beyond
that, of the possibility that life is meaningless and absurd" (154). Yes,
and both Lydia and Annie seem aware already, to a degree that the
Melanie we meet early in the film is not, of instability and fragility in
life. Consider that the diner owner's wife can routinely defer to him to
make critical judgments; that the ornithologist is both masculinized and
subject to the requirements, codes, and empowerments of (male-dominated) academic scholarship; that the frenzied mother has been sundered
from her protecting husband while she lunches with the children; and
that Melanie shows herself from the start to be, above all, daddy's girl.
It is as daddy's girl, after all, that she has been able to survive her own
reputation for socially reckless behavior. Many viewers have surmised
that Lydia Brenner, grieving for her dead husband, invokes an Oedipal
conflict wherein she attempts to possess her son as a replacement, this
apparently because she once rejected the presumed girlfriend, Annie,
and because she does not appear overly friendly to Melanie when first
they meet. But these are misreadings. Lydia is a citizen of the country,
not the city; she is not gregarious; she is slow to know and to trust,
and her feelings are held in, so her initial slightly distanced civility to
Melanie is absolutely in character and not a signal of antipathy. Annie,

she may well have seen, is too much like herself, a woman, that is, too sympathetic with Mitch to really find him interesting. Listen to the way Annie speaks of Mitch, with a voice that could be a sister's. Some have argued, nonsensically I think, that the extreme youth of Mitch's actual sister leads us to see him as being coupled with his mother, with Cathy as their progeny. Mitch is clearly a generation removed from his mother; and were Cathy to be his child by another marriage, it would hardly change the girl's relationship to anyone, Mitch's to his mother, or Mitch's to Melanie. The Brenner farm is typically removed from the town, in this case by a circuitous drive or a long row, and Lydia is thus distanced, from the moment we meet her, from the comforting place-bos of social intercourse. In a similar way, Annie's residence is secluded. Both of these women have come to learn the difficulties of living in this world and know the birds for precisely what Wood describes them to be. Given that Melanie comes to emulate these women, one of them martyred, indeed, in such a way that Melanie's consciousness of her can only be heightened, we can find her at the end of the film as a person standing beside, yet not subject to, a man she cares for. Far from being a treatise on women's abject hysteria, this film valorizes the women who bear up to the bird attacks stoically, resolutely, calmly. The little sister is included, a harbinger of generations to come.

5. Arabesque

And what a macabre little girl this is! Her brother, she tells Melanie with some delight, is defending a man who shot his wife in the head six times, and "even twice would be overdoing it!" One shot to the head, in short, is entirely sufficient, as she imagines the world. This sister (Veronica Cartwright) is nothing if not garrulous, chattering on and on, in her excitement to make friends with Melanie, about her brother's views on San Francisco being "like an anthill at the foot of a bridge," the deten-tion cells at the Hall of Justice, "all that democracy jazz," her birthday party, the proprieties of murder, Mitch's apartment in the city. The film displays a kind of continuum of female garrulousness, in fact, ranging from Melanie at one end; through Annie Hayworth and the ornithologist; to Lydia Brenner and the pet shop manager, Mrs. MacGruder (Ruth McDevitt), who chirps like a plump canary; and finally the gabby little sister and her countless squealing, cavorting agemates. All of these crea-tures are birds of a sort, tweeting urgently or merrily regardless of what else is going on, as though their message is more important to them than the context in which they send it. If it could be said to be true of Hitchcock, as Truffaut offered, that his "love scenes were filmed like murder scenes, and the murder scenes like love scenes" (345), it seems evident, too, that in *The Birds* the humans very frequently seem avian, and the birds very frequently seem human. The sound design of the postprandial scene in which Cathy is nattering to Melanie is part of its charm and its intrigue. Immediately before this, as a set-up, there is a long telephone conversation in which Lydia Brenner is complaining to Fred Brinkmeyer about the feed he has sold her for her chickens, because the chickens will not eat. We have Lydia in the foreground in a static shot, with Mitch and Melanie moving around behind her just out of focus and discussing the portrait of Mitch's father, which hangs above the piano. It is here, for example, in the background discussion between these two that occasionally punctuates the pauses in Lydia's foregrounded telephone call, that we first learn about the death of Mitch's father and thus have grounds for making surmises about the relations among Lydia, Mitch, and Cathy. The meat of Lydia's conversation, meanwhile, is that there is a problem with her birds, and this is perhaps the first time we have cause for suspicion and alarm, since it is the second instantiation of bird trouble in Bodega Bay (the first having been that gull attack while Melanie was in the row boat, an attack we might easily pass off as circumstantial until now, when it seems to have a strange reflection). Because Lydia's conversation is so crucial to our concerns about "the birds"—concerns raised by the film's title and promotion if not yet by the story onscreen—it is fascinating to observe how Hitchcock rhythmically draws it forward into, and drops it backward out of, our acoustic focus by using this background conversation as a kind of counterpoint. On the note that Fred sold Lydia's neighbor Dan Fawcett a different kind of feed and Fawcett's birds are not eating, either—"You don't think the birds could be sick, do you, Mitch?"—the scene slowly dissolves to the conversation between Melanie and Cathy at the piano. And again here, but this time even more distinctly, we can see a contrapuntal juxtaposition of two sound productions, one representing the expressiveness of the little girl in her eager delight and the other representing that of Melanie in her reserve and courteousness: Cathy prates—with Hitchcock turning his camera directly into her face to make this emphatic—while Melanie is absorbed in playing the piano. In short, the little girl is talking over Melanie's music making, with Melanie decidedly turning her head toward Cathy once in a while to respond with etiquette to her young hostess even as the hostess, perhaps in her youth and innocence— she cannot tell the male lovebird from the female—sees fit to interrupt the music. It is true that no one asked Melanie to play—at least not in the diegesis as we have it—and true, too, that in certain circumstances individuals who have no particular attraction to music might take it as nothing but acoustic wallpaper to fill in the background of the human interaction they consider more important. Nevertheless, Melanie's choice of music is a particular one, a piece of extreme apparent simplicity and melodiousness, not to say smooth and flowing tranquility, that turns out to be exactly the acoustic contradiction of Cathy's imperious and eager staccato outbursts of disconnected thought: Claude Debussy's *Arabesque No. 1.* ("A Debussy Arabesque" is specifically nominated in the final shooting script [Script, 53].) This piece, which some musicologists date from 1888 but which did not see print until 1891 or real popularity until early in the twentieth century (Richard Parks suggests the possibility that the piece was composed even earlier [5]), begins with a melody built upon an arpeggio, this a way for a pianist such as Melanie to show off some technique while at the same time not demanding bravura style of the sort she has not yet developed (Hitchcock paid several thousand dollars to have Hedren take piano lessons for twenty-one days so as to be able artfully to simulate these shots [Sullivan 270]; she does, but it is not the fingerings we see with our eyes that we hear on the soundtrack). Melanie can thus establish herself a little as a young woman whose reputation—as we cut to the kitchen, with the playing in the background off-scene, we see Lydia confronting Mitch about precisely this reputation—does not thoroughly cover over all of her talents; and, too, as an American who has been influenced by European culture (she apparently bathed nude in a fountain in Rome!) in a way that the modesties of the bourgeoisie would applaud: the Arabesque, after all, is a European form participating in the general project of Orientalist admiration that was flowering in the latter nineteenth century, and the particular selection of Debussy positions Melanie's music-making in the post-Wagnerian cycle of early French Impressionism. It is not, however, harmonically challenging in the way that Debussy's later music is—Parks calls the phrasing "square and blatantly articulated" (5)—and thus, refraining from challenging either the player or the listener, works both to define Melanie as exactly the sort of conventional girl Mitch might successfully bond with (within his mother's purview)—the *Arabesque* "is exceptional in Debussy's oeuvre for its adherence to certain traditional tonal and formal conventions," writes Parks (5)—and to make plausible a scene in which we can hear the beautiful progress of the musical notes while incessantly being interrupted by vocal information that intrudes without warning and at the same amplitude. In both the living room phone conversation and after-dinner piano scenes, then, enjambed through that dissolve, background and foreground acoustic events are placed in competition just in such a way that we can, and must, attend thoroughly to both. The first scene allows us to know that trouble is brewing with the birds but at the same time that trouble may already be brewed in the Brenner family; the second scene allows us to see Melanie's qualities, sensibilities, and tastes, all admirable, while simultaneously confronting us with the possibility there is something maudlin, even grotesque, about the people she is now befriending. Consider, then, that "innocent" little Cathy Brenner—who has a sharp gleam in her eye when she presses Melanie about her brother's legal business—thinks six shots in the head is excessive when "even twice would be overdoing it," that is, that it is necessary and permissible on some occasions to deliver *one* shot to the head; and that this same girl has been put in charge of the only two impeccably innocent birds we see in the film, birds, indeed, who cannot escape their cage to be free of her; that it is the Brenner house the birds seem concentrated upon attacking, the house not only of Lydia and Mitch Brenner and, now, their guest Melanie Daniels, but also of little Cathy with her imprisoned victims. Melanie's music is something like her birdsong, fluid and ephemeral. It is interrupted over and over by Cathy's innocent pecking. And now the birds come upon this house—after first having a try at the school where Cathy is to be found with her classmates. It is essential to have the Debussy. Were Cathy to be interrupting Bartok or even Mozart with her quips, we should not see her for the aggressive little thing that she is. Yet Cathy is only the human condition in development. Her little joke about shots to the head resonates with viewers. Anyone and everyone might say such a thing and mean it as she does: not that any shots would be overdoing it, but that two would. Not, by the way, "would *have been* overdoing it" as a way of referencing what this accused client of Mitch's is alleged to have done, but "would *be* overdoing it," as though this is an action currently in contemplation for future execution. Cathy is a rational planner, but Melanie and her Debussy seem to move along in an oneiric delight.

6. Class

Vertical alignment was a theme precious to Hitchcock. There is a widespread presumption shared in many cultures, he knew, that as a species the birds fall beneath human beings, occupy a humbler class. Thus, when we hear an outlandish piece of nonsense, when our attention is drawn to garbage, we delightedly proclaim it as belonging properly not to the human race at all but to "the birds"—those outcasts; this attitude is reflected in the assassin Gromek's (Wolfgang Kieling) menacing comments to Michael Armstrong (Paul Newman) in *Torn Curtain* (1966), as he prepares to turn him in as a spy. Armstrong has evaded Gromek's

pursuit by ducking into, then out of, the Kunstmuseum, but Gromek
has found him:

> GROMEK: What's wrong, Professor? In one door—(he whistles,
> making a swift movement with his hand)—out the other. You don't
> like our museum?

> ARMSTRONG: I've seen better ones.

> GROMEK: Strictly for the birds, huh? They still say that? We used
> to say it all the time. (quoting himself half-remembered Brooklynese)
> "Ah, dats strictly for de boids!" (Moore 69)

Melanie Daniels, who if she were from Brooklyn would never permit
herself to speak this way, has amassed some cultural credentials, and we
can see her self-possession, the pride of ownership she feels for her own
valuable accomplishments, in the fur coat, the carriage, the assertiveness
in finding out where Mitch Brenner has gone for the weekend, and
even the way she stiffens a tiny bit when Mitch's young sister rushes
up to embrace her to say thank you for the lovebirds. Yet as a cultural
exemplar Melanie may not stand alone. After the Brenner dinner she
returns to Annie Hayworth's, where she is spending the night, and we
are treated to the display of framed paintings (or reproductions) on
Annie's walls as well as to a framed program for Wagner's *Tristan und
Isolde* standing behind her phonograph. Annie, too, affiliates with the
postromantic movement that was sweeping Europe from 1870 onward,
and with modern art, and with literature. She is not, however, independently wealthy, even though, like Melanie, she had affection for
Mitch; even though, like Melanie, she affiliates with culture; there is a
class difference that separates the two women. Late in the film, Mitch
Brenner sets himself to remodeling the house, as Nat had done in the
story: "He made the children help him rearrange the furniture, and he
took the precaution of moving the dresser, with his wife's help, across
the window. It fitted well. It was an added safeguard. The mattresses
could now be lain, one beside the other, against the wall where the
dresser had stood" (Du Maurier 22). Mitch's work is nest building of a
special kind, since he has put a mind to defenses, not coziness. But like
any bird assiduously scraping together a home for a family's safety, he is
set to hammering and blockading, inspecting and worrying the future.
He is crafty, he is cagey, but in the end his nest is insecure, its attic
and upstairs bedroom an open roost. The theme of vertical dominance

that had been sounded with Melanie and Annie—an apparent equality trumped by class considerations—is now echoed as Mitch, putting
himself up against his adversaries in home design, comes out the loser.
Which species is the more advanced, avian or human? Who is left
onscreen at the end of the film, sweetly purring at the sunset, after the
troublesome humans have retreated? Now, the revolution having come,
Bodega Bay is strictly for de boids.

7. East

When Melanie is driving away from the Brenner house after dinner, a
horde of clucking birds has massed on the telephone wires along the
road. The next day, the sound of these birds is recalled by the sound
of the children squealing in play during Cathy's birthday party, all this
heard by Melanie and Mitch as they climb to the top of an adjacent hill
with a carafe of martinis. We are alerted, then, to the avian world during
this party and this conversation, and it is somewhat less shocking than
it might otherwise be that the party ends in catastrophe because of a
seagull attack. Were we not to be prepared at all, the relation between
the wildly attacking birds and the tame children with the pink birthday
cake might seem too extreme, too wildly improbable, and our attention thus might be slightly dampened by disbelief. But as it is, every
movement at this party is, in a way, a bird movement, every sound a
bird sound. Melanie and Mitch come to talk of mothers and mothers'
love. Melanie bitterly announces that her mother "ditched us when I
was eleven and ran off with some hotel man in the east. You know
what a mother's love is!" This hotel man, who makes no appearance
in this film or that one, had been present as well in *Psycho*, as the root
and cause of Norman Bates's troubles with his mother. But the east,
as a source of corruption, disruption, sexual incontinence, and allure
was also, of course, more broadly speaking, Europe, the center out of
which Melanie's culture flowed and the cauldron in which she became
"lost," hung out with the wrong people, was pushed into that fountain
in Rome. The West, on the other hand, is pure and untrammeled. Mitch
is a Western hero fallen for a woman affected by the East. Du Maurier's
story is set in England, to be sure, but in the west country, most likely
Cornwall since the protagonist, Nat Hocken, likes to sit on the cliff's
edge watching the birds while eating a pasty (a traditional Cornish
preparation). The birds who mass suddenly upon the sea and suddenly
attack—" 'Did you hear that?' he said. 'They went for me. Tried to peck
my eyes.' " (4)—don't, apparently, simply appear but are delivered to
civilization: "It's the weather," repeated Nat. "I tell you, it's the weather,"

but, more specifically, "It was the east wind brought them in" (6, 7). Later, Nat reflects that the bird attacks are "like air-raids in the war. No one down this end of the country knew what the Plymouth folk had seen and suffered" (9) in the face of attacks from Germany, which is to say, the East. Nat must soon announce what he has heard on the wireless, that "[i]n London, all over the country . . . something has happened to the birds" (11)—London, east of Cornwall. The source of contagion migrates ever eastward. A neighboring farmer confides to Nat, "They're saying in town the Russians have done it. The Russians have poisoned the birds" (19). "They've got reasoning powers," thinks Nat (24), calling up rationality, philosophy, intellect, culture—the product of the East; calling up, indeed, history and racial memory, all eastern, all original: "Nat listened to the tearing sound of splintering wood, and wondered how many million years of memory were stored in those little brains" (38). For Western man, after all, the East is "the place of origin of his old self, that original Adam, whom the New World presumably made a New Man," as Leslie Fiedler informs us (19). "The study of mental states of animals who cannot report their thoughts to us is beset with difficulties," report Bernd Heinrich and Thomas Bugnyar, "Indeed, we do not know and perhaps can never know what goes on in the mind of another animal or even other individual of our own species. Yet invoking Occam's razor and accepting the simplest explanation, as is traditional in science, we can conclude that our experiments provide a consistent affirmation that ravens use some kind of mental representation to guide their actions . . . Learning occurs, but it alone cannot account for all of the observed behavior, because the behavior is exhibited very fast, almost immediately, without any trials and errors" (71). And the production team found this true in practice: "Boyle: Oh, they were fantastic animals. We grew to have tremendous respect for the crows. We did not like gulls who . . . crows you could reason with, but the rest they were sheer greed. The gulls just came for food, so we put a little perch in front of the camera and they'd fly almost into the lens to get food. So that wasn't very difficult, but the crows were pretty wily. We had to work with them. Negotiate. Negotiate a deal" (Krohn 47).

But for his part, Mitch looks very much the New Man atop this hillock, the sunlight beaming off him and showing his every expression to be ingenuous, spontaneous, unmotivated by a perduring history. Even if she has recently been living in San Francisco, Melanie, with her culture and her sophistication, seems a creature of the East. One begins to have the sense, after she has confided in Annie Hayworth, that Melanie has knowledge, and in the culminating bird attacks, as beleaguered as she is, she is never mystified.

8. Value

Lydia drives her pick-up to Dan Fawcett's farm, finds the place in disarray. This is a recasting of Du Maurier's scene of the visit to Jim Trigg's farm—

> He went down alone to the farm. He pushed his way through the herd of bellowing cows, which turned this way and that, distressed, their udders full. He saw the car standing by the gate, not put away in the garage. The windows of the farm-house were smashed. There were many dead gulls lying in the yard and around the house. The living birds perched on the group of trees behind the farm and on the roof of the house. They were quite still. They watched him. Jim's body lay in the yard . . . what was left of it. When the birds had finished, the cows had trampled him. (34)

—insofar as anything in this film can be strictly called a "recasting," given Hitchcock's riposte to the zealous François Truffaut, eager to know how many times he had read the Du Maurier story, "What I do is to read a story only once, and if I like the basic idea, I just forget all about the book and start to create cinema" (qtd. in Du Maurier vi). Fawcett, at any rate, has no eyes. "The effect of the experience on Lydia," writes Robin Wood, stunningly, "calls to mind the effect on Mrs. Moore of her experience in the Marabar cave in E. M. Forster's *A Passage to India*. Hitchcock's image is more powerful and terrible than Forster's, it arises more naturally from its context and seems less 'applied': one is never quite convinced that an echo could mean all that" (164). Well, the elderly Mrs. Moore, who has come to India to visit her son, an official in the Raj, is surely hearing *something*, whereas Lydia is being confronted by an absence—say that she hears no echo when she believes she should and desires to. Along with Adela Quested, a young Englishwoman whom her son thinks to marry, Mrs. Moore has been invited by the kindly Dr. Aziz to a picnic in the Marabar Caves. Adela, too, hears the startling echo: she is a woman ethnocentric in the extreme, as it turns out, although she would be loathe to think of herself this way, whereas Mrs. Moore has made an attempt in all seriousness and sincerity to reach across the abyss and genuinely touch India, let herself be touched by it, and having failed, because the echo, suddenly giving her a sense of a formless universe—"The more she thought it over, the more disagreeable and frightening it became" (149)—has terrified her to her core she takes steps to leave the country. As to that echo the women hear: all the mystery in the world attaches to it, surely from Adela's perspective, as she has made herself terrified of every nuance of this territory and culture and is consequently ready to hear ghosts on every corner. An echo could, indeed, "mean all that" if it were sounded in the right place, at the right moment, to the right listener in the right frame of mind; it could mean at least as much as pictures of birds, which are what echo for us. After their discussion about Lydia, Annie and Melanie are getting ready to go to bed, Melanie showing off the rather hideous nightgown she purchased at the general store (and that we never see her wear). There is a knock at the door. Annie goes to open it, and Melanie sees a massive gull lying dead on the doorstep. "Poor thing!" says Annie, "It must have lost its way in the dark," but Melanie cannot take her eyes off the distant sky, which centers the shot, pulled through with streaks of pewter gray and ethereal white. "But it isn't dark at all, Annie!" says she. "The moon is out." This sky recalls the one we saw only moments before, ominous and yet still, with the masses of birds lined up on the telephone wire outside the Brenner farm; it is distant and yet far too proximate, the locus of possibility in a context where possibility has been defined, increasingly scene by scene, as dangerous and mortal. This sky is the equivalent of Forster's echo in the cave, an echo that presages what Adela Quested, later, in all her ignorance, is convinced is an instant of physical contact initiated by the putatively uncontainable Mr. Aziz. Just as Aziz represents the unknown heading our way for contact, so, too, do Hitchcock's birds offer the same thrill and frisson, present the same terrifying promise. "The more [Mrs. Moore] thought over it, the more disagreeable and frightening it became . . . Coming at a moment when she chanced to be fatigued, it had managed to murmur 'Pathos, piety, courage—they exist, but are identical, and so is filth. Everything exists, nothing has value.'" Worse, for old Mrs. Moore and for Lydia, too, one might well surmise: "Religion appeared, poor little talkative Christianity, and she knew that all its divine words from 'Let there be light' to 'It is finished' only amounted to 'boum.'" (139). "Boum" and the noiseless, vectorless, incomprehensible chatter of the birds.

9. Spectacle

While I may seem utterly simplistic in saying this, it bears repeating—especially in the context of this film (and of Hitchcock's work in general)—that we do not go to the movies in order to be told a story; we go in order to see. The eye itself does not have memory, does not comprehend time, and so the act of seeing is an engulfment in an extended present. The logic of narrative works in counterpoint to the energies of the visioning act, continually taking us away from what is presented here and now to enmesh us in memory traces that are not themselves within the optical field and in expectations as yet undefined and unclear for all their persistence. As with the Phantasmagoria of the early nineteenth century, what cinema provides for its viewers is a chain of "progressive appearances" (Mannoni 173), the spectacle inhering in both the continuous movement itself and the qualities of perspective and illusion that are managed in making depiction. When we watch *The Birds*, two contradictory trains of feeling and awareness are offered. First, we can understand clearly enough that the citizens of Bodega Bay, including that temporary citizen Melanie, the Brenners, and the many strangers we see in and around the café, are moving through the story with mounting desperation that the birds, for whatever reason and through whatever plan of nature, are bent on malevolence and destruction. The bird appearances, from this point of view, beginning with the gull swooping onto Melanie and proceeding through various intermediary stages to the conflagration near the dock, the school attack, and the final apocalyptic onset upon the Brenner home (even leading to what may be imagined as the cataclysm to take place after our protagonists have escaped and the credits have rolled), certainly seem increasingly potent, increasingly probable, increasingly awful, and precisely dramatic in the sense that actions are undertaken that imply and promise outcomes that seem inevitably to follow. At the same time, however, we sit in the theater and watch the birds and their motions with something of the same detachment, curiosity, pleasure, and engagement that Melanie shows in the opening scene of the film as, strolling among their pretty cages, she makes an entertainment of watching the docile birds on display in the little shop at Union Square. Melanie, Mitch, Mitch's family, the residents of the town—all these are as so many birds in a cage to us, as are the birds who fly at them, to be sure: the cage is the film. The birds and all that they do are spectacles for us, and in the way that Hitchcock has filmed their movements they constitute an essentially cinematic show, not a logical story. Our visual interest in the birds does not increase when we surmise that they are working upon a plan or when we tell ourselves their acts are random. Nor is it augmented when we see the destruction they have accomplished *as* an avian production, when we allow ourselves to be concerned, as the characters are, that more destruction of this kind is probable. The birds simply are, just as the echo in Forster's Marabar cave simply is: "The echo in Marabar cave is . . . entirely devoid of distinction," the learned Prof. Godbole intones. "Whatever is said, the same monotonous noise replies, and quivers up and down the walls" (147). The phenomenon of the echo is not enriched by virtue of what is said, then, and what is said disappears entirely into the phenomenon of its own ostensibly end-less repetition. In just such a way as this, the phenomenon of the birds is most emphatically spectacular because it is disconnected from logic, calculation, rationality, the future, the past.

10. Present

"Today is what's important to them, not the dollar that tomorrow might bring. I guess the Yankees might say that's lazy," Jim Bowie (Richard Widmark) says to Davy Crockett (John Wayne) in *The Alamo* (1960). Narrative is an investment, a northern preoccupation, always, until it is exhausted, invoking an important future. Spectacle, lazy and lovely, however it may bring nightmares and fears, is southern. In tone, in implication, in presentation, in characterization *The Birds* is Hitchcock's most southern film to date, if also, ironically, a rational and mechanical masterpiece—"*The Birds* is the most mechanical of all his films," claims Elisabeth Weis (145)—and a year later *Marnie* would follow and join it (163–69). What we experience in *The Birds* is a fluttering, extended, directionless, aggressive present.

11. Point of View

The shot looking down on Bodega Bay as the gas station explodes was required by Hitchcock's sensitivity to his audience always having a clear line of approach to the filmic material at each moment, a standard operat-ing directive that propelled him always. The sequence with the gasoline fire, he believed, had *too* many elements: it had the phone booth where Tippi went; it had the fire at the gas station, where the attendant was being attacked by the gulls. There was the man who was lighting his cigar. There were the other people in the café, so Hitchcock said, "We need here a shot to re-orient the audience." He always thought about the audience. He said, "It's getting too many places. We need something that will never be mistaken for anybody's viewpoint, except God's point of view." He very often would call these extreme objective shots God's point of view.

> Well, how are you going to get gulls under the camera? Of course, the simplest thing would have been to do it with animation and superimpose that animation over the thing, but to do it without getting too many dupe prints involved. Because we knew we were going to have to have a lot of different pieces of film to make up

that shot. One of the main things was how to look down on the
top of gulls flying. Well, we finally went out to Anacapa Island,
where there's a very tall hundred-foot cliff. And that was done by
shooting down and throwing fish out, and the gulls would come
down to grab the fish as we threw them. And now you got a down
shot. So you had real gulls. (Boyle 186–87)

In this shot, a few gulls are hovering over the burning town, seemingly
in conversation as down on the ground the flames consume the gas station; the viewer floats just above the birds, a member of their species and
conspirator in their success. The shot represents two accomplishments. It
offers, first, a stunning vision, perhaps a vision to outshine all the shocking and enervating visions of the film. The birds, after all, have a perfect
point of view, or at least one that seems boundless and ideally pleasurable.
So if the bird attacks in general are visions to galvanize us, this shot
permits us to see the birds reflecting our own spectatorial hunger; the
birds become viewers themselves for a vision that is beyond spectacular.
At the same time, however, this shot announces itself as presenting a
spectacular point of view. Beyond offering, and being, spectacle, then, it
affirms the principle of spectacle, all the while placing the flying gulls
in its center as our focal priority, as if to say not only, "spectacle is a
bird's-eye view" or even "spectacle is birds in flight" but, pronouncedly,
"See, note, calculate what a penchant the viewer has for spectacle itself."
Spectacle is the true spectacle of this film. The birds are spectacular.
Many viewers have tried to fathom, "What are the birds symbolic of?"
They are symbolic of nature overwhelming mankind, symbolic of transgression, symbolic of immorality, symbolic of love gone wrong, symbolic
of the fury of childhood withheld too long. The birds are not symbolic;
they are spectacular; they are the essence of cinema, something to look
at. It is looking we must consider as the central movement of the film,
not understanding, not decoding, not interpreting, not making sense.
Looking is before, above all these, as the birds are before, above all of
us. And looking is tactical, especially looking from on high: that is, the
high view has military value, and so does height itself. During the Civil
War, Jack Kelly notes, ingenious minds were devoted to the invention of
some infernal machine that could mechanically produce victory. "A man
named R. O. Davidson proposed a 'Bird of Art.' This was 'a machine for
aerial locomotion by man' carrying a 50-pound load of exploding shells.
A thousand of the birds, he was sure, would put an immediate end to
the war" (203). Our birds are even more advanced, warring but at the
same time envisioning a panorama.

12. Flight

In his science-fictional history of the human race, *Last and First Men*, Olaf Stapledon suggests the formation, more than 40 million years into our future, of "flying men." The Sixth Men, he writes, "had often been fascinated by the idea of flight. The bird was again and again their most sacred symbol" (195), and they invented flying machines and determined to produce a "true flying man" (196). The Seventh Men actually flew. "On the ground the Seventh Men walked much as other human beings, for the flight-membranes were folded close to the legs and body, and hung from the arms like exaggerated sleeves. In flight the legs were held extended as a flattened tail, with the feet locked together by the big toes . . . Their brains were given ample tracts for the organization of prowess in flight" (196). He goes on to stipulate how carefree these men were and that "[t]here was no occasion for them, as there had often been for some others, to regard the world as fundamentally hostile to life" (196). Their humanity was radically different on the ground and in the air:

> Life in the air was life at high pressure, and necessitated spells of recuperation on the ground. In their pedestrian phase the Seventh Men were sober folk, mildly bored, yet in the main cheerful, humorously impatient of the drabness and irk of pedestrian affairs, but ever supported by memory and anticipation of the vivid life of the air . . . [T]heir hearts were ever in the air. So long as they could have frequent periods of aviation, they remained bland even on the ground. But if for any reason such as illness they were confined to the ground for a long period, they pined, developed acute melancholia, and died. (197)

When we watch the human characters in *The Birds*, we see that they behave much like Seventh Men. Melanie and Mitch are at their most robust, their freshest, their most openly affecting, when they stand at the top of the hillock looking down on the birthday party from an airy position: this is not flight, but it comes close. The birds themselves might often be playing—the attack at the birthday party, watched objectively, yields many visions of birds swooping down onto the humans but not necessarily trying to injure them. The birds are squawking, and we have a tendency, unable as we are to comprehend this language, to guess that they are calling out war cries. The damage comes in the human projection. The birds surely wish to come close to the humans, and this is, physically speaking, a gesture that has its dangers, automatically, a savage intent entirely notwithstanding. What is profoundly revealed in this film, in scene after scene, is the debilitating effect of gravity on our spirits, our heavy attitude, our struggle to ascend. Stapledon tells us of the Flying Men's culture: "Of the arts, music, spoken lyric and epic verse, and the supreme art of winged dance, were constantly practiced," and in fact, "[t]he social order of the Seventh Men was in essence neither utilitarian, nor humanistic, nor religious, but aesthetic" (199). This aerial society lasted nearly 100 million years. As to Dan Fawcett, that poor victim: things sometimes go wrong. Here, it is clear, his eyes were the prize, and one may imagine birds not merely devouring them but instead trying to find a way to try them on. We are shown, with expert keylighting, astonishing visions of the other characters' eyes as they gaze at one another and at the sky—eyes that mimic the state of our own as, secretly in the darkness, we devour these visions. "*The Birds* is coming," Hitchcock gleefully caused the advertising for this film to (ungrammatically) read. Perhaps with their human eyes the birds is coming to watch Hitchcock's next film, *Marnie*.

13. Patterns

There is a scene outside the schoolhouse, with Melanie seated peacefully on the worn wooden bench smoking her cigarette while she waits for Annie's class to end, and the crows drop down onto the jungle gym behind her back, one then another and another and another . . . There is a creepy and irritating song she must be hearing, although she gives scant evidence, "Risseldy Rosseldy":

> I married my wife in the month of June,
> Risseldy, rosseldy, Mow, mow, mow,
> I carried her off in a silver spoon,
> Risseldy, Rosseldy,
> Hey bambassity,
> Nickety, nackety,
> Retrical quality,
> Willowby, wallowby,
> Mow, mow, mow,

It is a song of Irish origin, one perhaps influenced by "The Wee Cooper O' Fife,"

There was a wee cooper wha' lived in Fife,
Nickety nackety, noo, noo, noo
And he hae gotten a gentle wife,
Hey Willie Wallacky, Ho, John Dougal,
Alane quo' rushety roo, roo, roo.

We hear acousmetrically, it being apparent that the voices singing it belong to the children in the schoolroom whom we do not immediately see. Although Hitchcock does cut to the schoolroom, as John McCombe tells us: Annie has arranged the children into perfectly symmetrical rows, and they sing in perfect unison. The banality of all of this provides a counterpoint to the mayhem to come, but it also suggests the limits of imagination in the adult world of *The Birds*. The children's desks further provide a visual parallel to the equally orderly rows of bottles behind the bar in the Tides Restaurant, another conscious choice in the mise-en-scène that suggests humanity's futile attempt to impose order on the surrounding world. The process of imposing order and reason begins in school (75). The schoolroom is anything but the center of this scene, and the children's chanting becomes acousmetric as soon as we are watching Melanie outside, our true focus (see Chion). Is she, we can wonder, singing to herself, "Mow, mow, mow," and has she divided herself into a little chorus in order to do so—a little chorus in the way the crows form a little chorus? Is the melody something the crows are thinking of, willowby wallaby? It is so peaceful and quiet here in the open air of the country—that country air that is stifling Annie Hayworth but she will not admit it and that is stifling Melanie Daniels, so she loathes Bodega Bay, but the sounds from the schoolroom are wafting though the opened windows and penetrating this space in an irritating, repetitive, gnawing, snapping, erosive way. The sing-song up-and-down nature of the melody is blatantly pedagogical—"The process of imposing order . . . begins in school"—so pedagogy is suddenly everywhere. Even the playground is a schoolroom: the crows are certainly ready to impose, ready to imprint a lesson upon the bodies of those who can be made subject. A schoolroom becoming a playground: this interpenetration of interior and exterior is a modern development, Walter Benjamin, for one, having written about how the outside can be reflected upon an interior surface; but in this case, the penal interior extrudes, begins to imprint itself not only upon the birds but, through the agency of the birds, and once they have scattered into the street, upon the children. Melanie for one must take instruction. And now we can see that the birds, flocking together behind her, indeed also get the message. Perhaps they are coming to learn, to develop their native intelligence. Birds are certainly said to be sensitive to music—we often attribute human musicality to their utterances, calling them "birdsong"—so these ravens may be coming to hear the concert or learn the rhyme. Marry and carry, marrying and carrying—the film is full of references to housework or domesticity, marriage, elapsed marriage, troublesome marriage, wounded marriage, obstructed marriage, and much gets carried off in this film, lovebirds carried off, Annie's plans carried off, the innocence of children carried off, Dan Fawcett's eyes carried off. Perhaps the most pointed indication is the broken teacups that are hanging from little hooks in the kitchen of the Fawcett farm—domestic peace carried off, nickety nackety. But this sequence in the schoolyard has to be seen, not listened to. It strikes home because of the way the number of birds slowly increases, each bird in its turn seeming an ideal and logical addition to the forming crowd, and also natural, as it seeks a place to rest upon that appealing jungle gym, until—until what? Until a threshold is crossed. In Julio Cortázar's beautiful account of the crossing of thresholds, "A Small Story Tending to Illustrate the Uncertainty of the Stability within Which We Like to Believe We Exist, or Laws Could Give Ground to the Exceptions, Unforeseen Disasters, or Improbabilities, and I Want to See You There," a confidential memorandum from the secretary of OCLUSIOM has admitted to "terrible confusion" as the committee meets to elect replacements for the six office holders who all died as a result of being injected with overdoses of sulfanilamide accidentally:

> They elect unanimously Mr. Felix Voll (applause). They elect unanimously Mr. Felix Romero (applause). Another vote is called for, result, they unanimously elect Mr. Felix Lupescu (a certain uneasiness). The interim president takes the floor and makes a rather jocular allusion to the coincidence of first names. The Greek delegate requests the floor and declares that although it may seem somewhat peculiar, he has been instructed by his government to offer as candidate Mr. Felix Paparemologos. He is voted on and wins by a majority. The next vote comes up, and the Pakistani delegate, Mr. Felix Abib, carries it. At this point in the proceedings there is great confusion among the Committee, so it presses the final vote, with the result that the Argentine candidate, Mr. Felix Camusso, is elected. Amid the markedly uncomfortable applause of the present members, the senior Committee member welcomes the six new members, whom he qualifies cordially and designates as namesakes (stupefaction). The composition of the Committee

is read and ends up organized in the following order: reading from the left, President and oldest surviving member, Mr. Felix Smith. Members: Felix Voll, Felix Romero, Felix Lupescu, Felix Paparemologos, Felix Abib, and Felix Camusso. (69)

The "certain uneasiness" is delicious and a challenge to our understanding. At what point does random chance become probability? When are there too many Felixes, or, for that matter, too many crows to inspire the Felixes' salivation? There is a point, certainly, a moment, in which one bird too many heads for, flutters down toward, then—yes!—lands on that apparatus, the bird that makes the statement, in effect, "I am not alone." When are we alone, and when are we not alone? When is something organized? Cathy Brenner spells out to Melanie, while Melanie is playing Debussy for her, what the plans are for her "surprise" birthday party tomorrow: "I will go over to Michelle's house, and Michelle's mother will say she has a headache and she'd better drive me home, and when I come in all the kids will be there and will yell 'Surprise!' "—plans that are constituted of a series of casual events, each probable in its way, and yet the sum total of which seems to convey intention and direction. In the same way do we recognize the flights of the birds. In the same way do we recognize one another's actions as we drive on the road, visit a pet shop, borrow a dinghy, sit as guests at a dinner table. In the Cortázar story, three of the members decide peremptorily to resign, Camusso for his part requesting instructions "as to how his resignation should be worded; in effect, he has no valid reason to offer for his resignation from the Committee, and as with Mr. Voll and Mr. Lupescu, his sole wish and sincerest advice is that the Committee be composed of gentlemen who do not answer to the name of Felix" (70). Mitch, Lydia, Cathy, and Melanie abandon their home and flee Bodega Bay in resignation, it apparently being their sole wish and sincerest advice that the world should be populated less stringently (and less consistently) by creatures who can fly. Do they have a "valid reason" for departing, or in what province and by what authority greater than the human could such a question be arbitrated, it now being evident that some humans do not wish to endure in cages marshaled by birds? The moral conundrum is as great as any in Hitchcock, to be sure, and as great as any in Western philosophy: is man supreme, and, therefore, does he have just cause for abandoning this habitation, for presuming, as Mitch and his new family have clearly presumed, that they should somehow obviously *not* fall under the birds' dominion, at least for a while? And how many birds is enough to make you see that the balance has tipped, and which bird was it that first crossed the line?

Note

My sincere gratitude to Jay Glickman (Silver City NM), Bill Krohn (Los Angeles), and William Rothman (Miami).

Works Cited

Allen, Richard. "Avian Metaphor in *The Birds*." In *Framing Hitchcock: Selected Essays from The Hitchcock Annual*, ed. Sidney Gottlieb and Christopher Brookhouse. Detroit: Wayne State University Press, 2002, 281–309.

Boyle, Robert F. *Oral History with Robert F. Boyle*. Los Angeles: Margaret Herrick Library Oral History Series, 1998.

Chion, Michel. *La Voix au cinema*. Paris: Éditions de l'etoile, 1982.

Cortázar, Julio. *Cronopios and Famas*. Trans. Paul Blackburn. New York: Pantheon, 1969.

Du Maurier, Daphne. *The Birds and Other Stories*. London: Virago, 2004 © 1952.

Fiedler, Leslie A. *The Return of the Vanishing American*. New York: Stein and Day, 1969.

Forster, E. M. *A Passage to India*. New York: Penguin, 2005 © 1924.

Heinrich, Bernd, and Thomas Bugnyar. "Just How Smart Are Ravens?" *Scientific American* 296, no. 4 (April 2007), 64–71.

Hunter, Evan. Final shooting script for *The Birds*, Prod. #9402, January 26, 1962.

Kelly, Jack. *Gunpowder: Alchemy, Bombards, and Pyrotechnics: The History of the Explosive That Changed the World*. New York: Basic Books, 2004.

Krohn, Bill. "They Made *The Birds*: Round Table with Hitchcock's Designers Albert Whitlock, Robert Boyle, Harold Michelson, Richard Edlund." *Cahiers du cinéma* 337 (June 1982): 36–48. The English version is from the original tape transcription, courtesy of Bill Krohn.

Mannoni, Laurent. *The Great Art of Light and Shadow: Archaeology of the Cinema*. Trans. Richard Crangle. Exeter: University of Exeter Press, 2000.

McCombe, John P. "'Oh, I See. . . .': *The Birds* and the Culmination of Hitchcock's Hyper-Romantic Vision," *Cinema Journal* 44, no. 3 (Spring 2005): 64–80.

Moore, Brian. *Torn Curtain*, Revised shooting script, October 21, 1965.

Paglia, Camille. *The Birds*. London: BFI, 1978.

Parks, Richard S. *The Music of Claude Debussy*. New Haven and London: Yale University Press, 1989.

Pomerance, Murray. *An Eye for Hitchcock*. New Brunswick NJ: Rutgers University Press, 2004.

Scheler, Max. *Ressentiment*. Trans. Lewis B. Coser and William W. Holdheim. Milwaukee: Marquette University Press, 2003 (first published 1912).

Sobchack, Vivian. *Carnal Thoughts: Embodiment and Moving Image Culture*. Berkeley: University of California Press, 2004.

Stapledon, Olaf. *Last and First Men*. New York: Dover, 1968 © 1931.

Sullivan, Jack. *Hitchcock's Music*. New Haven and London: Yale University Press, 2006.

"This Town Is for The Birds," *Toronto Star*, August 31, 2006: H1–H2.

Thomas, William I. and Florian Znaniecki. *The Polish Peasant in Europe and America*. Urbana: University of Illinois Press, 1984 © 1927.

Truffaut, François. *Hitchcock*. Trans. Helen Scott. New York: Touchstone, 1985.

Weis, Elisabeth. *The Silent Scream: Alfred Hitchcock's Sound Track*. Rutherford: Fairleigh Dickinson University Press, 1982.

Wood, Robin. "*The Birds*." In *Hitchcock's Films Revisited*, rev. ed. New York: Columbia University Press, 2002, 152–172.

Žižek, Slavoj. *Looking Awry: An Introduction to Jacques Lacan through Popular Culture*. Cambridge: MIT Press, 1992.

20

LESLEY BRILL

A Brief Anatomy of *Family Plot*

W HEN I FIRST ENCOUNTERED *Family Plot* on television, it seemed mildly entertaining and little more. Clearly, it reflected its director's deterioration. Projecting it as a 16 millimeter print later, I was startled to see a film as dense and eloquent, as complex in its coherence, balance, and design, as any but the greatest of Hitchcock's masterpieces. My taped television version, I discovered, was thirty minutes shorter than the print. What had been cut was thematic material, the wit and dialogic irony that failed to advance the action and absorbed time better used for commercials. Nothing essential to the plot was gone, but most of what makes *Family Plot* a Hitchcock movie had disappeared.

This misadventure vividly illustrated how much there is to a Hitchcock movie beyond plot and characters, how good a film *Family Plot* is, and how little Hitchcock had declined. In retrospect, it is evident that when the director felt that he could not perform up to standard, he retired. Indeed, he resigned even though he had in hand another screenplay, *The Short Night*, its initial drafts written by Ernest Lehman, with whom he had previously made *North by Northwest* (1959) as well as *Family Plot*.[1]

Hitchcock's last movie "is not," according to Donald Spoto, "a 'summary film,' nor is it a creative résumé" (447). In his analysis of *Family Plot*, David Sterritt implies the opposite, noting that Hitchcock "found himself in the unique (for him) position of filming a death-related story while nearing the end of his own life" (3, 5). As is often the case in Hitchcock's fictions, two contradictory postulates manage to be true simultaneously. *Family Plot* does sum up much of its maker's career; but at the same time, it is the work of an artist who never stood still. Hitchcock always seemed to be asking himself, "How could one do this differently?" For his last film, Hitchcock continued to find new harmonies among his familiar melodies.

Among the aspects of *Family Plot* characteristic of Hitchcock is the freedom that he and Lehman took with the novel on which the screenplay is based. The director and his collaborator reworked Victor Canning's noirish story—a book that turns downright nasty in its conclusion—into a wry comedy. In this regard, it recalls Hitchcock's transformation of Patricia Highsmith's *Strangers on a Train*, a bleak, anxious, claustrophobic work that the film ventilated with wit, self-deprecating manipulations of its story, and comic insertions.

Thematically, *Family Plot* has the richness one expects of Hitchcock's work: the impingement of past into present; actions of performance and deceit; an emphasis on women, both as they are perceived by men in the film and as they are portrayed; religion; death and resurrection. Less familiar is the motif of magic, embodied in the "psychic" performances of Blanche (Barbara Harris). Also relatively unfamiliar are the symmetries between the central couples. I shall argue, however, that their mutual reflections ultimately underline their differences. Finally, the formal artistry of the film—its sets, camera work, music score, sounds and silences, costumes, props, and use of color—is playfully, tightly crafted.

Identity

Among concepts crucial for understanding art of any kind is the complex idea of "identity." That word can signify either the singular amalgam that makes a character unique, or it can mean the opposite: "the fact or condition," as one dictionary declares, "of being the same." In art, identity often includes both facts and conditions at once. For *Family Plot*, simultaneous uniqueness and mutuality apply to the two central couples, whose actions and characters are parallel and similar but also divergent and contrasting.

Sterritt and Spoto both emphasize numerous parallels among the members of the couples. Hitchcock, Sterritt argues, takes "complicated pleasure in muddling and partially erasing the boundaries . . . All four major characters are frauds . . ." (6, 7, 9). Both couples are contentious; they share the nexus of Joe Maloney; and, like the paths traversing the *Family Plot* cemetery, they come together, slide apart, and reconverge.

Joining other aspects of *Family Plot* that imply the similarity of its central couples are images of an ordinary human attribute, smiling and the teeth it exposes. In *Crowds and Power*, Elias Canetti begins his discussion of power with "Seizing and Incorporation." Canetti's subtitle illuminates a complex in *Family Plot* that includes its kidnappings and its imagery of food and eating. Of special consequence is what Canetti says about the mouth with its terrible teeth and about the dark secrets of digestion. For the kidnapped prey of Adamson (William Devane) and Fran (Karen Black), a hypodermic needle paralyzes like crushing teeth, a hidden room stands in for the intestines: "The final stage of power is excrement" (203–11). Fran and Adamson argue over the disposal of their prisoner's chemical toilet, his remaining trace and the last "evidence against us."

But sublimated teeth are overshadowed in *Family Plot* by teeth themselves, which are strongly associated with another prey, money. We may be deceived into regarding teeth in this film as benign, since we usually see them in smiles. Nonetheless, they do not typically communicate good cheer or friendliness, but rather greed or rage. Adamson appears archetypally as an elegant Big Bad Wolf. Roger Greenspun noticed "a wonderfully toothy William Devane" (22). Canetti also says, "Smoothness and order, the manifest attributes of the teeth, have entered into the very nature of power" (208). We see Adamson's dental grins when he contemplates ransoms, expresses contempt or frustration, or is enraged. Congratulating themselves on their first success, he and Fran show their teeth repeatedly. The teeth are again in evidence as they drive from the cathedral with the anesthetized bishop. At first their smiles are of self-congratulation; then Adamson's come to signify anger, as they discuss the unwelcome reappearance of George Lumley (Bruce Dern). During a third sequence in Adamson's car, his teeth are luminous as he inspects another extorted jewel.

Adamson sneers to express contempt, notably toward Joe Maloney (Ed Lauter). Treating his henchman with unconcealed disdain, Adamson flashes a sarcastic smile as he remarks, "Isn't it touching how a perfect murder's kept our friendship alive all these years?" He produces an angry grin when he learns of his inept executioner's fatal accident. Fran, too, shows teeth of anger when she rebels at the declaration, "Now we'll have to eliminate these two ourselves." When Adamson faces more resistance he flashes his teeth again, unsmiling but effective: "Will you do as I say!" And so she does, bringing him a fresh hypodermic, a dragon's tooth that he plunges into Blanche's arm.

Neither George nor Blanche is toothless, especially when contemplating money, a prey they share with their counterparts. When they talk about the prospect of "ten big ones," their teeth gleam in the dark. George can also show his teeth in anger, as he does after Maloney's first assassination attempt. Here and elsewhere, imagery of teeth underlines what the couples share, an irascibility and/or desire for the sublimated prey of cash. Simultaneously, it underscores what separates Fran and Adamson from Blanche and George, the former's unsublimated rapaciousness.

With Adamson and Fran, and with Maloney, a characteristic Hitchcockian use of the camera, the high shot, often introduces incidents of predation as well as less extreme occasions of greed. Hitchcock consistently used high angles to push characters down into danger and scenes that approach the infernal. In *Family Plot*, this optical suppression is associated with cupidity and, often, with the violence it engenders. The most brutal actions in *Family Plot*, Maloney's attempted murders, include three emphatic high-angle shots.

A motif of eating continues the pattern of mildly likening the two couples and then distinguishing them. At its most congenial, eating in Hitchcock's films becomes an act of communion; when that connotation is neglected or reversed, the implications are often dreadful. However fractiously, George and Blanche share food and drink. We never see Adamson and Fran together at table; for them, food serves primarily as part of their kidnappings, an instrument of their power.

Like the imagery of teeth or food, the amorous interactions of the two couples draw attention to both similarities and differences. With respect to sex, the likenesses are superficial, the differences deeply significant. For both couples, sex is consistently linked to the quest for riches. The course of love between George and Blanche does not run smooth, but their relationship strengthens in response to the strains caused by their search for the Rainbird heir. Between Adamson and Fran, on the contrary, contention steadily grows.

Blanche and George rehearse in a diminished version the romantic trials central to most Hitchcock films: the protagonists' simultaneous striving for and resistance to mutual trust and their need to attain mature identities. Our first glimpse of the "quarrelsome lovers" has them arguing in George's cab, and they continue squabbling throughout much of the film. A turning point comes after George has managed to thwart Maloney's first attempt to kill them. After momentary contention, they walk from Blanche's upturned car, arms around each other. This mutual tenderness and increasingly trusting partnership contrasts with the growing irritability between Adamson and Fran as their plans go awry.

Blanche's eventual ascendancy epitomizes Hitchcock's treatment of all the female characters. The women of *Family Plot* are more effective and shrewder than its men—despite the tendency of self-important males to belittle their female counterparts. George slightingly assumes that Julia Rainbird is "another one of your twenty-five-dollar sardines," and he dismisses Blanche's psychic powers as "bullshit." By the end of the film, however, he will be wide-eyed and convinced: "Blanche, you did it! You are psychic!" With paternal condescension, Adamson bosses and lectures Fran throughout the film. Ultimately, however, Fran's reluctance is fully validated.

Blanche anchors *Family Plot*. It begins and ends with her, and she functions as something like the director's proxy. Hitchcock thus ends his career, as he began it, with a plucky, resourceful heroine. Between Patsy in *The Pleasure Garden* (1925) and Blanche come a series of enterprising women. Among them we may count Daisy in *The Lodger* (1927), Emily in *Rich and Strange* (1931), the mothers in both versions of *The Man Who Knew Too Much* (1934 and 1956), Erica in *Young and Innocent*, Miss Froy in *The Lady Vanishes* (1938), young Charlie in *Shadow of a Doubt* (1943), Ingrid Bergman in her Hitchcock films, and Grace Kelly in hers. The notion of Hitchcock as a torturer of females—preferably blondes—and a probable misogynist is overdue for composting. Given the director's predilection for passionate, courageous women, one wonders how it took root in the first place. Finally, we should remember that Blanche's closing wink is also Hitchcock's closing wink. Through Blanche, Hitchcock both acknowledges a reciprocity of goals with the audience and retains some control.

Family Plot and The Rainbird Pattern

In *The Rainbird Pattern*, Eddie Shoebridge loves his adoptive parents, and he knows of his real origin and his prospects as heir to the Rainbird fortune. The superfluity of criminal activities that provides central ironies for *Family Plot* does not exist in the novel, nor does the reported incineration of the couple who adopted the Rainbird heir-to-be. The comedy of *Family Plot* depends upon far-fetched coincidences, while its tragic elements demonstrate the ironic operation of justice. From the point of view of Blanche and George, *Family Plot* plays as an indoor-outdoor drawing room comedy of mistaken identities. For Adamson and Fran, the same improbable intersections produce unhappy ironies. Since the first couple is on center stage more often, the overall feeling of the film is comic, and we are unlikely to suffer much anxiety, even at its scariest moment, when Blanche is captive and apparently destined to be murdered.

In *The Rainbird Pattern*, on the other hand, the kidnappers kill Blanche, a detail that makes clear the enormous difference between the

novel and its filmic transformation. The presentation of her death also
underlines the degree to which the novel takes seriously its female protagonist's powers. Miss Rainbird experiences an eerie psychic moment
when she sees her spiritualist occupying "the chair, deep in the shadows,
which Madame Blanche had always used during their sessions . . . And
at that moment, in a little wood on the barren lands of the western part
of Salisbury plain, Blanche died" (175–76).There is a sadistic manipulation about Canning's writing. As Hitchcock manipulates his audience for
mutual pleasure, Canning manipulates his to cause unexpected pain. The
kidnappers are first shot and then incinerated in their home by the police
(an action mutated in the movie into the report of Adamson's killing of
his adoptive parents). In the novel, Miss Rainbird adopts the kidnappers'
surviving son, her heir. "Miss Rainbird [was] happier than she had ever
been in her life before . . . Now there was a smooth, sweet relationship
between them." This comes from the novel's omniscient narrator. Two
pages later, however, at the top of a steep staircase, we are given a different picture: "Miss Rainbird of Reed Court, he thought, his great-aunt,
doting and half-tipsy as usual. His face tightened with disgust and cold
hate. He thrust out his right hand and pushed her violently . . . He
watched her as she lay there, sprawled out like a broken doll. If there
had been any sign of life from her he would have gone down and finished her off" (253).

The thematic point of the novel seems to be the persistence of evil.
Two government detectives who eventually execute the kidnappers make
the point explicit. "Bush stood up. 'It'll be good to have it all finished.'
Grandison shook his head, 'Nothing's ever finished. It's an endless pattern.'" The principal kidnapper makes the same point, "Adam and Eve
had stepped out of the paradise and within half a mile had taken the
wrong turning. There was no hope for mankind" (218, 228). We are
a long way from either the tone or the central themes of *Family Plot*.
Even though Adamson's name recalls the Fall, that allusion contributes
to a minority mood in the film; and its chief villain does not approach
in bitterness or merciless expedition the cops and criminals of the novel.

Performance: Religion and Magic;
Lying, Feigning, and Truth

Other than the kidnapper's summary of humankind's wickedness, there
is little about religion in *The Rainbird Pattern*. However, religious language and imagery permeate *Family Plot*. Some of it is simple, colloquial
cursing; but most contributes to a pattern of religious themes. Religious
language is insistently associated with Blanche: "I have to go through

heaven and hell, the great beyond . . ." Later, she responds to George's casual interjection—"Christ, no!"—with a less casual reproach, "Christ, yes. Now George, stop blaspheming."

Interjections of "Jesus!" and "Oh, my God" from Fran and Adamson appear casual and without significance, but in practice they define a complex mixture of belief and disbelief. As Adamson says about Blanche's possible ESP, "You and I know that's off-the-wall, but can we afford to be wrong?" The film makes clear that Adamson is largely of the devil's party; at the same time, it suggests that all humans carry the same taint. We are all sons (and daughters) of Adam. Further emphasizing the connection of Adamson's last name with this part of the Judeo-Christian tradition, his sales assistant is named "Mrs. Clay," the substance from which our mythological forebear was shaped.

The religious language associated with Maloney connects him to the lower portion of the afterworld. Recounting George's inquiries, Maloney assures his childhood coconspirator that he did not divulge "a goddamn thing." The car that forced Maloney off the cliff speeds away, one of its occupants exclaiming, "Hey guys, let's get the hell out of here!"

Uniquely in *Family Plot*, Maloney dies; but he, like other characters (and the director), is woven into another religious motif, the equivocal relation between life and death. Hitchcock's cameo is a silhouette of his famous profile behind a frosted glass door labeled, "REGISTRAR OF BIRTHS & DEATHS." The connection between life and death persists throughout the film. Entering the Barlow Creek cemetery, George passes gravesites that both hold the dead and await the living. "Dead end, Blanche. Dead and buried," he murmurs. At that moment, a man ascends from a grave in the background. Eddie Shoebridge "went up in smoke twenty-five years ago and came down in the city." As in *The Trouble with Harry* (1956), the dead neither remain buried nor cease to interact with the living.

Closely related to religion and resurrection is magic. Blanche the spiritualist is the purveyor of the supernatural. Analogous to Blanche's mystifications, Hitchcock's magic is that of motion pictures. Hitchcock plays a benign confidence game, one to which we bring eagerly suspended disbelief. The opening credits of *Family Plot* appear on a crystal ball, itself an image of the movie screen. Emphasizing Blanche's status as Hitchcock's surrogate, the director's credit is succeeded immediately by her image and voice.

In *Family Plot*, and for all of Hitchcock's many comic romances, genuine performance emerges triumphant and true. The honesty of its feigning is as far from self-interested mendaciousness as real diamonds are from paste. In his ironic films, performance equates with lying; it attempts to deceive rather than to give pleasure. Many of Hitchcock's films hover between the poles of irony and romance; and their performances include both the truth of art's feigning and the sham of deception. The working title of *Family Plot*, revealingly rejected, was *Deceit*.

Hitchcock's last film closes his career as he began it, with a meditation on honest and dishonest acting, on the arts of stage and cinema. As he set Patsy's straightforward dancing in *The Pleasure Garden* against the counterfeit performances of Jill and of Patsy's unfaithful husband, he embodies the honesty of art's make-believe in another tenacious heroine. George (a professed actor) cannot contain his admiration: "Blanche, you faked that one beautifully." High praise for well-executed, candid fakery. "You are still the champ!" Hitchcock allows himself a bit of a boast through praise for his surrogate. One is tempted to agree; he *is* still the champ.

The Designs of *Family Plot*: Color and Music

As I have noted elsewhere, "Chromatic associations in Hitchcock's color films have a tendency to replicate the conventions of traffic lights: green often indicates safety, yellow and orange suggest caution, and red signals danger" (126).[2] In *Family Plot*, red is the commonest color. White, too, has great importance, especially its connection with Blanche—as her name promises. Hitchcock uses blue systematically, correlating it with doing routine business. The chromatic design of *Family Plot* offers some surprises, notably in the associations it assigns to the color green. It is connected with the violent Maloney, and it accompanies danger or deception.

Red in *Family Plot* often signifies acute danger. The red gasoline container in Adamson's garage serves as an exemplar; capital letters on it spell out "WARNING." Blanche's troubles there begin because a corner of the drugged bishop's scarlet vestment is visible. When she cowers before the inside of the closed garage door, we see to the right of her a bright red tag. Elsewhere in the garage, strong reds proliferate: a tear-off day calendar with a bright red "16," the crimson of Blanche's blood on her white sleeve, and a pair of gas cans next to her when she slumps to the floor.

Disappointment and anger combine with sex and danger when Blanche and George sit in "Abe & Mabel's Cafe" awaiting Joe Maloney— who fails to appear but busies himself outside jamming the accelerator and cutting the brake lines of their car. The scene is overwhelmingly red: red checked table cloths, red lamps, a red counter, a red-haired waitress, red Coke signs, red window curtains, and a curveaceous young woman who arrives in a startling crimson dress for an assignation with a pastor. Red is associated with danger elsewhere as well. As Adamson and Fran drive away with the kidnapped bishop, they acknowledge their alarm at the presence of "the man with the pipe," George. A large red sign is suddenly visible. Earlier, Fran wore a red necklace and carried a red purse when she and Adamson staked out Blanche's apartment. But the last example is somewhat ambiguous. Fran, although accessorized in red during her prowling around Blanche's home, is dressed in a white pants suit, which strongly associates her with her quarry.

For Hitchcock's practice in *Family Plot*, such complicating of the suggestions of red is typical. Red is often connected with strong emotion, anger and occasionally sexual passion. But other colors or counter-significant objects, especially flowers, frequently balance the angry, passionate, or dangerous overtones of the red. Sterritt's perception of Hitchcock's "characteristic ambiguity" in *Family Plot* is confirmed by its use of color as well as in its plot and thematic structure (3).

Throughout his career, Hitchcock associated his heroines with an archetype of romantic fiction, Persephone, goddess of flowers and earthly abundance. In *Family Plot*, Blanche is entombed by Fran and Adamson in the underworld of their basement prison, from which she will escape to bring a profusion of rewards. She is also associated with flowers, almost always red roses, which thus have a double significance: promising fertility and wealth and hinting at danger and passion or anger. In the opening sequence, "Henry," Blanche's putative informant from the world of the dead, intones, "Too many memories, too much pain, too much sorrow." The camera pans past a red chair, a stack of red-bound books, and a vase filled with red roses. The film thus sets itself a task familiar from many of Hitchcock's other movies, the redemption or detoxification of an unquiet personal history; and it links the color red to this task, with its dangers and hopes.

Given its more usual connotations of safety and growth, green in *Family Plot* might be called the color of irony. Associated with Maloney, it is almost always dangerous. In a few contexts, its ironies are playful, though not necessarily benign. Driving away from the abortive meeting with Maloney, for example, George sighs, "Well, that's the end of that." Hitchcock's camera tracks the departing car. Fluid drips from a severed brake line and, just above, the green license plate cheerfully advises, "Drive Safely."

When Maloney first appears in dirty green coveralls, the colors of the set are hot red and orange: an American flag on the corner of the gas pump, a red can, a red truck in the background, red and orange cans visible through the service station window, Maloney's wife (Katherine

Helmond) in a red dress, and the brilliant red of the underside of the hood of Blanche's car. The green of Maloney's attire is thus powerfully connected with the color of danger.

White is strongly, but not exclusively, associated with Blanche. Yet neither the innocence and purity often symbolized by white nor the nothingness and disaster sometimes associated with it seem clearly to apply. Like Hitchcock's handling of other colors, his uses of white in *Family Plot* are systematic but complex. Tracing that color leads us to conclusions that first may strike us as surprising, then as apt. Associations of white with Blanche are pointed: the long white scarf she trails at the first séance, her white Mustang, her name, the white sweater she wears over a white shirt for the last quarter of the film, and so on. We might begin to make sense of the significance of white in *Family Plot* by noting Adamson's remark as he awaits Blanche's return, "The spirit is never at home." One of the associations of white is with "the spirit." Inside the cathedral—where the spirit is presumably always at home—huge white bouquets decorate the front of the pews and choir.

Beyond its association with the spirit world, Blanche's white ultimately signals a kind of innocence. This becomes evident when we compare her to her counterpart in Canning's novel. The heroine of the film is more vulgar, cynical, and self-consciously fraudulent than Canning's Blanche. In *The Rainbird Pattern*, Blanche is polished and professional; and she trusts the authenticity of her psychic powers. Her "Henry" is real, at least to her. Like her vulgarity, the unflagging appetite of Hitchcock's Blanche for sex (and for hamburgers, a desire that seems related to the sexual one) has little to do with the novel's heroine.[3] Blanche's association in Hitchcock's movie with white may at first seem ironic, but her dishonesty and "impurity" have a straightforwardness and simplicity about them that reironizes the irony back to innocence.[4]

Hitchcock's use of the camera as a character has been widely noted. Less discussed has been his use of music for the same purposes. Williams's music track qualifies as a sort of disembodied analog to the present-absence that Michel Chion has identified as an *acousmêtre*, a voice neither inside nor outside the image yet "implicated in the action, constantly about to be part of it" (129). *Family Plot* opens with the sound of female voices. These ethereal sounds float through the opening sequence. We hear them twice more: during the second séance in the Rainbird mansion and at the end of the film, when Blanche appears to fall into a trance that leads her to the ransom diamond taped among the pendants of Adamson's chandelier. In all three cases, the voices cooperate with Blanche's performances.[5]

The main musical theme begins when Miss Rainbird offers Blanche ten thousand dollars. When George goes off to claim their rewards at the end, it resumes and thus recalls its original association with money. It continues through Blanche's wink and the credits as the camera shifts to a close-up on the diamond. The theme remains connected with financial gain; but it now also includes the rewards accruing to the film company. The musical use of the Rainbird reward theme, then, associates the project of making the movie with the profit motives of its plot.

Like its visuals, the soundtrack of *Family Plot* has some typical Hitchcock ingenuity. As George unsuccessfully looks for Blanche in Adamson's apartment, the music acoustically fades into a high tone that sounds like an electronic alarm. Will he hear it? Did he trigger it? Unambiguously, it raises the sense of urgency for us and reminds us that Adamson and Fran are on their way. After a minute, the sound is taken over by a sustained note on a violin; at the same time, we hear the garage door open. The use of the electronic alarm and of the sustained high note recalls Bernard Herrmann, especially his work for *Psycho* and *The Birds*.

A final example of Hitchcock's attention to sound arises through a reference in the dialogue. Politically incorrect and in line with Hitchcock's evident misgivings about homosexuality, it involves a coded communication regarding the Bishop's ransom. Hitchcock avoided identifying the city of *Family Plot*, but most viewers will recognize it as San Francisco, a point relevant to Fran's announcement to her partner, "The message has come through on KFAG."

Joseph Maloney's Burial

The sequence of Maloney's burial service serves as the gravitational center of the entire film. There is no similar episode in *The Rainbird Pattern*—nor is there any character resembling Maloney. Virtually all the major themes and motifs important to *Family Plot* are present, and the sequence is as freighted with meaning as anything in Hitchcock's work. It begins after Fran storms out of Adamson's Jewelers, the color green providing continuity between the two shots. All the colors that are key to the film are evident during the initial pan across the cemetery. The dominant hue is green, altogether appropriate, given its strong association with Maloney. George, on assignment, wears his sporty but businesslike blue. Blanche is present, symbolically, with her white car; and touches of red remind us of ongoing danger. The presiding clergyman delivers a eulogy that recalls the irony Maloney attracts throughout the film: "Yes, . . . you were a generous man." Most of it sounds generic, and little of it accords with its scruffy, vindictive subject.

While he continues, we see Mrs. Maloney, surrounded by mourners. She notices a glowering Lumley and, feigning overwhelming grief, moves away. George follows her, as does the camera for roughly the next minute—a long time, given that "nothing happens." Lumley's pursuit serves as an emblem of the plot; their paths diverge, run parallel, draw closer together.

As the tracking-shot begins, the preacher's words become general. His ruminations on "mortal man" fit the religious ideas of *Family Plot*, and especially its motif of resurrection. They provide a commentary on central themes, while the image summarizes plot: "Behold, He suffereth the pains of all men . . . who belong to the family of Adam. And He suffereth this that the resurrection might pass among all men."

Joseph Maloney is but one of Adam's sons, Arthur Adamson another; neither is unique. Like Julia Rainbird's, the life of all humanity is made uneasy by a terrible mistake in our past. We are of Adam's family, on whom the camera looks down with quasidivine omniscience, irony, and, finally, amusement. The director and its audience are at once above the scene and part of it. The capability of art to render this double perspective was recognized by Philip Sidney, three centuries before the invention of motion pictures. The artist "bringeth things forth surpassing [nature's] doings—with no small arguments to the incredulous of that first accursed fall of Adam, since our erected wit maketh us know what perfection is, and yet our infected wil keepeth us from reaching unto it" (507).

Like Scheherazade, Hitchcock had as many stories as he needed. Had his vigor and life continued, he would almost certainly have made *The Short Night*. As the officiating clergyman says at Maloney's funeral (typical of Hitchcock to hide truth in dubious mouthpieces), "You gave the very best that was in you, and no more than that can be asked of mortal man on this earth." A less equivocal character, Miss Rainbird, offers an equally applicable declaration, "I'm seventy-eight years of age . . . I'm too old for trying. I've only time enough left for results." When *Family Plot* was released, Hitchcock was seventy-seven. If we take *Family Plot* to be, among other things, a light-hearted apologia *pro sua vita*, a meditation on a lifetime of performances, we also need to remember that Hitchcock's first completed feature contained a similar meditation. Indeed, few films among his fifty-three features lack depictions of performances—whether the feigning of art, the lies of deceivers and criminals, or, usually, both. Nonetheless, as Sterritt points out, we should notice "the film's extraordinary wealth of allusions to a wide range of works from his earlier career" (5). Such references, I suspect, make up in *Family Plot* part of the director's contemplation of his own life-long role as a filmmaker, a performer whose self-consciousness is reflected in his famous cameo appearances. One aspect of his thinking about the cinema remains constant: a deeply held conviction that for movies the distinction between the feigned and the real is irrelevant. Blanche's (Hitchcock's) closing wink includes us in her triumph. With this last gesture—at once sly and candid—we fully comprehend all the feigning.

As Hitchcock said, "Mr. Williams, murder can be fun."[6] Few storytellers have made that point more entertainingly than the dour, porky Englishman. Though murder was largely reduced to kidnapping, he was making it again, and remaking it anew. Much of *Family Plot* reprises the humor, verbal jousting of women and men, entertaining violence, and suspense on which Hitchcock made a career of unprecedented success. At the same time, it plays new variations on familiar themes and stylistic gestures. Of course, new variations were also Hitchcock's stock in trade. The audiences for any Hitchcock film expected that the old dog would trot out a few new tricks.

So he does in *Family Plot*. He once more transformed, in the heat and pressure of a movie set, the carbon black of a mediocre novel into a diamond of a film. Of *Family Plot* we may say, as its antagonist does when looking at the payoff from his second kidnapping, "Wow! It's gorgeous!" But let us go further in praise and back in the film to Adamson's inspection of his first extorted gem. For it is on the image of that sparkling diamond that *Family Plot* and Hitchcock's career end. "Brilliant! Absolutely perfect."

Notes

1. The screenplay has been published, with a substantial introduction, in David Freeman, *The Last Days of Alfred Hitchcock*. Mr. Freeman writes, "The screenwriter Ernest Lehman, who among other films wrote 'North by Northwest,' wrote several drafts of a script . . . and worked on the project until he and Hitchcock had a falling out" (8).

2. Richard Allen makes a similar, but somewhat more general assertion: "Hitchcock's films, like the work of many colorists, draw on a range of conventions that pertain to the symbolic and emotional significance of color that are deeply embedded in Western culture." "Hitchcock's Color Designs," in *Color: The Film Reader*, ed. Angela Dalle Vacche and Brian Price (New York and London: Routledge, 2006), 131.

3. Michael Walker writes, "When, in *Family Plot*, Blanche asks a reluctant George to cook her another hamburger, she is also referring to a matter alluded to elsewhere in the film: that her sexual desires exceed his." Michael Walker, *Hitchcock's Motifs*, 185.

4. As Sterritt notes, "For all their perfidy, Lumley and Blanche seek only reward money and not the inheritance nor the diamonds that cross their path" (7). A little later, he adds that her "dishonesty does no real harm" (9).

5. Jack Sullivan observes, "The cue is ironic, the ethereal chorus singing against Blanche's transparent fakery." *Hitchcock's Music*, 312.

6. As quoted in "Plotting *Family Plot*," a 1990 documentary written, directed, and produced by Laurent Bouzereau. It is available on the Universal Studio DVD of *Family Plot*; copyright 2000, ASIN B00055Y15.

Works Cited

Brill, Lesley. *Crowds, Power, and Transformation in Cinema*. Detroit, MI: Wayne State University Press, 2006.

Canetti, Elias. *Crowds and Power*. 1962. Trans. Carol Steward. New York: Farrar, Straus & Giroux, 1973.

Canning, Victor. *The Rainbird Pattern*. 1972. London: Pan Books, 1974.

Freeman, David. *The Last Days of Alfred Hitchcock*. Woodstock, NY: Overlook, 1984.

Greenspun, Roger. "Family Plot." *Film Comment* 12, no. 3 (May–June 1976): 20–22.

Chion, Michel. *Audio-Vision*. Ed. and trans. Claudia Gorbman. New York: Columbia University Press, 1994.

Sidney, Sir Philip. "The Defence of Poesy." Rpt. in *The Norton Anthology of English Literature*. Vol. 1 5th ed. Ed. M. H. Abrams. New York: Norton, 1986.

Spoto, Donald. *The Art of Alfred Hitchcock*. 1976. Garden City, NY: Doubleday & Company, 1979.

Sterritt, David. "Hitchcock: Registrar of Births and Deaths." *Hitchcock Annual*, 1997–98.

Sullivan, Jack. *Hitchcock's Music*. New Haven: Yale University Press, 2006.

Walker, Michael. *Hitchcock's Motifs*. Amsterdam: Amsterdam University Press, 2006.

Appendix

Hitchcock's Films and Their Sources

The Pleasure Garden (1926) Novel by "Oliver Sandys" (Marguerite Florence Barclay)

The Mountain Eagle (1926) Original story by Charles Lapworth

The Lodger (1926) Novel by Marie Belloc-Lowndes

Downhill (1927) Play by "David L'Estrange" (Ivor Novello and Constance Collier)

Easy Virtue (1927) Play by Noël Coward

The Ring (1927) Original story by Hitchcock

The Farmer's Wife (1928) Play by Eden Philpotts

Champagne (1928) Original story by Walter C. Mycroft

The Manxman (1929) Novel by Hall Caine

Blackmail (1929) Play by Charles Bennett

Juno and the Paycock (1929) Play by Sean O'Casey

Murder! (1930) Novel (*Enter Sir John*) by "Clemence Dane" (Winifred Ashton) and Helen Simpson

The Skin Game (1931) Play by John Galsworthy

Rich and Strange (1931) Novel by Dale Collins

Number Seventeen (1932) Play by J. Jefferson Farjeon

Waltzes from Vienna (1934) Play (*Walzerkrieg*) by A. M. Willner, Heinz Reichert, and Ernst Marischka

The Man Who Knew Too Much (1934) Original story by Charles Bennett and D. B.Wyndham Lewis, inspired by the Bulldog Drummond stories of H. C. McNeile

The 39 Steps (1935) Novel (*The Thirty-Nine Steps*) by John Buchan

Secret Agent (1936) Two short stories ("The Traitor" and "The Hairless Mexican") in the volume *Ashenden* by W. Somerset Maugham, and stage adaptation by Campbell Dixon

Sabotage (1936) Novel (*The Secret Agent*) by Joseph Conrad

Young and Innocent (1937) Novel (*A Shilling for Candles*) by "Josephine Tey" (Elizabeth Mackintosh)

The Lady Vanishes (1938) Novel (*The Wheel Spins*) by Ethel Lina White

Jamaica Inn (1939) Novel by Daphne du Maurier

Rebecca (1940) Novel by Daphne du Maurier

Foreign Correspondent (1940) Original screenplay

Mr. and Mrs. Smith (1941) Original screenplay

Suspicion (1941) Novel (*Before the Fact*) by Francis Iles

Saboteur (1942) Original screenplay

Shadow of a Doubt (1943) Original story by Gordon McDonell

Lifeboat (1943) Original story by John Steinbeck

Spellbound (1945) Novel (*The House of Dr. Edwardes*) by "Francis Beeding" (Hilary St. George Saunders and John Palmer)

Notorious (1946) Short story ("The Song of the Dragon") by George E. Wolfe

The Paradine Case (1947) Novel by Robert Hichens

Rope (1948) Play (*Rope's End*) by Patrick Hamilton

Under Capricorn (1949) Novel by Helen Simpson

Stage Fright (1950) Novel (*Outrun the Constable*) by Selwyn Jepson

Strangers on a Train (1951) Novel by Patricia Highsmith

I Confess (1952) Play (*Nos Deux Consciences*) by Paul Anthelme

Dial M for Murder (1954) Play by Frederick Knott

Rear Window (1954) Short story by Cornell Woolrich

To Catch a Thief (1955) Novel by David Dodge

The Trouble with Harry (1956) Novel by John Trevor Story

The Man Who Knew Too Much (1956) See *The Man Who Knew Too Much* (1934)

The Wrong Man (1956) Story by Maxwell Anderson, based on a true case

Vertigo (1958) Novel (*D'entre les morts*) by Pierre Boileau and Thomas Narcejac

North by Northwest (1959) Original screenplay

Psycho (1960) Novel by Robert Bloch

The Birds (1963) Short story by Daphne du Maurier

Marnie (1964) Novel by Winston Graham

Torn Curtain (1966) Original screenplay

Topaz (1969) Novel by Leon Uris

Frenzy (1972) Novel (*Goodbye Piccadilly, Farewell Leicester Square*) by Arthur La Bern

Family Plot (1976) Novel (*The Rainbow Pattern*) by Victor Canning

This list is limited to feature-length theatrical films directed by Hitchcock, excluding his wartime propaganda films (*Bon Voyage* and *Aventure Malgache*), *Elstree Calling* (to which he contributed some short segments), and the episodes he directed for the television series *Alfred Hitchcock Presents* and *The Alfred Hitchcock Hour*.

Contributors

Charles Barr taught for many years at the University of East Anglia in Norwich, England, and has since worked in the USA (Washington University in St Louis) and in Ireland (University College Dublin, and the John Huston School in Galway). His publications include books on *Ealing Studios*, *English Hitchcock*, and, for the BFI Classics series, *Vertigo*.

Matthew H. Bernstein currently chairs the Film and Media Studies Department at Emory University, where he teaches courses on Hollywood, European and Japanese cinemas. He is the co-editor of *Visions of the East: Orientalism in Film* (Rutgers, 1997) and *John Ford Made Westerns* (Indiana, 2001), editor of *Controlling Hollywood* (Rutgers, 1999) and *Michael Moore: Filmmaker, Newsmaker, Cultural Icon* (University of Michigan Press, 2010). He is also the author of *Walter Wanger, Hollywood Independent* (University of Minnesota Press, 2000) and *Screening a Lynching: The Leo Frank Case on Film and TV* (University of Georgia Press, 2009), as well as numerous articles on film history and criticism.

David Boyd is a Conjoint Associate Professor of English and Film at the University of Newcastle in Australia. He is author of *Film and the Interpretive Process* (Peter Lang, 1989), editor of *Perspectives on Alfred Hitchcock* (G.K. Hall, 1995), and co-editor of *Re-Reading Frye: The Published and* Unpublished *Works* (University of Toronto Press, 1999) and of *After Hitchcock: Influence, Imitation, and Intertextuality* (University of Texas Press, 2006).

Lesley Brill is the author of *The Hitchcock Romance* (Princeton, 1988), *John Huston's Filmmaking* (Cambridge, 1997), *Crowds, Power, and Transformation in Cinema* (Wayne State, 2006), and numerous essays on film, photography, and literature. He teaches at Wayne State University in Detroit.

Barbara Creed is Professor of Cinema Studies and Head of the School of Culture & Communication at the University of Melbourne. She saw *Psycho* when it was first released and has been a Hitchcock devotee ever since. Her books include *The Monstrous-Feminine: Film, Feminism, Psychoanalysis (Routledge, 1993)*; Phallic *Panic: Film, Horror and the Primal Uncanny (Melbourne University Press 2005)*; and Darwin's *Screens: Evolutionary Aesthetics, Time and Sexual Display in the Cinema (Melbourne University Press, 2009)*. She is currently working on film and human rights.

Mark Glancy teaches film history courses at Queen Mary University of London. He is a regular contributor to *BBC History Magazine* and his books include *The 39 Steps: A British Film Guide* (I.B. Tauris, 2003).

Sidney Gottlieb is Professor of Media Studies at Sacred Heart University in Fairfield, Connecticut. He co-edits the *Hitchcock Annual* (distributed by Columbia University Press) with Richard Allen. His publications include *Hitchcock on Hitchcock: Selected Writings and Interviews* (University of California Press, 1995), *Alfred Hitchcock: Interviews* (University of Mississippi Press, 2003), and *The Hitchcock Annual Anthology: Selected Essays from Volumes 10-15*, co-edited with Richard Allen (Wallflower, 2009).

Mary Hammond is Senior Lecturer in Nineteenth-Century Literature at the University of Southampton, UK, where she specializes in Book History. She is the author of *Reading, Publishing, and the Formation of Literary Taste in England 1880-1914* (Ashgate, 2006) and many articles on 19th-century literature and culture. She is also co-editor with Shafquat Towheed of *Publishing in the First World War: Essays in Book History* (Palgrave, 2007), and co-editor with Robert Fraser of *Books Without Borders Volume 1: The Cross-National Dimension in Print Culture* and *Books Without Borders Volume 2: Perspectives from South Asia* (Palgrave, 2009). She is currently working on a project on the global migrations of Victorian print workers, and writing a publishing history of Charles Dickens' *Great Expectations*.

Ina Rae Hark is Distinguished Professor Emerita of English and Film/Media Studies at the University of South Carolina. Her previous work on Hitchcock has appeared in *Cinema Journal*, *Hitchcock's Re-Released Films*, *Hitchcock Centenary Essays*, *After Hitchcock*, and *A Companion to Hitchcock Studies*. She has also written monographs on *Star Trek* and *Deadwood* and edited four other books of film scholarship

Noel King teaches in the Department of Media, Music, Communication and Cultural Studies at Macquarie University, Sydney, NSW, Australia. His recent publications include articles on "Dennis Hopper and American Dreamer" for Studies in Documentary Film, and "Remembering Manuel Alvarado" for a special issue of Television and New Media devoted to the work of Manuel Alvarado. He edited a dossier on "Bob Dylan and Martin Scorsese's No Direction Home" for Studies in Documentary Film (2007) and also edited an issue of that journal on music and documentary (vol 2, 3, 2008). His current research concerns Don DeLillo and film, and Richard Hugo and film, as part of a larger exploration of "literary cinephilia."

Thomas Leitch teaches English and directs the Film Studies program at the University of Delaware. His most recent books are *Film Adaptation and Its Discontents* and *A Companion to Alfred Hitchcock*, co-edited with Leland Poague.

Brian McFarlane, an Honorary Adjunct Professor at Monash University, Australia, and former Visiting Professor (Film) at the University of Hull is the author of many articles on film and literature, and of books including *Words and Images: Australian Novels into Film* (Heinemann, 1983), *New Australian Cinema: Sources and Parallels in American and British Film* (1987), *Novel to Film: An Introduction to the Theory of Adaptation* (Clarendon, OUP, 1996), *An Autobiography of British Cinema* (Methuen/BFI, 1997), *The Oxford Companion to Australian Film* (co-edited—OUP, 1999), *Screen Adaptations: Charles Dickens'* Great Expectations (A&C Black/Methuen Drama, 2008, and (as compiler, editor and chief author) *The Encyclopedia of British Film* (Methuen/BFI, 2003, 4th ed. due 2011). His most recent book is a light-hearted and ironic memoir, *Real and Reel* (Sid Harta, 2010), focusing on a lifetime's obsession with the cinema.

Douglas McFarland is professor of English at Flagler College. His many publications on film include essays on the Coen brothers, literary adaptation, and Peter Bogdanovich.

Toby Miller works at the University of California, Riverside and is the author and editor of over 30 books, has published essays in more than 100 journals and edited collections, and is a frequent guest commentator on television and radio programs. His teaching and research cover the media, sports, labor, gender, race, citizenship, politics, and cultural policy, as well as the success of Hollywood overseas and the adverse effects of electronic waste. Miller's work has been translated into Chinese, Japanese, Swedish, German, Spanish and Portuguese.

R. Barton Palmer is Calhoun Lemon Professor of Literature and director of film studies at Clemson University. Palmer is the author, editor, or general editor of more than forty books on various literary and cinematic subjects and the founding/general editor of book series at four university presses. His most recent film books include (with Robert Bray) *Hollywood's Tennessee: The Williams Films and Postwar America* and *To Kill a Mockingbird: The Relationship between the Text and the Film*. He has recently edited (with Steven M. Sanders) *The Philosophy of Steven Soderbergh*, (with Murray Pomerance) *"A Little Solitaire": John Frankenheimer and American Film*, and *Larger than Life: Movie Stars of the 1950s*.

Murray Pomerance is Professor in the Department of Sociology at Ryerson University and the author of *Michelangelo Red Antonioni Blue: Eight Reflections on Cinema, Edith Valmaine, The Horse Who Drank the Sky: Film Experience Beyond Narrative and Theory, Johnny Depp Starts Here, Savage Time*, and *An Eye for Hitchcock*. He has edited or co-edited more than fourteen volumes, including *"A Little Solitaire": John Frankenheimer and American Film, Shining in Shadows: Movie Stars of the 2000s*, and *Cinema and Modernity*. He edits the "Techniques of the Moving Image" series at Rutgers University Press, the "Horizons of Cinema" series at SUNY Press, and co-edits, with Lester D. Friedman and Adrienne L. McLean respectively, the "Screen Decades" and "Star Decades" series at Rutgers.

Hilary Radner is Professor of Film and Media Studies at the University of Otago. Her books include two monographs on feminine culture and subjectivity: *Shopping Around: Feminine Culture and the Pursuit of Pleasure* (Routledge, 1995) and *Neo-Feminist Cinema: Girly Films, Chick Flicks, and Consumer Culture* (Routledge, 2010). She is also a co-editor of: *Film Theory Goes to the Movies* (Routledge, 1993); *Constructing the New Consumer Society* (St. Martin's Press, 1997); *Swinging Single: Representing Sexuality in the 1960s* (University of Minnesota Press, 1999); *Jane Campion: Cinema, Nation, Identity* (Wayne State Press, 2009); *New Zealand Cinema: Interpreting the Past* (Intellect, 2011, forthcoming); *Feminism at the Movies* (Routledge, 2011, forthcoming).

David Sterritt is chair of the National Society of Film Critics, film professor at Columbia University and the Maryland Institute College of Art, professor emeritus at Long Island University, chief book critic of *Film Quarterly*, and film critic of *Tikkun*, and is co-chair of the Columbia

University Seminar on Cinema and Interdisciplinary Interpretation. He has twice been chair of the New York Film Critics Circle and has served on the New York Film Festival selection committee. His books include *The Films of Alfred Hitchcock*, published by Cambridge University Press in 1993 and translated into Chinese (2007) and Greek (1998). His writing on Hitchcock has appeared in the *Hitchcock Annual*, *Film-Philosophy*, *The Chronicle of Higher Education*, *Film Quarterly*, *Moving Image Source*, Blackwell's *Companion to Hitchcock Studies*, *PopMatters*, and elsewhere, and he has lectured on Hitchcock at the National Gallery of Art, the Brooklyn Museum, the Boston Museum of Fine Arts, and other venues.

Constantine Verevis is Senior Lecturer in Film and Television Studies at the School of English, Communications and Performance Studies at Monash University, Melbourne. He is the author of *Film Remakes* (Edinburgh UP, 2006), and co-editor of *Second Takes: Critical Approaches to the Film Sequel* (SUNY P, 2010).

Pamela Robertson Wojcik is Associate Professor in the Department of Film, TV and Theatre and Director of Gender Studies at the University of Notre Dame. She is the author of *The Apartment Plot: Urban_Living in American Film and Popular Culture, 1945 to 1975* and *Guilty Pleasures: Feminist Camp from_Mae West to Madonna*; editor of *Movie Acting: The Film Reader*, *New Constellations: Movie Stars of the 1960s*, and co-editor, with Arthur Knight, of *Soundtrack Available: Essays on Film and Popular Music*.

Alan Woolfolk is Dean of Academic Affairs at Flagler College in Saint Augustine, Florida. He holds a Ph.D. in sociology from the University of Pennsylvania and has previously taught at Oglethorpe University and Southern Methodist University. He has recently edited with an introduction *The Crisis of the Officer Class* by Philip Rieff (University of Virginia Press) and published extensively on contemporary culture, public intellectuals, and film. Woolfolk has twice been a National Endowment for the Humanities Fellow and is a member of the editorial board of *Society*.

Index